Lecture Notes in Artificial Intelligence 2322

Subseries of Lecture Notes in Computer Science
Edited by J. G. Carbonell and J. Siekmann

Lecture Notes in Computer Science

Edited by G. Goos, J. Hartmanis, and J. van Leeuwen

W0049857

Springer
Berlin
Heidelberg
New York
Barcelona
Hong Kong
London
Milan
Paris
Tokyo

Vladimír Mařík   Olga Štěpánková
Hana Krautwurmová   Michael Luck (Eds.)

Multi-Agent Systems and Applications II

9th ECCAI-ACAI / EASSS 2001, AEMAS 2001, HoloMAS 2001
Selected Revised Papers

 Springer

Volume Editors

Vladimír Mařík
Czech Technical University
Faculty of Electrical Engineering, Department of Cybernetics
166 27 Prague 6, Czech Republic
E-mail: marik@labe.felk.cvut.cz
and
Rockwell Automation Research Center Prague
Americka 22, 120 00 Prague 2, Czech Republic

Olga Štěpánková
Hana Krautwurmová
Czech Technical University
Faculty of Electrical Engineering, Department of Cybernetics
166 27 Prague 6, Czech Republic
E-mail: {step,hakraut}@labe.felk.cvut.cz

Michael Luck
University of Southampton, Department of Electronics and Computer Science
Highfield, Southampton SO17 1BJ, UK
E-mail: mml@ecs.soton.uk

Cataloging-in-Publication Data applied for

Die Deutsche Bibliothek - CIP-Einheitsaufnahme

Multi-agent systems and applications : selected revised papers /
9th ECCAI ACAI/EASSS 2001 ... Vladimír Marik ... (ed.). -
Berlin ; Heidelberg ; New York ; Barcelona ; Hong Kong ; Milan ;
Paris ; Tokyo : Springer
2 . - (2002)
    (Lecture notes in computer science ; Vol. 2322 : Lecture notes
    in artificial intelligence)
    ISBN 3-540-43377-5

CR Subject Classification (1998): I.2.11, I.2, J.1

ISSN 0302-9743
ISBN 3-540-43377-5 Springer-Verlag Berlin Heidelberg New York

This work is subject to copyright. All rights are reserved, whether the whole or part of the material is
concerned, specifically the rights of translation, reprinting, re-use of illustrations, recitation, broadcasting,
reproduction on microfilms or in any other way, and storage in data banks. Duplication of this publication
or parts thereof is permitted only under the provisions of the German Copyright Law of September 9, 1965,
in its current version, and permission for use must always be obtained from Springer-Verlag. Violations are
liable for prosecution under the German Copyright Law.

Springer-Verlag Berlin Heidelberg New York
a member of BertelsmannSpringer Science+Business Media GmbH

http://www.springer.de

© Springer-Verlag Berlin Heidelberg 2002

Typesetting: Camera-ready by author, data conversion by PTP-Berlin, Stefan Sossna
Printed on acid-free paper   SPIN: 10846686   06/3142   5 4 3 2 1 0

Preface

The Advanced Course on Artificial Intelligence ACAI 2001, with the subtitle of "Multi-Agent Systems and Their Applications", held in Prague, Czech Republic, represented a joint event of ECCAI (the European Coordinating Committee for Artificial Intelligence) and AgentLink, the European Network of Excellence for Agent-Based Computing. Whereas ECCAI organizes two-week ACAI courses on different topics each second year, AgentLink's European Agent Systems Summer School (EASSS) has been an annual event since 1999. In 2001, both of these important events were merged, giving weight to the fact that multi-agent systems currently represent one of the hottest topics of AI research. The name, *ACAI 2001 Summer School*, was intended to emphasize that this event continued the tradition of regular ECCAI activities (ACAI), as well as that of the EASSS summer schools of AgentLink.

The Prague ACAI Summer School was proposed and initiated by both the Gerstner Laboratory, Czech Technical University, Prague (GL-CTU) and the Czech Society for Cybernetics and Informatics (CSKI), with the support of the Austrian Research Institute for Artificial Intelligence in Vienna (OFAI).

One of the most important stimulating factors behind the organization of ACAI 2001 was the support provided by the European Commission to the Gerstner Laboratory within the frame of the MIRACLE Centre of Excellence project (No. ICA1-CT-2000-70002). Additional support was later provided by both the Commission's AgentLink II project (IST-1999-29003) and ECCAI. The combined financial and conceptual participation of these important international bodies enabled the invitation of a large number of truly world-class lecturers in this field, who added a unique flavor to the event.

The main goal of the Summer School was to present the current state of the art in the theoretical foundations of multi-agent systems as well as to demonstrate the applicability of these systems in many practical tasks. The choice of the topics and lecturers was driven by the desire to cover the field of multi-agent systems with the maximum breadth, while maintaining the utmost quality. As a result, the presentations highlight many different but complementary aspects and viewpoints of this recently established and very active scientific field.

In total, 29 invited speakers presented tutorials and lectures focusing on the current state of the art in the theoretical foundations and practical applications of multi-agent systems. For the ACAI Summer School, 175 participants from 29 countries registered (73% PhD students, 10% industry). Three student sessions, together containing 26 student papers, which were selected through a regular refereeing process, were organized within the frame of ACAI.

Twenty tutorial papers were included in a special tutorial volume (LNAI No. 2086, Springer-Verlag). Five additional ACAI tutorial papers represent the first part of this volume. These are followed by seven further papers, selected as the best contributions to the ACAI student sessions.

In addition to the combined Summer School, there were four affiliated workshops/meetings that were co-located: the AEMAS 2001 workshop (Adaptability and Embodiment Using Multi-Agent Systems), the ESAW 2001 workshop (Engineering Societies in the Agents' World), the AgentLink II SIG meetings, and the meeting of the FIPA Working Group on "Product Modeling and Manufacturing". Three selected papers from the AEMAS 2001 workshop are included in this volume as the third part.

The last part gathers the most valuable papers from the HoloMAS 2001 workshop (Industrial Applications of Holonic and Multi-Agent Systems) held within the framework of the DEXA conference in Munich on September 6, 2002. This series of workshops (with the earlier HoloMAS 2000 held in London, and HoloMAS 2002 expected to be held in Aix-en-Provence in September 2002) concentrates on holonic manufacturing systems as a very attractive application area of the multi-agent paradigm. It seems that industrial manufacturing applications of MAS technology are currently outside the main focus of attention of the MAS research community which, to a large extent, has focused primarily on e-business and e-services of various kinds. However, the potential economic and social effects of holonic and MAS solutions in manufacturing, as well as in virtual enterprising, is huge. The papers included in the last part of this volume report both promising perspectives and the first positive experiences.

Finally, we would like to thank all the contributors to this "joint" volume, as well as the numerous collaborators who helped substantially to shape and complete the book, especially Jiří Lažanský who carried out the main portion of the computer work related to the preparation of both the camera-ready and electronic versions of this volume.

January 2002

Vladimír Mařík
Olga Štěpánková
Hana Krautwurmová
Michael Luck

ACAI 2001

Nineth ECCAI Advanced Course
&
AgentLink's Third European Agent Systems Summer School
(EASSS 2001)

Multi-Agent Systems and Applications II

Prague, Czech Republic, July 2–13, 2001

Program Co-chairs:

Michael LUCK	University of Southampton, UK
Vladimír MAŘÍK	Czech Technical University, Czech Republic
Olga ŠTEPÁNKOVÁ	Czech Technical University, Czech Republic
Robert TRAPPL	Austrian Research Institute for AI, Austria

Invited Speakers:

Hamideh AFSARMANESH	University of Amsterdam, The Netherlands
Elisabeth ANDRÉ	Universität Augsburg, Germany
Luis M. CAMARINHA-MATOS	New University of Lisbon, Portugal
S. Misbah DEEN	University of Keele, UK
Yves DEMAZEAU	Leibnitz-Institute IMAG, France
Jim DORAN	University of Essex, UK
Edmund H. DURFEE	University of Michigan, USA
Klaus FISCHER	DFKI GmbH, Germany
Les GASSER	University of Illinois, USA
Jozef KELEMEN	Silesian University, Czech Republic
Matthias KLUSCH	DFKI GmbH, Germany
Sarit KRAUS	University of Maryland, USA
Yannis LABROU	University of Maryland, USA
Jörg P. MÜLLER	Siemens AG, Germany
Bernhard NEBEL	University of Freiburg, Germany
Eugénio OLIVEIRA	University of Porto, Portugal
Paolo PETTA	Austrian Research Institute for AI, Austria
Stefan POSLAD	University of London, UK
Katia SYCARA	Carnegie Mellon University, USA
Milind TAMBE	University of Southern California, USA
Paul VALCKENAERS	Catholic University of Leuven, Belgium
Wolfgang WAHLSTER	DFKI GmbH, Germany
Hendrik VAN BRUSSEL	Catholic University of Leuven, Belgium
Wiebe VAN DER HOEK	Utrecht University, The Netherlands
Michael WOOLDRIDGE	University of Liverpool, UK

Contributors:

Stephan BALDES	DFKI GmbH, Germany
Bernhard BAUER	Siemens AG, Germany
Michael BERGER	Siemens AG, Germany
Olaf BOCHMANN	Catholic University of Leuven, Belgium
Patricia CHARLTON	University of London, UK
Kurt DRIESSENS	Catholic University of Leuven, Belgium
Petra FUNK	DFKI GmbH, Germany
Dimitar KAZAKOV	University of York, UK
Martin KOLLINGBAUM	Catholic University of Leuven, Belgium
Daniel KUDENKO	University of York, UK
Vladimír KVASNICKA	Slovak Technical University, Slovakia
Sorabain W. DE LIONCOURT	University of Warwick, UK
Michal PĚCHOUČEK	Czech Technical University, Czech Republic
Jiří POSPÍCHAL	Slovak Technical University, Slovakia
David V. PYNADATH	University of Southern California, USA
Thomas RIST	DFKI GmbH, Germany
Christian RUSS	DFKI GmbH, Germany

Organizing Committee:

Hana KRAUTWURMOVÁ	Czech Technical University, Czech Republic
Jiří LAŽANSKÝ	Czech Technical University, Czech Republic
Zuzana HOCHMEISTEROVÁ	Czech Technical University, Czech Republic
Eva KUBRYCHTOVÁ	EKU Agency, Czech Republic
Jiří PALOUŠ	Czech Technical University, Czech Republic

AEMAS 2001

International Workshop on
Adaptability and Embodiment Using Multi-Agent Systems

Prague, Czech Republic, September 7, 2001

Program Committee:

Alexis DROGOUL	Chair, Université Paris 6, France
Kerstin DAUTENHAHN	University of Hertfordshire, UK
Les GASSER	University of Illinois, USA
Yves DEMAZEAU	Institut d'Informatique et Mathématiques Appliquées de Grenoble, France
Toru ISHIDA	University of Kyoto, Japan
Jean-Pierre MÜLLER	Centre de Coopération Internationale en Recherche Agronomique pour le Développement, France

Organizing Committee:

Alain CARDON	Université du Havre LIP6, Université Paris 6 – CNRS, France
Jean-Pierre BRIOT	LIP6, Université Paris 6 – CNRS, France

HoloMAS 2001

Second International Workshop on
Industrial Applications of Holononic and Multi-Agent Systems

Munich, Germany, September 6, 2001

Workshop Co-chairs:

Vladimír MAŘÍK   Czech Technical University, Czech Republic
                             Rockwell Automation, Czech Republic
Michal PECHOUCEK   Czech Technical University, Czech Republic

Program Committee:

Luis M.CAMARINHA-MATOS   New University of Lisbon, Portugal
James CHRISTENSEN   Rockwell Automation, USA
S. Misbah DEEN   University of Keele, UK
Klaus FISCHER   DFKI GmbH, Germany
William A. GRUVER   Simon Fraser University, Canada
Duncan McFARLANE   University of Cambridge, UK
Rainer MITTMANN   Softing GmbH, Germany
Jörg P. MÜLLER   Siemens AG, Germany
Douglas H. NORRIE   University of Calgary, Canada
Paul VALCKENAERS   Catholic University of Leuven, Belgium
Jianbing WU   University of Calgary, Canada

Table of Contents

Multi-Agent Systems and Applications

ACAI 2001: Selected Tutorial Papers

Intelligent Agents: The Key Concepts

Michael Wooldridge

Department of Computer Science
University of Liverpool
Liverpool L69 7ZF, UK
mjw@csc.liv.ac.uk

Abstract. This chapter aims to introduce the reader to the basic issues surrounding the design and implementation of intelligent agents. It begins by motivating the idea of an agent, presents a definition of agents and intelligent agents. The article then goes on to discuss four major approaches to building agents. First, logic based architectures are reviewed, in which decision-making is viewed as logical deduction. Second, reactive architectures are discussed, in which symbolic representations and models are eschewed in favour of a closer relationship between agent perception and action. Third, we discuss belief-desire-intention architectures, in which decision making is viewed as practical reasoning from beliefs about how the world is and will be to the options available to an agent, and finally to intentions and actions. Fourth, we review layered agent architectures, in which decision making is partitioned into a number of different decision making layers, each dealing with the agent's environment at a different level of abstraction.

1 Introduction

Computers are not very good at knowing what to do: every action a computer performs must be explicitly anticipated, planned for, and coded by a programmer. If a computer program ever encounters a situation that its designer did not anticipate, then the result is not usually pretty – a system crash at best, multiple loss of life at worst. This mundane fact is at the heart of our relationship with computers. It is so self-evident to the computer literate that it is rarely mentioned. And yet it comes as a complete surprise to those encountering computers for the first time.

For the most part, we are happy to accept computers as obedient, literal, unimaginative servants. For many applications (such as payroll processing), it is entirely acceptable. However, for an increasingly large number of applications, we require systems that can *decide for themselves* what they need to do in order to satisfy their design objectives. Such computer systems are known as *agents*. Agents that must operate robustly in rapidly changing, unpredictable, or open environments, where there is a significant possibility that actions can *fail* are known as *intelligent agents*, or sometimes *autonomous agents*. Here are examples of recent application areas for intelligent agents:

V. Mařík et al. (Eds.): MASA 2001, LNAI 2322, pp. 3–43, 2002.
© Springer-Verlag Berlin Heidelberg 2002

- When a space probe makes its long flight from Earth to the outer planets, a ground crew is usually required to continually track its progress, and decide how to deal with unexpected eventualities. This is costly and, if decisions are required *quickly*, it is simply not practicable. For these reasons, organisations like NASA are seriously investigating the possibility of making probes more autonomous – giving them richer decision making capabilities and responsibilities.
- Searching the Internet for the answer to a specific query can be a long and tedious process. So, why not allow a computer program – an agent – do searches for us? The agent would typically be given a query that would require synthesising pieces of information from various different Internet information sources. Failure would occur when a particular resource was unavailable, (perhaps due to network failure), or where results could not be obtained.

This chapter is about intelligent agents. Specifically, it aims to give you a thorough introduction to the main issues associated with the design and implementation of intelligent agents. After reading it, you will understand:

- why agents are believed to be an important new way of conceptualising and implementing certain types of software application;
- what intelligent agents are (and are not);
- the main approaches that have been advocated for designing and implementing intelligent agents, the issues surrounding these approaches, their relative merits, and the challenges that face the agent implementor.

The chapter is structured as follows. First, Sect. 2 describes what is meant by the term *agent*. Section 3, presents some *abstract architectures* for agents. That is, some general models and properties of agents are discussed without regard to how they might be implemented. Section 4, discusses *concrete* architectures for agents. The various major design routes that one can follow in implementing an agent system are outlined in this section. In particular, *logic-based* architectures, *reactive* architectures, *belief-desire-intention* architectures, and finally, *layered* architectures for intelligent agents are described in detail.

Comments on Notation. This chapter makes use of simple mathematical notation in order to make ideas precise. The formalism used is that of discrete maths: a basic grounding in sets and first-order logic should be quite sufficient to make sense of the various definitions presented. In addition: if S is an arbitrary set, then $\wp(S)$ is the powerset of S, and S^* is the set of sequences of elements of S; the symbol $\neg$ is used for logical negation (so $\neg p$ is read "not p"); $\wedge$ is used for conjunction (so $p \wedge q$ is read "p and q"); $\vee$ is used for disjunction (so $p \vee q$ is read "p or q"); and finally, $\Rightarrow$ is used for material implication (so $p \Rightarrow q$ is read "p implies q").

2   What Are Agents?

An obvious way to open this chapter would be by presenting a definition of the term *agent*. After all, this is a book about multi-agent systems – surely we must all agree on what an agent is? Surprisingly, there is no such agreement: there is no universally accepted definition of the term agent, and indeed there is a good deal of ongoing debate and controversy on this very subject. Essentially, while there is a general consensus that *autonomy* is central to the notion of agency, there is little agreement beyond this. Part of the difficulty is that various attributes associated with agency are of differing importance for different domains. Thus, for some applications, the ability of agents to *learn* from their experiences is of paramount importance; for other applications, learning is not only unimportant, it is undesirable.

Nevertheless, some sort of definition is important – otherwise, there is a danger that the term will lose all meaning (cf. "user friendly"). The definition presented here is adapted from [55]: An *agent* is a computer system that is *situated* in some *environment*, and that is capable of *autonomous action* in this environment in order to meet its design objectives.

There are several points to note about this definition. First, the definition refers to "agents" and not "intelligent agents". The distinction is deliberate: it is discussed in more detail below. Second, the definition does not say anything about what *type* of environment an agent occupies. Again, this is deliberate: agents can occupy many different types of environment, as we shall see below. Third, we have not defined *autonomy*. Like agency itself, autonomy is a somewhat tricky concept to tie down precisely. In this chapter, it is used to mean that agents are able to act without the intervention of humans or other systems: they have control both over their own internal state, and over their behavior.

Figure 1 gives an abstract, top-level view of an agent. In this diagram, we can see the action output generated by the agent in order to affect its environment. In most domains of reasonable complexity, an agent will not have *complete* control over its environment. It will have at best *partial* control, in that it can *influence* it. From the point of view of the agent, this means that the same action performed twice in apparently identical circumstances might appear to have entirely different effects, and in particular, it may *fail* to have the desired effect. Thus agents in all but the most trivial of environments must be prepared for the possibility of *failure*. We can sum this situation up formally by saying that environments are *non-deterministic*.

Normally, an agent will have a repertoire of actions available to it. This set of possible actions represents the agents *effectoric capability*: its ability to modify its environments. Note that not all actions can be performed in all situations. For example, an action "lift table" is only applicable in situations where the weight of the table is sufficiently small that the agent *can* lift it. Similarly, the action "purchase a Ferrari" will fail if insufficient funds area available to do so. Actions therefore have *pre-conditions* associated with them, which define the possible situations in which they can be applied.

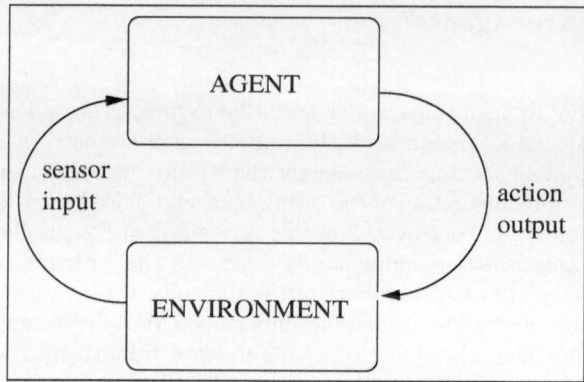

Fig. 1. An agent in its environment. The agent takes sensory input from the environment, and produces as output actions that affect it. The interaction is usually an ongoing, non-terminating one.

The key problem facing an agent is that of deciding *which* of its actions it should perform in order to best satisfy its design objectives. *Agent architectures*, of which we shall see several examples later in this chapter, are really software architectures for decision making systems that are embedded in an environment. The complexity of the decision-making process can be affected by a number of different environmental properties. Russell and Norvig suggest the following classification of environment properties [49, p46]:

- *Accessible* vs *inaccessible*.
  An accessible environment is one in which the agent can obtain complete, accurate, up-to-date information about the environment's state. Most moderately complex environments (including, for example, the everyday physical world and the Internet) are inaccessible. The more accessible an environment is, the simpler it is to build agents to operate in it.
- *Deterministic* vs *non-deterministic*.
  As we have already mentioned, a deterministic environment is one in which any action has a single guaranteed effect – there is no uncertainty about the state that will result from performing an action. The physical world can to all intents and purposes be regarded as non-deterministic. Non-deterministic environments present greater problems for the agent designer.
- *Episodic* vs *non-episodic*.
  In an episodic environment, the performance of an agent is dependent on a number of discrete episodes, with no link between the performance of an agent in different scenarios. An example of an episodic environment would be a mail sorting system [50]. Episodic environments are simpler from the agent developer's perspective because the agent can decide what action to perform based only on the current episode – it need not reason about the interactions between this and future episodes.

- *Static* vs *dynamic*.
  A static environment is one that can be assumed to remain unchanged except by the performance of actions by the agent. A dynamic environment is one that has other processes operating on it, and which hence changes in ways beyond the agent's control. The physical world is a highly dynamic environment.
- *Discrete* vs *continuous*.
  An environment is discrete if there are a fixed, finite number of actions and percepts in it. Russell and Norvig give a chess game as an example of a discrete environment, and taxi driving as an example of a continuous one.

As Russell and Norvig observe [49, p46], if an environment is sufficiently complex, then the fact that it is *actually* deterministic is not much help: to all intents and purposes, it may as well be non-deterministic. The most complex general class of environments are those that are inaccessible, non-deterministic, non-episodic, dynamic, and continuous.

2.1   Examples of Agents

At this point, it is worth pausing to consider some examples of agents (though not, as yet, intelligent agents):

- Any *control* system can be viewed as an agent. A simple (and overused) example of such a system is a thermostat. Thermostats have a sensor for detecting room temperature. This sensor is directly embedded within the environment (i.e., the room), and it produces as output one of two signals: one that indicates that the temperature is too low, another which indicates that the temperature is OK. The actions available to the thermostat are "heating on" or "heating off". The action "heating on" will generally have the effect of raising the room temperature, but this cannot be a *guaranteed* effect – if the door to the room is open, for example, switching on the heater may have no effect. The (extremely simple) decision making component of the thermostat implements (usually in electro-mechanical hardware) the following rules:

$$\text{too cold} \longrightarrow \text{heating on}$$
$$\text{temperature OK} \longrightarrow \text{heating off}$$

  More complex environment control systems, of course, have considerably richer decision structures. Examples include autonomous space probes, fly-by-wire aircraft, nuclear reactor control systems, and so on.
- Most software daemons, (such as background processes in the UNIX operating system), which monitor a software environment and perform actions to modify it, can be viewed as agents. An example is the X Windows program `xbiff`. This utility continually monitors a user's incoming email, and indicates via a GUI icon whether or not they have unread messages. Whereas our thermostat agent in the previous example inhabited a *physical* environment

– the physical world – the xbiff program inhabits a *software* environment. It obtains information about this environment by carrying out software functions (by executing system programs such as ls, for example), and the actions it performs are software actions (changing an icon on the screen, or executing a program). The decision making component is just as simple as our thermostat example.

To summarize, agents are simply computer systems that are capable of autonomous action in some environment in order to meet their design objectives. An agent will typically sense its environment (by physical sensors in the case of agents situated in part of the real world, or by software sensors in the case of software agents), and will have available a repertoire of actions that can be executed to modify the environment, which may appear to respond non-deterministically to the execution of these actions.

2.2   Intelligent Agents

We are not used to thinking of thermostats or UNIX daemons as agents, and certainly not as *intelligent* agents. So, when do we consider an agent to be intelligent? The question, like the question *what is intelligence?* itself, is not an easy one to answer. But for the purposes of this chapter, an intelligent agent is one that is capable of *flexible* autonomous action in order to meet its design objectives, where flexibility means three things [55]:

- *reactivity*: intelligent agents are able to perceive their environment, and respond in a timely fashion to changes that occur in it in order to satisfy their design objectives;
- *pro-activeness*: intelligent agents are able to exhibit goal-directed behavior by *taking the initiative* in order to satisfy their design objectives;
- *social ability*: intelligent agents are capable of interacting with other agents (and possibly humans) in order to satisfy their design objectives.

These properties are more demanding than they might at first appear. To see why, let us consider them in turn. First, consider *pro-activeness*: goal directed behavior. It is not hard to build a system that exhibits goal directed behavior – we do it every time we write a procedure in PASCAL, a function in C, or a method in JAVA. When we write such a procedure, we describe it in terms of the *assumptions* on which it relies (formally, its *pre-condition*) and the *effect* it has if the assumptions are valid (its *post-condition*). The effects of the procedure are its *goal*: what the author of the software intends the procedure to achieve. If the pre-condition holds when the procedure is invoked, then we expect that the procedure will execute *correctly*: that it will terminate, and that upon termination, the post-condition will be true, i.e., the goal will be achieved. This is goal directed behavior: the procedure is simply a plan or recipe for achieving the goal. This programming model is fine for many environments. For example, its works well when we consider *functional systems* – those that simply take some input x, and produce as output some some function $f(x)$ of this input. Compilers are a classic example of functional systems.

But for non-functional systems, this simple model of goal directed programming is not acceptable, as it makes some important limiting assumptions. In particular, it assumes that the environment *does not change* while the procedure is executing. If the environment does change, and in particular, if the assumptions (pre-condition) underlying the procedure become false while the procedure is executing, then the behavior of the procedure may not be defined – often, it will simply crash. Also, it is assumed that the goal, that is, the reason for executing the procedure, remains valid at least until the procedure terminates. If the goal does *not* remain valid, then there is simply no reason to continue executing the procedure.

In many environments, neither of these assumptions are valid. In particular, in domains that are *too complex* for an agent to observe completely, that are *multi-agent* (i.e., they are populated with more than one agent that can change the environment), or where there is *uncertainty* in the environment, these assumptions are not reasonable. In such environments, blindly executing a procedure without regard to whether the assumptions underpinning the procedure are valid is a poor strategy. In such dynamic environments, an agent must be *reactive*, in just the way that we described above. That is, it must be responsive to events that occur in its environment, where these events affect either the agent's goals or the assumptions which underpin the procedures that the agent is executing in order to achieve its goals.

As we have seen, building purely goal directed systems is not hard. As we shall see later in this chapter, building *purely reactive* systems – ones that *continually* respond to their environment – is also not difficult. However, what turns out to be hard is building a system that achieves an effective *balance* between goal-directed and reactive behavior. We want agents that will attempt to achieve their goals systematically, perhaps by making use of complex procedure-like patterns of action. But we don't want our agents to continue blindly executing these procedures in an attempt to achieve a goal either when it is clear that the procedure will not work, or when the goal is for some reason no longer valid. In such circumstances, we want our agent to be able to react to the new situation, in time for the reaction to be of some use. However, we do not want our agent to be *continually* reacting, and hence never focussing on a goal long enough to actually achieve it.

On reflection, it should come as little surprise that achieving a good balance between goal directed and reactive behavior is hard. After all, it is comparatively rare to find humans that do this very well. How many of us have had a manager who stayed blindly focussed on some project long after the relevance of the project was passed, or it was clear that the project plan was doomed to failure? Similarly, how many have encountered managers who seem unable to stay focussed at all, who flit from one project to another without ever managing to pursue a goal long enough to achieve *anything*? This problem – of effectively integrating goal-directed and reactive behavior – is one of the key problems facing the agent designer. As we shall see, a great many proposals have been made for how to build agents that can do this – but the problem is essentially still open.

Finally, let us say something about *social ability*, the final component of flexible autonomous action as defined here. In one sense, social ability is trivial: every day, millions of computers across the world routinely exchange information with both humans and other computers. But the ability to exchange bit streams is not really social ability. Consider that in the human world, comparatively few of our meaningful goals can be achieved without the *cooperation* of other people, who cannot be assumed to *share* our goals – in other words, they are themselves autonomous, with their own agenda to pursue. To achieve our goals in such situations, we must *negotiate* and *cooperate* with others. We may be required to understand and reason about the goals of others, and to perform actions (such as paying them money) that we would not otherwise choose to perform, in order to get them to cooperate with us, and achieve our goals. This type of social ability is much more complex, and much less well understood, than simply the ability to exchange binary information. Social ability in general (and topics such as negotiation and cooperation in particular) are dealt with elsewhere in this book, and will not therefore be considered here. In this chapter, we will be concerned with the decision making of *individual* intelligent agents in environments which may be dynamic, unpredictable, and uncertain, but do not contain other agents.

Sources and Further Reading. A view of artificial intelligence as the process of agent design is presented in [49], and in particular, Chapter 2 of [49] presents much useful material. The definition of agents presented here is based on [55], which also contains an extensive review of agent architectures and programming languages. In addition, [55] contains a detailed survey of *agent theories* – formalisms for reasoning about intelligent, rational agents, which is outside the scope of this chapter. This question of "what is an agent" is one that continues to generate some debate; a collection of answers may be found in [39]. The relationship between agents and objects has not been widely discussed in the literature, but see [20]. Other readable introductions to the idea of intelligent agents include [26] and [11].

3   Abstract Architectures for Intelligent Agents

We can easily formalize the abstract view of agents presented so far. First, we will assume that the state of the agent's environment can be characterized as a set $S = \{s_1, s_2, \ldots\}$ of *environment states*. At any given instant, the environment is assumed to be in one of these states. The effectoric capability of an agent is assumed to be represented by a set $A = \{a_1, a_2, \ldots\}$ of *actions*. Then abstractly, an agent can be viewed as a function

$$action : S^* \rightarrow A$$

which maps sequences of environment states to actions. We will refer to an agent modelled by a function of this form as a *standard agent*. The intuition is that an agent decides what action to perform on the basis of its history – its experiences to date. These experiences are represented as a sequence of environment states – those that the agent has thus far encountered.

The (non-deterministic) behavior of an an environment can be modelled as a function

$$env : S \times A \to \wp(S)$$

which takes the current state of the environment $s \in S$ and an action $a \in A$ (performed by the agent), and maps them to a set of environment states $env(s, a)$ – those that could result from performing action a in state s. If all the sets in the range of env are all singletons, (i.e., if the result of performing any action in any state is a set containing a single member), then the environment is *deterministic*, and its behavior can be accurately predicted.

We can represent the interaction of agent and environment as a *history*. A history h is a sequence:

$$h : s_0 \xrightarrow{a_0} s_1 \xrightarrow{a_1} s_2 \xrightarrow{a_2} s_3 \xrightarrow{a_3} \cdots \xrightarrow{a_{u-1}} s_u \xrightarrow{a_u} \cdots$$

where s_0 is the initial state of the environment (i.e., its state when the agent starts executing), a_u is the u'th action that the agent chose to perform, and s_u is the u'th environment state (which is one of the possible results of executing action a_{u-1} in state s_{u-1}). If $action : S^* \to A$ is an agent, $env : S \times A \to \wp(S)$ is an environment, and s_0 is the initial state of the environment, then the sequence

$$h : s_0 \xrightarrow{a_0} s_1 \xrightarrow{a_1} s_2 \xrightarrow{a_2} s_3 \xrightarrow{a_3} \cdots \xrightarrow{a_{u-1}} s_u \xrightarrow{a_u} \cdots$$

will represent a possible history of the agent in the environment iff the following two conditions hold:

$$\forall u \in I\!N, a_u = action((s_0, s_1, \ldots, s_u))$$

and

$$\forall u \in I\!N \text{ such that } u > 0, s_u \in env(s_{u-1}, a_{u-1}).$$

The *characteristic behavior* of an agent $action : S^* \to A$ in an environment $env : S \times A \to \wp(S)$ is the set of all the histories that satisfy these properties. If some property ϕ holds of all these histories, this property can be regarded as an invariant property of the agent in the environment. For example, if our agent is a nuclear reactor controller, (i.e., the environment is a nuclear reactor), and in all possible histories of the controller/reactor, the reactor does not blow up, then this can be regarded as a (desirable) invariant property. We will denote by $hist(agent, environment)$ the set of all histories of $agent$ in $environment$. Two agents ag_1 and ag_2 are said to be *behaviorally equivalent* with respect to environment env iff $hist(ag_1, env) = hist(ag_2, env)$, and simply behaviorally equivalent iff they are behaviorally equivalent with respect to all environments.

In general, we are interested in agents whose interaction with their environment *does not end*, i.e., they are *non-terminating*. In such cases, the histories that we consider will be infinite.

3.1   Purely Reactive Agents

Certain types of agents decide what to do without reference to their history. They base their decision making entirely on the present, with no reference at all to the past. We will call such agents *purely reactive*, since they simply respond directly to their environment. Formally, the behavior of a purely reactive agent can be represented by a function

$$action : S \rightarrow A.$$

It should be easy to see that for every purely reactive agent, there is an equivalent standard agent; the reverse, however, is not generally the case.

Our thermostat agent is an example of a purely reactive agent. Assume, without loss of generality, that the thermostat's environment can be in one of two states – either too cold, or temperature OK. Then the thermostat's action function is simply

$$action(s) = \begin{cases} \text{heater off if } s = \text{temperature OK} \\ \text{heater on otherwise.} \end{cases}$$

3.2   Perception

Viewing agents at this abstract level makes for a pleasantly simply analysis. However, it does not help us to construct them, since it gives us no clues about how to design the decision function *action*. For this reason, we will now begin to *refine* our abstract model of agents, by breaking it down into sub-systems in exactly the way that one does in standard software engineering. As we refine our view of agents, we find ourselves making *design choices* that mostly relate to the subsystems that go to make up an agent – what data and control structures will be present. An *agent architecture* is essentially a map of the internals of an agent – its data structures, the operations that may be performed on these data structures, and the control flow between these data structures. Later in this chapter, we will discuss a number of different types of agent architecture, with very different views on the data structures and algorithms that will be present within an agent. In the remainder of this section, however, we will survey some fairly high-level design decisions. The first of these is the separation of an agent's decision function into *perception* and *action* subsystems: see Fig. 2.

The idea is that the function *see* captures the agent's ability to observe its environment, whereas the *action* function represents the agent's decision making process. The *see* function might be implemented in hardware in the case of an agent situated in the physical world: for example, it might be a video camera or an infra-red sensor on a mobile robot. For a software agent, the sensors might be system commands that obtain information about the software environment, such as `ls`, `finger`, or suchlike. The *output* of the *see* function is a *percept* – a perceptual input. Let P be a (non-empty) set of percepts. Then *see* is a function

$$see : S \rightarrow P$$

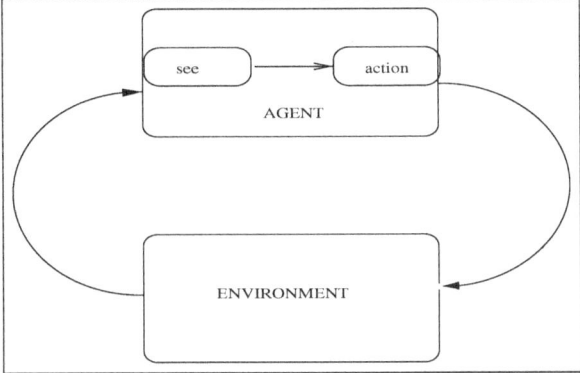

Fig. 2. Perception and action subsystems.

which maps environment states to percepts, and *action* is now a function

$$action : P^* \to A$$

which maps sequences of percepts to actions.

These simple definitions allow us to explore some interesting properties of agents and perception. Suppose that we have two environment states, $s_1 \in S$ and $s_2 \in S$, such that $s_1 \neq s_2$, but $see(s_1) = see(s_2)$. Then two *different* environment states are mapped to the *same* percept, and hence the agent would receive the same perceptual information from different environment states. As far as the agent is concerned, therefore, s_1 and s_2 are *indistinguishable*. To make this example concrete, let us return to the thermostat example. Let x represent the statement

"the room temperature is OK"

and let y represent the statement

"John Major is Prime Minister".

If these are the only two facts about our environment that we are concerned with, then the set S of environment states contains exactly four elements:

$$S = \{\underbrace{\{\neg x, \neg y\}}_{s_1}, \underbrace{\{\neg x, y\}}_{s_2}, \underbrace{\{x, \neg y\}}_{s_3}, \underbrace{\{x, y\}}_{s_4}\}$$

Thus in state s_1, the room temperature is not OK, and John Major is not Prime Minister; in state s_2, the room temperature is not OK, and John Major *is* Prime Minister. Now, our thermostat is sensitive *only* to temperatures in the room. This room temperature is not causally related to whether or not John Major is Prime Minister. Thus the states where John Major is and is not

Prime Minister are literally *indistinguishable* to the thermostat. Formally, the *see* function for the thermostat would have two percepts in its range, p_1 and p_2, indicating that the temperature is too cold or OK respectively. The *see* function for the thermostat would behave as follows:

$$see(s) = \begin{cases} p_1 \text{ if } s = s_1 \text{ or } s = s_2 \\ p_2 \text{ if } s = s_3 \text{ or } s = s_4. \end{cases}$$

Given two environment states $s \in S$ and $s' \in S$, let us write $s \equiv s'$ if $see(s) = see(s')$. It is not hard to see that $\equiv$ is an *equivalence relation* over environment states, which partitions S into mutually indistinguishable sets of states. Intuitively, the coarser these equivalence classes are, the less effective is the agent's perception. If $| \equiv | = |S|$, (i.e., the number of distinct percepts is equal to the number of different environment states), then the agent can distinguish *every* state – the agent has perfect perception in the environment; it is *omniscient*. At the other extreme, if $| \equiv | = 1$, then the agent's perceptual ability is non-existent – it cannot distinguish between *any* different states. In this case, as far as the agent is concerned, all environment states are identical.

3.3   Agents with State

We have so far been modelling an agent's decision function *action* as from *sequences* of environment states or percepts to actions. This allows us to represent agents whose decision making is influenced by history. However, this is a somewhat unintuitive representation, and we shall now replace it by an equivalent, but somewhat more natural scheme. The idea is that we now consider agents that *maintain state* – see Fig. 3.

These agents have some internal data structure, which is typically used to record information about the environment state and history. Let I be the set

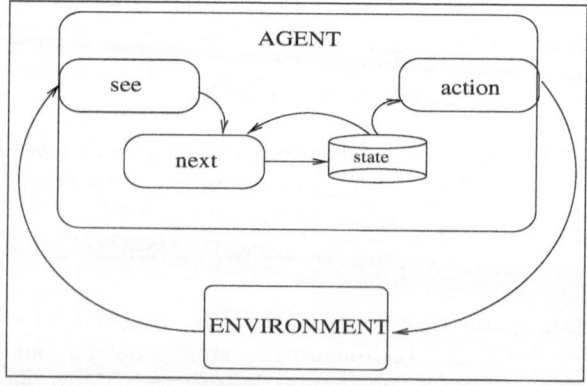

Fig. 3. Agents that maintain state.

of all internal states of the agent. An agent's decision making process is then based, at least in part, on this information. The perception function *see* for a state-based agent is unchanged, mapping environment states to percepts as before:

$$see : S \rightarrow P$$

The action-selection function *action* is now defined as a mapping

$$action : I \rightarrow A$$

from internal states to actions. An additional function *next* is introduced, which maps an internal state and percept to an internal state:

$$next : I \times P \rightarrow I$$

The behavior of a state-based agent can be summarized as follows. The agent starts in some initial internal state i_0. It then observes its environment state s, and generates a percept $see(s)$. The internal state of the agent is then updated via the *next* function, becoming set to $next(i_0, see(s))$. The action selected by the agent is then $action(next(i_0, see(s)))$. This action is then performed, and the agent enters another cycle, perceiving the world via *see*, updating its state via *next*, and choosing an action to perform via *action*.

It is worth observing that state-based agents as defined here are in fact no more powerful than the standard agents we introduced earlier. In fact, they are *identical* in their expressive power – every state-based agent can be transformed into a standard agent that is behaviorally equivalent.

Sources and Further Reading. The abstract model of agents presented here is based on that given in [21, Chapter 13], and also makes use of some ideas from [51,50]. The properties of perception as discussed in this section lead to *knowledge theory*, a formal analysis of the information implicit within the state of computer processes, which has had a profound effect in theoretical computer science. The definitive reference is [12], and an introductory survey is [25].

4   Concrete Architectures for Intelligent Agents

Thus far, we have considered agents only in the abstract. So while we have examined the properties of agents that do and do not maintain state, we have not stopped to consider what this state might look like. Similarly, we have modelled an agent's decision making as an abstract function *action*, which somehow manages to indicate which action to perform – but we have not discussed how this function might be implemented. In this section, we will rectify this omission. We will consider four classes of agents:

– *logic based agents* – in which decision making is realized through logical deduction;

- *reactive agents* – in which decision making is implemented in some form of direct mapping from situation to action;
- *belief-desire-intention agents* – in which decision making depends upon the manipulation of data structures representing the beliefs, desires, and intentions of the agent; and finally,
- *layered architectures* – in which decision making is realized via various software layers, each of which is more-or-less explicitly reasoning about the environment at different levels of abstraction.

In each of these cases, we are moving away from the abstract view of agents, and beginning to make quite specific commitments about the internal structure and operation of agents. Each section explains the nature of these commitments, the assumptions upon which the architectures depend, and the relative advantages and disadvantages of each.

4.1   Logic-Based Architectures

The "traditional" approach to building artificially intelligent systems, (known as *symbolic AI*) suggests that intelligent behavior can be generated in a system by giving that system a *symbolic* representation of its environment and its desired behavior, and syntactically manipulating this representation. In this section, we focus on the apotheosis of this tradition, in which these symbolic representations are *logical formulae*, and the syntactic manipulation corresponds to *logical deduction*, or *theorem proving*.

The idea of agents as theorem provers is seductive. Suppose we have some theory of agency – some theory that explains how an intelligent agent should behave. This theory might explain, for example, how an agent generates goals so as to satisfy its design objective, how it interleaves goal-directed and reactive behavior in order to achieve these goals, and so on. Then this theory ϕ can be considered as a *specification* for how an agent should behave. The traditional approach to implementing a system that will satisfy this specification would involve *refining* the specification through a series of progressively more concrete stages, until finally an implementation was reached. In the view of agents as theorem provers, however, no such refinement takes place. Instead, ϕ is viewed as an *executable specification*: it is *directly executed* in order to produce the agent's behavior.

To see how such an idea might work, we shall develop a simple model of logic-based agents, which we shall call *deliberate* agents. In such agents, the internal state is assumed to be a database of formulae of classical first-order predicate logic. For example, the agent's database might contain formulae such as:

$$Open(valve221)$$
$$Temperature(reactor4726, 321)$$
$$Pressure(tank776, 28)$$

It is not difficult to see how formulae such as these can be used to represent the properties of some environment. The database is the *information* that the agent has about its environment. An agent's database plays a somewhat analogous role to that of *belief* in humans. Thus a person might have a belief that valve 221 is open – the agent might have the predicate $Open(valve221)$ in its database. Of course, just like humans, agents can be wrong. Thus I might believe that valve 221 is open when it is in fact closed; the fact that an agent has $Open(valve221)$ in its database does not mean that valve 221 (or indeed any valve) is open. The agent's sensors may be faulty, its reasoning may be faulty, the information may be out of date, or the interpretation of the formula $Open(valve221)$ intended by the agent's designer may be something entirely different.

Let L be the set of sentences of classical first-order logic, and let $D = \wp(L)$ be the set of L *databases*, i.e., the set of sets of L-formulae. The internal state of an agent is then an element of D. We write $\Delta, \Delta_1, \ldots$ for members of D. The internal state of an agent is then simply a member of the set D. An agent's decision making process is modelled through a set of *deduction rules*, ρ. These are simply rules of inference for the logic. We write $\Delta \vdash_\rho \phi$ if the formula ϕ can be proved from the database Δ using only the deduction rules ρ. An agents perception function *see* remains unchanged:

$$see : S \rightarrow P.$$

Similarly, our *next* function has the form

$$next : D \times P \rightarrow D$$

It thus maps a database and a percept to a new database. However, an agent's action selection function, which has the signature

$$action : D \rightarrow A$$

is defined in terms of its deduction rules. The pseudo-code definition of this function is as follows.

```
1.    function action(Δ : D) : A
2.    begin
3.            for each a ∈ A do
4.                    if Δ ⊢ρ Do(a) then
5.                            return a
6.                    end-if
7.            end-for
8.            for each a ∈ A do
9.                    if Δ ⊬ρ ¬Do(a) then
10.                           return a
11.                   end-if
12.           end-for
13.           return null
14.   end function action
```

The idea is that the agent programmer will encode the deduction rules ρ and database Δ in such a way that if a formula $Do(a)$ can be derived, where a is a term that denotes an action, then a is the best action to perform. Thus, in the first part of the function (lines (3)–(7)), the agent takes each of its possible actions a in turn, and attempts to prove the form the formula $Do(a)$ from its database (passed as a parameter to the function) using its deduction rules ρ. If the agent succeeds in proving $Do(a)$, then a is returned as the action to be performed.

What happens if the agent fails to prove $Do(a)$, for all actions $a \in A$? In this case, it attempts to find an action that is *consistent* with the rules and database, i.e., one that is not explicitly forbidden. In lines (8)–(12), therefore, the agent attempts to find an action $a \in A$ such that $\neg Do(a)$ cannot be derived from its database using its deduction rules. If it can find such an action, then this is returned as the action to be performed. If, however, the agent fails to find an action that is at least consistent, then it returns a special action *null* (or *noop*), indicating that no action has been selected.

In this way, the agent's behavior is determined by the agent's deduction rules (its "program") and its current database (representing the information the agent has about its environment).

To illustrate these ideas, let us consider a small example (based on the vacuum cleaning world example of [49, p51]). The idea is that we have a small robotic agent that will clean up a house. The robot is equipped with a sensor that will tell it whether it is over any dirt, and a vacuum cleaner that can be used to suck up dirt. In addition, the robot always has a definite orientation (one of *north*, *south*, *east*, or *west*). In addition to being able to suck up dirt, the agent can move forward one "step" or turn right 90°. The agent moves around a room, which is divided grid-like into a number of equally sized squares (conveniently corresponding to the unit of movement of the agent). We will assume that our agent does nothing but clean – it never leaves the room, and further, we will assume in the interests of simplicity that the room is a 3×3 grid, and the agent always starts in grid square $(0,0)$ facing north.

To summarize, our agent can receive a percept *dirt* (signifying that there is dirt beneath it), or *null* (indicating no special information). It can perform any one of three possible actions: *forward*, *suck*, or *turn*. The goal is to traverse the room continually searching for and removing dirt. See Fig. 4 for an illustration of the vacuum world.

First, note that we make use of three simple *domain predicates* in this exercise:

$In(x, y)$ agent is at (x, y)
$Dirt(x, y)$ there is dirt at (x, y)
$Facing(d)$ the agent is facing direction d

Now we specify our *next* function. This function must look at the perceptual information obtained from the environment (either *dirt* or *null*), and generate a new database which includes this information. But in addition, it must *remove* old or irrelevant information, and also, it must try to figure out the new location

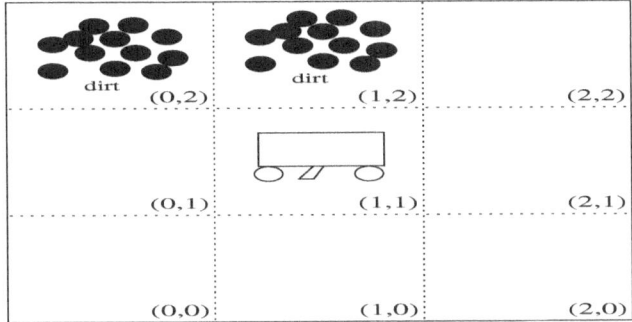

Fig. 4. Vacuum world

and orientation of the agent. We will therefore specify the *next* function in several parts. First, let us write $old(\Delta)$ to denote the set of "old" information in a database, which we want the update function *next* to remove:

$$old(\Delta) = \{P(t_1, \ldots, t_n) \mid P \in \{ \textit{In}, \textit{Dirt}, \textit{Facing}\} \text{ and } P(t_1, \ldots, t_n) \in \Delta\}$$

Next, we require a function *new*, which gives the set of new predicates to add to the database. This function has the signature

$$new : D \times P \rightarrow D$$

The definition of this function is not difficult, but it is rather lengthy, and so we will leave it as an exercise. (It must generate the predicates $\textit{In}(\ldots)$, describing the new position of the agent, $\textit{Facing}(\ldots)$ describing the orientation of the agent, and $\textit{Dirt}(\ldots)$ if dirt has been detected at the new position.) Given the *new* and *old* functions, the *next* function is defined as follows:

$$next(\Delta, p) = (\Delta \setminus old(\Delta)) \cup new(\Delta, p)$$

Now we can move on to the rules that govern our agent's behavior. The deduction rules have the form

$$\phi(\ldots) \longrightarrow \psi(\ldots)$$

where ϕ and ψ are predicates over some arbitrary list of constants and variables. The idea being that if ϕ matches against the agent's database, then ψ can be concluded, with any variables in ψ instantiated.

The first rule deals with the basic cleaning action of the agent: this rule will take priority over all other possible behaviors of the agent (such as navigation).

$$In(x, y) \wedge Dirt(x, y) \longrightarrow Do(suck) \tag{1}$$

Hence if the agent is at location (x, y) and it perceives dirt, then the prescribed action will be to suck up dirt. Otherwise, the basic action of the agent will be to traverse the world. Taking advantage of the simplicity of our environment, we will hardwire the basic navigation algorithm, so that the robot will always move from $(0,0)$ to $(0,1)$ to $(0,2)$ and then to $(1,2)$, $(1,1)$ and so on. Once the agent reaches $(2,2)$, it must head back to $(0,0)$. The rules dealing with the traversal up to $(0,2)$ are very simple.

$$In(0,0) \wedge Facing(north) \wedge \neg Dirt(0,0) \longrightarrow Do(forward) \qquad (2)$$

$$In(0,1) \wedge Facing(north) \wedge \neg Dirt(0,1) \longrightarrow Do(forward) \qquad (3)$$

$$In(0,2) \wedge Facing(north) \wedge \neg Dirt(0,2) \longrightarrow Do(turn) \qquad (4)$$

$$In(0,2) \wedge Facing(east) \longrightarrow Do(forward) \qquad (5)$$

Notice that in each rule, we must explicitly check whether the antecedent of rule (1) fires. This is to ensure that we only ever prescribe one action via the $Do(\ldots)$ predicate. Similar rules can easily be generated that will get the agent to $(2,2)$, and once at $(2,2)$ back to $(0,0)$. It is not difficult to see that these rules, together with the *next* function, will generate the required behavior of our agent.

At this point, it is worth stepping back and examining the pragmatics of the logic-based approach to building agents. Probably the most important point to make is that a literal, naive attempt to build agents in this way would be more or less entirely impractical. To see why, suppose we have designed out agent's rule set ρ such that for any database Δ, if we can prove $Do(a)$ then a is an *optimal* action – that is, a is the best action that could be performed when the environment is as described in Δ. Then imagine we start running our agent. At time t_1, the agent has generated some database Δ_1, and begins to apply its rules ρ in order to find which action to perform. Some time later, at time t_2, it manages to establish $\Delta_1 \vdash_\rho Do(a)$ for some $a \in A$, and so a is the optimal action that the agent could perform at time t_1. But if the environment has *changed* between t_1 and t_2, then there is no guarantee that a will *still* be optimal. It could be far from optimal, particularly if much time has elapsed between t_1 and t_2. If $t_2 - t_1$ is infinitesimal – that is, if decision making is effectively instantaneous – then we could safely disregard this problem. But in fact, we know that reasoning of the kind our logic-based agents use will be anything *but* instantaneous. (If our agent uses classical first-order predicate logic to represent the environment, and its rules are sound and complete, then there is no guarantee that the decision making procedure will even *terminate*.) An agent is said to enjoy the property of *calculative rationality* if and only if its decision making apparatus will suggest an action that was optimal *when the decision making process began*. Calculative rationality is clearly not acceptable in environments that change faster than the agent can make decisions – we shall return to this point later.

One might argue that this problem is an artifact of the pure logic-based approach adopted here. There is an element of truth in this. By moving away from strictly logical representation languages and complete sets of deduction rules, one can build agents that enjoy respectable performance. But one also loses what is arguably the greatest advantage that the logical approach brings: a simple, elegant logical semantics.

There are several other problems associated with the logical approach to agency. First, the *see* function of an agent, (its perception component), maps its environment to a percept. In the case of a logic-based agent, this percept is likely to be symbolic – typically, a set of formulae in the agent's representation language. But for many environments, it is not obvious how the mapping from environment to symbolic percept might be realized. For example, the problem of transforming an image to a set of declarative statements representing that image has been the object of study in AI for decades, and is still essentially open. Another problem is that actually *representing* properties of dynamic, real-world environments is extremely hard. As an example, representing and reasoning about *temporal information* – how a situation changes over time – turns out to be extraordinarily difficult. Finally, as the simple vacuum world example illustrates, representing even rather simple *procedural* knowledge (i.e., knowledge about "what to do") in traditional logic can be rather unintuitive and cumbersome.

To summarize, in logic-based approaches to building agents, decision making is viewed as deduction. An agent's "program" – that is, its decision making strategy – is encoded as a logical theory, and the process of selecting an action reduces to a problem of proof. Logic-based approaches are elegant, and have a clean (logical) semantics – wherein lies much of their long-lived appeal. But logic-based approaches have many disadvantages. In particular, the inherent computational complexity of theorem proving makes it questionable whether agents as theorem provers can operate effectively in time-constrained environments. Decision making in such agents is predicated on the assumption of calculative rationality – the assumption that the world will not change in any significant way while the agent is deciding what to do, and that an action which is rational when decision making begins will be rational when it concludes. The problems associated with representing and reasoning about complex, dynamic, possibly physical environments are also essentially unsolved.

Sources and Further Reading. My presentation of logic based agents is based largely on the discussion of *deliberate agents* presented in [21, Chapter 13], which represents the logic-centric view of AI and agents very well. The discussion is also partly based on [30]. A number of more-or-less "pure" logical approaches to agent programming have been developed. Well-known examples include the CONGOLOG system of Lespérance and colleagues [31] (which is based on the *situation calculus* [36]) and the METATEM and Concurrent METATEM programming languages developed by Fisher and colleagues [3,19] (in which agents are programmed by giving them *temporal logic* specifications of the behavior they should exhibit). Note that these architectures (and the discussion above) assume that if one adopts a logical approach to agent-building, then this means agents are essentially theorem provers, employing explicit symbolic reasoning (theorem proving) in order to make decisions. But just because we find logic a useful tool for conceptualising or specifying agents, this does not mean that we must view decision-making as logical manipulation. An alternative is to *compile* the logical specification of an agent into a form more amenable to efficient decision making. The difference is rather like the distinction between interpreted and compiled programming languages. The best-known example of this work is the *situated automata* paradigm of Leslie Kaelbling and Stanley Rosenschein [48]. A review of the role of logic in intelligent agents may be found in [54]. Finally, for a detailed discussion of calculative rationality and the way that it has affected thinking in AI, see [50].

4.2   Reactive Architectures

The seemingly intractable problems with symbolic/logical approaches to building agents led some researchers to question, and ultimately reject, the assumptions upon which such approaches are based. These researchers have argued that minor changes to the symbolic approach, such as weakening the logical representation language, will not be sufficient to build agents that can operate in time-constrained environments: nothing less than a whole new approach is required. In the mid-to-late 1980s, these researchers began to investigate alternatives to the symbolic AI paradigm. It is difficult to neatly characterize these different approaches, since their advocates are united mainly by a rejection of symbolic AI, rather than by a common manifesto. However, certain themes do recur:

- the rejection of symbolic representations, and of decision making based on syntactic manipulation of such representations;
- the idea that intelligent, rational behavior is seen as innately linked to the *environment* an agent occupies – intelligent behavior is not disembodied, but is a product of the *interaction* the agent maintains with its environment;
- the idea that intelligent behavior *emerges* from the interaction of various simpler behaviors.

Alternative approaches to agency are sometime referred to as *behavioral* (since a common theme is that of developing and combining individual behaviors), *situated* (since a common theme is that of agents actually situated in some environment, rather than being disembodied from it), and finally – the term used in this chapter – *reactive* (because such systems are often perceived as simply reacting to an environment, without reasoning about it). This section presents a survey of the *subsumption architecture*, which is arguably the best-known reactive agent architecture. It was developed by Rodney Brooks – one of the most vocal and influential critics of the symbolic approach to agency to have emerged in recent years.

There are two defining characteristics of the subsumption architecture. The first is that an agent's decision-making is realized through a set of *task accomplishing behaviors*; each behavior may be thought of as an individual *action* function, as we defined above, which continually takes perceptual input and maps it to an action to perform. Each of these behavior modules is intended to achieve some particular task. In Brooks' implementation, the behavior modules are finite state machines. An important point to note is that these task accomplishing modules are assumed to include *no* complex symbolic representations, and are assumed to do *no* symbolic reasoning at all. In many implementations, these behaviors are implemented as rules of the form

$$\text{situation} \longrightarrow \text{action}$$

which simply map perceptual input directly to actions.

The second defining characteristic of the subsumption architecture is that many behaviors can "fire" simultaneously. There must obviously be a mechanism to choose between the different actions selected by these multiple actions. Brooks proposed arranging the modules into a *subsumption hierarchy*, with the behaviors arranged into *layers*. Lower layers in the hierarchy are able to *inhibit* higher layers: the lower a layer is, the higher is its priority. The idea is that higher layers represent more abstract behaviors. For example, one might desire a behavior in a mobile robot for the behavior "avoid obstacles". It makes sense to give obstacle avoidance a high priority – hence this behavior will typically be encoded in a *low-level* layer, which has *high* priority. To illustrate the subsumption architecture in more detail, we will now present a simple formal model of it, and illustrate how it works by means of a short example. We then discuss its relative advantages and shortcomings, and point at other similar reactive architectures.

The *see* function, which represents the agent's perceptual ability, is assumed to remain unchanged. However, in implemented subsumption architecture systems, there is assumed to be quite tight coupling between perception and action – raw sensor input is not processed or transformed much, and there is certainly no attempt to transform images to symbolic representations.

The decision function *action* is realized through a set of behaviors, together with an *inhibition* relation holding between these behaviors. A behavior is a pair (c, a), where $c \subseteq P$ is a set of percepts called the *condition*, and $a \in A$ is an action. A behavior (c, a) will *fire* when the environment is in state $s \in S$ iff $see(s) \in c$. Let $Beh = \{(c, a) \mid c \subseteq P \text{ and } a \in A\}$ be the set of all such rules.

Associated with an agent's set of behavior rules $R \subseteq Beh$ is a binary *inhibition relation* on the set of behaviors: $\prec \subseteq R \times R$. This relation is assumed to be a total ordering on R (i.e., it is transitive, irreflexive, and antisymmetric). We write $b_1 \prec b_2$ if $(b_1, b_2) \in \prec$, and read this as "b_1 inhibits b_2", that is, b_1 is lower in the hierarchy than b_2, and will hence get priority over b_2. The action function is then defined as follows:

```
1.    function action(p : P) : A
2.    var fired : ℘(R)
3.    var selected : A
4.    begin
5.        fired := {(c, a) | (c, a) ∈ R and p ∈ c}
6.        for each (c, a) ∈ fired do
7.            if ¬(∃(c′, a′) ∈ fired such that (c′, a′) ≺ (c, a)) then
8.                return a
```

```
9.                    end-if
10.         end-for
11.         return null
12.   end function action
```

Thus action selection begins by first computing the set *fired* of all behaviors that fire (5). Then, each behavior (c, a) that fires is checked, to determine whether there is some other higher priority behavior that fires. If not, then the action part of the behavior, a, is returned as the selected action (8). If no behavior fires, then the distinguished action *null* will be returned, indicating that no action has been chosen.

Given that one of our main concerns with logic-based decision making was its theoretical complexity, it is worth pausing to examine how well our simple behavior-based system performs. The overall time complexity of the subsumption action function is no worse than $O(n^2)$, where n is the larger of the number of behaviors or number of percepts. Thus, even with the naive algorithm above, decision making is tractable. In practice, we can do *considerably* better than this: the decision making logic can be encoded into hardware, giving *constant* decision time. For modern hardware, this means that an agent can be guaranteed to select an action within nano-seconds. Perhaps more than anything else, this computational simplicity is the strength of the subsumption architecture.

To illustrate how the subsumption architecture in more detail, we will show how subsumption architecture agents were built for the following scenario (this example is adapted from [53]):

> *The objective is to explore a distant planet, more concretely, to collect samples of a particular type of precious rock. The location of the rock samples is not known in advance, but they are typically clustered in certain spots. A number of autonomous vehicles are available that can drive around the planet collecting samples and later reenter the a mothership spacecraft to go back to earth. There is no detailed map of the planet available, although it is known that the terrain is full of obstacles – hills, valleys, etc. – which prevent the vehicles from exchanging any communication.*

The problem we are faced with is that of building an agent control architecture for each vehicle, so that they will cooperate to collect rock samples from the planet surface as efficiently as possible. Luc Steels argues that logic-based agents, of the type we described above, are "entirely unrealistic" for this problem [53]. Instead, he proposes a solution using the subsumption architecture.

The solution makes use of two mechanisms introduced by Steels: The first is a *gradient field*. In order that agents can know in which direction the mothership lies, the mothership generates a radio signal. Now this signal will obviously weaken as distance to the source increases – to find the direction of the mothership, an agent need therefore only travel "up the gradient" of signal strength. The signal need not carry any information – it need only exist.

The second mechanism enables agents to communicate with one another. The characteristics of the terrain prevent direct communication (such as message passing), so Steels adopted an *indirect* communication method. The idea is that agents will carry "radioactive crumbs", which can be dropped, picked up, and detected by passing robots. Thus if an agent drops some of these crumbs in a particular location, then later, another agent happening upon this location will be able to detect them. This simple mechanism enables a quite sophisticated form of cooperation.

The behavior of an individual agent is then built up from a number of behaviors, as we indicated above. First, we will see how agents can be programmed to *individually* collect samples. We will then see how agents can be programmed to generate a *cooperative* solution.

For individual (non-cooperative) agents, the lowest-level behavior, (and hence the behavior with the highest "priority") is obstacle avoidance. This behavior can can be represented in the rule:

$$\text{\textit{if} detect an obstacle \textit{then} change direction.} \qquad (6)$$

The second behavior ensures that any samples carried by agents are dropped back at the mother-ship.

$$\text{\textit{if} carrying samples \textit{and} at the base \textit{then} drop samples} \qquad (7)$$

$$\text{\textit{if} carrying samples and \textit{not} at the base \textit{then} travel up gradient.} \qquad (8)$$

Behavior (8) ensures that agents carrying samples will return to the mother-ship (by heading towards the origin of the gradient field). The next behavior ensures that agents will collect samples they find.

$$\text{\textit{if} detect a sample \textit{then} pick sample up.} \qquad (9)$$

The final behavior ensures that an agent with "nothing better to do" will explore randomly.

$$\text{\textit{if} true \textit{then} move randomly.} \qquad (10)$$

The pre-condition of this rule is thus assumed to always fire. These behaviors are arranged into the following hierarchy:

$$(6) \prec (7) \prec (8) \prec (9) \prec (10)$$

The subsumption hierarchy for this example ensures that, for example, an agent will *always* turn if any obstacles are detected; if the agent is at the mother-ship and is carrying samples, then it will *always* drop them if it is not in any immediate danger of crashing, and so on. The "top level" behavior – a random walk – will only ever be carried out if the agent has nothing more urgent to do. It is not difficult to see how this simple set of behaviors will solve the problem: agents will search for samples (ultimately by searching randomly), and when they find them, will return them to the mother-ship.

If the samples are distributed across the terrain entirely at random, then equipping a large number of robots with these very simple behaviors will work extremely well. But we know from the problem specification, above, that this is not the case: the samples tend to be located in clusters. In this case, it makes sense to have agents *cooperate* with one-another in order to find the samples. Thus when one agent finds a large sample, it would be helpful for it to communicate this to the other agents, so they can help it collect the rocks. Unfortunately, we also know from the problem specification that *direct* communication is impossible. Steels developed a simple solution to this problem, partly inspired by the foraging behavior of ants. The idea revolves around an agent creating a "trail" of radioactive crumbs whenever it finds a rock sample. The trail will be created when the agent returns the rock samples to the mother ship. If at some later point, another agent comes across this trail, then it need only follow it down the gradient field to locate the source of the rock samples. Some small refinements improve the efficiency of this ingenious scheme still further. First, as an agent follows a trail to the rock sample source, it picks up some of the crumbs it finds, hence making the trail fainter. Secondly, the trail is *only* laid by agents returning to the mothership. Hence if an agent follows the trail out to the source of the nominal rock sample only to find that it contains no samples, it will reduce the trail on the way out, and will not return with samples to reinforce it. After a few agents have followed the trail to find no sample at the end of it, the trail will in fact have been removed.

The modified behaviors for this example are as follows. Obstacle avoidance, (6), remains unchanged. However, the two rules determining what to do if carrying a sample are modified as follows.

$$if \text{ carrying samples } and \text{ at the base } then \text{ drop samples} \qquad (11)$$

$$
\begin{aligned}
&if \text{ carrying samples and } not \text{ at the base} \\
&then \text{ drop 2 crumbs } and \text{ travel up gradient.}
\end{aligned} \qquad (12)
$$

The behavior (12) requires an agent to drop crumbs when returning to base with a sample, thus either reinforcing or creating a trail. The "pick up sample" behavior, (9), remains unchanged. However, an additional behavior is required for dealing with crumbs.

$$if \text{ sense crumbs } then \text{ pick up 1 crumb } and \text{ travel down gradient} \qquad (13)$$

Finally, the random movement behavior, (10), remains unchanged. These behavior are then arranged into the following subsumption hierarchy.

$$(6) \prec (11) \prec (12) \prec (9) \prec (13) \prec (10)$$

Steels shows how this simple adjustment achieves near-optimal performance in many situations. Moreover, the solution is *cheap* (the computing power required by each agent is minimal) and *robust* (the loss of a single agent will not affect the overall system significantly).

In summary, there are obvious advantages to reactive approaches such as that Brooks' subsumption architecture: simplicity, economy, computational tractability, robustness against failure, and elegance all make such architectures appealing. But there are some fundamental, unsolved problems, not just with the subsumption architecture, but with other purely reactive architectures:

- If agents do not employ models of their environment, then they must have sufficient information available in their *local* environment for them to determine an acceptable action.
- Since purely reactive agents make decisions based on *local* information, (i.e., information about the agents *current* state), it is difficult to see how such decision making could take into account *non-local* information – it must inherently take a "short term" view.
- It is difficult to see how purely reactive agents can be designed that *learn* from experience, and improve their performance over time.
- A major selling point of purely reactive systems is that overall behavior *emerges* from the interaction of the component behaviors when the agent is placed in its environment. But the very term "emerges" suggests that the relationship between individual behaviors, environment, and overall behavior is not understandable. This necessarily makes it very hard to *engineer* agents to fulfill specific tasks. Ultimately, there is no principled *methodology* for building such agents: one must use a laborious process of experimentation, trial, and error to engineer an agent.
- While effective agents can be generated with small numbers of behaviors (typically less than ten layers), it is *much* harder to build agents that contain many layers. The dynamics of the interactions between the different behaviors become too complex to understand.

Various solutions to these problems have been proposed. One of the most popular of these is the idea of *evolving* agents to perform certain tasks. This area of work has largely broken away from the mainstream AI tradition in which work on, for example, logic-based agents is carried out, and is documented primarily in the *artificial life* (alife) literature.

Sources and Further Reading. Brooks' original paper on the subsumption architecture – the one that started all the fuss – was published as [7]. The description and discussion here is partly based on [13]. This original paper seems to be somewhat less radical than many of his later ones, which include [8,10,9]. The version of the subsumption architecture used in this chapter is actually a simplification of that presented by Brooks. The subsumption architecture is probably the best-known reactive architecture around – but there are many others. The collection of papers edited by Pattie Maes [33] contains papers that describe many of these, as does the collection by Agre and Rosenschein [2]. Other approaches include:

- the *agent network architecture* developed by Pattie Maes [32,34,35];

- Nilsson's *teleo reactive programs* [40];
- Rosenchein and Kaelbling's *situated automata* approach, which is particularly interesting in that it shows how agents can be *specified* in an abstract, logical framework, and *compiled* into equivalent, but computationally very simple machines [47,28,27,48];
- Agre and Chapman's PENGI system [1];
- Schoppers' *universal plans* – which are essentially decision trees that can be used to efficiently determine an appropriate action in any situation [52];
- Firby's *reactive action packages* [17].

Kaelbling [26] gives a good discussion of the issues associated with developing resource-bounded rational agents, and proposes an agent architecture somewhat similar to that developed by Brooks.

4.3   Belief-Desire-Intention Architectures

In this section, we shall discuss *belief-desire-intention* (BDI) architectures. These architectures have their roots in the philosophical tradition of understanding *practical reasoning* – the process of deciding, moment by moment, which action to perform in the furtherance of our goals.

Practical reasoning involves two important processes: deciding *what* goals we want to achieve, and *how* we are going to achieve these goals. The former process is known as *deliberation*, the latter as *means-ends* reasoning. To gain an understanding of the BDI model, it is worth considering a simple example of practical reasoning. When you leave university with a first degree, you are faced with a decision to make – about what to do with your life. The decision process typically begins by trying to understand what the *options* available to you are. For example, if you gain a good first degree, then one option is that of becoming an academic. (If you fail to obtain a good degree, this option is not available to you.) Another option is entering industry. After generating this set of alternatives, you must *choose between them*, and *commit* to some. These chosen options become *intentions*, which then determine the agent's actions. Intentions then feed back into the agent's future practical reasoning. For example, if I decide I want to be an academic, then I should commit to this objective, and devote time and effort to bringing it about.

Intentions play a crucial role in the practical reasoning process. Perhaps the most obvious property of intentions is that they tend to lead to action. If I truly have an intention to become an academic, then you would expect me to *act* on that intention – to try to achieve it. For example, you might expect me to apply to various PhD programs. You would expect to make a *reasonable attempt* to achieve the intention. Thus you would expect me to carry out some course of action that I believed would best satisfy the intention. Moreover, if a course of action fails to achieve the intention, then you would expect me to *try again* – you would not expect me to simply give up. For example, if my first application for a PhD programme is rejected, then you might expect me to apply to alternative universities.

In addition, once I have adopted an intention, then the very fact of having this intention will constrain my future practical reasoning. For example, while I hold some particular intention, I will not entertain options that are inconsistent with that intention. Intending to become an academic, for example, would preclude the option of partying every night: the two are mutually exclusive.

Next, intentions *persist*. If I adopt an intention to become an academic, then I should *persist* with this intention and attempt to achieve it. For if I immediately drop my intentions without devoting resources to achieving them, then I will never achieve anything. However, I should not persist with my intention for too long – if it becomes clear to me that I will *never* become an academic, then it is only rational to drop my intention to do so. Similarly, if the reason for having an intention goes away, then it is rational of me to drop the intention. For example, if I adopted the intention to become an academic because I believed it would be an easy life, but then discover that I would be expected to actually *teach*, then the justification for the intention is no longer present, and I should drop the intention.

Finally, intentions are closely related to beliefs about the future. For example, if I intend to become an academic, then I should believe that I will indeed become an academic. For if I truly believe that I will never be an academic, it would be non-sensical of me to have an intention to become one. Thus if I intend to become an academic, I should at least believe that there is a good chance I will indeed become one.

From this discussion, we can see that intentions play a number of important roles in practical reasoning:

- *Intentions drive means-ends reasoning.*
  If I have formed an intention to become an academic, then I will attempt to achieve the intention, which involves, amongst other things, deciding *how* to achieve it, for example, by applying for a PhD programme. Moreover, if one particular course of action fails to achieve an intention, then I will typically attempt others. Thus if I fail to gain a PhD place at one university, I might try another university.
- *Intentions constrain future deliberation.*
  If I intend to become an academic, then I will not entertain options that are inconsistent with this intention. For example, a rational agent would not consider being rich as an option while simultaneously intending to be an academic. (While the two are not actually mutually exclusive, the probability of simultaneously achieving both is infinitesimal.)
- *Intentions persist.*
  I will not usually give up on my intentions without good reason – they will persist, typically until either I believe I have successfully achieved them, I believe I cannot achieve them, or else because the purpose for the intention is no longer present.
- *Intentions influence beliefs upon which future practical reasoning is based.*
  If I adopt the intention to become an academic, then I can plan for the future on the assumption that I *will* be an academic. For if I intend to be

an academic while simultaneously believing that I will never be one, then I am being irrational.

A key problem in the design of practical reasoning agents is that of achieving a good *balance* between these different concerns. Specifically, it seems clear that an agent should at times drop some intentions (because it comes to believe that either they will never be achieved, they are achieved, or else because the reason for having the intention is no longer present). It follows that, from time to time, it is worth an agent stopping to *reconsider* its intentions. But reconsideration has a cost – in terms of both time and computational resources. But this presents us with a dilemma:

- an agent that does not stop to reconsider sufficiently often will continue attempting to achieve its intentions even after it is clear that they cannot be achieved, or that there is no longer any reason for achieving them;
- an agent that *constantly* reconsiders its attentions may spend insufficient time actually working to achieve them, and hence runs the risk of never actually achieving them.

This dilemma is essentially the problem of balancing pro-active (goal directed) and reactive (event driven) behavior, that we introduced in section 2.2.

There is clearly a tradeoff to be struck between the degree of commitment and reconsideration at work here. The nature of this tradeoff was examined by David Kinny and Michael Georgeff, in a number of experiments carried out with a BDI agent framework called dMARS [29]. They investigate how *bold* agents (those that never stop to reconsider) and *cautious* agents (those that are constantly stopping to reconsider) perform in a variety of different environments. The most important parameter in these experiments was the *rate of world change*, γ. The key results of Kinny and Georgeff were as follows.

- If γ is low, (i.e., the environment does not change quickly), then bold agents do well compared to cautious ones, because cautious ones waste time reconsidering their commitments while bold agents are busy working towards – and achieving – their goals.
- If γ is high, (i.e., the environment changes frequently), then cautious agents tend to outperform bold agents, because they are able to recognize when intentions are doomed, and also to take advantage of serendipitous situations and new opportunities.

The lesson is that different types of environment require different types of decision strategies. In static, unchanging environment, purely pro-active, goal directed behavior is adequate. But in more dynamic environments, the ability to react to changes by modifying intentions becomes more important.

The process of practical reasoning in a BDI agent is summarized in Fig. 5. As this figure illustrates, there are seven main components to a BDI agent:

- a set of current *beliefs*, representing information the agent has about its current environment;

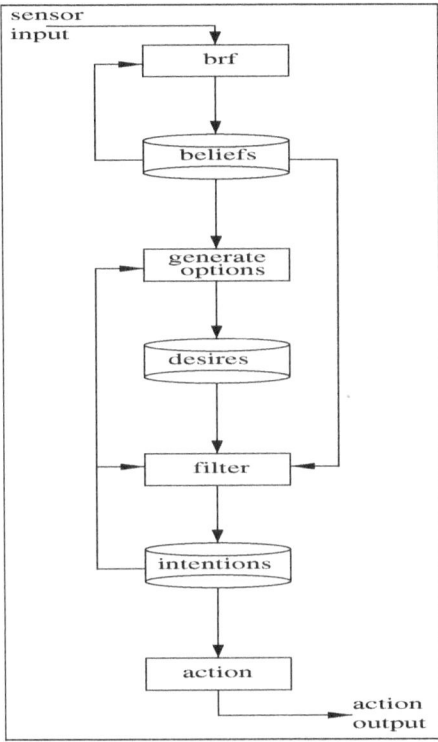

Fig. 5. Schematic diagram of a generic belief-desire-intention architecture.

- a *belief revision function*, (*brf*), which takes a perceptual input and the agent's current beliefs, and on the basis of these, determines a new set of beliefs;
- an *option generation function*, (*options*), which determines the options available to the agent (its desires), on the basis of its current beliefs about its environment and its current *intentions*;
- a set of *current options*, representing possible courses of actions available to the agent;
- a *filter* function (*filter*), which represents the agent's *deliberation* process, and which determines the agent's intentions on the basis of its current beliefs, desires, and intentions;
- a set of current *intentions*, representing the agent's current focus – those states of affairs that it has committed to trying to bring about;
- an *action selection function* (*execute*), which determines an action to perform on the basis of current intentions.

It is straightforward to formally define these components. First, let *Bel* be the set of all possible beliefs, *Des* be the set of all possible desires, and *Int* be the set of all possible intentions. For the purposes of this chapter, the content of these sets is not important. (Often, beliefs, desires, and intentions are represented as logical formulae, perhaps of first-order logic.) Whatever the content of these sets, its is worth noting that they should have some notion of *consistency* defined upon them, so that one can answer the question of, for example, whether having an intention to achieve x is consistent with the belief that y. Representing beliefs, desires, and intentions as logical formulae permits us to recast such questions as problems of determining whether logical formulae are consistent – a well known and well-understood problem. The state of a BDI agent at any given moment is, unsurprisingly, a triple (B, D, I), where $B \subseteq Bel$, $D \subseteq Des$, and $I \subseteq Int$.

An agent's belief revision function is a mapping

$$brf : \wp(Bel) \times P \to \wp(Bel)$$

which on the basis of the current percept and current beliefs determines a new set of beliefs. Belief revision is out of the scope of this chapter (and indeed this book), and so we shall say no more about it here.

The option generation function, *options*, maps a set of beliefs and a set of intentions to a set of desires.

$$options : \wp(Bel) \times \wp(Int) \to \wp(Des)$$

This function plays several roles. First, it must be responsible for the agent's means-ends reasoning – the process of deciding how to achieve intentions. Thus, once an agent has formed an intention to x, it must subsequently consider options to *achieve* x. These options will be more concrete – less abstract – than x. As some of these options then become intentions themselves, they will also feedback into option generation, resulting in yet more concrete options being generated. We can thus think of a BDI agent's option generation process as one of recursively elaborating a hierarchical plan structure, considering and committing to progressively more specific intentions, until finally it reaches the intentions that correspond to immediately executable actions.

While the main purpose of the *options* function is thus means-ends reasoning, it must in addition satisfy several other constraints. First, it must be *consistent*: any options generated must be consistent with both the agent's current beliefs and current intentions. Secondly, it must be *opportunistic*, in that it should recognize when environmental circumstances change advantageously, to offer the agent new ways of achieving intentions, or the possibility of achieving intentions that were otherwise unachievable.

A BDI agent's deliberation process (deciding *what* to do) is represented in the *filter* function,

$$filter : \wp(Bel) \times \wp(Des) \times \wp(Int) \to \wp(Int)$$

which updates the agent's intentions on the basis of its previously-held intentions and current beliefs and desires. This function must fulfill two roles. First, it must *drop* any intentions that are no longer achievable, or for which the expected cost of achieving them exceeds the expected gain associated with successfully achieving them. Second, it should *retain* intentions that are not achieved, and that are still expected to have a positive overall benefit. Finally, it should *adopt* new intentions, either to achieve existing intentions, or to exploit new opportunities.

Notice that we do not expect this function to introduce intentions from nowhere. Thus *filter* should satisfy the following constraint:

$$\forall B \in \wp(Bel), \forall D \in \wp(Des), \forall I \in \wp(Int), filter(B, D, I) \subseteq I \cup D.$$

In other words, current intentions are either previously held intentions or newly adopted options.

The *execute* function is assumed to simply return any executable intentions – one that corresponds to a directly executable action:

$$execute : \wp(Int) \rightarrow A$$

The agent decision function, *action* of a BDI agent is then a function

$$action : P \rightarrow A$$

and is defined by the following pseudo-code.

```
1.    function action(p : P) : A
2.    begin
3.            B := brf(B, p)
4.            D := options(D, I)
5.            I := filter(B, D, I)
6.            return execute(I)
7.    end function action
```

Note that representing an agent's intentions as a *set* (i.e., as an unstructured collection) is generally too simplistic in practice. A simple alternative is to associate a *priority* with each intention, indicating its relative importance. Another natural idea is to represent intentions as a *stack*. An intention is pushed on to the stack when it is adopted, and popped when it is either achieved or else not achievable. More abstract intentions will tend to be at the bottom of the stack, with more concrete intentions towards the top.

To summarize, BDI architectures are practical reasoning architectures, in which the process of deciding what to do resembles the kind of practical reasoning that we appear to use in our everyday lives. The basic components of a BDI architecture are data structures representing the beliefs, desires, and intentions of the agent, and functions that represent its deliberation (deciding *what* intentions to have – i.e., deciding what to do) and means-ends reasoning (deciding *how* to do it). Intentions play a central role in the BDI model: they provide stability for decision making, and act to focus the agent's practical reasoning. A major issue in BDI architectures is the problem of striking a *balance* between being committed to and overcommitted to one's intentions: the deliberation process must be finely tuned to its environment, ensuring that in more dynamic, highly unpredictable domains, it reconsiders its intentions relatively frequently – in more static environments, less frequent reconsideration is necessary.

The BDI model is attractive for several reasons. First, it is intuitive – we all recognize the processes of deciding what to do and then how to do it, and we all have an informal understanding of the notions of belief, desire, and intention. Second, it gives us a clear functional decomposition, which indicates what sorts of subsystems might be required to build an agent. But the main difficulty, as ever, is knowing how to efficiently implement these functions.

Sources and Further Reading. Belief-desire-intention architectures originated in the work of the Rational Agency project at Stanford Research Institute in the mid 1980s. The origins of the model lie in the theory of human practical reasoning developed by the philosopher Michael Bratman [5], which focusses particularly on the role of intentions in practical reasoning. The conceptual framework of the BDI model is described in [6], which also describes a specific BDI agent architecture called IRMA. The description of the BDI model given here (and in particular Fig. 5) is adapted from [6]. One of the interesting aspects of the BDI model is that it has been used in one of the most successful agent architectures to date. The Procedural Resoning System (PRS), originally developed by Michael Georgeff and Amy Lansky [22], has been used to build some of the most exacting agent applications to date, including fault diagnosis for the reaction control system of the space shuttle, and an air traffic management system at Sydney airport in Australia – overviews of these systems are described in [23]. In the PRS, an agent is equipped with a library of *plans* which are used to perform means-ends reasoning. Deliberation is achieved by the use of *meta-level plans*, which are able to modify an agent's intention structure at run-time, in order to change the focus of the agent's practical reasoning. Beliefs in the PRS are represented as PROLOG-like facts – essentially, as atoms of first-order logic.

The BDI model is also interesting because a great deal of effort has been devoted to formalising it. In particular, Anand Rao and Michael Georgeff have developed a range of BDI logics, which they use to axiomatize properties of BDI-based practical reasoning agents [42,46,43,44,45,41]. These models have been extended by others to deal with, for example, communication between agents [24].

4.4   Layered Architectures

Given the requirement that an agent be capable of reactive and pro-active behavior, an obvious decomposition involves creating separate subsystems to deal with these different types of behaviors. This idea leads naturally to a class of architectures in which the various subsystems are arranged into a hierarchy of interacting *layers*. In this section, we will consider some general aspects of layered architectures, and then go on to consider two examples of such architectures: INTERRAP and TOURINGMACHINES.

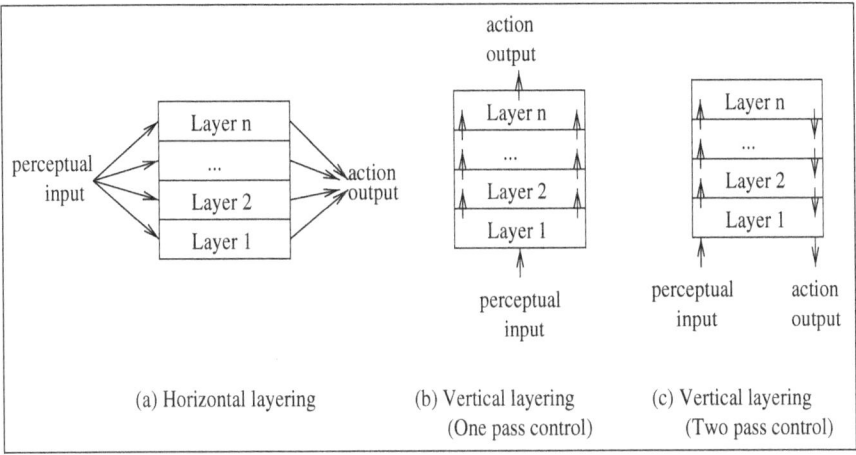

action

perceptual
input

action

Layer n

...

Layer 2

Layer 1

Layer n

...

Layer 2

Layer 1

perceptual
input

Layer n

...

Layer 2

Layer 1

perceptual
input

action
output

(a) Horizontal layering

(b) Vertical layering
(One pass control)

(c) Vertical layering
(Two pass control)

Fig. 6. Information and control flows in three types of layered agent architecture (Source: [38, p263]).

Typically, there will be at least two layers, to deal with reactive and pro-active behaviors respectively. In principle, there is no reason why there should not be many more layers. However many layers there are, a useful typology for such architectures is by the information and control flows within them. Broadly speaking, we can identify two types of control flow within layered architectures (see Fig. 6):

- *Horizontal layering.*
  In horizontally layered architectures (Fig. 6a), the software layers are each directly connected to the sensory input and action output. In effect, each layer itself acts like an agent, producing suggestions as to what action to perform.
- *Vertical layering.*
  In vertically layered architectures (Fig. 6b and 6c), sensory input and action output are each dealt with by at most one layer each.

The great advantage of horizontally layered architectures is their conceptual simplicity: if we need an agent to exhibit n different types of behavior, then we implement n different layers. However, because the layers are each in effect competing with one-another to generate action suggestions, there is a danger that the *overall* behavior of the agent will not be coherent. In order to ensure that horizontally layered architectures *are* consistent, they generally include a *mediator* function, which makes decisions about which layer has "control" of the agent at any given time. The need for such central control is problematic: it means that the designer must potentially consider all possible interactions between layers. If there are n layers in the architecture, and each layer is capable of suggesting m possible actions, then this means there are m^n such interactions to be considered. This is clearly difficult from a design point of view in any but the most simple system. The introduction of a central control system also introduces a *bottleneck* into the agent's decision making.

These problems are partly alleviated in a vertically layered architecture. We can subdivide vertically layered architectures into *one pass* architectures (Fig. 6b) and *two pass* architectures (Fig. 6c). In one-pass architectures, control flows sequentially through each layer, until the final layer generates action output. In two-pass architectures, information flows up the architecture (the first pass) and control then flows back down. There are some interesting similarities between the idea of two-pass vertically layered architectures and the way that organisations work, with information flowing up to the highest levels of the organisation, and commands then flowing down. In both one pass and two pass vertically layered architectures, the complexity of interactions between layers is reduced: since there are $n-1$ interfaces between n layers, then if each layer is capable of suggesting m actions, there are at most $m^2(n-1)$ interactions to be considered between layers. This is clearly much simpler than the horizontally layered case. However, this simplicity comes at the cost of some flexibility: in order for a vertically layered architecture to make a decision, control must pass between *each* different layer. This is not fault tolerant: failures in any one layer are likely to have serious consequences for agent performance.

In the remainder of this section, we will consider two examples of layered architectures: Innes Ferguson's TOURINGMACHINES, and Jörg Müller's INTERRAP. The former is an example of a horizontally layered architecture; the latter is a (two pass) vertically layered architecture.

TouringMachines. The TOURINGMACHINES architecture is illustrated in Fig. 7. As this figure shows, TOURINGMACHINES consists of three *activity producing layers*. That is, each layer continually produces "suggestions" for what actions the agent should perform. The *reactive layer* provides a more-or-less immediate response to changes that occur in the environment. It is implemented as a set of situation-action rules, like the behaviors in Brooks' subsumption architecture (Sect. 4.2). These rules map sensor input directly to effector output. The original demonstration scenario for TOURINGMACHINES was that of autonomous vehicles driving between locations through streets populated by other similar agents. In this scenario, reactive rules typically deal with functions like obstacle avoidance. For example, here is an example of a reactive rule for avoiding the kerb (from [14, p59]):

```
rule-1: kerb-avoidance
    if
        is-in-front(Kerb, Observer) and
        speed(Observer) > 0 and
        separation(Kerb, Observer) < KerbThreshHold
    then
        change-orientation(KerbAvoidanceAngle)
```

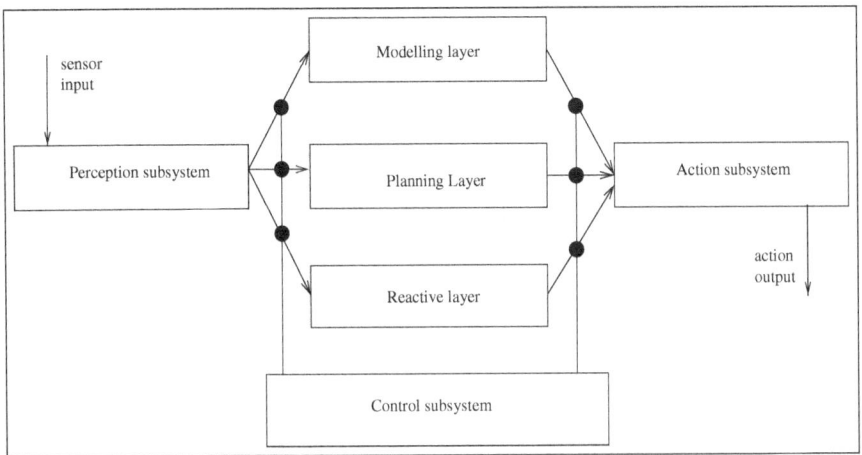

Fig. 7. TOURINGMACHINES: a horizontally layered agent architecture

Here `change-orientation(...)` is the action suggested if the rule fires. The rules can only make references to the agent's current state – they cannot do any explicit reasoning about the world, and on the right hand side of rules are *actions*, not predicates. Thus if this rule fired, it would not result in any central environment model being updated, but would just result in an action being suggested by the reactive layer.

The TOURINGMACHINES *planning layer* achieves the agent's pro-active behavior. Specifically, the planning layer is responsible for the "day-to-day" running of the agent – under normal circumstances, the planning layer will be responsible for deciding what the agent does. However, the planning layer does not do "first-principles" planning. That is, it does not attempt to generate plans from scratch. Rather, the planning layer employs a *library* of plan "skeletons" called *schemas*. These skeletons are in essence hierarchically structured plans, which the TOURINGMACHINES planning layer elaborates at run time in order to decide what to do. So, in order to achieve a goal, the planning layer attempts to find a schema in its library which matches that goal. This schema will contain sub-goals, which the planning layer elaborates by attempting to find other schemas in its plan library that match these sub-goals.

The *modeling* layer represents the various entities in the world (including the agent itself, as well as other agents). The modeling layer thus predicts conflicts between agents, and generates new goals to be achieved in order to resolve these conflicts. These new goals are then posted down to the planning layer, which makes use of its plan library in order to determine how to satisfy them.

The three control layers are embedded within a *control subsystem*, which is effectively responsible for deciding which of the layers should have control over the agent. This control subsystem is implemented as a set of *control rules*.

Control rules can either *suppress* sensor information between the control rules and the control layers, or else *censor* action outputs from the control layers. Here is an example censor rule [16, p207]:

```
censor-rule-1:
    if
        entity(obstacle-6) in perception-buffer
    then
        remove-sensory-record(layer-R, entity(obstacle-6))
```

This rule prevents the reactive layer from ever knowing about whether `obstacle-6` has been perceived. The intuition is that although the reactive layer will in general be the most appropriate layer for dealing with obstacle avoidance, there are certain obstacles for which other layers are more appropriate. This rule ensures that the reactive layer never comes to know about these obstacles.

InteRRaP. INTERRAP is an example of a vertically layered two-pass agent architecture – see Fig. 8.

As Fig. 8 shows, INTERRAP contains three control layers, as in TOURING-MACHINES. Moreover, the purpose of each INTERRAP layer appears to be rather similar to the purpose of each corresponding TOURINGMACHINES layer. Thus the lowest (*behavior based*) layer deals with reactive behavior; the middle (*local planning*) layer deals with everyday planning to achieve the agent's goals, and the uppermost (*cooperative planning*) layer deals with social interactions. Each layer has associated with it a *knowledge base*, i.e., a representation of the world appropriate for that layer. These different knowledge bases represent the agent and its environment at different levels of abstraction. Thus the highest

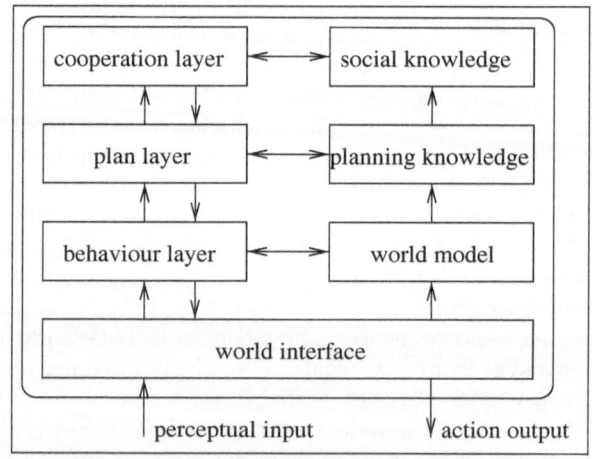

Fig. 8. INTERRAP – a vertically layered two-pass agent architecture.

level knowledge base represents the plans and actions of other agents in the environment; the middle-level knowledge base represents the plans and actions of the agent itself; and the lowest level knowledge base represents "raw" information about the environment. The explicit introduction of these knowledge bases distinguishes TOURINGMACHINES from INTERRAP.

The way the different layers in INTERRAP conspire to produce behavior is also quite different from TOURINGMACHINES. The main difference is in the way the layers interract with the environment. In TOURINGMACHINES, each layer was directly coupled to perceptual input and action output. This necessitated the introduction of a supervisory control framework, to deal with conflicts or problems between layers. In INTERRAP, layers interact with *each other* to achieve the same end. The two main types of interaction between layers are *bottom-up activation* and *top-down execution*. Bottom-up activation occurs when a lower layer passes control to a higher layer because it is not *competent* to deal with the current situation. Top-down execution occurs when a higher layer makes use of the facilities provided by a lower layer to achieve one of its goals. The basic flow of control in INTERRAP begins when perceptual input arrives at the lowest layer in the achitecture. If the reactive layer can deal with this input, then it will do so; otherwise, bottom-up activation will occur, and control will be passed to the local planning layer. If the local planning layer can handle the situation, then it will do so, typically by making use of top-down execution. Otherwise, it will use bottom-up activation to pass control to the highest layer. In this way, control in INTERRAP will flow from the lowest layer to higher layers of the architecture, and then back down again.

The internals of each layer are not important for the purposes of this chapter. However, it is worth noting that each layer implements two general functions. The first of these is a *situation recognition and goal activation* function. This function acts rather like the *options* function in a BDI architecture (see Sect. 4.3). It maps a knowledge base (one of the three layers) and current goals to a new set of goals. The second function is responsible for *planning and scheduling* – it is responsible for selecting which plans to execute, based on the current plans, goals, and knowledge base of that layer.

Layered architectures are currently the most popular general class of agent architecture available. Layering represents a natural decomposition of functionality: it is easy to see how reactive, pro-active, social behavior can be generated by the reactive, pro-active, and social layers in an architecture. The main problem with layered architectures is that while they are arguably a *pragmatic* solution, they lack the conceptual and semantic clarity of unlayered approaches. In particular, while logic-based approaches have a clear logical semantics, it is difficult to see how such a semantics could be devised for a layered architecture. Another issue is that of interactions between layers. If each layer is an independent activity producing process (as in TOURINGMACHINES), then it is necessary to consider all possible ways that the layers can interact with one another. This problem is partly alleviated in two-pass vertically layered architecture such as INTERRAP.

Sources and Further Reading. The introductory discussion of layered architectures given here draws heavily upon [38, pp262–264]. The best reference to TOURINGMACHINES is [14]; more accessible references include [15,16]. The definitive reference to INTERRAP is [37], although [18] is also a useful reference. Other examples of layered architectures include the subsumption architecture [7] (see also Sect. 4.2), and the 3T architecture [4].

5   Conclusions

I hope that after reading this chapter, you understand what agents are and why they are considered to be an important area of research and development. The requirement for systems that can operate autonomously is very common. The requirement for systems capable of *flexible* autonomous action, in the sense that I have described in this chapter, is similarly common. This leads me to conclude that intelligent agents have the potential to play a significant role in the future of software engineering. Intelligent agent research is about the theory, design, construction, and application of such systems. This chapter has focussed on the design of intelligent agents. It has presented a high-level, abstract view of intelligent agents, and described the sort of properties that one would expect such an agent to enjoy. It went on to show how this view of an agent could be refined into various different types of agent architecture – purely logical agents, purely reactive/behavioral agents, BDI agents, and layered agent architectures.

References

1. P. Agre and D. Chapman. PENGI: An implementation of a theory of activity. In *Proceedings of the Sixth National Conference on Artificial Intelligence (AAAI-87)*, pages 268–272, Seattle, WA, 1987.
2. P. E. Agre and S. J. Rosenschein, editors. *Computational Theories of Interaction and Agency.* The MIT Press: Cambridge, MA, 1996.
3. H. Barringer, M. Fisher, D. Gabbay, G. Gough, and R. Owens. METATEM: A framework for programming in temporal logic. In *REX Workshop on Stepwise Refinement of Distributed Systems: Models, Formalisms, Correctness (LNCS Volume 430)*, pages 94–129. Springer-Verlag: Berlin, Germany, June 1989.
4. R. P. Bonasso, D. Kortenkamp, D. P. Miller, and M. Slack. Experiences with an architecture for intelligent, reactive agents. In M. Wooldridge, J. P. Müller, and M. Tambe, editors, *Intelligent Agents II (LNAI Volume 1037)*, pages 187–202. Springer-Verlag: Berlin, Germany, 1996.
5. M. E. Bratman. *Intentions, Plans, and Practical Reason.* Harvard University Press: Cambridge, MA, 1987.
6. M. E. Bratman, D. J. Israel, and M. E. Pollack. Plans and resource-bounded practical reasoning. *Computational Intelligence*, 4:349–355, 1988.
7. R. A. Brooks. A robust layered control system for a mobile robot. *IEEE Journal of Robotics and Automation*, 2(1):14–23, 1986.
8. R. A. Brooks. Elephants don't play chess. In P. Maes, editor, *Designing Autonomous Agents*, pages 3–15. The MIT Press: Cambridge, MA, 1990.

9. R. A. Brooks. Intelligence without reason. In *Proceedings of the Twelfth International Joint Conference on Artificial Intelligence (IJCAI-91)*, pages 569–595, Sydney, Australia, 1991.

10. R. A. Brooks. Intelligence without representation. *Artificial Intelligence*, 47:139–159, 1991.

11. Oren Etzioni. Intelligence without robots. *AI Magazine*, 14(4), December 1993.

12. R. Fagin, J. Y. Halpern, Y. Moses, and M. Y. Vardi. *Reasoning About Knowledge*. The MIT Press: Cambridge, MA, 1995.

13. J. Ferber. Reactive distributed artificial intelligence. In G. M. P. O'Hare and N. R. Jennings, editors, *Foundations of Distributed Artificial Intelligence*, pages 287–317. John Wiley, 1996.

14. I. A. Ferguson. *TouringMachines: An Architecture for Dynamic, Rational, Mobile Agents*. PhD thesis, Clare Hall, University of Cambridge, UK, November 1992. (Also available as Technical Report No. 273, University of Cambridge Computer Laboratory).

15. I. A. Ferguson. Towards an architecture for adaptive, rational, mobile agents. In E. Werner and Y. Demazeau, editors, *Decentralized AI 3 – Proceedings of the Third European Workshop on Modelling Autonomous Agents in a Multi-Agent World (MAAMAW-91)*, pages 249–262. Elsevier Science Publishers B.V.: Amsterdam, The Netherlands, 1992.

16. I. A. Ferguson. Integrated control and coordinated behaviour: A case for agent models. In M. Wooldridge and N. R. Jennings, editors, *Intelligent Agents: Theories, Architectures, and Languages (LNAI Volume 890)*, pages 203–218. Springer-Verlag: Berlin, Germany, January 1995.

17. J. A. Firby. An investigation into reactive planning in complex domains. In *Proceedings of the Tenth International Joint Conference on Artificial Intelligence (IJCAI-87)*, pages 202–206, Milan, Italy, 1987.

18. K. Fischer, J. P. Müller, and M. Pischel. A pragmatic BDI architecture. In M. Wooldridge, J. P. Müller, and M. Tambe, editors, *Intelligent Agents II (LNAI Volume 1037)*, pages 203–218. Springer-Verlag: Berlin, Germany, 1996.

19. M. Fisher. A survey of Concurrent METATEM – the language and its applications. In D. M. Gabbay and H. J. Ohlbach, editors, *Temporal Logic – Proceedings of the First International Conference (LNAI Volume 827)*, pages 480–505. Springer-Verlag: Berlin, Germany, July 1994.

20. L. Gasser and J. P. Briot. Object-based concurrent programming and DAI. In *Distributed Artificial Intelligence: Theory and Praxis*, pages 81–108. Kluwer Academic Publishers: Boston, MA, 1992.

21. M. R. Genesereth and N. Nilsson. *Logical Foundations of Artificial Intelligence*. Morgan Kaufmann Publishers: San Mateo, CA, 1987.

22. M. P. Georgeff and A. L. Lansky. Reactive reasoning and planning. In *Proceedings of the Sixth National Conference on Artificial Intelligence (AAAI-87)*, pages 677–682, Seattle, WA, 1987.

23. M. P. Georgeff and A. S. Rao. A profile of the Australian AI Institute. *IEEE Expert*, 11(6):89–92, December 1996.

24. A. Haddadi. *Communication and Cooperation in Agent Systems (LNAI Volume 1056)*. Springer-Verlag: Berlin, Germany, 1996.

25. J. Y. Halpern. Using reasoning about knowledge to analyze distributed systems. *Annual Review of Computer Science*, 2:37–68, 1987.

26. L. P. Kaelbling. An architecture for intelligent reactive systems. In M. P. Georgeff and A. L. Lansky, editors, *Reasoning About Actions & Plans – Proceedings of the 1986 Workshop*, pages 395–410. Morgan Kaufmann Publishers: San Mateo, CA, 1986.

27. L. P. Kaelbling. A situated automata approach to the design of embedded agents. *SIGART Bulletin*, 2(4):85–88, 1991.

28. L. P. Kaelbling and S. J. Rosenschein. Action and planning in embedded agents. In P. Maes, editor, *Designing Autonomous Agents*, pages 35–48. The MIT Press: Cambridge, MA, 1990.

29. D. Kinny and M. Georgeff. Commitment and effectiveness of situated agents. In *Proceedings of the Twelfth International Joint Conference on Artificial Intelligence (IJCAI-91)*, pages 82–88, Sydney, Australia, 1991.

30. K. Konolige. *A Deduction Model of Belief.* Pitman Publishing: London and Morgan Kaufmann: San Mateo, CA, 1986.

31. Y. Lésperance, H. J. Levesque, F. Lin, D. Marcu, R. Reiter, and R. B. Scherl. Foundations of a logical approach to agent programming. In M. Wooldridge, J. P. Müller, and M. Tambe, editors, *Intelligent Agents II (LNAI Volume 1037)*, pages 331–346. Springer-Verlag: Berlin, Germany, 1996.

32. P. Maes. The dynamics of action selection. In *Proceedings of the Eleventh International Joint Conference on Artificial Intelligence (IJCAI-89)*, pages 991–997, Detroit, MI, 1989.

33. P. Maes, editor. *Designing Autonomous Agents*. The MIT Press: Cambridge, MA, 1990.

34. P. Maes. Situated agents can have goals. In P. Maes, editor, *Designing Autonomous Agents*, pages 49–70. The MIT Press: Cambridge, MA, 1990.

35. P. Maes. The agent network architecture (ANA). *SIGART Bulletin*, 2(4):115–120, 1991.

36. J. McCarthy and P. J. Hayes. Some philosophical problems from the standpoint of artificial intelligence. In B. Meltzer and D. Michie, editors, *Machine Intelligence 4*. Edinburgh University Press, 1969.

37. J. P. Müller. *The Design of Intelligent Agents*. Springer-Verlag: Berlin, Germany, 1997.

38. J. P. Müller, M. Pischel, and M. Thiel. Modelling reactive behaviour in vertically layered agent architectures. In M. Wooldridge and N. R. Jennings, editors, *Intelligent Agents: Theories, Architectures, and Languages (LNAI Volume 890)*, pages 261–276. Springer-Verlag: Berlin, Germany, January 1995.

39. J. P. Müller, M. Wooldridge, and N. R. Jennings, editors. *Intelligent Agents III (LNAI Volume 1193)*. Springer-Verlag: Berlin, Germany, 1995.

40. N. J. Nilsson. Towards agent programs with circuit semantics. Technical Report STAN–CS–92–1412, Computer Science Department, Stanford University, Stanford, CA 94305, January 1992.

41. A. S. Rao. Decision procedures for propositional linear-time Belief-Desire-Intention logics. In M. Wooldridge, J. P. Müller, and M. Tambe, editors, *Intelligent Agents II (LNAI Volume 1037)*, pages 33–48. Springer-Verlag: Berlin, Germany, 1996.

42. A. S. Rao and M. P. Georgeff. Asymmetry thesis and side-effect problems in linear time and branching time intention logics. In *Proceedings of the Twelfth International Joint Conference on Artificial Intelligence (IJCAI-91)*, pages 498–504, Sydney, Australia, 1991.

43. A. S. Rao and M. P. Georgeff. Modeling rational agents within a BDI-architecture. In R. Fikes and E. Sandewall, editors, *Proceedings of Knowledge Representation and Reasoning (KR&R-91)*, pages 473–484. Morgan Kaufmann Publishers: San Mateo, CA, April 1991.

44. A. S. Rao and M. P. Georgeff. An abstract architecture for rational agents. In C. Rich, W. Swartout, and B. Nebel, editors, *Proceedings of Knowledge Representation and Reasoning (KR&R-92)*, pages 439–449, 1992.

45. A. S. Rao and M. P. Georgeff. A model-theoretic approach to the verification of situated reasoning systems. In *Proceedings of the Thirteenth International Joint Conference on Artificial Intelligence (IJCAI-93)*, pages 318–324, Chambéry, France, 1993.

46. A. S. Rao, M. P. Georgeff, and E. A. Sonenberg. Social plans: A preliminary report. In E. Werner and Y. Demazeau, editors, *Decentralized AI 3 – Proceedings of the Third European Workshop on Modelling Autonomous Agents in a Multi-Agent World (MAAMAW-91)*, pages 57–76. Elsevier Science Publishers B.V.: Amsterdam, The Netherlands, 1992.

47. S. Rosenschein and L. P. Kaelbling. The synthesis of digital machines with provable epistemic properties. In J. Y. Halpern, editor, *Proceedings of the 1986 Conference on Theoretical Aspects of Reasoning About Knowledge*, pages 83–98. Morgan Kaufmann Publishers: San Mateo, CA, 1986.

48. S. J. Rosenschein and L. P. Kaelbling. A situated view of representation and control. In P. E. Agre and S. J. Rosenschein, editors, *Computational Theories of Interaction and Agency*, pages 515–540. The MIT Press: Cambridge, MA, 1996.

49. S. Russell and P. Norvig. *Artificial Intelligence: A Modern Approach*. Prentice-Hall, 1995.

50. S. Russell and D. Subramanian. Provably bounded-optimal agents. *Journal of AI Research*, 2:575–609, 1995.

51. S. J. Russell and E. Wefald. *Do the Right Thing – Studies in Limited Rationality*. The MIT Press: Cambridge, MA, 1991.

52. M. J. Schoppers. Universal plans for reactive robots in unpredictable environments. In *Proceedings of the Tenth International Joint Conference on Artificial Intelligence (IJCAI-87)*, pages 1039–1046, Milan, Italy, 1987.

53. L. Steels. Cooperation between distributed agents through self organization. In Y. Demazeau and J.-P. Müller, editors, *Decentralized AI – Proceedings of the First European Workshop on Modelling Autonomous Agents in a Multi-Agent World (MAAMAW-89)*, pages 175–196. Elsevier Science Publishers B.V.: Amsterdam, The Netherlands, 1990.

54. M. Wooldridge. Agent-based software engineering. *IEE Transactions on Software Engineering*, 144(1):26–37, February 1997.

55. M. Wooldridge and N. R. Jennings. Intelligent agents: Theory and practice. *The Knowledge Engineering Review*, 10(2):115–152, 1995.

Motivated Agent Behaviour and Requirements Applied to Virtual Emergencies

Sorabain Wolfheart de Lioncourt[1] and Michael Luck[2]

[1] Department of Computer Science, University of Warwick, Coventry, CV4 7AL, UK
bane@dcs.warwick.ac.uk
[2] Department of Electronics and Computer Science, University of Southampton, UK
mml@ecs.soton.ac.uk

Abstract. Virtual environments provide a rich and varied domain for intelligent agents, but questions of design and development in this context are still to be answered. An agent with multiple requirements and limited or constrained resources must be able to make decisions as to how to divide those resources in order to satisfy its requirements. It may not be possible to satisfy all of them at once, so some may have to be sacrificed for the sake of those that are more important; in other cases a compromise may be possible in which all requirements are partially satisfied. This paper examines the kinds of requirements we may expect to have of an agent in virtual environments, and describes how we can measure an agent's preformance in this light. Such an analysis can be used as a conceptual design tool and as the basis of an agent specification. An agent architecture based on the BDI model is proposed in which design and implementation is decomposed in terms of requirements, and which allows the intuitive development of sophisticated agents with multiple requirements in a dynamic virtual environment.

1 Introduction

While much work in the field of intelligent agents has sought to develop sophisticated agent architectures capable of reasoning and acting in addressing a range of tasks, it has largely ignored the issues involved in situating such agents in virtual environments. Similarly, work in virtual environments has tended to focus on lower-level agent capabilities more closely related to situatedness and embodiment [4]. As these fields converge, however, the dividing line between them is beginning to be erased, with increasingly sophisticated agent models being developed specifically for use in virtual environments.

On the one hand, virtual agents are no different from agents in any other context or domain, with the same characteristics and properties, yet on the other hand, they require consideration of some issues that might not otherwise be necessary, or might not be as significant. As pointed out by Aylett and Luck [1], for example, work on virtual agents has given a new impetus to the field of motivation and emotion in agents, because there is a greater potential for its useful representation, and because such explicit representation may also be necessary. These physical effects of internal motivators can be matched by similar impact at a cognitive level, by which the reasoning of an agent is determined to some extent by its internal mental state.

Though the work in this area has been increasing, it is limited. In particular, there is a tendency for new agents and architectures to be constructed for each new application,

V. Mařík et al. (Eds.): MASA 2001, LNAI 2322, pp. 44–60, 2002.
© Springer-Verlag Berlin Heidelberg 2002

so that much of benefit of reuse is lost, and incremental advances are difficult. If the application of intelligent agents in virtual environments is to progress adequately, work must focus on understanding the specific demands of the problem domains – what extra constraints are imposed on agents in rich synthetic environments that have implications for design – and on the development of agent architectures suited to such domains that can be reused across multiple applications. In this paper, we address exactly these points by describing our work towards the development of a sophisticated agent architecture that

- extends an existing model so that it offers flexibility of control and is suitable for use in a dynamic virtual environment, and
- is based on a set of architectural analysis and design templates that provide guidelines for the development of any specific agent within this model.

The paper begins by introducing the behavioural analysis needed for directing autonomous agents in virtual environments, through an examination of requirements imposed by design and by the domain, leading to a preference ordering on design constraints. To deal with violations of these constraints, cost functions are then described, before moving on to the details of the architecture itself. The base architecture is inspired by, and derived from, an example of possibly the best-known class of agent architecture, the belief-desire-intention (BDI) model. dMARS [6] is an implemented and deployed commercial system that underlies this work, and is extended through the inclusion of mechanisms for motivated behaviour similar to artificial life approaches. Finally, the application of the architecture in an emergency services scenario in a virtual city, where emergency services must be coordinated to deal with situations of varying urgency, is used to illustrate the previous sections, and to show how the architecure thus derived may be implemented.

2   Directing Autonomous Agent Behaviour

An intelligent autonomous agent is expected to act for extended periods without human intervention. Although the agent is free to set its own goals and decide how best to achieve them, it has particular rôles and is expected to act accordingly. In this section we consider the kinds of behavioural requirement that might be placed on an autonomous agent, based on the treatment in [5]. To introduce the different kinds of requirements we consider a hypothetical squirrel-like virtual creature that must survive in a hostile environment.

Ideally an agent will avoid the violation of any of its requirements, but in general this may not be possible where the agent has limited resources and the different requirements compete over them. Where an agent cannot avoid the violation of some of its requirements the designer may have some preferences as to which violations should be avoided with greater effort.

Given a list of requirements, the strongest kind of preference ordering we can impose is that of lexicographic preferences [12]. A pure lexicographic preference ranking of n requirements, $r_1, r_2, \ldots, r_n$ treats a requirement r_i as infinitely more important than any requirement r_j with $j > i$. In terms of violations, an agent will not tolerate any kind of violation (even a flexible violation of minimal duration) of a more important requirement in preference to any combination of violations of requirements lower in the lexicographic ranking. For example, we would not want our squirrel to suffer death by starvation, no matter how well groomed it can keep itself. Note that a violation of a requirement does not imply that all requirements of lower importance are also violated, or that more important violations are necessarily rectified before less important ones. It may be the case that a violation with lower importance can be rectified by using resources that cannot be used to rectify the more important violation.

Lexicographic preferences can be used to model default behaviours where we want our agent only to perform certain behaviours when it has nothing better to do, such as grooming [2]. A default behaviour is placed after all non-default behaviours in the lexicographic preference ordering. If more than one default behaviour is present then we consider lexicographic dominance between them as for non-default behaviours.

In general we will not be able to produce a pure lexicographic preference ordering between the agent's requirements. Some requirements may have equal importance to others, such as avoiding death by starvation, and avoiding death by dehydration. In other cases we may wish to allow a trade-off between violations, where we consider one requirement to be more important than others, but we may tolerate a flexible violation of it if we can satisfy several less important requirements at once. In cases where no pure lexicographic preference exists between requirements we place them both on the same level in the lexicographic ordering.

The general lexicographic ordering we produce is between sets of requirements. A requirement is considered infinitely more important than those requirements in lower levels, and the current situation the agent finds itself in dictates the relative importance of requirements at the same level.

For the squirrel we came up with the following requirements.

- avoid death by dehydration;
- avoid death by starvation;
- avoid having a poor condition coat;
- avoid being far from cover;
- avoid not having performed environment scanning in last 60-seconds.

From these requirements we might produce the general lexicographic ordering shown in Fig. 1. Since we have specified that grooming is a default behaviour it should clearly inhabit the least important level in the lexicographic ordering. Avoiding death by starvation and death by dehydration are both equally important, and we would not want to risk a chance of death by either in preference to scanning the surroundings or remaining close to cover, so these both inhabit the highest level of the lexicographic ordering. There is no clear dominance between scanning the surroundings and remaining close to cover, so these are placed together in the middle level.

Note that the placing of the requirements to scan the environment and maintain proximity to cover on a lower level to that of avoiding death by starvation or dehydration does not mean that the desire to stay near cover does not influence the agent's behaviour in approaching food or water. Should an agent perceive a food source the top level requirement of avoiding death by starvation is indifferent to whether the agent approaches directly and nonchalantly, or by staying close to cover and remaining alert. Due to this

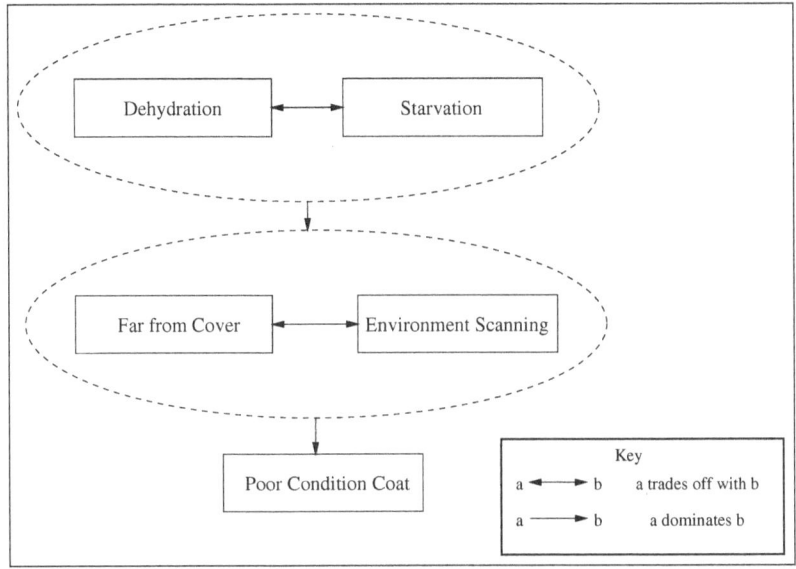

Fig. 1. General lexicographic ordering for a virtual squirrel.

indifference, the lower level requirements to stay close to cover and scan the environment regularly dictate that the latter method is more desirable.

3   Measuring Performance

An agent may not be able to satisfy all of its requirements over its lifetime, and it may suffer from many combinations of violations. In order to rate the agent's overall performance, and possible compare different agent architectures in the same environment with the same requirements we would like a measure of how well an agent has satisfied its requirements over its lifetime. We develop such a measure based on the notion of *cost*. At any instant the agent may have several violated requirements, and each violated requirement will have an instantaneous associated cost that is accrued over the agents lifetime. An ideal agent will minimize this measure over its lifetime given the resources that it has.

The instantaneous cost of a violation will depend on how important the requirement is, and the nature of the violation. Some requirements may have differing levels of violation. For example, a squirrel that is required to maintain a good coat may meet or violate this requirement at varying levels.

To distinguish between levels of violation we introduce a variable x_r for each requirement r, which measures the extent of the violation. In the case where all violations of a requirement are considered equal (such as death) the variable x_r takes the values *true* or *false* indicating the presence or absence of a violation.

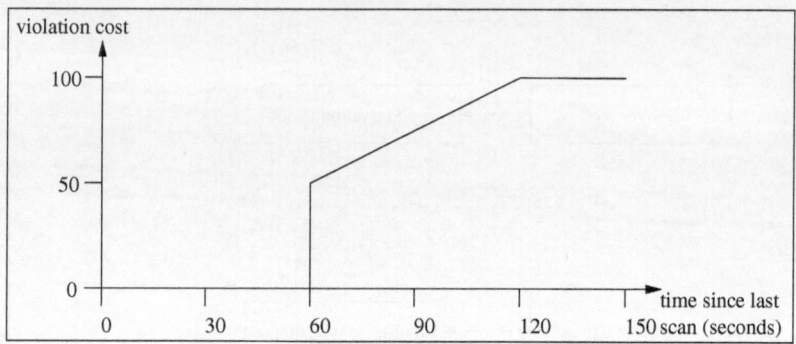

Fig. 2. Cost of violating a scanning requirement

In the case of a requirement that constrains the value of some measurable variable in the environment we can use that variable directly. In Fig. 2 we show the violation cost function for the squirrel's requirement to scan its surroundings periodically. For this requirement the instantaneous cost of violation increases with the time since violation, making it less desirable to avoid scanning for four minutes in a row, than to avoid it for two minutes twice. The exact shape of the function will depend on the chance of a predator sneaking up on the squirrel in the time since the last scan.

Even in the case of requirements that are not periodic we may wish to increase the cost of a violation as time goes on. For example, we may wish to consider an agent's death 10 minutes before the required lifetime as more than twice as bad as an agent's death 5 minutes before the required lifetime.

The general form of an instantaneous violation cost function of a requirement r is a function of x_r and v_r, where v_r is the time since violation.

We can define the total instantaneous violation cost, V_l, at each level, l, of the lexicographic preference ordering as simply the sum of the instantaneous violation costs of the requirements at that level. We obtain the overall violation cost, C_l, at at each level is by integrating the instantaneous violation cost with respect to time.

$$C_l = \int_0^L V_l(t) \, dt$$

where L is the desired lifetime of the agent. Then to compare the performance of two agents we begin by comparing the overall violation costs at each level of the lexicographic ordering in turn. We consider each level in turn, from the most important to the least important, until we find a level at which the agent's overall violation cost differs. The agent that performed best is that agent which achieved a lower overall violation cost at this level, irrespective of performance on lower levels. We disregard the agent's performance at lower levels since these are defined to be infinitely less important than the requirements at the level in which the agents are first found to differ.

In trying to minimize the overall violation cost at any level of the lexicographic ordering the agent must consider trade-offs between the requirements at that level. An agent may pursue a course of action that allows it to maintain several requirements that are individually less important than another requirement at that level, but in conjunction are more important. Developing an architecture that is capable of predicting and taking advantage of such trade-offs is the subject of the next section.

4 Motivating Autonomous Agents

In the previous sections we described the kinds of requirements we may have of an autonomous agent, and how to measure an agent's performance with respect to these requirements. This gives us an intuitive conceptual model of how an autonomous agent should behave that is independent of the specific agent architecture employed. To prove the value of this conceptual model it should be closely married with equally intuitive design and implementation methods. The need for intuitive modelling techniques in agent-oriented programming has been noted elsewhere [7]. In this section we present an agent architecture specifically developed for autonomous agents with the kinds of requirements discussed. The architecture is inspired by the distributed Multi-Agent Reasoning System (dMARS) [6], a highly successful commercial architecture based on the belief-desire-intention (BDI) model [3,11,10].

Our conceptual model of autonomous agent behaviour revolves around its requirements. Up to now we have discussed the requirements of an agent without reference to its capabilities. Any implemented autonomous agent will have limited resources over which its requirements will compete. For the squirrel the primary resource is the physical embodiment of the agent itself, it can only be in one place at any given moment. The requirement to avoid death by starvation will be best satisfied if the agent maintains close proximity to a plentiful supply of food, but at the same the requirement to avoid death by dehydration will be best satisfied if the agent stays close to a supply of fresh water. In cases where it is not possible to maintain both these conditions at the same time a choice must be made as to which requirement takes control of the agent's position. It is the reconcilliation of such competition that is the main problem addressed by this architecture.

4.1 Motivators and Resource Controllers

The primary components of this architecture are *motivators* and *resource controllers*. A motivator serves as an encapsulation of all the information needed to satisfy a single requirement, and serves as that requirement's representative in the system. A resource controller is provided for each of the agent's resources that one or more motivators may want to control. Intuitively, when a motivator wishes to use a resource it makes a request to the appropriate resource controller. The controller passes on the details of the request to all other motivators that can be affected by that resource who are then free to criticize the proposed use of the resource. The dependencies between motivators and resource controllers are represented explicitly, so that the resource controller knows exactly which motivators can be affected by the use of its resource. We use the resource controller to arbitrate between competing motivators so that each motivator only has to understand the interface of the resource controllers that it needs or can be affected by, it does not

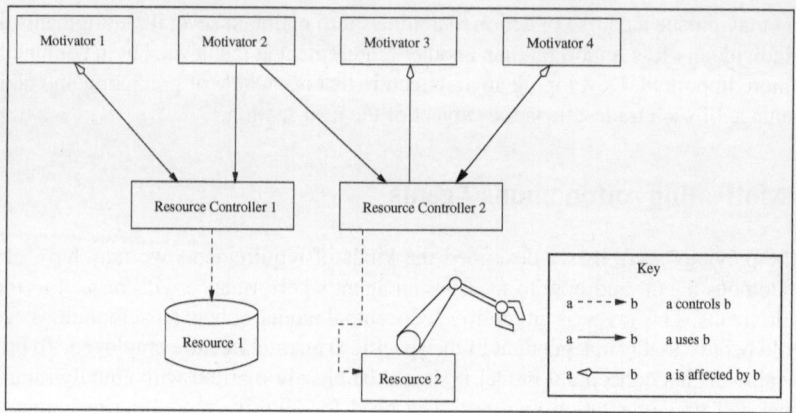

Fig. 3. Relationships between motivators and resource controllers

need to know any details about other motivators in the system. Motivators and resource controllers are considered to exist in their own namespace and communicate by message passing. As such, they can be seen as agents in their own right, and the overall behaviour of the agent can be seen as governed by a multi-agent system. An example organization of motivators and resource controllers is shown in Fig. 3.

Individual motivators are implemented as an augmented dMARS agent as shown in Fig. 4. A standard dMARS agent consists of a set of beliefs, intentions, and a plan library. Each plan in its library has a triggering condition and a context. The triggering condition determines when the plan is considered *relevant* for execution, with plans being triggered by events either received from the environment or generated internally. The plan's context determines whether a relevant plan is *applicable* for taking on as an intention, and consists of a logical sentence that must be a logical consequence of the agent's beliefs for the plan to be considered applicable. A plan that is both relevant and applicable is taken on as an intention. More detail on the workings of dMARS agents can be found in [6].

4.2   Benefit Calculation

Motivators differ from dMARS agents in that a relevant and applicable plan is not immediately taken on as an intention, it is still only a candidate for execution. Should the plan involve the use of a resource that is contended between motivators then it must request the use of that resource from its resource controller. In order to decide whether the plan is in the best interests of the agent as a whole all of the motivators that can be affected by the plan must be allowed to criticize it. To enable this, each motivator is provided with a benefit calculation mechanism, which may depend on the agent's current beliefs and intentions. Note that the calculation of benefit could be performed in a standard dMARS agent by using special plans in its plan library that are applicable when the motivator receives a request for a benefit calculation. However, we choose to

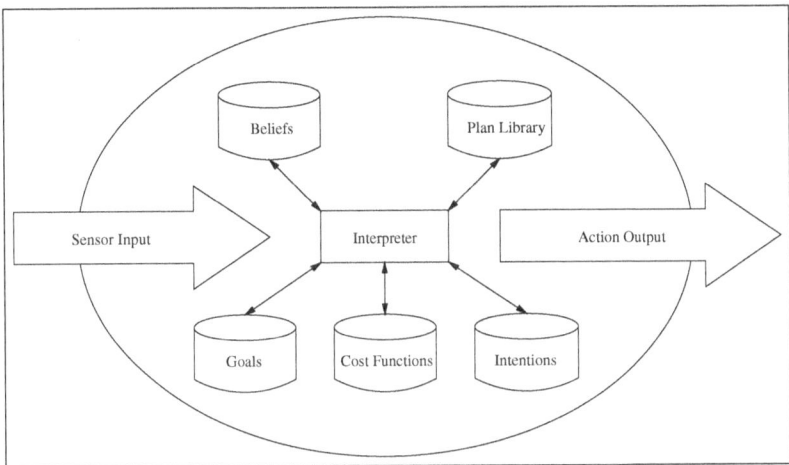

Fig. 4. An augmented dMARS agent

seperate out the benefit calculation mechanism because it performs such a critical role in this architecture and thus the mechanism used should be readily identifiable.

A motivator calculates the benefit of a resource use, U, using the following formula.

$$benefit = cost\ of\ not\ doing\ U\ -\ cost\ of\ doing\ U$$

We take into account the cost of not doing U to allow for situations when even the best thing we can do is expected to incur some cost, but doing nothing will incur a greater cost. An example of such a situation is given in Sect. 5.

Resource controllers receive proposals for use from motivators, along with an expected benefit. The details of the proposed use are passed on to all motivators that can be affected by it. These motivators return an expected benefit of the use, which may be negative if the use increases the risk of violation of the motivator's requirement. The benefits returned by the motivators are compared on the basis of their ranking in the lexicographic ordering, starting with the greatest level of importance. The individual benefits of the motivators at each level are summed to get the overall benefit. This overall benefit is compared with the overall benefit of the current activity using the resource. Should there be no current activity using the resource then we consider this benefit to be zero. If the overall benefit of the proposed use is greater than the overall benefit of the current activity using the resource at that level then the proposed use is accepted, and the current activity is suspended, otherwise it is refused. If the expected overall benefits are equal then we consider the next level. If after considering all levels we are still indifferent between the proposed use and the current use then we choose to continue with the current use.

The resource controller maintains a record of the expected benefit of the current activity using the resource, and it is the responsibility of individual motivators to inform the resource controller should their disposition towards the current activity change.

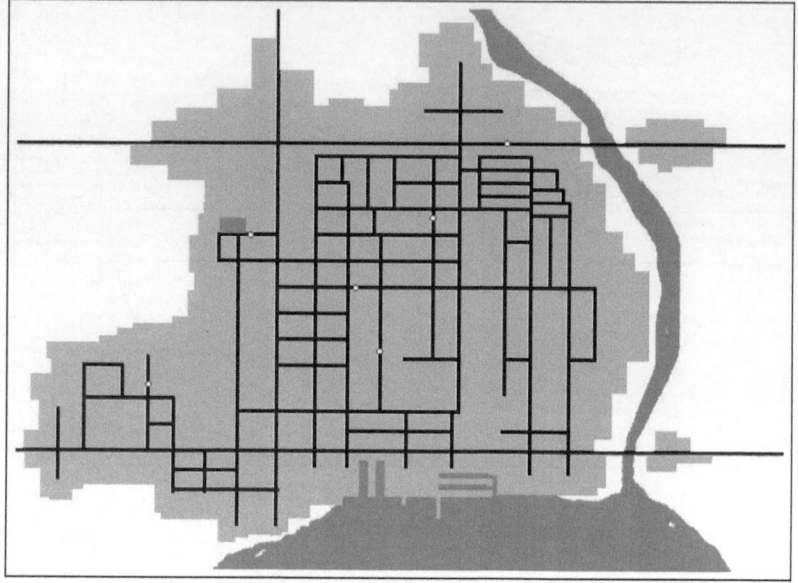

Fig. 5. Virtual City Layout

The architecture described in this section has been successfully applied to a simplifed version of an emergency services coordination problem. The details of this application are given in the next section.

5 Emergency Services Coordination

To demonstrate the diversity of behaviours an agent may have it was intuitive to discuss them in relation to a squirrel with the same needs as a real, biological creature. However, the kinds of behaviour specified can also be applied to real-world applications where the agents have no direct similarity with biological creatures. In this section we look at one such application, that of *emergency services coordination*, which might be found in scenarios based on *RoboCup Rescue* [8], for example

The system developed in this section is intended as an illustrative example of the potential of the architecture described. As such, we take a simplified view of the problem of emergency services coordination, concentrating on the role of ambulances in responding to clients from the public in a simulated city. The city road layout is shown in Fig. 5, and is loosely based on the layout of a city in the United States. The hospital is the dark grey box in the north-western portion of the city. While the environment does not in itself have detailed visual representations of agents, the strong agent model enables such graphical representations to be easily developed at a later date.

All roads in the city are two-way, and the traffic flow is constant and uniform throughout the city. A single hospital exists in the city, which deals with all of the city's needs.

Emergencies will occur at random intervals and at random points within the city, but always at a point that an ambulance can access. We refer to the object of the emergency as the *client*. Every emergency is considered severe enough to warrant transport to hospital, but the urgency of such transport may vary. In this simulation we provide three levels of urgency.

Level 1 emergencies are the most urgent with the client's condition expected to deteriorate rapidly;

level 2 emergencies are urgent with the client's condition deteriorating over time, but not as rapidly as a level 1 emergency; and

level 3 emergencies are relatively stable with some deterioration over time, but not as pronounced as for a level 1 or level 2 emergency.

A number of ambulances will be available for picking up and ferrying clients to a hospital.

5.1 Desired System Behaviour

Clearly the desired behaviour of the system is to deliver clients to the hospital promptly. We might choose to measure the overall performance as the mean time between an emergency request and delivery to the hospital. However, since we distinguish between several types of emergency, each with a differing level of urgency, we construct a more sophisticated measure. We assume that there is some measure of cost associated with the time taken to deliver a client to hospital. This measure of cost is linked to the client's chance of survival, and also perhaps the resources required to save their life. The cost functions for the three levels of emergency are given in Fig. 6.

Given such a set of cost functions, the desired performance of the system as a whole is to minimize the accumulated cost.

5.2 An Agent-Oriented Approach

The primary entities within the system are the ambulances and clients. We consider both as a kind of autonomous agent, where ambulance agents and client agents will coordinate in order to ensure the prompt delivery of high urgency clients to the hospital.

A client agent's rôle is to provide the ambulance agents with up to date information concerning the urgency of the emergency, and the time the client has been waiting. The client agent receives offers from the ambulance agents for a possible pick up, along with an estimated time of arrival. The client agent selects the nearest ambulance and requests a commitment to the pick up. Since the ambulance agents are autonomous and have the final say over their use, such a commitment may not be forthcoming, in which case the client agent requests a commitment from the next best ambulances until such a commitment is gained. The client agent will try to ensure that at most one ambulance is en route at any given moment.

The ambulance agents make the final choice as to which client to attend to. The decision is based on the urgency of the emergencies and the estimated time that the ambulance can get the client to the hospital. Each ambulance has a limited fuel load and must ensure that it is sufficient before committing to picking up a client. Should

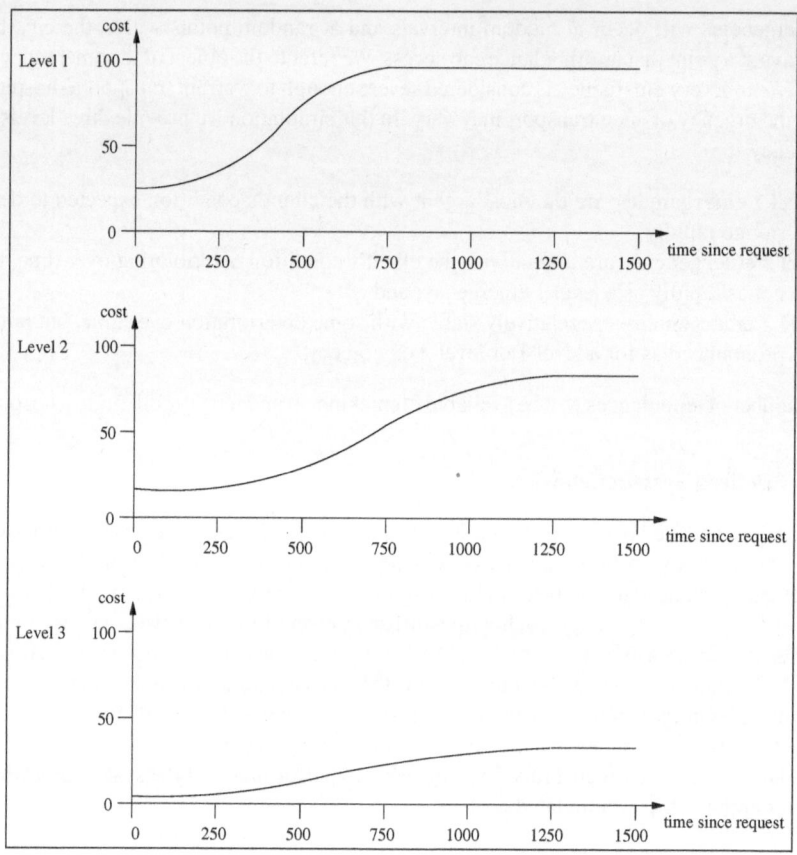

Fig. 6. Cost functions for each level of emergency

there be no clients to pick up the ambulances roam to different parts of the city, thereby reducing the expected journey time for any new client compared to if the ambulances remained at the hospital at such times. This roaming behaviour is only effective if the ambulance maintains enough fuel to provide full coverage of the city, otherwise the expected journey time will be increased due to the need to refuel first. Since the overall system performance measure does not incorporate fuel costs, we are justified in using the roaming behaviour to reduce the expected delivery times and hence the overall accrued cost. In this simulation we only allow the ambulances to refuel at the hospital. In the following sections we describe the requirements of each kind of agent.

5.3   Ambulance Agents

The complete list of requirements for our ambulance agents are given below.

– Do not run out of fuel.

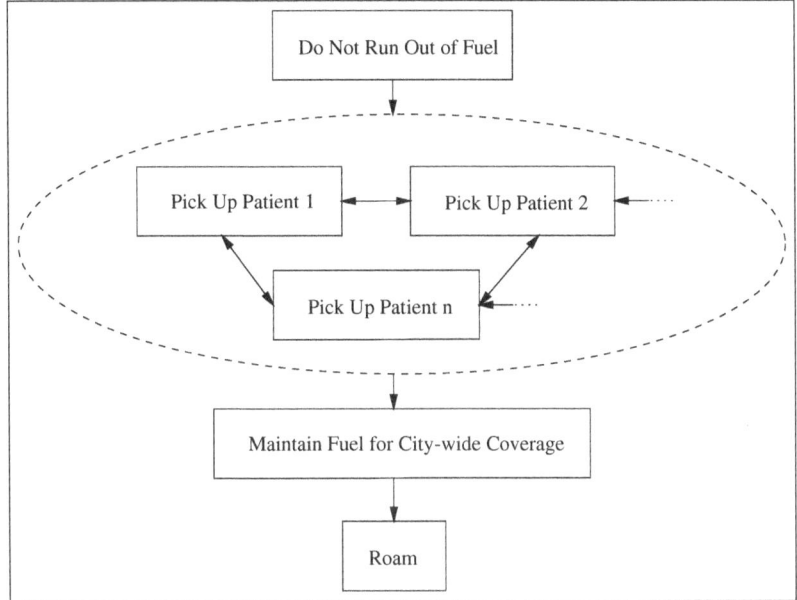

Fig. 7. Lexicographic ordering of ambulance requirements

- Pick up clients.
- Roam.
- Maintain enough fuel to provide city-wide coverage.

The requirements to pick up clients may be satisfied by any of the ambulances in the system, although at any time we will only have one ambulance committed to picking up that client. The lexicographic ordering of these requirements is given in Fig. 7.

Do Not Run Out of Fuel. Since the requirement to avoid running out of fuel is the sole occupoant of the top level of the lexicographic ordering we do not need to consider any trade-offs. As such, the choice of the level cost for requirement violation is arbitrary, and any cost greater than zero will suffice since behaviours defending this requirement will automatically dominate all others when a violation is predicted. In this case we set the cost of violation at 100.

In this simulation, the ambulance agents are aware of their fuel load with complete accuracy, and are also able to predict the fuel used in travelling between two points with complete accuracy. In addition, there are no possible circumstances arising that may unexpectedly alter the rate of fuel usage. Due to the lack of uncertainty in this situation; the expected cost (in relation to the fuel requirement) for any journey that terminates with the ambulance at the hospital with any positive amount of fuel left is zero. The expected cost only becomes non-zero if the ambulance is predicted to arrive at the hospital with

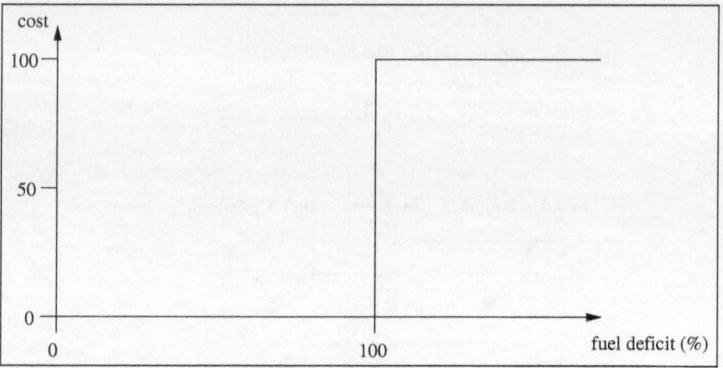

Fig. 8. Expected cost of a journey terminating at the hospital, dependent on predicted fuel deficit.

a negative amount of fuel, i.e. it will run out on the way. This cost function is shown in Fig. 8. If the measurement of fuel load or fuel usage was susceptible to error then the expected cost of a journey terminating at the hospital would increase as a function of the fuel deficit [9].

Pick Up Clients. A new requirement to pick up a client is instantiated every time a new emergency request is received, and is open for consideration by all of the ambulances present in the system. At any time the number of requirements to pick up clients is exactly equal to the number of clients waiting to be picked up. Each ambulance maintains beliefs about the location, emergency level, and time of request for each pending client so that they can calculate the expected costs of potential action sequences using the cost functions given in Fig. 6.

Plans to pick up a client are considered *relevant* whenever a new emergency request is received, or whenever the ambulance becomes available after dropping off a client. When a plan to pick up a client becomes *applicable* the ambulance will send an offer to the client agent of a pickup, together with the expected journey time. These offers are regarded as prospective and without commitment. The client agent can then send a message back asking for the nearest ambulance to commit to picking it up, together with the next best offer it has received. At this stage the ambulance agent calculates the cost of picking up that client, and if the expected cost is less than the expected cost of not picking up the client then the ambulance agent commits to doing so, possibly dropping other commitments to other client agents in the process. This communication process is shown in Fig. 9. How the estimated cost of these plans is calculated is outlined below.

The motivator proposing the intention to pick up a client, E_1, calculates the benefit of the intention by considering how long it will take for this ambulance to pick up the client, and how long it estimates it will take for another ambulance to pick up the client. This benefit is given by the following formula.

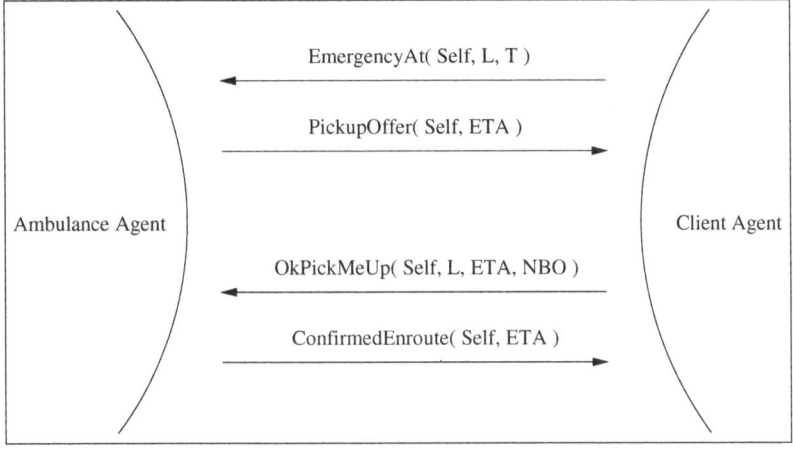

Fig. 9. Ambulance Agent – Client Agent Communication

$$benefit = cost\ of\ not\ picking\ up\ E_1\ -\ cost\ of\ picking\ up\ E_1$$
$$= c_{l(E_1)}(t_j(E_1) + t_{nbo}(E_1)) -$$
$$c_{l(E_1)}(t_j(E_1) + t_p(E_1))$$

where $c_{l(E_1)}$ is the cost function associated with the emergency level, $t_j(E_1)$ is the expected journey time from the scene of the emergency to the hospital, $t_p(E_1)$ is the estimated time of pickup if we deal with the request, and $t_{nbo}(E_1)$ is the estimated time of pickup by the next best offer that the client has received. Since $t_{nbo}(E_1)$ is greater than $t_p(E_1)$ the expected benefit will be greater than zero.

In the case where the client agent has not received another offer then we need to estimate $t_{nbo}(E_1)$, and to ensure that commitment is beneficial this estimate of $t_{nbo}(E_1)$ must be greater than $t_p(E_1)$. The client will receive another offer when another ambulance has returned to the hospital with a client, and since we know the expected journey time from the hospital to the client is $t_j(E_1)$, which will be the offer received. Given this we can estimate $t_{nbo}(E_1)$ as $t_j(E_1) + t_{interval}$, where $t_{interval}$ is the mean interval between ambulances returning to the hospital. However, in the case where the hospital is between the ambulance and the client this estimate of $t_{nbo}(E_1)$ may be less than $t_p(E_1)$. To ensure that commitment is always beneficial we take the estimate of $t_{nbo}(E_1)$ to be the maximum of $t_j(E_1) + t_{interval}$ and $t_p(E_1) + 20$. If a client agent receives a better offer then it will release the currently committed ambulance and take on this better offer.

When considering the expected costs of picking up a client, only those motivators that are committed to a client are allowed to criticize a suggested intention to pick up another client. Those requirements that have not been committed to will already have been considered earlier in the process and intentions to pick up those clients will have been found to be inferior to those currently committed to. Thus, we do not need to consider every client in the system each time we consider a new intention to pick up a client.

If a motivator is committed to picking up a client, E_2, then this motivator will criticize proposed intentions to pick up another client using the following formula.

$$benefit = cost\ of\ picking\ up\ E_2\ -\ cost\ of\ not\ picking\ up\ E_2$$
$$= c_{l(E_2)}(2 * t_j(E_2) + t_{interval}) -$$
$$c_{l(E_2)}(t_j(E_2) + t_p(E_2))$$

Since the commitment to E_2 will have been given some time in the past E_2 will not have an up to date next best offer. As before, the expected time for another ambulance to pick up that client is based on the interval between ambulances returning to hospital and the expected journey time between hospital and client, and back again.

Maintain Fuel for City-Wide Coverage. This requirement ensures that a roaming ambulance will be able to pick up a new client from anywhere within the city. It is dominated by the requirements to pick up and deliver clients should the ambulance be able to. Although the ambulance may not have enough fuel for city-wide coverage it may still be able to ferry a particular client back to the hospital.

Since this requirement is alone in its level in the lexicographic ordering, the cost we associate with violation is arbitrary, and in this case we again set it at 100. The cost function for this requirement is identical to that given in Fig. 8, where we predict the amount of fuel left after a hypothetical journey taking us from our current position to the farthest point in the city, and back to the hospital.

Roam. Roaming is a default behaviour that is the sole inhabitant of the bottom level of the lexicographic ordering. If no other requirement is currently directing the ambulance then the roaming requirement will generate an intention to travel to a part of the city that is not currently well covered by other ambulances. As before, we choose the value 100.

5.4   Client Agents

Each new emergency request is embodied within an agent that maintains information about the level of the emergency and the time of the request. This agent has a single requirement, to be picked up promptly.

Be Picked Up Promptly. On creation the client agent broadcasts the nature of the emergency and its location to all ambulances, and each ambulance that is not already carrying a client will supply a prospective offer of a pickup to this agent, supplying an estimated time of arrival. The emergency agent allows 5 seconds for offers to be received, and should any ambulance take longer than this to reply then it is likely to be involved in dealing with other clients and not the best candidate for picking this client up promptly. Should no offers be received in this time then we assume that all the ambulance are busy, and each ambulance will supply offers to all pending clients as soon as it becomes free.

As the cost of being delivered to the hospital increases monotonically with time (see Fig. 6) the best offer is the one from the ambulance that will arrive first. The nearest

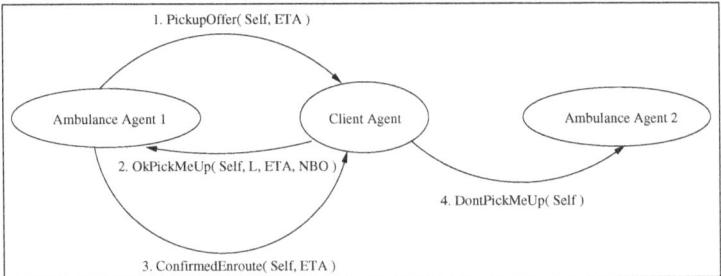

Fig. 10. Ambulance Agent – Client Agent Communication. Client agent decides

ambulance is asked to commit to picking the client up, as shown in Fig. 9. If the ambulance refuses to commit (because it has decided that it can handle another client better) then the ambulance that provided the next best offer is asked to commit, and so on until we receive a commitment. Should no ambulance commit to picking the client up then again they must all be busy serving other clients and will have to wait until one becomes free, at which time it will offer to this client agent again.

While the currently committed ambulance is en-route a better offer may be provided by another ambulance that has just dropped off a client. In this case that ambulance is asked to commit to the client agent, and if such a commitment is gained then the first ambulance is released from its commitment to this client. Once released from its commitment that ambulance will make offers to other pending clients. The communication involved in this situation is given in Fig. 10.

It is possible that an ambulance currently committed to pick us up may change its mind en-route, usually because another emergency request has been received that that ambulance is better able to deal with. In this case it is possible that there are other ambulances able to respond that we have already refused offers from, so we broadcast the fact that we are again open to new offers to all ambulances.

6   Conclusion

This paper has demonstrated the beginnings of a framework for specifying, designing, and implementing autonomous agents. Using the requirements of an agent as the central notion throughout means that each stage of the process remains intuitive and progresses naturally from the others.

We have presented a method for deriving a quantitative performance measure for an agent's behaviour, and illustrated this by considering a virtual squirrel that must survive in a hostile environment. To show the wide applicability of this method we then describe in detail the specification and implementation of an emergency services coordination application that is suitable for serious real world applications.

The architecture presented allows the designer of an autonomous agent with limited resources and multiple requirements to specify the relative importance of its requirements, varying from strict dominance to a flexible trade-off mechanism. A major benefit of the architecture is that the relative importance of the requirements is determined by a mechanism entirely seperate from the procedural knowledge of the agent. This allows changes in the relative importance of the requirements to be performed without possibility of affecting the agents overall capabilities, and vice versa, and also enables new requirements to be added or existing ones removed without affecting any other requirements.

References

1. R. Aylett and M. Luck. Applying artificial intelligence to virtual reality: Intelligent virtual environments. *Applied Artificial Intelligence*, 14(1):3–32, 2000.
2. C. Balkenius. *Natural Intelligence in Artificial Creatures*. PhD thesis, Lund University Cognitive Studies, 1995.
3. M. E. Bratman. *Intentions, Plans, and Practical Reason*. Harvard University Press: Cambridge, MA, 1987.
4. R. A. Brooks. Intelligence without reason. In *Proceedings of the Twelfth International Joint Conference on Artificial Intelligence (IJCAI-91)*, pages 569–595, Sydney, Australia, 1991.
5. S. de Lioncourt and M. Luck. Towards requirements analysis for autonomous agent behaviour. In *Proceedings of the First International Workshop of Central and Eastern Europe on Multi-Agent Systems*, to appear.
6. M. d'Inverno, D. Kinny, M. Luck, and M. Wooldridge. A formal specification of dMARS. In *Intelligent Agents IV: Proceedings of the Fourth International Workshop on Agent Theories, Architectures and Languages*, volume 1365, pages 155–176. Springer-Verlag, 1998.
7. D. Kinny, M. Georgeff, and A. Rao. A methodology and modelling technique for systems of BDI agents. In Y. Demazeau and J.-P. Müller, editors, *Agents Breaking Away: Proceedings of the Seventh European Workshop on Modelling Autonomous Agents in a Multi-Agent World, Lecture Notes in Artificial Intelligence 1038*, pages 56–71. Springer-Verlag, 1996.
8. H. Kitano. Robocup rescue: A grand challenge for multi-agent systems. In *Proceedings of the Fourth International Conference on Multi-Agent Systems*, pages 5–12, 2000.
9. D. McFarland and T. Bösser. *Intelligent Behaviour in Animals and Robots*. MIT Press, Cambridge, MA, 1993.
10. A. S. Rao and M. Georgeff. BDI Agents: from theory to practice. In *Proceedings of the First International Conference on Multi-Agent Systems*, pages 312–319, San Francisco, CA, June 1995.
11. A. S. Rao and M. P. Georgeff. Modeling rational agents within a BDI-architecture. In R. Fikes and E. Sandewall, editors, *Proceedings of Knowledge Representation and Reasoning (KR&R-91)*, pages 473–484. Morgan Kaufmann Publishers: San Mateo, CA, April 1991.
12. S. Russell and P. Norvig. *Artificial Intelligence: a modern approach*. Prentice-Hall, 1995.

Software Agents for Electronic Business: Opportunities and Challenges

Jörg P. Müller, Bernhard Bauer, and Michael Berger

Siemens AG, Corporate Technology, CT IC 6, D-81730 Munich, Germany
Joerg.mueller{bernhard.bauer,michael.berger}@mchp.siemens.de

Abstract. Electronic business (eBusiness) is one of the main global drivers of information technology. In this paper, we investigate how eBusiness can benefit from methods, components and solutions based on software agent technology. We give an overview of the current electronic business mainstreams and outline a number of important the challenges eBusiness has to tackle. We then describe how agent technology can be applied to in eBusiness to resolve some of these challenges. We discuss related work and the need for integration of any agent technologies into existing eBusiness landscapes and infrastructures. We describe the opportunities for agent technology in this area. In addition risks and areas of future work are discussed.

1 Introduction

Since the early nineties the Internet usage has been growing exponentially. Stationary and, increasingly, mobile information services are reaching users world-wide at anytime. Based on these facilities for communication and data exchange, many kinds of businesses are moving to the electronic world of the web to connect customers, suppliers and partners to respect the globalization of markets. For *electronic business (eBusiness)*, the Internet is much more than just a mine of information. It is capable of helping to attract a whole new customer base whilst ensuring that existing customers remain. It can enable an increase in efficiency and better cost control by allowing customers, as well as nominated suppliers and distributors, to work together and share applications and knowledge in a secure environment, based on a uniform platform.

eBusiness is the overall term for the complex integration / transformation of existing infrastructures, business processes, enterprise applications, and organizational structures into a high-performance business model using information technology based on electronic media such as the Internet, other computer networks, and wireless transmission to facilitate the business. eBusiness is changing the traditional business landscape and the way business is done in general. The future success of a company depends largely on their ability to transform themselves into eBusiness companies. This means the implementation of new business strategies and the introduction of innovative marketing techniques, as well as the better management of information and the reduction of time-wasting paper-based processes. The aim of this e-transformation is increased speed of service, improved customer satisfaction, integrated solutions, convergence of sales and service chains, leveraging legacy systems, connecting the entire corporate, contract manufacturing, information

V. Mařík et al. (Eds.): MASA 2001, LNAI 2322, pp. 61-106, 2002.
© Springer-Verlag Berlin Heidelberg 2002

security, and protection of intellectual property. A special trend is mobile business (mBusiness). That's the overall term for eBusiness based on mobile electronic media and wireless networks. Beside and on top of the traditional eBusiness applications mBusiness can provide additional value through e.g. location based services.

An important branch of eBusiness are electronic marketplaces (e-marketplaces). An e-marketplace is a central place on the Internet functioning as a meeting place for buyers and sellers of specific products. Buyers and sellers can form interest groups to bundle their capacity. An electronic marketplace can be open or closed. It has intermediary functions like auctioning and negotiation. Additionally, electronic marketplaces usually have a portal functionality as well providing e.g. catalogues, availability information, and supply order. Parts of a marketplace are seller and buyer sites (e.g. e-procurement at the buyer site).

eBusiness is the most growing market in the world. The world-wide business-to-business (B2B) Internet commerce market is on pace to total $8.5 trillion in 2005, according to Gartner Group in March 2001 [25]. In 2000, the value of world-wide B2B Internet commerce sales transactions surpassed $433 billion, a 189 percent increase over 1999 sales transactions. World-wide B2B Internet commerce is projected to reach $919 billion in 2001, followed by $1.9 trillion in 2002. Forrester Research expected in February 2000, that 75 percent of B2B will migrate to e-marketplaces over the next five years and that e-marketplaces will capture 53% of all online business trade by 2004 [22]. The same company predicted in January 2001 that businesses world-wide would increase their spending on B2B e-marketplaces from $2.6 billion in 2000 to $137.2 billion by 2005. Despite the disillusionment brought by the dot-com crisis, this will still be a huge market.

Today, many different software components and systems offer a wide range of standard business services and partially isolated eBusiness solutions. No single vendor can offer software, which covers all eBusiness services. Thus, a distributed global architecture based on open architectural standards, such as Java, HTTP, EJB, and XML, is needed. This architecture will offer component based functionality, wide range of scalability, interoperability between applications, and secure access. Furthermore, a more personalized and intelligent support of the eBusiness processes is becoming more and more important.

In this paper, we investigate how *software agent technologies* can help enterprises tackle the challenges of eBusiness. Software agents are software components characterized by *autonomy* (to act on their own), *re-activity* (to process external events), *pro-activity* (to reach goals), *co-operation* (to efficiently and effectively solve tasks), *adaptation* (to learn by experience) and *mobility* (migration to new places). Agents can be individualized to act on behalf of users, teams, or organizations. They coordinate their activities and collaborate with humans, other agents and external components in order to achieve their goals (see e.g. [31], [39], [43]).

Agent technology has the potential to play a key role in combining the existing heterogeneous eBusiness solutions, adding advanced functionality and automating standard processes. For that, agents provide task delegation, enriched higher level communication, enable more intelligent service provision and process management, provide individualization (also personalized visualizations and avatars), provide service integration to value added services to deal with the enlarging amount of information and functions, and allow self-organization of processes and systems.

To realize this big potential, agents need an infrastructure that allows them to communicate, to discover service-peers, to negotiate and to co-operate in open environments [48]. This requires standards to ensure the interoperability between agents of different vendors and domains (see e.g. FIPA [19]). Most importantly, agents will need to build on and interface with a variety of existing and upcoming developments and standards, like DAML+OIL [7] and ebXML [11]. Establishing agents as enabling technology will touch on supporting a wide range of devices, integrating telecommunication and Internet, and interfacing with Enterprise Resource Planning (ERP) and supply chain management systems and eBusiness platforms.

Another important precondition for the acceptance of agent technology in eBusiness is the availability of generic added-value services, such as team coordination, process scheduling, recommendation engines, mobility support and location-aware services. Such services are designed for multiple reuses and cover areas requiring higher levels of flexibility, individualization, or intelligence. In addition, successfully bringing agent technology to market, techniques that reduce the perceived risk inherent in any new technology are required. Such a technique is to present the new technology as an incremental extension of known and trusted methods, and to provide explicit engineering tools to support proven methods of technology deployment.

In this paper we give an overview over agent-based approaches to eBusiness and show the main advantages in building agent based eBusiness systems. Section 2 gives a short introduction on eBusiness providing several views: a process view, an architectural view, and a functional view. Based on these views, we will investigate current limitations of eBusiness, and look at fields where we believe agent technology can play an important role over the next few years. Section 3 provides an introduction to agent technology and gives a detailed view on agent enabled eBusiness architectures, in particular having a focus on the benefits of agent technology for eBusiness. Section 4 illustrates three case studies in the domains of Human Resource Matching, Distributed Team Management and Travel Support. Section 5 describes agent standards and outlines relationships between agent technologies and related and integration technologies. Section 6 concludes and outlines areas for future work.

2   Areas and Challenges of eBusiness

In this section, we will outline several views on eBusiness: a process view, an architectural view, and a functional view. Based on these views, we will investigate current limitations of eBusiness, and have look at fields where we believe agent technology can play an important role over the next few years.

2.1   Process View

Electronic business, as far as regarded from a corporate perspective, is neither driven by specific functions nor by technologies. It is mainly driven by processes: the objective of electronic business is to support and optimize business processes. Hence, any discussion of eBusiness will be incomplete without taking a process-oriented stance.

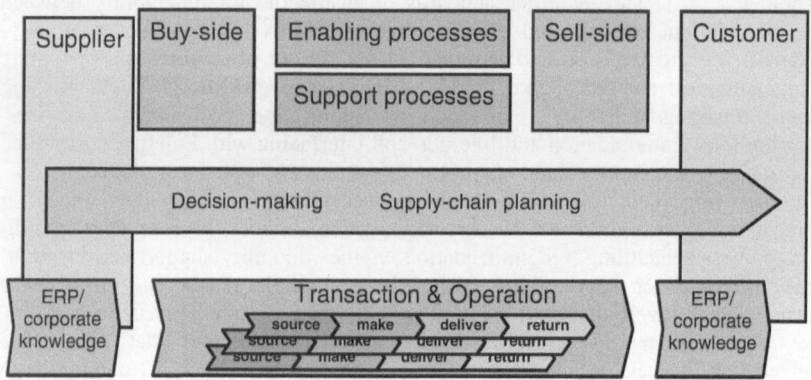

Fig. 1. eBusiness Process Architecture

Fig. 1 outlines the process view of eBusiness. It shows the basic application domains for eBusiness, from the perspective of an enterprise. It depicts the value chain, from suppliers (buy-side, procurement) to customers (sell-side, customer relationship management). The transaction layer that describes the value chain forms the basis of a companies' eBusiness process. It feeds on information from Enterprise Resource Planning (ERP) systems and corporate knowledge bases. On top of this process, there is a decision-making and supply-chain planning flow. Furthermore, a number of *enabling processes* such as content/knowledge management, e-payment, registration and single login management as well as *support processes* including travel management and Human Resources (eHR) round up the corporate eBusiness picture.

2.2   Architecture View

A second important perspective of an eBusiness system is in terms of its underlying software architecture. The software architecture and the technologies used in its different tiers have a great influence on the flexibility and scalability of such a system.

eBusiness systems are typically based on multi-tier architectures. A typical example is illustrated in Fig. 2. In the following, we briefly describe the individual tiers.

2.2.1 Client Tier

The client tier contains the part of the system that runs on client-side hardware. It typically provides a Web / WAP browser interface but may also incorporate a fat-client approach to facilitate rich functionality and personalization on the client side. There typically is a trade-off between rich client-side functionality on the one hand, favoring a fat-client approach, and ease of change, maintenance and administration, favoring a thin-client solution.

Especially in the context of mobile business, more powerful mobile devices and networks, and of new software paradigms such as peer-to-peer technology, fat client solutions are attractive. However, we perceive a strong trend to thin client solutions in many corporate, intranet-based eBusiness environments, mainly for the above mentioned reasons.

2.2.2 Client Interaction Tier

The role of the client interaction tier is to process client requests and to transform results produced by the business logic tier (see below) into presentations that are tailored with respect to the requesting user and its context (preferences, location, device, etc.). At the time of writing, using XSL transformation engines and Java-based front-end technologies such as Java Server pages appears a state-of-the art solution. Having said this, we must state that up to our knowledge, it is still rather the exception than the rule that this technology is actually used in practice.

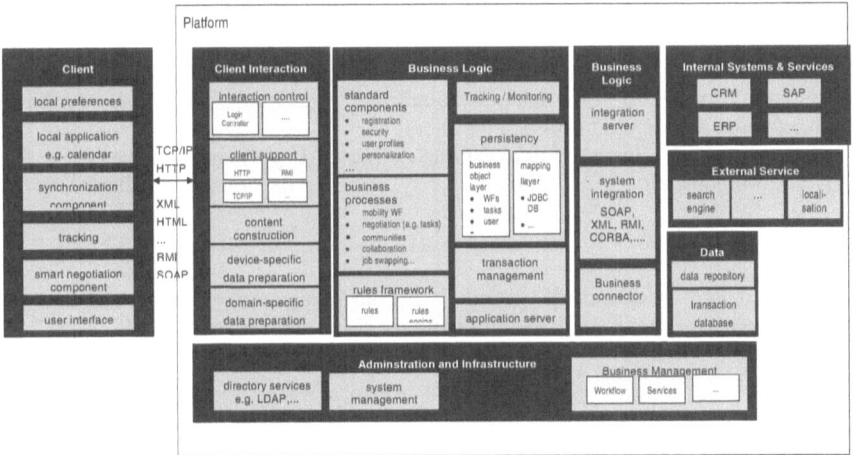

Fig. 2. Software Architecture of an eBusiness System

2.2.3 Business Logic Tier

This tier is the core of an eBusiness architecture, implementing the business objects (e.g., users, customers, orders) and the basic business processes and transactions (e.g., register, order, search). Scalability and flexibility are the most important requirements to be satisfied by the business logic tier. On the one hand, these objects and processes may be requested a large number of times by applications; on the other hand, as the processes in a company change, their implementation needs to be updated. Also, the attempt to standardize interfaces and processes in eBusiness and the need to reuse existing building blocks throughout multiple applications brings about the need and the possibility to reuse pieces of business logic. The dominant solutions today are based on Enterprise Java Beans Application Servers. These Application Servers offer good performance and availability and provide support for transactions and persistence. They often play the role of wrappers to ERP systems or other external or legacy applications.

2.2.4 Integration Tier

More advanced eBusiness architectures provide an extra layer of abstraction for interaction with / integration of legacy systems and external business applications. The integration tier offers uniform interfaces for enterprise application integration to the business tier (often based on XML/SOAP); furthermore, it provides single login support (e.g., based on LDAP) to deal with the authentication regimes of multiple external systems. For asynchronous communication between applications, the integration tier will usually support messaging. Towards the backend, adapters for different legacy systems are provided (e.g., SAP). Today, there are a growing number of products available to implement the integration (e.g., WebMethods, IBM MQSeries).

2.2.5 Systems and Services Tier

This tier provides the physical connectivity between an eBusiness system and the information it accesses, in the form of connectors to data bases and legacy systems, but in addition to external information systems.

State of the art eBusiness architectures define generic invocation interfaces for flexible communication between the tiers, e.g., based on the command pattern.

2.3   Functional View

One way to look at eBusiness systems is by the functions they perform, from the perspective of the parties involved. Figure 3 illustrates these functions. They are briefly discussed in the following:

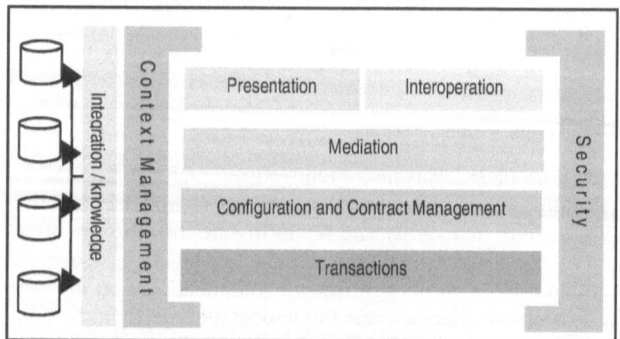

Fig. 3. Functional eBusiness Architecture

2.3.1 Communication: Presentation and Interoperation

The first function of eBusiness is to make communication between enterprises, customers, partners and suppliers across the value chain more efficient. This involves **presentation** (e.g., attractive web shops, efficient marketing strategies, sales campaigns, communities) but also **interoperation**, i.e., the ability of business applications to communicate with each other across the borders of departments and enterprises. Providing this function offers visibility and thus the basis for mutual attraction and interaction.

2.3.2 Mediation

By mediation we mean the solicitation of demand and supply in eBusiness systems and marketplaces. Mediation allows customers to find and contact potential products, partners or merchants[1].

2.3.3 Configuration and Contract Management

This function subsumes the phase of negotiation between buyer(s) and seller(s) with the goal to achieve a business agreement, i.e., a signed contract on some matter. This typically involves the configuration of the product and the negotiation of the contract for the selected product configuration. In practice, however, negotiation may involve modification of the product configuration; hence, the two phases can be inter-linked.

2.3.4 Transactions

Once an agreement has been reached, the actual business transaction is carried out, connected with processes such as charging, payment, order fulfillment, and delivery. Typically, transactions require interactions with ERP systems or with external systems (such as payment servers).

These core functions need to be supported by a number of supporting functions.

2.3.5 Context Management

In order to automate any eBusiness activity, eBusiness systems need access to the context in which the activity is located. In particular, that means the access to and maintenance of user profiles. E.g., to provide personalized services, a Customer Relationship Management system will store information about a customer and derive information about the users' preferences from this history, which is then used for dedicated marketing campaigns, or to deal with complaints and requests by that customer quicker and more efficiently. Another example is the use of location information for mobiles personalized services.

2.3.6 Security

For technical, business and psychological reasons, the provision of a secure infrastructure is (e-)business critical. Security needs to cover all levels, ranging from security of information transfer to application-level security, and requires appropriate measures to be taken at the hardware, software, and process level.

---

[1] In [28] Guttman et al. split this function into Product Brokering and Merchant Brokering.

2.3.7 Integration and Knowledge Management

For companies, the core of eBusiness is information about their products, customers and processes (normally stored in ERP systems) and the implicit and explicit corporate knowledge available in numerous databases, document repositories, and in addition in the heads of the employees. The ability to access eBusiness relevant information from legacy systems and organize the knowledge within a company in an easily accessible form is crucial.

2.4   Challenges in eBusiness

Today, there are well-established product suites to support these eBusiness functions. E.g., *IBM Websphere* for sell-side, *i2* for Supply Chain Planning and Procurement, *CommerceOne* for procurement and trade exchanges, *Siebel* for Customer Relationship Management, and *SAP* for ERP systems (see also Sect. 5.3).

In this section, we will outline some of the remaining challenges and opportunities for research on eBusiness. We believe that in order for a technology to succeed in eBusiness it will be necessary to take an incremental approach, thus adding value on top of existing platforms and services.

2.4.1 Challenge: Individualization and Privacy

How can eBusiness systems provide individualized content and services while at the same time ensuring adequate (and user-defined) levels of privacy? How can user profiles be created, maintained, and adapted to cope with multiple threads of a user's activity, with disruptive events, and with longer term changes in the user's preference and activity structure? How can teams and organizations be profiled?

The importance of this question has been recognized. P3P is an attempt to provide a uniform representation of privacy preferences for an individual or company. However, it only covers privacy related preferences, and not the individualization of presentation, content, and services.

2.4.2 Challenge: Secure Delegation

How can humans delegate complex tasks to machines? How can they be sure the machine has understood the task correctly? How can they specify the permissions and limitations of authorization of machines during task execution? How can they monitor the progress of task execution? How can a flexible hand-over between humans and machines be implemented to guarantee human and machine abilities are used for their best? How can transactions done by machines be verified and liabilities be enforced? What are legal aspects to be observed?

While many researchers investigate secure protocols and efficient strategies e.g., for automating negotiation, it is our firm belief that the most difficult part of the problem is at the user interface layer in developing appropriate models for efficient delegation and transparent collaboration between humans and machines.

2.4.3 Challenge: Semantic Interoperability

How can machines better understand the content of communication with humans or other machines? How can eBusiness consumers find supply matching their demand? How can suppliers find potential customers? How can applications created by different companies interoperate more smoothly even if there is no explicit standard for the interaction? How can techniques for achieving interoperability at the level of semantics be used to add value to existing platforms and standards in eBusiness?

We believe that semantic interoperability is maybe the hardest of all challenges to be overcome, because it requires the understanding of semantics by machines which is still in its beginnings.

2.4.4 Challenge: Support for Flexible Organization Structures

How can eBusiness infrastructures keep up with ever changing structures of enterprises? When departments change their responsibility or structure, when a partner becomes a competitor or vice versa, how can communication and security policies be maintained smoothly? How can the participants in the value chain communicate and collaborate securely and efficiently over firewalls and enterprise boundaries? How do suppliers know which events in their internal supply chain are of relevance and need to be communicated to their (downstream) partners? How can an existing IT infrastructure migrate towards this functionality?

While various theoretical approaches exist, supporting flexible organization structures in practice is a huge challenge.

2.4.5 Challenge: Intelligent Collaboration and Coordination

How can distributed individuals, teams, departments, and enterprises collaborate and coordinate their activity? How can the information necessary for this be exchanged efficiently? How can tasks be formulated, associated with skills, responsibilities, and permissions, and be allocated? How can humans collaborate with applications acting on their behalf or on behalf of other humans?

In particular in a corporate context, huge efforts are made to set up infrastructures that allow humans to share information, resources, and applications, and to work towards a common goal. Still, the problem remains hard due to its dynamic nature and through increased mobility.

2.4.6 Challenge: Mobility Support

How can mobile users be ensured effective access to corporate processes and knowledge? How can they find and communicate with team members remotely? How can location and situation information be used to make services more useful and intelligent? How can information be routed, transported and presented in a way that accommodates available networks and devices? What infrastructure is necessary to leverage the potential of ubiquitous computing for enterprises and individuals?

In a society where mobility plays a more and more important role, providing answers to these questions is crucial.

2.4.7 Challenge: Pro-active, Adaptive Processes

How can complex, distributed processes be modeled as active, situated entities that can interoperate with other processes that can monitor their environments and change their behavior on demand? How can these processes deal with change? What needs to be done to implement (pro-)active processes based on existing process models, e.g., in distributed, flexible manufacturing and supply chain management.

While many approaches to process modeling exist, automating them still remains a challenge due to the required level of introspection (i.e., a process needs to be able to judge a situation with respect to its competence, e.g., to recognize unforeseen conditions) and due to incomplete sensor-actor loops (i.e., decisions relevant to the process are often made by entities outside the control (and visibility) of that process.

2.4.8 Challenge: Adaptive Decision-Making Assistance

As machines change their role from slaves to assistants, more complex domain models are required to enable them to provide assistance in complex decision situations such as contract negotiations. How can these models be defined? How can machines be effectively instructed for these decision-making assistance tasks? How can decisions (or suggestions for decisions) by machines be made transparent to humans?

This challenge is closely related to Challenges 2.4.2 (Secure Delegation) and 2.4.5 (Intelligent Collaboration and Coordination).

2.4.9 Challenge: Intelligent Selection and Evaluation of Products and Services

How can configuration and purchasing processes be automated? How can machines support users in finding products and services matching a demand profile? How can they evaluate different configuration and product offers? How can they interoperate with existing eBusiness platforms? How can transactions made by machines be tracked down to the users? How can fraud be prevented? How can the risk for users or enterprises be minimized that faulty software makes wrong suggestions or buys the wrong items at too high a price?

Finding answers to these questions will be a precondition to any automation of matchmaking, contracting, or shopping / procurement processes in eBusiness.

In the following section we shall investigate where and how agent technology can provide means for dealing with these challenges.

3 Agents in eBusiness

In this section we define our notion of agent technology and then elaborate opportunities for agent technology to tackle the eBusiness challenges defined in Sect. 2.

3.1   Agents Definitions and Characteristics

In [1], an agent is defined as

> ... *a computer system, situated   in some environment, that is capable of flexible, autonomous action in order to meet its design objectives.*

We would like to enhance this definition by one aspect. Put more simply:

> *an agent is an intelligent autonomous computer system that does something useful on behalf of a human or an organization.*

With software agents usually special properties are associated, see e.g., [44], [43] for an overview. Fig. 4 illustrates the most important properties and dimensions of agents. These properties are well reflected in the different dimensions of agents, namely mobility, intelligence, cooperation and distribution, showing moreover that agent technologies combines these functions with the existing base technologies in agent-oriented integrated development environments supporting agent platforms and agent-oriented software engineering to develop agent-based frameworks and applications.

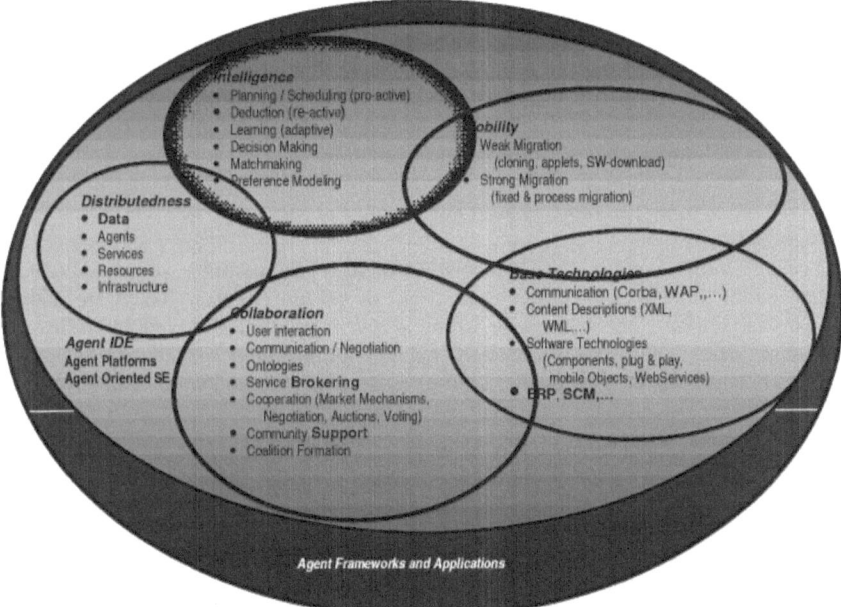

Fig. 4. Dimensions of agents

It becomes clear from Fig. 4 that agent technology is based on and needs to be developed in the context of existing basic technologies, such as software technologies. Content is described using standards like XML or RDF; existing communication mechanisms, like SOAP or WAP, are applied within agent technology. In the case of eBusiness we also view platforms as those described in Sect. 2.1 as base technology.

Software agents add a number of additional features to these technologies:

- Agents enable **collaboration** between humans and machines, thus providing a new metaphor for multimodal *user interaction*. Users instruct agents to act on their behalf instead of having to program them. Two core areas within the discipline of intelligent user interfaces include intelligent dialog systems, and believable virtual personalities. At the same time, agents introduce the notion of *machine-machine collaboration. negotiation and communication* on a semantics level allowing agents to coordinate their tasks and resources. In order to support the communication at a semantics level *ontologies* are applied to assign meaning to symbols and expressions within a given domain language. Based on negotiation, communication and ontologies *cooperation* between different agents can take place. *Coalition formation* is useful in eCommerce where virtual purchasing cooperative societies can be built to obtain quantity discount. *Organizational models* can be applied for the mapping of real organizations within a company to software organizations based on agents.
- The **intelligence** of an agent is manifested by its ability to adapt its behavior to changing environmental conditions, and to employ *planning and decision-making*, e.g., for process scheduling and resource planning based on negotiation techniques. In particular planning can be performed by a single agent or in cooperation with several agents. *Learning* can be applied in several dimensions, e.g. learning of user preferences, learning of negotiation strategies of other agents up to adapting processes in the context of eBusiness. *Matchmaking* is the process of mediating demand and supply based on profile information. Matchmaking (see Sect. 3.4.9) plays a crucial role, e.g. in agent based electronic marketplaces: the task to be solved is to find the most appropriate agents, products, or services for a task, negotiation, or market transaction.
- Agent technology supports **mobility** at different levels: mobility of users, devices, and code. In the latter case we speak of *mobile agents*. They are either characterized by *weak mobility* or *strong mobility*. Examples of weak mobility are cloning where an agent is deployed on another machine with the initial state. Applets can be seen as a specific kind of cloning. The download of a new version of software on an agent platform is another kind of weak migration. Strong migration is characterized by the complete movement of the execution state of an agent to another machine; this can be obtained either through real process migration or through specific migration points where an agent is allowed to migrate.
- Multi-agent systems are **distributed** systems; therefore distribution is an inherent feature of agent-based systems. In this context both agents and resources can be distributed. The agent infrastructure enables transparent access to distributed resources and transparent interaction among distributed agents.

These pillars of agent technology result in individualized added value services, supporting a possible nomadic user with intelligent assistance, based on search, integration and presentation of distributed information and knowledge management, advanced process control support, and eBusiness and enterprise applications. To conclude, agent technology provides

- the integration of distributed heterogeneous systems
- the mobility of persons and software

- the coordination of heterogeneous components and services
- the support of users for routine tasks
- the personalization of tasks and the exchange of personalized information and
- the easy integration of additional components and frameworks

Based on these potential benefits, we will now investigate how agent technology can help us tackle the eBusiness challenges identified in Sect. 2.4.

3.2   Agents in eBusiness: Areas of Application

With the broad acceptance of the Internet technology, future business processes will increasingly access electronic market places. The fact that these business processes will involve larger number of different parties from different organizations makes multi-agent systems a very promising approach for the management of these processes. Agents must be able to make autonomous decisions, e.g., in electronic negotiations or auctions. The intelligence of the agents will be essentially determined by the degree of their adaptability, covering the intelligent evaluation of the data, the adaptive reaction to changes of the environment, matchmaking, distributed planning, negotiation protocols and strategies (see Sect. 3.1).

As we have seen in Sect. 2, the today's landscape of eBusiness platforms and architectures is very heterogeneous. eBusiness architectures need to support the integration of the existing products, solutions, processes with new functionality, such as those supported by agent technology to enable end-to-end eBusiness. Within the different views of eBusiness depicted in Sect. 2, we see the following focus areas of application for agents:

- **Sell-Side / Customer Relationship Management:** the electronic networking of business relations with the customers of a company can be essentially supported by agent technology. When applied wisely, avatar technology supports appealing personal assistance functionality based on virtual characters. Negotiations with customers can be supported by assistant agents – participating e.g. in an auction – to help a user through the negotiation process. In this context learning techniques can be applied to optimize the negotiation strategy of the user agent. Furthermore mobile agents can migrate to electronic marketplace to minimize communication costs and time delays and to ensure maximum flexibility and expressiveness of negotiation strategies. Security issues are fundamental in this context; therefore we believe that marketplace agents will only succeed in the market within a timeframe of three to five years. Another topic in sell-side eCommerce is the search and evaluation of existing shops and products with respect to their qualities. Here agents can be applied using matchmaking and act as recommendation engines.
- **Knowledge Management:** the electronic networking of all knowledge within a company and across companies. An important agent-related activity that has the potential to leverage knowledge management to a new quality is the semantic web initiative. Agents can use the metadata included in the semantic web to perform better quality searches and to provide users with better explanations for their decisions.
- **Buy-Side eBusiness (eProcurement):** the electronic networking of business relationships with the suppliers of a company. Software agents are geared to

support a company to automate (pre-)negotiation with existing suppliers based on given framework agreements and contracts. Details of these contracts can be negotiated automatically, like the amount of goods and the delivery date, based on the knowledge of the agents about production capacity and orders on the supplier side and the supply chain management information on the buyer side. Intelligent sourcing techniques and automated negotiation can be used for obtaining required goods or services on spot markets, e.g., if demand increases or an existing supplier has delivery problems. Recommendation engines based on matchmaking can provide sufficient information to select new potential suppliers.

- **Process Optimization:** adapting processes for end-to-end networking. Processes within a company can be optimized by integrating different single solutions into a company-wide network. Agent technology helps enterprises to optimize their business processes by (a) reacting quickly and autonomously to extraordinary events (e.g. breakdown of a machine); (b) ad-hoc planning and scheduling of processes; (c) using the available resources optimal or working to capacity; (d) integrating existing solutions on the interface and process side; (e) applying learning techniques to optimize the planned and scheduled processes; (f) dynamic negotiation and skills-based assignment of tasks; or (g) collective decision making.

- **eManufacturing:** lean manufacturing supporting cost-efficient, customer-driven management of operations. Agent technology can be applied for developing distributed intelligent manufacturing systems, including manufacturing enterprise integration, manufacturing planning, scheduling and control, materials handling, and holonic manufacturing systems. The key issues for developing agent-based manufacturing systems are enterprise integration and supply chain management, agent encapsulation, system architectures, dynamic system reconfiguration, design and manufacturability assessments, distributed dynamic and concurrent scheduling and execution, and factory control structures.

- **Supply Chain Management:** the networking from the purchase of raw goods and materials for manufacturing to the delivery of a finished product to an end user and cash flow. It includes eProcurement/eSourcing and eManufacturing (see above), and logistics. In the area of logistics dynamic advanced market and negotiation based resource management can be applied to achieve vertical (within a company) and horizontal coordination (task distribution across companies). Tracking information of the ordered goods and materials can help optimizing (re-scheduling) the processes dynamically in case of unexpected events, like traffic jams. Organizational techniques can be applied for forming teams and coalitions and to re-organize the supply chain.

- **mBusiness:** the mobile networking of eBusiness including mCommerce with additional value like location based services. Software agents can add advanced functionality for supporting the workflow of mobile employees by being situation-aware (including e.g., device, location, tasks, and time). It can be used to automate, optimize, enable or create mobility-supporting businesses and processes through individualization and process scheduling on the fly.

Today, many different software components and systems offer a wide range of standard business services and partially isolated eBusiness solutions. The objective of using agent technology in this area is to combine the heterogeneous solutions, to add advanced functionality and automating standard processes to connect companies worldwide. Thus, the major contributions of agent technology will be to help *em-*

power eBusiness users, and to *connect enterprises* internally and with their customers and partners world-wide

Agent technology must not reinvent the wheel; therefore it is necessary that these agent architectures are based on open standards, like XML or WebServices (see Sect. 5.3.3), allowing us to deploy their functions as components, and to provide wide scalability from mobile phones up to server farms, interoperability between applications, and secure access.

3.3   Agent Enabled eBusiness Architecture

Recalling the typical eBusiness software architecture presented in Sect. 2.2, we now discuss how agents can support the design of eBusiness systems on the individual tiers:

On the **client tier,** intelligent dialog systems and believable virtual personalities assist users in interacting effectively with the eBusiness systems. User agents can be instructed to provide a wide range of assistance services, to perform searches, negotiations, and transactions on behalf of their users. The instructed agent can reside on the end-user device and cooperate with other agents on end-user devices, servers, or marketplaces. Alternatively, it can migrate to the servers or marketplaces. This flexibility is supported by scalable agent platforms (see Sect. 4.2.1) that run on client devices (ranging from mobile phones up to usual personal computers). Individualized services such as personal negotiation support will be available to users on their **devices**. User agent on the device will increasingly monitor and learn user preferences from observing the user's behavior. In addition personal agents can support the user in planning and scheduling of tasks and managing appointments on behalf of the user. Tracking the user's tasks, appointments, time and positions allows a situation aware reaction of the user agent.

Client interaction can be integrated and extended with agent technology. At the moment this tier mainly deals with the device and domain specific representation and physical communication with the end-user device. The communication can support agent communication languages and in particular interaction protocols. The device specific content preparation can be improved using learning techniques about the user's behavior and interaction with the graphical user interface; in particular in the context of mobile devices with small displays the presentation can be optimized. This tier can perform ontology translations for different domains. The client interaction tier can support code mobility and provides the necessary security infrastructure, allowing mobile agents to migrate between servers and end-user devices.

At the **business logic tier,** agent technology can be applied for preference modeling of users and communities, and for collaboration and integration of business processes. Individualization is supported on different levels, like tasks, processes, services, and negotiations. The business logic tier can provide market places where agents can participate in auctions or other negotiations. The agents' collaboration facilities can be used to integrate with internal and external services and solutions. Distributed, on the fly planning and scheduling can be managed by agents using smart planning and scheduling techniques based on market mechanisms. Ontologies in connection with catalogue systems and ontology mapping enable the integration of heterogeneous data, workflow and processes. Negotiation and communication on a semantics level allow agents to coordinate their tasks and resources. eBusiness specific user preferences can be learnt, leading to better negotiation strategies and improved processes. Matchmaking allows agents to find the most appropriate agents, products, or services for a task, negotiation, or market transaction and support decision making.

Within the **integration tier** agent wrappers can be applied as a specific technique for the integration of heterogeneous components, systems and services. Moreover on this layer process scheduling, dynamic reaction and on the fly scheduling like in the business logic tier can be done if appropriate. In addition agents can control the usage of appropriate services depending on their quality of service (QoS). In particular the agent can learn about the reliability of services and function as recommendation engines for external services and data providers.

Internal and external **systems and services** can be agentified and thus integrated into the agent framework or can provide agent-based services.

In the following section we will investigate how agent technology can overcome the shortcomings of today's eBusiness solutions.

3.4   Benefits of Agent Technology

The promises of agent technology in eBusiness are:

- To achieve enriched, higher level communication
- To enable more intelligence service provision, and process management e.g. by personalization and integration of different services to value-added
- To deal with the enlarging amount of information and functions, and
- To allow self-organizing of processes.

To realize this potential, agents need to communicate to discover their peers, to negotiate and to co-operate in open environments where everybody can add their contribution when and how it is deemed appropriate. Most importantly, agent systems will need to build on and interface with a variety of existing and upcoming developments and standards, like DAML+OIL, ebXML or WebServices. This includes support for a wide range of devices, but also integration of telecommunication and internet, and the integration with ERP, supply chain management systems, m/eCommerce platforms up to application servers and WebServices.

Thus, agents will only be able to fulfil their potential if they provide a standardized, open and generic infrastructure (see Sect. 5.1). Another important requirement for the success of agent technology is the availability of generic services, like for virtual team coordination, self-organization of processes, recommendation engines, mobility support and location-aware services. Such services are designed for multiple reuses and cover areas where higher level of intelligence is needed and agents seem more relevant than ever. In addition successfully marketing agent technology requires presenting it as an incremental extension of known and trusted technologies (e.g., object-oriented programming), and providing explicit engineering tools to support proven methods of technology deployment.

3.4.1 Challenge: Individualization and Privacy

Agent technology can support different kinds of personalization and individualization. First of all agent technology can support end-to-end processes from the end-user to some service and their scheduling using planning and scheduling mechanisms based on market-based resource management. These processes can be optimized according to the users' preferences like preferred working times.

Tracking the user, i.e. taking the actual time, the actual position and the actual tasks of the user into consideration and comparing these information with the planned activities can result in *situation awareness and reaction*, i.e. depending on the current situation, e.g. time, position, tasks to be performed in the future; specific action options are triggered in order to help to fulfil the schedule of a user if some extraordinary events occur like a traffic jam on the way to the next customer or if tasks take longer than expected. In particular *automating standard procedures*, e.g. appointment scheduling, using knowledge about the working and travel times, the position of a user, the performed work or the consumption of some material, e.g. semi-automatic ordering of new material could be included in the supply chain.

At the service level user preferences, like preferred jobs, hotels or brands, can be taken into consideration and adapted depending on user behavior. User agents can select what information to present and how to present it depending on the user's profile.

An important topic is *privacy*. Using agent technology ensures adequate user privacy, since user-side agents hold the private data and decide (based on instructions by the user) which information are given to others. The same holds for user agents on trusted server which can guarantee that user information is kept private. The user agent is the instance which selects the appropriate information for the user depending on their preferences.

3.4.2 Challenge: Secure Delegation

In order to be able to accomplish tasks (e.g., negotiations) automatically, user agents have to be equipped with knowledge (e.g., negotiation strategies). In addition, models of user preferences and profiles can be developed, to better seize dependencies between individual dimensions by mapping domain-specific attributes (e.g. price, material, extras) to general preference dimensions (security, comfort, thriftiness, achievement). This allows users to express their preferences via these general dimensions.

Distributed planning and optimization as well as coalition formation are other important components in multi-agent systems for delegating tasks. An interesting point in purchasing in electronic market places represents the formation of a buyers' coalition to achieve better prices in negotiations. In automated negotiation, planning and optimization can be applied to deal with global dependencies between different processes or supply chains, e.g. several parts have to be available for the construction of a larger product. In this case a constraint could be to have either all kinds of raw material available or the constructed product out of these different parts. I.e. the negotiation with all raw material suppliers can be seen as one transaction which has to be successful either for all parts or for none. The transaction paradigm is well known from data base applications and is supported by all major data bases. This technology allows applications to place a transaction e.g. from one account to another account and obtain even in the case of some error a consistent state. In the case of an error a rollback is used to obtain a consistent state otherwise the transaction is committed and fixed. Agent systems are decentralized, distributed applications, thus transaction are important concepts for agents, too, in particular in the context of automated negotiations, where either an auction is completely accomplished or has to be set back under certain conditions.

3.4.3   Challenge: Semantic Interoperability

Usually agents are not closed units, but cooperate with each other to solve their tasks. The important issue concerning the cooperation between agents is that they should be domain independent and cooperate dynamically with unknown partners. Two levels of cooperation can be considered: The first level - some kind of meta-level - supports mechanisms for searching for cooperating agents, to analyze their features and to start cooperating with them depending on their domain specific behavior. At the second level of the cooperation the agents need a language to solve their domain specific tasks.

In such an open cooperation between software modules one problem arises, namely the usage of a common language between the partners with identical syntax and semantics. Agents can have different terms for the same concept and identical terms for different concepts. A common *ontology*, then, is required for representing the knowledge from various domains of discourse.

As a first approximation an ontology is a collection of well-defined terms of a specific domain, i.e. an ontology is a specification of the objects, concepts, and relationships in an area of interest. Moreover within an ontology semantic constraints can be defined. FIPA 98 states [17]:

> *An ontology gives meanings to symbols and expressions within a given domain language. In order for a message from one agent to be properly understood by another, the agents must ascribe the same meaning to the constants used in the message. The ontology performs the function of mapping a given constant to some well-understood meaning. For a given domain, the ontology may be an explicit construct or implicitly encoded with the implementation of the agent.*

The *knowledge model* is a specification of the set of primitives used by a certain class of representation languages. As such, a knowledge model can be considered a meta-ontology, i.e. an ontology can be defined using some knowledge model. The *ontology sharing problem* is the problem of ensuring that two agents who wish to converse do share a common ontology for the domain of discourse. Minimally, agents should be able to discover whether or not they share a mutual understanding of the domain constants.

In the area of ontologies we usually distinguish between *ontology* and *conceptualization*. A conceptualization is not concerned with meaning assignments, but just with the formal *structure* of reality as perceived and organized by an agent, independently of the language used to describe it and the current occurrence of a specific situation. An ontology, on the other hand, is first of all a vocabulary. Besides that, an ontology must specify the *intended meaning* of such vocabulary, i.e. its underlying conceptualization.

Currently, quite a few web ontology languages are available, including SHOE, OML, XPL, ONTOBROKER, RDF, and RDF Schemas, DAML, and OIL. The most influential ones are the FIPA 98 ontology service based on Ontolingua, and OKBC, DAML, and OIL. The standardization of DAML and OIL is based on existing languages, and the combination of both, namely DAML+OIL, was published [7] and submitted to the world wide web consortium.

In eBusiness semantic interoperability is a crucial point. The standardization efforts shown in the related work can help to manage part of these problems. Semantic Web activities (see Sect. 5.4) and the ontology work in the area of agent-based systems can help to overcome additional interoperability issues.

In addition agent technology supports standardized interaction protocols as pattern of communication which are also in the focus of W3C's Protocol working group and of WSCL. These protocols are a necessity for the interoperability of standardized automated negotiations.

3.4.4 Challenge: Support for Flexible Organization Structures

Organizational models and their representation and support are a core topic in eBusiness research. In [20], the notion of an organization is defined as *all regulations, which provide for a co-ordination of the enterprise and for its adjustment at the company target.* Current research in organizational models focus on techniques to analyze organizations and their processes.

Due to the nature of agents as decentralized, autonomous entities, organizational modeling technique can be transferred to multi-agent systems (for details see e.g. [65]; parts of the section are based on this reference). As already stated not all agents can perform all activities, but some agents are specialized for appropriate tasked. Organizational models are a structuring mechanism to obtain results which are not achievable by an individual agent, but need coordination of the individual agents. One rationale for the existence of organizations is to overcome the limitations of individuals (agents). Transferring this to agents we have four basic limitations [65]:

- **Cognitive Limitations:** agents have cognitive limitations and need to cooperate to achieve higher levels of performance

- **Physical Limitations:** agents have only limited resources and therefore must coordinate their actions, especially accessing non-local resources

- **Temporal Limitations:** agents are temporally limited and therefore must join together to achieve goals which transcend the lifetime of a single agent

- **Institutional Limitations:** agents are legally or politically limited and therefore must attain organizational status to act as a corporate actor rather than as an individual actor

However there is no individual organizational model which fits all problem domains. E.g. in some domains specialization tasks whereas in other domains division of labor can be appropriate. But over-specialization and excessive division of labor can reduce performance and flexibility by de-skilling individuals, decreasing attention due to boredom and increasing decision making time and increasing coordination costs in situations of uncertainty or failure. These facts are also reflected in eBusiness.

Research in the field of computational organizational theory uses computational and mathematical methods to study both human and automated organizations as computational entities, in particular necessary in the eBusiness domain and can be solved using agent technology:

- Human organizational models are characterized by acquiring, manipulating and producing information through joint, interlocked activities of human beings and automated information processing.
- Automated organizational models are characterized by multiple distributed agents which exhibit collective organizational properties
- For the modeling of an organization usually the following points have to be considered:
  - agents - humans as well as artificial - comprising the organization by modeling their organizational roles and decision making influenced by their capabilities and knowledge
  - the organization's design or structure specifying the aspects like tasks, roles, skills, collaborative teams, agents hierarchies, and resources.
  - tasks the organization carries out, especially taking into consideration temporal constraints or other dependencies on the single tasks, and similarities of tasks
  - any environment of the organization, and the organization is involved in.
  - the organizational material transformation and / or information processing technology
  - any stressors, like time pressure, deadlines, and turnover, on the organization.

Thus, virtual organizations and flexible organizational structures show many of the characteristics that make an agent-based approach seem adequate. However, any agent-based solution must build on established standards, especially in the area of process modeling and enterprise application integration (see Sect. 5.3).

3.4.5 Challenge: Intelligent Collaboration and Coordination

Communication is a key feature in multi agent systems. The communication between different agents is necessary to exchange information, to distribute tasks, plans and goals, to coordinate actions, to negotiate prices and resources, to manage shared resources and to recognize, avoid and manage conflicts.

The easiest way of communication between two agents is simple method or remote method invocation. More complex interaction would include those agents that can react to observable events within the environment, i.e. they receive events regarding the state of the environment. Even more complex interaction is found in systems where agents can be engaged in multiple, parallel interactions with other agents. Here, agents begin to act as a society. Based on these considerations one can distinguish different levels of abstraction as shown in Fig. 5.

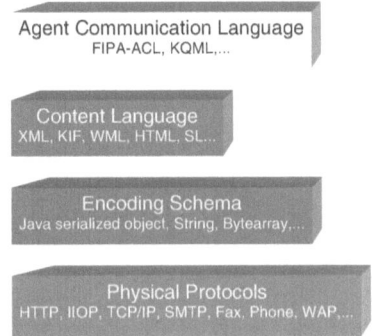

Fig. 5. Levels of abstraction for communication

At the lowest level, communication is done via physical protocols. Messages can be sent synchronously or asynchronously. Transportation mechanisms support unique addressing as well as role based addresses (i.e., "white page" versus "yellow page" addressing). Furthermore, they should support unicast, multicast, and broadcast modes and services like broadcast behavior, non-repudiation of messages, and logging. On top of this level different programming languages and tools provide different encoding of information, namely in the case of Java for example as serialized objects, strings or other programming specific representation of information. In the context of agent based systems an abstraction is made from this programming language specific coding by defining *content languages*: content languages can be XML, WML/HTML, or logic based languages like KIF or the FIPA content language SL. To enable negotiation between different agents, e.g. for task delegation, communicative acts are used, grounding on speech act theory. Examples of communicative acts are *cfp* (call for proposals) starting a contract negotiation between agents, or *request* to request an agent to perform some task. These communicative acts and additional information, like sender or receiver of a message, are covered by agent communication languages (ACLs). The main representatives of ACLs are FIPA-ACL [16] from the standardization committee FIPA, and KQML [15]. Within ACL messages the content languages are used to code the real content of the message, e.g. the starting of an auction or the proposed price of a good.

Agents can interact in various patterns called *interaction protocols* also known as *conversation* or *communication* protocols which are built on top of the communicative acts. Agent interaction protocols as defined e.g. by FIPA can be seen as pattern for interaction between different agents that is formally defined and abstracted from any particular sequence of execution steps. Whichever kind of conversation is chosen, the pattern or protocol of that conversation must be understood by the participating agents. The behavior of an agent how to participate in some auction, for example, is fixed by the agent interaction strategies.

In eBusiness, the communicative act, interaction protocol and interaction strategy layer are important for the automation of business processes and automated supply chain management.

3.4.6 Challenge: Mobility Support

Agent technology supports human mobility at different levels. Code mobility is provided by mobile agents, which can migrate from one machine to another. Because of their migration capabilities mobile agents can (1) benefit from the capabilities of a visited computer. This can be data of a special database, or services, such as online banking or the connection to wireless networks which are only accessible on the visited computer; (2) take part in auctions on a user's behalf while the user is offline, for instance because of areas with no reception. Moreover in this scenario the response times are shorter than when using mobile communication; (3) profit from the resources of different servers to calculate solutions in parallel. The performance of the client machine can be low, however the server machines have to be powerful; (4) be supported by the client as well as by the server and the dynamic adaptation to the requirements of the user. This proceeding allows installing the necessary software (dynamic software update); (5) allow independent, off-line operation, e.g., after agents have migrated to some server to perform their tasks a notebook can be switched off. This fact results again in higher availability and robustness, since the agents change their environment system and in contrast to typical client-server approaches no permanent connection to the server has to be established; (6) save bandwidth if the agent as a software program and all its data needs less resources than the data which have to be processed by the agent; (7) communicate fast because of the local communication via e.g. shared memory; (8) support load balancing.

As already stated situation-aware services can be supported by software agents. Moreover the upcoming lightweight agent platforms (see Sect. 4.2.1) deal with mobile communication and mobile collaboration supporting agents on small (mobile) devices.

3.4.7 Challenge: Pro-active, Adaptive Processes

Agent-oriented systems are based on small units with negotiation facilities as shown above which can coordinate the tasks and goals independent of some central process, self-organization is one of the key issues agent-based systems can support. Moreover, the pro-active behavior of agents based on planning and scheduling together with autonomous behavior allow agents to organize complex tasks and processes in agents' inherent distributed environments on their own. In particular with organizational concepts agents can support pro-active processes. Applying learning techniques can improve the process formation.

In particular agents are applied for eManufacturing. According to [29], the scheduling and manufacturing control structure used within the MABES system is a distributed autonomous agent framework. Thereby each agent is responsible for monitoring and acting on a component of the manufacturing process. A component may be a process, such as a press; or a stack of pre-processed components. The agents interact to control the flow of parts through either a traditional push or a lean pull or takt system. Within the adopted approach, the overall desired behavior for a manufacturing line emerges from individual behaviors of, and interactions among, distributed agents. For other research on agent-based manufacturing we refer to [21], [6], [47].

3.4.8 Challenge: Adaptive Decision-Making Assistance

Beyond the benefit of agent technology described in Sects. 3.4.2 and 3.4.5, matchmaking can be applied to deal with the topic of adaptive decision-making assistance. Matchmaking is the process of mediating demand and supply based on profile information. The task to be solved is to find the most appropriate agents, products, or services for a task, negotiation, or market transaction. Most real-world problems require multi-attribute matchmaking, i.e., the ability to combine various dimensions of decision-making to define an overall solution to a matchmaking problem, requiring the interplay of multiple matchmaking algorithms. In addition, in order to be applicable for real-world applications, the matchmaking component must be easily integrated into standard industrial marketplace platforms. The essential requirements to be met by a matchmaking framework are the following:

- Demand and supply profiles in electronic marketplaces are often complex (e.g., matching job profiles against applicant profiles) and require multi-dimensional matchmaking. Often, a combination of existing methods is adequate to deal with different aspects of matchmaking.

- Demand and supply information is distributed and heterogeneous. Thus, distributed search and ontology mapping may be required to achieve comparable profiles.

- Demand and supply profiles differ depending on the application domain; also the underlying business logic to determine the quality of a match (distance functions) is very domain specific in part. A framework must support this variety.

- A framework should restrict the effort of developing new marketplace solutions by enabling reuse of existing profiles and business logic. In particular, developing a matchmaking solution should require only little coding, and should be done mainly through customization.

- The matchmaking framework should assist marketplace developers by supporting a clear process for building matchmaking solutions; appropriate tools should support the enforcement of this process.

- Beyond relying on agent standards such as FIPA, which can be achieved by using FIPA-compliant agent platforms (see Sect. 5.1), it is necessary to serve the integration needs and capabilities of today's eBusiness platforms, which are mostly based on Enterprise Java Beans (EJB) application servers.

In Sect. 4.1 we present an agent-based approach to sourcing and matchmaking in the human resources domain.

3.4.9 Challenge: Intelligent Selection and Evaluation of Products and Services

Helping individuals and organizations to find what they need in distributed electronic marketplaces and vast heterogeneous content repositories requires a number of tasks to be accomplished well: (1) individualization of requests; (2) automation of search; and (3) interpretation and evaluation of candidates. Agents have the potential to contribute to each of these challenges. By maintaining and learning user profiles, agents can construct appropriate demand profiles. By using brokering services (e.g., yellow pages) and by doing query planning to combine multiple services, agents can find possible matches for a demand profile. In this context, they make use of existing services as described e.g., by [3]. Finally, matchmaking combined with the ability to negotiate provides the means for evaluating possible candidates and helping the user to get the best deal.

The interoperability with existing eBusiness platforms is largely based on the usage of standards and enabling technologies as described in Sect. 5. Lately, we have observed that eBusiness software companies enter the market with products the features of which contain agent support for personalization and marketplace inter-action (e.g., [38], [37]). While it is not always easy to see how much of this is marketing and how much is technology, we believe that this is an encouraging sign that agents will play a considerable role to tackle this challenge within the next three to five years, and that the big players in the market might include agent features into their products and solutions once the basic foundations for eBusiness has been established in enterprises.

4   Agents for eBusiness Applications: Case Studies

In this section we describe some case studies for the use of agents in eBusiness applications. The examples include the use of agents for intelligent human resources matchmaking, distributed team coordination, and personal travel assistance.

4.1   Agents for Human Resource Matching

In this section we describe the GRAPPA system for agent-based matchmaking, and an agent-supported tool for e-recruiting based on GRAPPA.

4.1.1 Agent-Based Matchmaking

Matchmaking is not only a key task in multi-agent systems, it is also a crucial function in industrial portals and marketplaces. The provider who will enable the most effective matches between demand and supply will gain a competitive advantage and increase the acceptance and popularity of their marketplaces.

Fig. 6 illustrates a usage scenario for a matchmaking agent in an electronic marketplace. On the supply side, providers of services or products make themselves known to the matchmaker (which can be based on push (e.g., by registering) or pull (e.g., by search initiated by the matchmaker). In Step 2, a requester requests a service (by issuing a demand profile) and the matchmaker returns a list of the k best matching providers. In Step 3, the requester and the selected provider will negotiate a contract and upon agreement the service or product is delivered. Here, we will focus on the matchmaking phase (step 2).

We understand matchmaking as a function which accepts as input a set of offers (supply profiles, candidates) and a request (demand profile) and provides as output a ranked list of the k best offers with respect to the request.

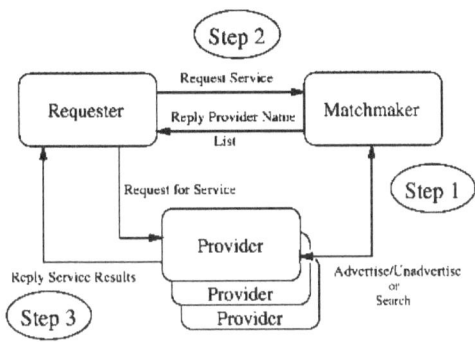

Fig. 6. Matchmaking Procedure

4.1.2 The GRAPPA Matchmaking Framework

Fig. 7 illustrates the structure of the GRAPPA matchmaking framework. It consists of three major parts. Its core is the *matchmaking engine*. It is complemented by the *matchmaking library* and the *matchmaking toolkit*.

4.1.2.1   GRAPPA Matchmaking Engine

The matchmaking engine accepts a set of supply profiles (candidate instances) and a demand profile as input. The supply profiles which have to be provided as instances of the matchmakers candidate class are either stored in the matchmakers service repository (see Fig. 8) or – in case the matchmaker does not keep a service repository – retrieved from different data sources. The request which has to be provided as an instance of the matchmakers demand profile class is matched against each of the candidate instances. The candidate structure as well as the demand profile structure are multidimensional. They consist of complex types constructed from a domain specific set of basic types under application of four complex type constructors: list, array, record and set.

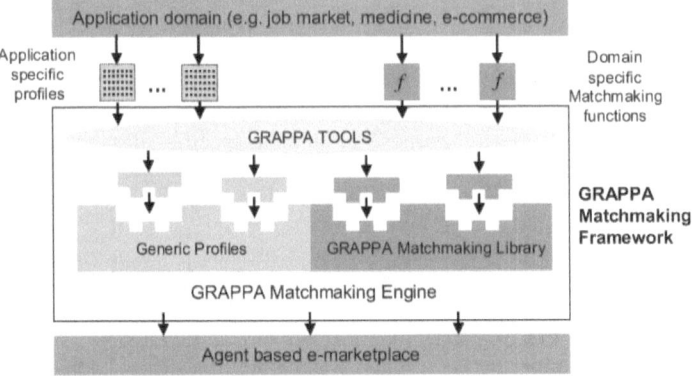

Fig. 7. GRAPPA Matchmaking Framework

The procedure performed by the matchmaking engine is illustrated in Fig. 8.

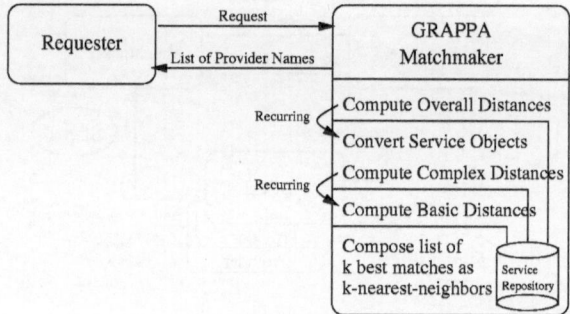

Fig. 8. GRAPPA Matchmaking procedure

The overall distance, a real value between 0 and 1, is computed by recursively computing the distance values for different profile sub-types and propagating them upwards to compute the values for their parents. For the basic types (the atomic attributes of the demand and the supply profile), the specific distance function for the particular type is applied and the result is propagated upwards. Then, at the next higher level, all basic distances between the atomic types in this level are merged to one distance value for this complex type under application of aggregate functions.

The result of the recursive computation of distance values is
* an overall distance (real value between 0 and 1) which reflects the quality of the considered candidate instance for the current demand profile instance.
* a structure (in XML) which consists the individual distance results in each layer.

The best k candidates (with respect to the current demand profile) are returned as the result of the match. This list is ranked using the value the overall distance
   The agent (or the agent's principal) can then recur into the XML structure to obtain an explanation how the particular overall result arose (e.g., which aspects of the match contributed to a good or bad overall result).

4.1.2.2   GRAPPA Matchmaking Library

The GRAPPA Matchmaking Library hosts an extensible collection of predefined profile schemas and (general-purpose or domain-specific) distance functions. The profiles schemas can be used as a basis for application-specific profiles; the distance functions provide uniform interfaces that allow us to flexibly combine them to develop specific matchmaking solutions.

It is essential for a matchmaking system to provide powerful distance functions. Currently, we provide distance functions for FreeText, WeightedKeyword, Interval, TimeInterval, DateInterval, Boolean, and Number basic values (i.e. instances of basic types). All distance functions have the property to take two basic values as input and to provide a real number between 0 and 1 as output (distance). Additionally, domain specific distance functions can be easily integrated to accommodate the requirements of different matchmaking applications.

On top of these basic functions, we can define aggregate distance functions. Currently, WeightedAverage, Average, Minimum, Maximum are supported as predefined aggregate functions. As for basic functions, it is possible to define domain specific aggregate functions and integrate them into a domain specific matchmaker.

4.1.2.3   GRAPPA TOOLKIT

The GRAPPA Toolkit provides a set of tools which enable the development of a multidimensional matchmaker for specific applications mainly through configuration without much coding work. To guide the marketplace designer we have defined a 5-step process to obtain a domain specific matchmaking solution:

- Define the demand and supply profile schemas (basic entries) in XML;
- Define the clusters of attributes in XML (pseudo-orthogonalization); clustering can be recursive;
- Associate the clusters of the demand profile with clusters of the candidate by applying appropriate distance function;
- Combine the results of the distance functions to an overall distance value (e.g., weighted sum);
- Apply feedback regarding the quality of the matches, e.g., by adaptively changing weights or matching functions.

4.1.3 Application: HRNetAgent

Due to the open, flexible architecture of the GRAPPA framework, it can be applied to a wide range of matchmaking problems in all sorts of (agent- or human-operated) electronic marketplaces. In this section, we provide a brief description of two industrial projects in which GRAPPA has been applied successfully: The Siemens Cooperation Market (CoMa) and the Human Resource Network project (HRNetAgent).

4.1.3.1   Siemens Cooperation Market

CoMa is a Siemens corporate service where individuals and teams describe their capabilities, including competence and availability, as service offers and supply this information to some designated provider agent. Departments or customers in need for teams to take over certain projects or tasks forward their project profiles to a requester agent. The CoMa matchmaker keeps a repository of all available provider agents and processes the incoming requests using the GRAPPA matchmaking framework.

4.1.3.2   Human Resource Network (HRNetAgent)

The Human Resource Network (HRNetAgent) is an application of GRAPPA for matching corporate job profiles with profiles of job applicants (i.e., unemployed persons), stored in various data bases. The current version of HRNetAgent is a prototype system that has been developed for the German Labor Exchange Office, and demonstrates the feasibility of a partially automated approach to employment relaying. Based on its success, a full-fledged system is planned for the near future. The potential return on investment is huge: reducing the relaying time of unemployed persons (towards the end of 2001, there are almost 4 million people in Germany without employment) just by one day on average will save the German government more than a hundred million dollars a year.

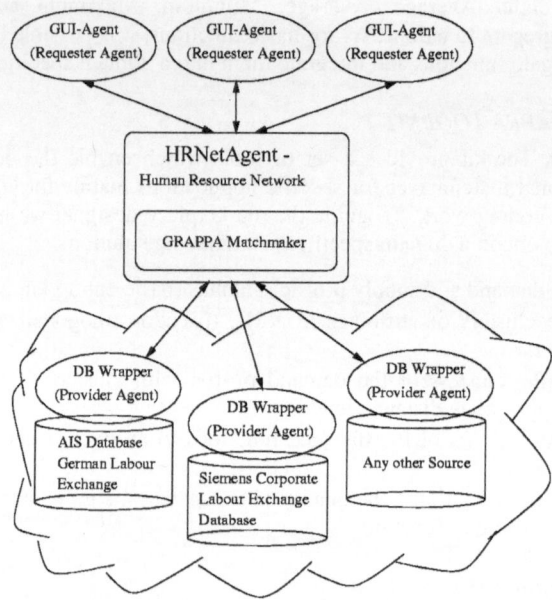

Fig. 9. HRNetAgent System overview

Fig. 9 shows the architecture of the HRNetAgent system. A company specifies its job profiles to a designated GUI-Agent, which takes the role of a requester agent in the system. The GUI-Agent queries the matchmaker by sending to HRNetAgent the description of the open position which should be filled. The scheme for specifying the open positions is the demand profile.

The backend of HRNetAgent consists of a collection of data sources wrapped by information agents, and by a search controller that coordinates a number of search agents. E.g., one data source is the central database of the German Federal Labor Exchange Office, in which all currently unemployed persons in Germany are stored. Others may be corporate skills databases, additional databases can be easily integrated. Note, that the database wrapper agents play the role of virtual provider agents in our architecture.

Wrapper agents perform the task of query translation, connection handling, and result translation. They return a pre-selection of profiles to the matchmaker based on conditions extracted from the demand profile. In HRNetAgent, the demand and candidate schemes are converted to XML-DTDs which are considered as the document classes of these types. Matchmaking thus is done on a pre-selection of candidates. The most successful candidates for a job profile are stored in the local service repository for fast access by the application. In addition, HRNetAgent offers an automated notification service via SMS, Fax, or Email.

4.2   Agents for Corporate Team Management

Within the European project LEAP ([34], [4]) a lightweight extensible agent platform is developed and applied being the precursor of the second generation of FIPA-compliant platforms. It solves a major technical challenge - it is the first integrated agent development environment capable of generating agent applications and executing them on run-time environments implemented over a large family of devices (personal computers, PDAs, mobile phones like the Siemens SL45i etc.) and communication mechanisms (TCP/IP, HTTP, etc.). The feasibility and real-world evaluation of the LEAP platform is performed by field trials dealing with an integrated solution on de-centralized work co-ordination, travel management and knowledge management.

4.2.1   The Platform JADE/LEAP

LEAP emerged as an independent development branch of JADE (see [30]) under the LGPL license and was merged with the JADE mainstream in September 2001, at which point LEAP transformed JADE's kernel. As such, LEAP concentrates on lightweight and extensible aspects, whereas JADE continues independently its evolution towards environmental functions such as monitoring facilities, visualization packages, ontologies and policies. The JADE APIs remain unchanged. Therefore all existing applications continue to run as before. In addition, developers can use JADE/LEAP to migrate existing applications to, or develop a new generation of applications for small wireless devices. The LEAP applications on virtual mobile team management are a good illustration of these new capabilities.

The LEAP activity focused on restructuring the JADE core, compliant to Java 2 Standard Edition (J2SE), in order to match the LEAP requirements and to obtain a single platform that is:

- Lightweight enough to be deployed on small devices, such as mobile phones, supporting only a KVM with Java 2 Micro Edition / Connected, Limited Device Configuration (J2ME/CLDC) and MIDP, instead of a standard JVM.
- Transport layer independent and in particular supporting transport protocols suitable for both the wired and wireless environment, thus providing an homogeneous layer to agent application developers.
- Compliant to the last FIPA specifications.
- Extensible such that, when deployed on a powerful machine, it can provide a number of optional functions such as agent mobility, user-defined ontology's, and platform management GUIs.

The complete external view of the LEAP platform is a distributed system. A JADE agent platform consists of so-called containers, being either an agent container or a main container. All components and agents of a container are loaded into the Java Virtual Machine (JVM). An agent container is a container for agents, which can be either empty or containing one or more agents. The amount of agents running in a container can change during execution time. Each agent container may consist, beyond the agents, of a message dispatcher responsible for the delivering of agents' messages to other containers, and an Agent Communication Channel (ACC) responsible for the message passing between different agent platforms. A main container is a special case of an agent container. For each JADE platform exists exactly one main container, containing an Agent Management Service (AMS) and Directory Facilitator (DF) agent and a RMI registry, since in JADE the intra platform communication is done using RMI. Therefore, a main container builds up a complete FIPA compliant agent platform. Arbitrary agent containers can register at the main container and thus the agent platform can be distributed over several computers.

Tasks in LEAP are implemented using behaviors. A behavior can be execution and terminated and must be removed from the agent pool of behaviors. Behaviors can be added and removed to/from the agent both during agent initialization and from within other behaviors. All agent behaviors are managed by a scheduler that, at each round, decides which behavior to select for execution.

LEAP is deployable on different types of device and different types of network. The part of a container that handles communication (both intra-platform and inter-platform) is isolated and different implementations dealing with different transport protocol are plug-able without affecting the rest of the container:

- With the outside world, to send and receive FIPA messages to and from other FIPA compliant platforms. This inter-platform exchange of information occurs over one or more Message Transport Protocol (MTP)
- With the other containers in the platform e.g. to dispatch an ACL message to an agent on another container. This intra-platform exchange of information is carried out through platform management commands that the containers send and receive and occurs over one or more Internal Transport Protocol (ITP).
- Inter platform communication (involving a container and a remote platform) where FIPA messages, with a well defined structure (envelop plus payload), are exchanged. This is handled by the ACC in Jade which is already able to manage different transport protocols. Therefore, no modification is required as far as this type of communication is concerned.
- Intra platform communication (involving two containers in the same platform) where platform management information are exchanged. In JADE the implementation is done directly performing RMI calls to the container where some information has to be transferred/retrieved. It has to be noticed that ACL message dispatching to an agent residing on a remote container falls in this type of communication. The exchanged information in this case is an ACL message.

The command dispatcher manages different transport protocol objects to which it delegates the operations related to actually sending/receiving data over the network. The transport protocol interface abstracts from the details related to a given transport protocol (HTTP, IIOP, RMI, etc.).

Agent mobility allows agents moving within a LEAP platform exploiting a LEAP-proprietary mechanism. This kind of mobility, that we call *intra-platform*, is fundamental to cope with mobile devices because it might be quite common for agents to move from the fixed network to the mobile device to allow the user disconnecting the device and having the agent running on it. Nevertheless, the implementation of such functionality requires implementing a Java class loader and the J2ME CLDC/MIDP does not allow this. Therefore, we consider intra-platform mobility as part of the optional functionality.

Inter-platform mobility allows agents migrating between different FIPA agent platforms and it requires a precise FIPA specification describing the messages which must be exchanged by platforms in order to implement such a migration. Currently

FIPA does not provide specifications for this type of interoperability. Hence, the LEAP platform design does not currently support inter-platform mobility as part of the optional functionality.

4.2.2 LEAP Field Trials

LEAP is addressing the need for open infrastructures and services which support dynamic enterprises and mobile teams, against a backdrop of information overload, increasing competition and globalization. The project develops key enabling technologies that facilitate virtual team working and managed risk-taking through decentralized policy-based management and workforce empowerment.

The goals of the LEAP agent-based services and applications are:

- prove that agent technology can add value in the management of mobile teams. Three kinds of problems are tackled: knowledge management, work co-ordination, and travel assistance;
- demonstrate the advantage of locally based agents on small devices as part of a distributed application. Agents increase the autonomy of devices and applications;
- prove the viability of both the infrastructure and agent-based services through two independent field trials deployed in Germany (ADAC) and the UK (British Telecommunications), running the same services, but in different operational contexts. Each field trial will involve users in vehicles, roaming over large areas, for a duration of several weeks;
- demonstrate the use of a number of device/operating system combinations, during the field trials.

The agent-based services which address the following key requirements:

- knowledge management - anticipating a user's knowledge requirements by accessing and customizing knowledge (based on the users skill, location, current job and type of display) and providing access to collective knowledge assets in the team (by networking individuals with each other, based on their current needs);
- decentralized work co-ordination - empowering individuals to collectively co-ordinate activities (e.g. by trading jobs, automatically negotiating for work, and expressing personal preferences) within an agreed policy framework;
- travel management - anticipating a user's travel needs, providing guidance and time estimation so as to synchronize the movements of virtual teams working over vast geographic areas.

The field trials are carried out in the open air, using mobile devices such as PDAs and mobile phones. In the case of the BT field trial, the domain is that of telecommunications engineers performing field-based installation and repair task. The domain of the ADAC field trial is roadside assistance for stranded motorists. Each field trial will last approximately several weeks. As the field trials will be carried out in two different countries they will use different existing communications infrastructures, access different knowledge sources, and most important of all, involve users with different cultural backgrounds. The field trials will not only assess the technical quality of the LEAP applications but also the usability and "soft systems" aspects in the context of mobile remote workforces.

4.3   Personal Travel Assistance

The increasing demand for mobility in today's society is leading to drastic increases in traffic volumes, causing undesirable effects such as traffic jams and overcrowded transport system restricting mobility (for details see [3]).

More and more services are becoming available electronically (in particular via the Internet), offering information and support in planning a journey. Unfortunately the typical user is currently overwhelmed with the large number of travel information and booking services, with too many user interfaces and individual offerings. The services which were integrated into a unified system are rarely. Today, in order to plan a trip, the user must initiate an extra session for each transport mode (e.g. automobile, train or plane) and for each layover (e.g. hotel, parking, car rental). These services are mostly offered separately from each other and are seldom individualized for the user. For example, the user needs to enter all of his/her data, such as home address, as well as individual preferences for the travel means (e.g. business class) more than once. When the traveler is on the way, things get even worse: the services are most often not available, especially when the traveler needs those most, such as when the travel plan need to be changed due to traffic jams or delays.

PTA offers a new perspective for individualized and automated handling of the vast amount of information and services, in order to support the traveler effectively in planning and during a journey. PTA is a comprehensive agent-based system comprising the complete chain from basic services up to the end user devices. PTA was part of the MoTiV-initiative of the German industry, for details see [3]. The project has been successfully finished in late 2000 and now the partners are encouraged to develop their own business based on the research results. Project partners included Siemens, BMW, Bosch, DaimlerChrysler, debis, IBM, Opel, VDO car systems, and VW. The agent architecture was an essential part of this prototype. The system architecture of the PTA system is illustrated in Fig. 10.

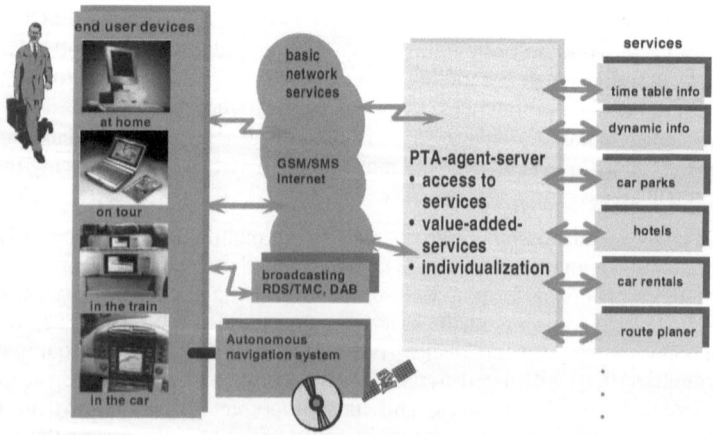

Fig. 10. PTA system architecture

The PTA system offers support for the user at any place and at any time. At home the user access PTA via personal computer and the internet; on tour handheld PCs can be used. Special end user devices support the traveller in the train with information about the delays of the current train, or the surrounding of the destination railway station. Calculated routes based on dynamic traffic information as well as other dynamic information (e.g. positions of car parks with free parking slots) can be loaded into the car navigation system and on-trip usual traffic messages via standard broadcasting mechanism are taken into consideration by the routing system. All the communication is done using standard communication channels.

The heart of the PTA system, namely the PTA agent server accesses the different services, combines the results to value-added information and takes personal preferences and travels into consideration.

The PTA system uses existing travel services, e.g., time table information from the German railway company "Deutsche Bahn", Lufthansa, and the public transportation of Hamburg and Munich. Dynamic information about traffic jams and reservations of car parks are accessible for distinguished areas of Germany. One car rental service supporting car rentals all over Germany is integrated too. Two hotel reservation services supporting hotel search and booking nearly all over the world are connected to the PTA server. An individual (car) route planner takes dynamic information, like traffic jams and building sites on roads in consideration. A new developed service, called "tracking"-service, informs the user on-trip about traffic jams and delays of trains, depending on the current position of the travel, i.e. only information about travel segments in the future are interesting for the traveler. If e.g. a plain cannot be caught any more, a new travel planning can be started. Fig. 11 illustrates the agent architecture underlying PTA.

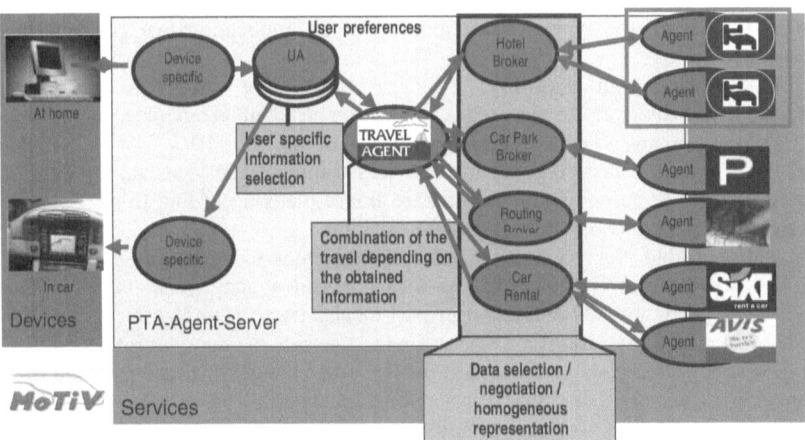

Fig. 11. Agents in PTA

User Device Agents: For each kind of end user device there exists a specialized version of a generic user device agent (UDA). The task of the UDA is to process the information depending on the end user device, like the generation of dynamic HTML pages for some usual handheld PCs or palm-size devices; or generating WAP compliant pages. Thus the presentation is disconnected from the user agent and it is very easy to add new and different as well as additional end user devices without changing the rest of the system. Adding a new end user device agent can be done during the normal operation of the PTA system.

User Agents: For each human user a user agents exists. The user agent is started on login into the system and is stopped, if all tasks of the user agent are finished and the user is logged out. The user agent (UA) stores and manages all the already planned and booked travels for the user. It knows the preferences of the user and does the selection of calculated travels according to them. Moreover, it analyzes the selections of the user and adapts the user preferences accordingly.

Travel Agent: The travel agent works as a virtual travel agency. It asks the different brokers to prepare information, to book hotel reservations or to make a route planning. It combines the travel results according to special user preferences which are known to the travel agency. The user agent has all the preferences and does the selection or ordering of the travels alternatives for the user.

Broker: The different broker agents access the service agents to get the information or do the booking. The main task of the broker agents is to perform the requests on behalf of the virtual travel agency and combine the results of different data sources e.g. hotel data shops, while the information of this data shops is in a unique representation.

Agent Wrapper: The different kinds of agent wrappers are adapted to already existing travel services (e.g. hotel or airways information services) and access these services directly. Different services support heterogeneous interfaces, like RPC, CORBA, or proprietary interfaces. The task of an agent wrapper is to support the different interfaces and map the information into a unique representation, namely the agent communication language, used internally in the PTA agent system.

PTA reveals all the typical characteristics of an application that can benefit from agent technology:

Distribution and Mobility: Services as well as users are geographically distributed. Moreover, queries to the system can be set up at any place, at any time.

Heterogeneous and Autonomous Components: The PTA system is a heterogeneous system concerning end user devices, supported services and interfaces. The used agents are autonomous and prepare travel plans according to user preferences and other external constraints using coordination.

Value-Added Services: By combining different existing services, new value-added services are created, like the virtual travel agency or an inter-modal route planer, which combines different transport means, like car, train or airlines.

Queries and Booking: PTA allows on the one side the query of information about, e.g. hotels, train schedules, etc. and on the other hand the booking of the different travel services, based on transactions among agents.

User Profiles: The planning of a travel is performed taking the individual preferences of the travelers into account, like preferring the car or a special airline with distinguished rates for companies. The preferences are learned according to the selected travels out of a set of possible travels.

Different Communication Channels and End User Devices: The access to the PTA server can take place using different end user devices and communication channels, ranging from hand-held PCs, to the integration into car navigation systems or distinguished seats of a train.

Robustness, Extensibility, and Modification: Using multi-agent systems the PTA system is robust wrt. error of components. It can dynamically be extended and modified.

The PTA system supports about 25 different kinds of interfaces to services and user interfaces; about 200 different requests to the services and answers from the services; about 20 parameterized interaction protocols, e.g. for information retrieval, booking, etc.; many non-parameterized protocols, e.g. for the communication with yellow and white pages. It has been shown with the project that an agent-based realization is ideal for connecting services or other existing software with different, heterogeneous interfaces using wrapper technology. The applications of brokers allow an implementation which is easy to grasp, because of the modular implementation. In order to support the dynamic integration of new similar services, like travel monitoring, the implementation is based on specific generic, domain-dependent pattern of interaction, not only taken the interaction protocols into account, but also the content of the communicative acts. Moreover agent technology was an appropriate software engineering paradigm to cope with the complexity of the system; in particular agent technology supports the necessary abstraction mechanisms, like interaction protocols or abstracting from the concrete physical communication between the agents using the underlying FIPA compliant agent infrastructure.

The experience with the application of a FIPA compliant agent platform was two-fold. First of all the underlying infrastructure is ideal for the dynamic starting and stopping of services and user agents, also for the connection of different PTA servers supported by different vendors. But the use of the content language FIPA-SL in the framework of a Java-based agent platform makes things more complicated than necessary, although MECCA supports automatic generation of FIPA-SL terms out of arbitrary Java objects.

Within the European project Leonet [36] we added a learning component based on reinforcement learning and evolutionary algorithms to the PTA system to allow the adaptation of the user preferences according to the selections of the user.

5 Related Work

In this section we will have first of all a closer look at agent standardization activities. Afterwards the enabling technologies are presented. We show current state of the art in integration technologies and finish with the semantic web initiative, matchmaking and agent-based marketplaces.

5.1 Agent Standardization

The main standardization efforts relevant for agent technology are the OMG viewing agents as extensions of agents, KQML a de-facto standard for agent communication, FIPA – the standardization organization for agents and the World Wide Web consortium dealing with negotiation protocols and security aspects. Moreover the

Java community process deals with standardizing Java interfaces for agent name services and agent yellow pages.

KQML was the first de-facto standard of ACLs (Agent Communication Languages) supporting a wide variety of interesting agent architectures. Therefore a small number of KQML performatives were introduced used by agents to describe the meta-data specifying the information requirements and capabilities and then to introduce a special class of agents called communication facilitators performing various useful communication services, like maintaining a registry of service names, and providing "matchmaking" between information providers and clients.

FIPA (Foundation for Intelligent Physical Agents [19]) the first standardization effort in agent technology with the remit of producing software standards for heterogeneous and interacting agents and agent-based systems across multiple vendors' platforms. The main focus of FIPA is the interface between the agents and the units of their environment, e.g. human beings, physical surrounding, and existing software. The technical parts address the following issues: agent management; agent communication language; agent software integration; agent management support for mobility; agent security management; ontology service; human/agent interaction and field trial specifications for the verification of the technical specifications. Moreover the FIPA Abstract Architecture specification, identifying architectural abstractions, has been published.

Java^{TM} **Agent Services** [18] were established within the Java Community Process with the focus on the specification of a set of objects and service interfaces to support the deployment and operation of autonomous communicative agents based upon the FIPA Abstract Architecture defining how agents may register and discover each other, and how agents interact by exchanging messages based on the communicative acts. Only the interface for agent management is standardized via a Java API, but nothing is said about how an agent platform has to look like.

OMG (Object Management Group, [46]) has two activities within the area of agent technology: **MASIF** a mobile agent standard [40], deals with the necessity of interoperation between mobile agent platforms. It defines standardized interfaces for agent transfer, class transfer, and agent management. MASIF does not deal with agent communication. **Agent Platform Special Interest Group** (Agent PSIG) [1] has the identified tasks to extend the OMG Object Management Architecture (OMA) to better support agent technology, to create new OMG specifications or extend existing OMG specifications in the agent area, and to deal with agent modeling techniques like Agent UML to allow a better understanding of how to develop agent based applications. There is a liaison between FIPA and OMG in order to transfer FIPA specifications to the OMG.

Activities of the **World Wide Web Consortium** [60] include the **XML Protocol Working Group** and **P3P.** The goal of the former [59] is to automate negotiations and to standardize application-to-application messaging, especially in the business-to-business e-commerce area, and to satisfy requirements for a lightweight, simple network protocol for distributed applications. **P3P** [58] is a standard for privacy preferences allow servers and clients to automatically check whether the privacy preferences of a user are kept by the information service or the web trader. P3P is a standardized set of multiple-choice questions, covering all the major aspects of a Web site's privacy policies presenting a clear snapshot of how a site handles personal information about its users.

5.2   Enabling Technologies

The Extensible Markup Language (**XML**, [106]) is the universal format for structured documents and data on the Web. XML is a subset of SGML. XML has been designed for ease of implementation and for interoperability with both SGML and HTML. XML is a technology for web applications. Thus XML simplifies business-to-business transactions on the web. It describes a class of data objects called XML documents and partially describes the behavior of computer programs which process them. Markup encodes a description of the document's storage layout and logical structure. XML provides a mechanism to impose constraints on the storage layout and logical structure.

The Resource Description Framework (**RDF** [61]) supported by W3C is a foundation for processing meta-data; it provides interoperability between applications that exchange machine-understandable information on the web. RDF emphasizes facilities to enable automated processing of web resources. The RDF Data Model is described by means of resources, properties and their values. A specific resource together with one or more named properties plus the values of these properties is an RDF description (a collection of RDF statements). RDF properties may be thought of as attributes of resources and in this sense correspond to traditional attribute-value pairs. RDF properties also represent relationships between resources. In addition to the RDF Data Model, the **RDF Schemas specification** (see [62]) provides a typing system for the resources and properties used in the RDF data. It defines concepts such as classes, subclasses, properties or sub-properties. It also allows expressing constraints. Both the RDF Data Model and RDF Schema propose XML as serialization syntax. In object oriented design terminology, resources correspond to objects and properties correspond to instance variables

At the level of underlying representations, **SMIL** [53], the Synchronized Multimedia Integration Language, is a major standard supported by W3C. SMIL is an XML application for synchronizing television-like audio and video with text and animation. It can be expected that this representation format will also have an important influence on future software solutions for multimedia information presentation within intelligent user interfaces.

SOAP [54] is a lightweight protocol for exchange of information in a decentralized, distributed environment. It is an XML based protocol that consists of three parts: (1) an envelope that defines a framework for describing what is in a message and how to process it; (2) a set of encoding rules for expressing instances of application-defined data types, and (3) a convention for representing remote procedure calls. SOAP messages are fundamentally one-way transmissions from a sender to a receiver, but SOAP messages are often combined to implement patterns such as request/response. A SOAP message does not have to contain a Document Type Declaration, but must contain Processing Instructions. Thus SOAP can be used for encoding messages between agents.

WSDL [67] is becoming a standard for describing Web Services. WSDL is an XML format for describing network services as a set of endpoints operating on messages containing either document-oriented or procedure-oriented information. It attempts to separate services, defined in abstract terms, from the concrete data formats and protocols used for implementation, and define bindings between the abstract description and its specific realization. There are four basic types of operations in

WSDL: a one-way, a (two-way) request-response, a (two-way) solicit-response and a (one-way) notification message.

The Web Services Conversation Language (**WSCL**) [66] provides a standard way to model the public processes of a service, thus enabling network services to participate in dynamic and complex inter-enterprise interactions. WSCL provides an XML schema for defining legal sequences of documents that web-services can exchange, comparable to interaction protocols. I.e., a conversation specification is defined to be a formal description of valid message type-based conversations that a service supports.

The goal of the **DAML** program and the **OIL** project [7] is to create technologies that enable software agents to dynamically identify and understand information sources, and to provide interoperability between agents in a semantic manner. DAML+OIL is a semantic markup language for Web resources (see e.g., [14]). Moreover it has an inference layer for ontologies, which combines the widely used modeling primitives from frame based languages with the formal semantics and reasoning services provided by description logic. Furthermore, OIL is properly grounded in W3C standards such as RDF/RDF-schema, XML/XML-Schema, Extensible Markup Language and Uniform Resource Identifiers and extends these languages with richer modeling primitives. The partners of DAML-OIL have submitted there technology to FIPA and more over to world-wide web consortium (W3C). In particular because of the liaison with W3C it can be assumed that DAML-OIL will also have a major impact in the eBusiness area.

BizTalk [5] is a community of standards users mainly driven by Microsoft, with the goal of a consistent adoption of XML to enable electronic commerce. In particular it defines the BizTalk framework, a set of guidelines for how to publish schemas in XML and how to use XML messages to easily integrate software programs together in order to build rich new solutions. The BizTalk Framework assumes that applications are distinct entities, and application integration takes place using a loosely coupled approach to exchange messages. The message flow between two or more applications integrates applications at the business-process level by defining a loosely coupled communication process that is based on requests.

xCBL (XML Common Business Library, [69]), is a set of XML business components and a document framework that allows the creation of robust, reusable, XML documents to facilitate global trading. xCBL is based on well-known standards like Electronic Data Interchange (EDI), RosettaNet, and Open Buying on the Internet (OBI). They can be obtained from public repositories like XML.org and BizTalk.org. Based on these building blocks companies can build their own documents out of the component library. The idea is that this promotes interoperability between applications and allows corporate parties to easily exchange documents across multiple e-marketplaces, giving global access to buyers, suppliers, and providers of business services. xCBL is made available as a set of SOX schemas (SOX is the schema language for Object-Oriented XML), as a single XML DTD, and in XDR schema forms. xCBL will be able to support all essential documents and transactions for global e-commerce including multi-company supply chain automation, direct and indirect procurement, planning, auctions, and invoicing and payment in an international multi-currency environment.

The Universal Description, Discovery and Integration (**UDDI** [57]) standard (registry) is an industry initiative (IBM, Microsoft, Ariba) creating a platform-independent, open framework for describing services, discovering businesses, and integrating business services using the Internet. UDDI is the first cross-industry effort driven by platform and software providers, marketplace operators and eBusiness leaders. UDDI could be regarded as an upper layer in an emerging stack of enabling rich Web Services based on TCP/IP, HTTP, XML, and SOAP to create a uniform service description format and service discovery protocol. The UDDI specifications define a way to publish and discover information about Web Services, to define the interaction with each other over the Internet and to share information in a global registry. This UDDI business registry is simply spoken an XML file storing white pages, yellow pages and green pages describing a business entity and its Web Services. In the focus of UDDI is sharing business information, making it easier to publish preferred means of doing business, find trading partners, and interoperate with these trading partners over the Internet.

The **eCo** (electronic COmmerce, [12]) specification is an architectural framework for interoperability among XML-based application standards and key electronic commerce environments that enables businesses to discover each other on the World Wide Web and determine how they can do business. Following [104] future eCo market places will feature multiple sellers or sources of products and services. Moreover the buyers want to compare these products, their prices and alternatives in order to make the best purchase decision. Sources will include multiple types of product content from multiple seller sources. Agent technology can help to set up such electronic commerce environment or at least can help to add functionality to such platforms, supporting matchmaking facilities or negotiation protocols and strategies for interacting on behalf of the user.

RosettaNet [50] works to create and deploy industry-wide, open eBusiness process standards, in particular the common business processes between trading partners in high tech supply chain. It allows manufacturers, suppliers and end-users to exchange business documents across the entire supply chain based on a comprehensive set of XML based standard business document schemas and data dictionaries. Interoperable protocols for the networked applications are specified that execute the business processes. RosettaNet standards can be divided into three broad groups of data format, business process and protocol specifications. They include the (1) *Business Dictionary* defining the properties used in basic business activities between trading partners; (2) *Technical Dictionaries* defining properties for products, components/devices and services; (3) *Implementation Framework* (RNIF) providing the fundamental prerequisites to execute business processes between the trading partners; (4) *Partner Interface Processes*™ (PIPs™) defining the sequence of steps required to execute a business processes between supply-chain partners, including e.g. purchase order management and distribution of new product information. Structure and content format of the exchanged business documents is specified based on XML DTDs and the time, security, authentication and performance constraints on these interactions.

ebXML [11] has the goal to provide an open XML based infrastructure enabling the use of electronic business information in an interoperable, secure and consistent manner, in particular from a workflow perspective. The main components ebXML deals with (1) Registries and Repositories (in particular an ebXML Registry can be published to UDDI). (2) Business Processes; (3) Collaboration Protocol Profiles;

Business Messages and Business Service Interfaces; (4) Core Library / Core Components, and (5) Collaboration Protocol Agreement.

5.3   Integration Technologies

Crosswolds or WebMethods as any other business integration platform deal with the integration of back-office legacy software, e.g., SAP or SIEBEL, with application interfaces independent of the underlying legacy system. A special type of platforms are e/m Commerce platforms allowing the integration of back-office solutions for electronic commerce.

5.3.1 eBusiness Integration Platforms

eBusiness integration (EBI) platforms define a general category of platform solutions that enable companies to link internal applications and processes with applications and processes of external partners, suppliers and customers. EBI platforms include EAI (Enterprise Application Integration) products and the newer B2B (Business to Business) integration platforms.

Integration platforms bring together the functions of standard application packages, new business logic (components), parts of legacy applications and required data to meet the needs of business processes. Integration platforms often use non-invasive wrapping mechanisms or standard component connectors from various vendors (SAP R/3, Oracle, IBM/CICS, etc).

The inclusion of both EAI and B2B in this category reflects the growing convergence of EAI and B2B integration worlds. Most integration solutions come with a library of pre-built or pre-configured adapters for connecting with packaged applications and other environments. Integration solutions include a set of GUI-based tools for defining and managing the various aspects of the integration process. These tools can be used for defining business process and how the business process integrates with existing applications and external partner applications and processes. There are the following main points which are supported by most of these systems: transactional real-time component integration, a queued messaging model, a publish-and-subscribe messaging or component model and bulk data movement (often as database replication). Usually business process management is support both for internal processes (EAI) and external processes (B2B). Moreover the solution support industry-standard documents, e.g., Open Applications Group (OAG) business object documents (BODs) and process definitions, e.g., RosettaNet (see Sect. 5.2).

An e/mBusiness platform – a specific kind of eBusiness integration platforms - is a software server offering basic selling features on a foundation designed for customizability. Commerce sites must tie into other systems like inventory management, partners' extranets, and eMarketplace software. To do this, a commerce platform, like agent technology used in eBusiness, needs to support integration standards like XML, EDI, .NET, and Java 2 Enterprise Edition (J2EE).

5.3.2 Application Server Platforms

The purpose of application servers is to provide a robust middleware infrastructure to develop and run eBusiness applications. The most important characteristics are scalability, load balancing, persistency, recovery, and fail-over. Further, the application server provides middleware services (APIs) for communication, transaction control, security and component management. However they are no direct integration technologies, but agents could run on such application server platforms to satisfy the above mentioned requirements.

5.3.3 WebServices

Web services are a new way of building Web application. Web Services can be understood as components in the Internet; they are self-contained, self-describing, modular applications that can be published, located, and invoked across the Web. They are mainly based on XML and HTTP with the specific notions of WSDL and UDDI for describing the services and providing the white, yellow and green pages; and SOAP on the protocol level for a Remote Procedure Call function over XML.

Web services perform functions ranging from simple requests to complicated business processes, like in the BizTalk environment. Like a web page a web service can be used by a human user but in the same way by another web service or program, i.e. once a Web service is deployed, it can be discovered - via WSDL and UDDI - and the deployed service can be invoked using SOAP. Despite the name "service", a web service is not restricted to be a server, it can act as well as a client to other web services. In this way widely distributed applications can be built where the services locate each other dynamically.

With the increase of the bandwidth and the decrease of the costs in the last few years more dynamic content, the pervasiveness and diversity of computing devices up to mobile devices like mobile phones or PDAs with multi-access make the need for a glue more important.

Viewed from a software architecture perspective (see Sect. 2.2), the web service is a veneer for programmatic access to a service which is then implemented by other kinds of middleware. Access consists of service-agnostic request handling (a listener) and a facade that exposes the operations supported by the business logic. The logic itself is implemented by a traditional middleware platform.

Web Services can be seen as the next step of development towards agent based services, since WebServices support only the infrastructure and syntactical level of communication, whereas agent technology adds additional functionality like negotiation or communication on a semantic level. Agents can be seen as individual peers which communicate with other peers (agents). It can be assumed that agent technology and peer-to-peer approaches are techniques that can benefit from each other and in the long run both technologies will come together.

5.4   Semantic Web

The Semantic Web will bring structure to the meaningful content of Web pages. The Semantic Web is an extension of the WWW, in which information is given well-defined meaning by providing metadata, for better enabling computers and people to work in cooperation. The first steps in weaving the Semantic Web into the structure of the existing Web are already defined. In the near future, these developments will usher in significant new functionality as machines become much better able to process and "understand" the data that they merely display at present.

For the semantic web to be operable computers must have access to structured collections of information and sets of inference rules that they can use to conduct automated reasoning. Two important technologies for developing the Semantic Web are already in place: eXtensible Markup Language (XML) and the Resource Description Framework (RDF). Another knowledgeable technique is the DAML+OIL approach. Two important question to be resolved is who will define the ontologies required, and, probably more seriously, how the billions of existing pages of web content can be provided with the metadata required for processing by agents in the Semantic Web.

5.5   Matchmaking and Agent-Based Marketplaces

Kuokka and Harada [33] considered matchmaking in the context of emerging information integration technologies, where potential providers and requesters send messages describing their capabilities and needs of information (or goods). They presented two matchmakers: COINS (COmmon INterest Seeker), which is based on free text matchmaking using a distance measure from information retrieval (Salton [51]), and SHADE (SHared DEpendency Engineering), which uses a subset of KIF ([26]) and a structured logic text representation called MAX ([32]). While COINS aimed at e-commerce, SHADE aimed at the engineering domain.

Complementing the theoretical work in ([9],[10]), Sycara and co-workers addressed the matchmaking problem in practice. They developed and implemented the LARKS matchmaker (LAnguage for Advertisement and Request for Knowledge Sharing, see [56]). In LARKS, the matchmaking process runs through three major steps: (1) Context matching, (2) syntactical matching, and (3) semantic matching. Step 2 is divided into a comparison of profiles, a similarity matching, and a signature matching. Compared to previous approaches, LARKS provides higher expressiveness for service descriptions.

In the context of electronic auctions, we refer to Sandholm's theoretical results on the properties of different market protocols and to a number of prototype systems constructed based on these results (see e.g., [52]). Weinstein and Birmingham ([64]) introduce a service classification agent which has meta-knowledge and access to nested ontologies. This agent dynamically generates unique agent and auction descriptions which classify an agent's services and auction subjects, respectively. A requester obtains from it the name of the best auction to its needs. In [49], Reeves et al. describe ContractBot, an interesting approach of automating negotiation based on declarative descriptions of contracts. ContractBot can be viewed as a further development of AuctionBot [68].

In [42], Müller and Pischel present a case study of employing an agent-based approach to a real-world solution in the area of digital libraries and web-publishing.

In IMPACT ([2]), so called Yellow Pages Servers play the role of matchmaker agents. Offers and requests are described in a simple data structure which represents a service by a verb and one or two nouns (e.g., *sell:car*, *create:plan(flight)*). The matchmaking process computes the similarity of descriptions from shortest paths in directed acyclic graphs that are built over the sets of verbs and nouns, respectively, where edges have weights reflecting their distance.

6 Conclusions and Outlook

The contribution of this paper is twofold: Firstly, we outlined what we believe are the key challenges in today's eBusiness. Secondly, we investigated how agent technology can help tackling some of these challenges. We demonstrated possible approaches in using agent technology for eBusiness solutions as well as main advantages in building agent based eBusiness systems. The paper shows that agent technology is well suited to develop highly dynamic, generic and intelligent integration frameworks for eBusiness based on standard vertical and horizontal services on top of existing standard platforms.

We believe that agent technology will play an important role in the development of the next generation eBusiness systems over the next few years. Agent technology first of all plays a key role in combining the existing heterogeneous eBusiness solutions, adding smart functionality and automating standard processes. This becomes also clear if we look at the main abilities which agents provide in contrast to other technologies. The four main abilities are the following:

- Enriched, higher level communication (agent communication languages, based on existing transport encoding and underlying networking protocols, co-ordination of tasks, collaboration based on semantics and ontology's)
- Enabling more intelligence service provision, and process management e.g. by personalization and integration of different services to value-added services (service wrapping, brokering, matchmaking, negotiation, auctioning, preference modeling, adaptive behavior by learning mechanisms)
- Dealing with the enlarging amount of information and functions (agent mobility, intelligent filtering, personalization, presentation)
- Allowing self-organizing of processes (autonomous, flexible and pro-active behavior by planning, scheduling, and learning functionality)

One point this paper makes is to show that agent technology has much to offer to next-generation eBusiness solutions. We believe that the main benefit of agents in eBusiness will be reached in the following application areas:

- Better customer relation by attractive user interfaces and personalized presentations
- Effective and fast assignment of supply and demand in electronic market places by intelligent matchmaking
- Optimization of processes by dynamic negotiations for configuration and contract management
- Integration of heterogeneous software systems by wrapping legacy software using agent standards, e.g. the FIPA standard, for co-ordination and co-operation between software agents

However, we should end with a word of caution. For agents to satisfy the expectations there are some important preconditions. Firstly, the research community needs to establish a focus on pragmatic solutions that build on existing standards. Secondly, existing solutions and technologies need to be used efficiently and enhanced incrementally instead of re-inventing the wheel. Thirdly, while agents are an important enabling technology, they do not liberate software engineers and system developers from making a careful requirement analysis and design of processes and systems; Fourthly, for some areas, such as advanced supply-chain management, automated negotiations and collaborations, new architectures and methods will be required to achieve the necessary level of scalability and flexibility. Self-organizing manufacturing and supply-chain whose nodes consist of autonomous collaborating agents seem to be appropriate building blocks for these solutions.

References

[1] APSIG: http://www.objs.com/agent/index.html
[2] Arisha, K., T. Eiter, S. Kraus, F.Ozcan, R. Ross, and V.S. Subrahmanian (1999, March/April). IMPACT: A Platform for Collaborating Agents. IEEE Intelligent Systems 14(2), 64-72
[3] Bauer, B.; Berger, M.: Agent-Based Personal Travel Assistance, Proceedings of International ICSC Symposium on Multi-Agents and Mobile Agents in Virtual Organizations and E-Commerce (MAMA 2000), Wollongong, Australia, 2000
[4] Berger, M, Bauer, B, Watzke, M.: Towards an Agent based Infrastructure for Distributed Virtual Organizations, Proceeding 3rd International WetICE Workshop on Web-Based Infrastructure and Coordination - Architectures for Collaborative Enterprises, MIT, Cambridge, 2001.
[5] BizTalk: http://www.biztalk.org
[6] Bussmann, S.: A Multi-Agent Approach to Dynamic, Adaptive Scheduling of Material Flow. MAAMAW 1994: 191-205.
[7] DAML(-OIL): http://www.daml.org
[8] Daniels, M.: Integrating Simulation Technologies with Swarm paper delivered to the "Agent Simulation: Applications, Models and Tools" conference held at University of Chicago in October of 1999, URL http://www.santafe.edu/~mgd/anl/anlchicago.html
[9] Decker, K., K. Sycara, and M. Williamson (1996, December). Matchmaking and Brokering. In International Conference on Multi-Agent Systems (ICMAS96)
[10] Decker, K., K. Sycara, and M. Williamson (1997, August). Middle-agents for the internet. In Proceedings of the Fifteenth International Joint Conference on Artificial Intelligence (IJCAI-97), pp.578-583.
[11] ebXML http://www.ebxml.org
[12] eCommerce, http://eco.commerce.net
[13] Etzioni, O. Moving Up the Information Food Chain: Deploying Softbots on the World Wide Web. Proceedings of AAAI-96 (Abstract of Invited Talk), 1996.
[14] Fensel D., I. Horrocks, F. Van Harmelen, S. Decker, M. Erdmann and M. Klein: OIL in a nutshell In: Knowledge Acquisition, Modeling, and Management, Proceedings of the European Knowledge Acquisition Conference (EKAW-2000), R. Dieng et al. (eds.), Lecture Notes in Artificial Intelligence, LNAI, Springer-Verlag, October 2000
[15] Finin, T. and Fritzson, R.: KQML - a language and protocol for knowledge and information exchange, In Proceedings of the 13th Intl. Distributed Artificial Intelligence Workshop, LNAI 890, Seatle, WA, USA, 1994]
[16] FIPA 97 specification: http://www.fipa.org/repository/fipa97.html
[17] FIPA 98 specification: http://www.fipa.org/repository/fipa98.html
[18] FIPA AGENT: http://www.java-agent.org
[19] FIPA: http://www.fipa.org
[20] Fischer Wirtschaftslexikon.
[21] Fischer, K.: Holonic Multiagent Systems - Theory and Applications. In Proceedings Portuguese Conference on Artificial Intelligence (EPIA) 1999: 34-48.
[22] Forrester Research: http://www.forrester.com

[23] Frey, R.: Agent technology is making the transition from research labs into industry, invited talk, PAAM 2000, 2000.

[24] Gamma, E., Helm, R., Johnson R., Vlissides J. Design Patterns, Addison Wesley, 1997.

[25] GartnerGroup: http://www.gartner.com

[26] Genesereth, M.R. and R.E. Fikes (1992, June). Knowledge Interchange Format, Version 3.0 Reference Manual. Technical Report Logic-92-1, Computer Science Department, Stanford University. http://www-ksl.stanford.edu/knowledge-sharing/papers/kif.ps

[27] Gerber Ch., B. Bauer, D. Steiner: Resource Adaptation for a Scalable Agent Society, (chapter in) Software Agents for Future Communication Systems, ed. Hayzelden, Bigham, Springer, 1999

[28] Guttman R., A. Moukas, and P. Maes. "Agent-mediated Electronic Commerce: A Survey." Knowledge Engineering Review, Vol. 13:3, June 1998.

[29] Ivezic N., Tom Potok, and Line Pouchard. Multiagent Transitional Operations, Autonomous Agents 2000

[30] JADE: http://sharon.cselt.it/projects/jade/

[31] Jennings N. R., K. Sycara, and M.J.Wooldridge. A Roadmap of Agent Research and Development. Journal of Autonomous Agents and Multi-Agent Systems. 1(1), pages 7-36. July 1998.

[32] Kuokka, D. (1990). The Deliberative Integration of Planning, Execution, and Learning. Ph.D. thesis, School of Computer Science, Carnegie Mellon University.

[33] Kuokka, D. and L. Harada (1996). Integration information via matchmaking. Journal of Intelligent Information Systems 6(2/3), 261-279.

[34] LEAP: http://leap.crm-paris.com

[35] Leonet: http://www.nm.informatik.uni-muenchen.de/~leonet

[36] Leonet: http://www.nm.informatik.uni-muenchen.de/~leonet

[37] LivingSystems: www.livingsystems.com

[38] LostWax: www.lostwax.com

[39] Maes, P.: Modeling Adaptive Autonomous Agents. In: Langton, C. (ed.): Artificial Life Journal, Vol. 1, No. 182, MIT Press, pp. 135-162, 1994.

[40] MASIF: http://www.omg.org/cgi-bin/doc?orbos/97-10-05

[41] MoTiV: http://www.motiv.de

[42] Müller, J. P. and M. Pischel. Doing business in the information marketplace: a case study. In Proceedings of the 3rd Intl. Conference on Autonomous Agents (Agents-1999), ACM Press, 1999.

[43] Müller, J. P. The design of intelligent agents. Lecture Notes of Artificial Intelligence, Vol. 1077. Springer-Verlag, 1997.

[44] Odell, J. ed., Agent Technology, OMG, green paper produced by the OMG Agent Working Group, 2000

[45] OIL http://www.ontoknowledge.org/oil

[46] OMG: http://www.omg.org

[47] Parunak, H. Van Dyke: A Practitioners Review of Industrial Agent Applications. Autonomous Agents and Multi-Agent Systems 3(4): 389-407 (2000)

[48] Raymond, E.S. "The Cathedral and the Bazaar – Musings on Linux and Open Source by an accidental Revolutionary"; O'Reilly & Associates, Inc., Sebastopol, CA, 1999.

[49] Reeves, D.M., Wellman, M.P., Grosof B.N. Automated negotiation from declarative contract descriptions. In Proceedings of the 5th Intl. Conference on Autonomous Agents, pp. 51-58. ACM Press, 2001.

[50] RosettaNet http://www.rosettanet.org

[51] Salton, G. (1989). Automatic Text Processing. Addison-Wesley. (ISBN 0-201-12227-8)

[52] Sandholm, T. eMediator: a next generation electronic commerce server. In Proceedings of the 4th Intl. Conference on Autonomous Agents (Agents-2000), pp.341-348, ACM Press, 2000.

[53] SMIL: http://www.w3.org/TR/REC-smil/

[54] SOAP: http://www.w3.org/TR/SOAP/

[55] SWARM http://www.swarm.org
[56] Sycara, K., J. Lu, M. Klusch, and S. Widoff (1999). Dynamic service matchmaking among agents in open information environments. ACM SIGMOD Record 28 (1), Special Issue on Semantic Interoperability in Global Information Systems, 47-53.
[57] UDDI http://www.uddi.org
[58] W3C P3P: www.w3c.org/P3P/
[59] W3C XML Protocol: http://www.w3.org/2000/xp
[60] W3C: www.w3c.org
[61] W3CRDF: http://www.w3c.org/Metadata/
[62] W3CRDFSchema: http://www.w3.org/TR/2000/CR-rdf-schema-20000327/
[63] Wayflow: http://www.wayflow.de
[64] Weinstein, P. and W. Birmingham (1997). Service classification in a proto-organic society of agents. In Proceedings of the IJCAI-97 Workshop on Artificial Intelligence in Digital Libraries.
[65] Weiss G., Multiagent Systems - A modern approach to Distributed Artificial Intelligence. Cambridge: MIT Press, 1999.
[66] WSCL: http://www.hp.com/go/e-speak
[67] WSDL: http://www.w3.org/TR/wsdl
[68] Wurman P.R., Wellman M.P., Walsh W.E. The Michigan Internet AuctionBot: A configurable auction server for human and software agents. In Proc. Of the 2nd Intl. Conference on Autonomous Agents, pp.301-308, ACM Press, 1998.
[69] XCBL: http://www.xcbl.org
[70] XML: http://www.w3.org/XML/

From Simulated Dialogues to Interactive Performances

Elisabeth André[1], Thomas Rist[2], and Stephan Baldes[2]

[1]Universität Augsburg, Eichleitnerstr. 30, D-86135 Augsburg, Germany
andre@informatik.uni-augsburg.de
[2]DFKI GmbH, Stuhlsatzenhausweg 3, D-66123 Saarbrücken, Germany
{rist,baldes}@dfki.de

Abstract. In this contribution, we argue in favor of a shift from applications with single presentation agents towards flexible performances given by a team of characters as a new presentation style. We will illustrate our approach by means of two subsequent versions of a test-bed called the "Inhabited Market Place" (IMP1 and IMP2). In IMP1, the attribute "flexible" refers to the system's ability to adapt a presentation to the needs and preferences of a particular user. In IMP2, flexibility additionally refers to the user's option of actively participating in a computer-based performance and influencing the behavior of the involved characters at runtime. While a plan-based approach has proven appropriate in both versions to automatically control the behavior of the agents, IMP2 calls for highly reactive and distributed behavior planning.

1   Introduction

Lifelike characters, or animated agents, provide a promising option for interface development as they allow us to draw on communication and interaction styles with which humans are already familiar. During the last years, animated characters have been used in a number of different application fields including educational software, help systems, and virtual representatives on commercial web pages that act as product presenters and sales assistants (see [1] for an overview). Most of these applications assume settings in which the agent addresses the user directly as if it were a face-to-face conversation between human beings. Such a setting seems quite appropriate for a number of applications that draw on a distinguished agent-user relationship. For example, an agent may serve as a personal guide or assistant in information spaces like the world-wide web.

However, there are also situations in which the emulation of a direct agent-to-user communication - from the perspective of the user - is not necessarily the most effective and most convenient way to present information. For example, an empirical study by Craig and colleagues [5] suggests that indirect interaction can have a positive effect on the user's performance. They found that, in tutoring sessions, users who overheard dialogues between virtual tutors and tutees, subsequently asked significantly more questions and also memorized the information significantly better. In other situations the user may just feel more comfortable in the role of an observer rather than in the role of an active questioner.

V. Mařík et al. (Eds.): MASA 2001, LNAI 2322, pp. 107–118, 2002.
© Springer-Verlag Berlin Heidelberg 2002

In this paper we propose a shift from single character settings towards interactive performances given by a team of characters as a new form of presentation. The use of presentation teams bears a number of advantages. First of all, they enrich the repertoire of possible communication strategies. For example, they allow us to convey certain rhetorical relationships, such as pros and cons, in a more canonical manner. Furthermore, they can serve as a rhetorical device that allows for a reinforcement of beliefs. For instance, they enable us to repeat the same piece of information in a less monotonous and perhaps more convincing manner simply by employing different agents to convey it. Last but not least, the single members of a presentation team can serve as indices which help the user to organize the conveyed information. For instance, we may convey meta-information, such as the origin of information, or present information from different points of view, e.g. from the point of view of a businessman or the point of view of a traveler.

Our proposal is inspired by the evolution of TV commercials over the past 40 years. A typical commercial of the early days featured a sales person who presented a product by enumerating its positive features – quite similar to what synthetic characters do on web pages today. On TV, however, this format has almost completely been replaced by formats that draw on the concept of short, but entertaining episodes or sketches. Typically, such performances embed product information into a narrative context that involves two or more human actors. One of the reasons that may have contributed to the evolution of commercial formats is certainly the fact that episodic formats offer a much richer basis compared to the plain enumeration of product features, and thus meet the commercial industry's high de- mand for originality and unseen spots. In this context, we also refer to psychological work that emphasizes the strength of episodic memory [21].

The goal of our research, however, is not to simply imitate episodic formats from TV commercials for information presentation. Rather, we aim at new formats which bring in *adaptivity* and *interactivity*. By adaptivity, we mean a system's ability to adapt a presentation to the needs and preferences of a particular user. Interactivity refers to the user's option of actively participating in a performance. We will illustrate our approach by means of two subsequent versions of a test-bed called the "Inhabited Market Place" (IMP). We will use the abbreviations IMP1 and IMP2 to refer to version 1 or 2 respectively.

2   The Inhabited Market Place

As the name indicates, the Inhabited Market Place [2] is a virtual place in which seller agents provide product information to potential buyer agents in form of a typical multi-party sales dialogue. Figure 1 illustrates the scenario: the characters Merlin and Robby on the left-hand side play the role of car dealers who present information about the displayed car, and answer questions posed by the two buyer agents Peedy and James on the right-hand side. The user has the option of joining the discussion as well

– either as a buyer or a seller. In Fig. 1, the user is represented by the agent in the middle.[1]

Fig. 1. The Inhabited Market Place

2.1   Structure and Representation of the Product Data

Part of the domain knowledge is an ordinary product database, e.g., organized in the form of an n-dimensional attribute vector per product. In our current scenario, the products are cars with attributes, such as model type, maximum speed, horsepower, fuel consumption, price, air conditioning, electric window lifters, airbag type etc. Thus, to a large extent, the contents of the database determines what an agent can say about a product. However, products and their attributes are described in a technical language which the user may not be familiar with. Therefore, it seems much more

---

[1] Apart from the user's avatar which was created by DFKI GmbH, all other agents have been taken from the Microsoft Agent Ring (see http://www.msagentring.org).

appropriate to maintain a further description of the products - one that reflects the impact of the product attributes on the value dimensions of potential customers. Such an approach can be modeled in the framework of multi-attribute utility theory (e.g. see [24]), and has already been used for the identification of customer profiles in an electronic bourse for used cars [16]. In this project, the car database was provided from a large German/American car producer and retailer, whereas the value dimensions for the product "car" have been adopted from a study of the German car market [19] that suggests that safety, economy, comfort, sportiness, prestige, family and environmental friendliness are the most relevant. In addition, it was represented how difficult it is to infer such implications. The work presented here follows this approach even though we employ a simplified model. For instance, we use the expressions:

```
FACT value "consumptioncar1" 8;
FACT polarity "consumptioncar1" "environment" "neg";
FACT difficulty "consumptioncar1" "environment" "low";
```

to represent that a certain car consumes 8 liters, that this fact has a negative impact on the dimension "environment" and that this implication is not difficult to infer.

2.2 Setting the Parameters for the Presentation

In the scenario shown in Fig. 1, the salesman Merlin is trying to convince the buyers of the potential benefits of the displayed car. From the point of view of the system, the presentation goal is to provide the user with facts about a certain car. However, the presentation is neither just a mere enumeration of the plain facts about the car, nor does it assume a fixed course of the dialogue between the involved agents. Rather, IMP1 supports the concept of adaptivity. It allows the user to specify prior to a presentation (a) the agents' role, (b) their attitude towards the product (in our case a car), (c) their initial status, (d) their personality profile and (e) their interests. Taking into account these settings, a variety of different sales dialogues will be generated for one and the same product. Figure 2 shows the interface that allows the user to input these settings.

The interest profile is used to determine those attributes of the car that should be addressed in the dialogue. Depending on the agents' attitude towards the product, their status and personality, positive or negative evaluations about these attributes are added.

To model the characters' personality, we adopt the so-called Five-Factor Model [15]. The FFM is a descriptive model, with the five dimensions (*Extraversion, Agreeableness, Conscientiousness, Neuroticism,* and *Openness*) being derived from a factor analysis of a large number of self- and peer reports on personality-relevant adjectives. We decided to focus on the dimensions: *Extraversion, Agreeableness,* and *Neuroticism* which seem to be most relevant for social interactions.

3   Automated Script Generation for Simulated Sales Dialogues

In IMP I, the system takes on the role of a screen writer that scripts the behavior of a group of actors that participate in a dialogue. We follow a communication-theoretic view and consider the automated generation of such scripts a planning task. The implementation of the planning approach is based on the Java[TM]-based JAM agent architecture [9]. To model the knowledge used for script generation, we defined plan-operators that code a decomposition of a complex communicative goal into dialogue acts for the single agents.

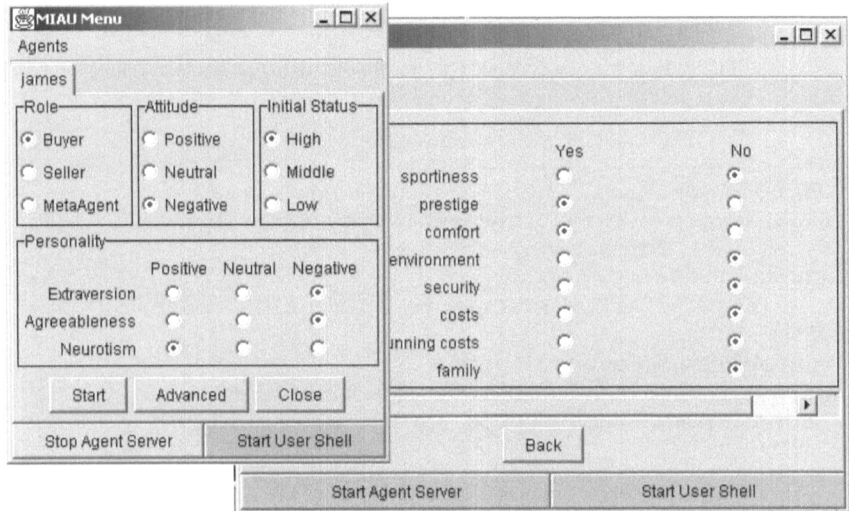

Fig. 2. Interface for Specifying a Character Profile

An example of a dialogue operator is listed in Fig. 3. It represents a scenario where two agents discuss a feature of an object. The operator only applies if the feature has a negative impact on any value dimension and if this relationship can be easily inferred. According to the operator, any disagreeable buyer produces a negative comment referring to this dimension (NegativeResponse). The negative response is followed by a response from a seller (ResponseNegativeResp).

One possible response is listed in Fig. 4. It only applies if there is an attribute that has a positive impact on the dimension under discussion. In this case, the seller first tells the buyer(s) that it disagrees and then lists attributes with a positive impact on the dimension. Note that our plan operators include both the propositional contents of an utterance and its communicative function. This is in line with Cassell and colleagues, who regard conversational behaviors as fulfilling propositional and interactional conversational functions [4]. For instance, we explicitly represent that "Bad for the " $dimension "?" is a response to a negative comment.

```
NAME: "DiscussValue1"
GOAL: PERFORM DiscussValue $attribute;
PRECONDITION:
      FACT polarity $attribute $dimension "neg";
      FACT difficulty $attribute $dimension "low";
      FACT Buyer $buyer;
      FACT Disagreeable $buyer;
      FACT Seller $seller;
BODY:
      PERFORM NegativeResponse $buyer $dimension;
      PERFORM ResponseNegativeResp $seller $attribute
           $dimension;
```

Fig. 3. Example of a dialogue operator for discussing an attribute value

```
NAME: "ResponseNegativeResponse2"
GOAL:
PERFORM ResponseNegativeResp $agent $attribute
           $dimension;
PRECONDITION:
      FACT Polarity $attribute $dimension "pos";
BODY:
      PERFORM Respond $agent
           (+ "Bad for the " $dimension "?");
      PERFORM EnumeratePos $agent $dimension;
```

Fig. 4. Example of a plan operator for responding to a negative comment

The character's profile is considered by treating it as an additional filter during the selection instantiation and rendering of dialogue strategies. In particular, we define specific dialogue strategies for characters of a certain personality and formulate constraints that restrict their applicability. The script planning mechanism ensures that the generated scripts entail for each character only role-appropriate or role-neutral behaviors that do not conflict with its personality profile. For instance, a customer in a sales situation usually tries to get information on a certain product in order to make a decision, while the seller aims at presenting this product in a positive light. In contrast to an extrovert agent, an introvert agent will less likely take the initiative in a dialogue.

To illustrate the adaptive features of our system, let's have a look at the two sample dialogues listed in Fig. 5. For expository reasons, we use extreme parameter settings so that differences in the behavior of the characters are readily distinguishable. The dialogues partially discuss the same car attributes, but from different points of view. In both cases, one of the buyers criticizes the high gas consumption of the car. But in the first case, it is concerned about the environment, while, in the second case, it is thinking of the high costs.

Robby:
Role: seller;
Personality: agreeable, extravert;
Interests: environmental issues
Peedy:
Role: customer;
Personality: disagreeable, introvert;
Interests: environmental issues

Peedy:
How much gas does it consume?
;;; wants to know more about gas
;;; consumption because this feature has an
;;; impact on "environment," which is
;;; important to him
Robby:
It consumes 8 liters per 100 km.
;;; retrieves the value from the car database
Peedy:
Isn't that bad for the environment?
;;; the value of the attribute "gas
;;; consumption" has a negative impact on
;;; "environment," Peedy is disagreeable
;;; and therefore makes a negative
;;; comment, less direct speech since it is
;;; introvert
Robby:
Bad for the environment?
;;; questions negative impact
It has a catalytic converter. It is made of
recyclable material.
;;; provides counterarguments
...

Robby:
Role: seller;
Personality: agreeable, extravert;
Interests: sportiness
Peedy:
Role: customer;
Personality: disagreeable, extrovert;
Interests: economy

Peedy:
How much gas does it consume?
;;; wants to know more about gas
;;; consumption because this feature has an
;;; impact on the dimension "economy,"
;;; which is important to him
Robby:
It consumes 8 liters per 100 km.
;;; retrieves the value from the car database
Peedy:
I'm worrying about the running costs.
;;; the value of the attribute "gas
;;; consumption" has a negative impact on
;;; "economy," Peedy is disagreeable and
;;; therefore makes a negative comment
Robby:
Forget the running costs. Think of the
prestige.
;;; tries to distract the buyer by
;;; mentioning any positive implication.
;;; "prestige" has been chosen since there
;;; is no other easier-to-infer positive
;;; implication
...

Fig. 5. Dialogues for different parameter settings

4   Structuring Interactive Performances

The presentation task and scenario of IMP II are similar to IMP I. In addition, IMP II provides the user with the option of taking an active role in the performance if she or he wishes to do so. If not, however, the characters will give a performance on their own – maybe encouraging the user to give feedback from time to time. At each point in time, the user has the option of joining the discussion again. The novelty of the approach lies in the fact that it allows the user to dynamically switch between active and passive viewing styles. Such a scenario bears a lot of similarities to improvisational theatre (cf. [10]). First of all, there is no pre-defined script. Instead the dialogue between the user and the characters evolves while time progresses. Furthermore, the scenario is open-ended. Neither the characters nor the users are able to tell what exactly may happen next.

Since user reactions cannot be anticipated prior to a presentation, it is no longer possible to pre-script utterances. Instead scripting has to be done at runtime, e.g. either by a centralized script writing component or by the single agents themselves. For IMP II, we decided to use a self-scripting approach and realize our characters as autonomous agents. That is, the behavior of each agent is triggered by events occurring in the scene and the dialogue contributions of the other agents and the user. Fig. 6 provides an overview of the architecture we developed for IMP II.

The *Jimpro* module implements an interface between the agents' body (which is realized by the Microsoft Agent Technology [17]) and their mind (which is realized by different JAM clients). It consists of an agent server which registers all agents that participate in a conversation and handles the communication between them. The agent handler is responsible for the execution of the elementary animations and speaking actions provided by the underlying audio-visual interface (in our case the Microsoft agents). In addition, it informs the JAM clients about the status of the executed actions and the audio-visual interface.

The *Dialogue Management Component* maintains the dialogue history and a list of dialogue goals stored on a goal board that still need to be addressed by the agents. All agents have access to the goal board and may apply for the right to accomplish goals. Which agent will succeed depends on the given dialogue protocol. As a first step, we implemented a protocol that supports well-organized conversations. Among other things, this protocol prescribes that questions should be addressed before new dialogue contributions are made (unless none of the agents is able to provide an answer). Furthermore, if an agent is addressed directly, he will get the right of speaking with a higher probability than any other agent. In addition, we consider the agents' status and personality when allocating dialogue turns. For instance, extrovert agents with a high status get a word in with a higher probability than introvert agents with a low status.

The *JAM clients* represent the agents' mind. We assign each agent its own reactive planner and a data base which contains its world knowledge. Furthermore, each agent has a repertoire of dialogue strategies at its disposal that are coded as plan operators. We were able to reuse most dialogue operators from IMP I that represent the behavior of a single agent (like the plan operator listed in Fig. 4). However, these operators are no longer employed by a central script-writing component, but now belong to an agent's individual repertoire of dialogue behaviors. Plan operators that specify a dialogue sequence between several agents, such as the plan operator listed in Fig. 3, have been replaced in IMP II by rules that map dialogue events onto dialogue goals for the single agents. For instance, if one of the agents (or the human user) asks a question, the dialogue management component puts the goal to respond to that question onto the goal board.

Dialogue contributions result from autonomous characters trying to achieve their individual goals. The goals of the single agents are derived from their role and personality profile. For instance, an agent that takes on the role of a car seller is initialized with the goal to sell a car. In addition, we associate with agreeable and

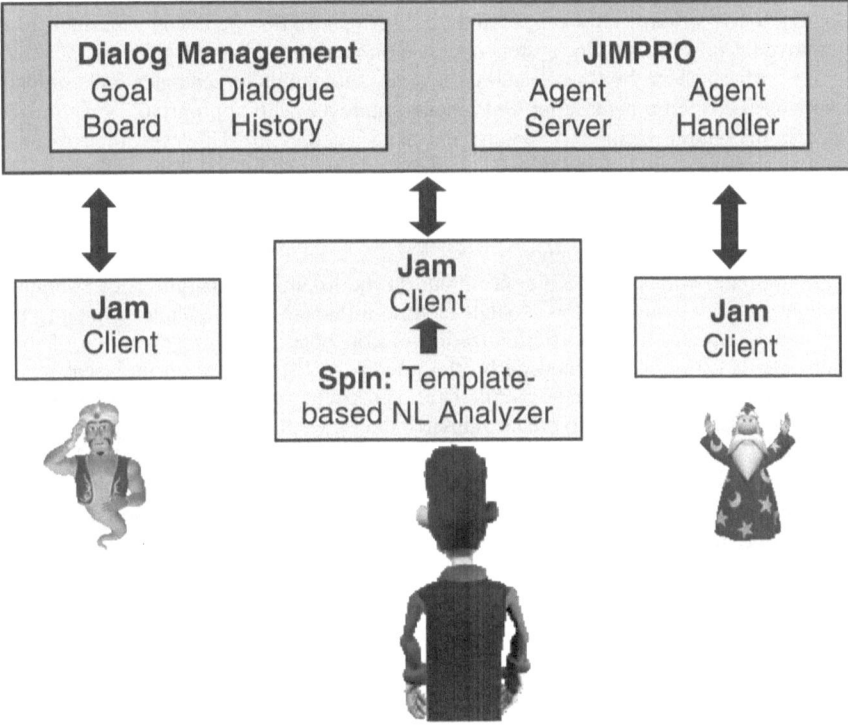

Fig. 6. Architecture for IMP II

extrovert agents the goal to perform polite behaviors which means among other things that they start a greeting behavior whenever they come across another agent for the first time. Unless an agent is both disagreeable and introvert, it adopts the goal to respond to a question whenever it kknows the answer.

As shown in Fig. 6, the user's avatar is assigned a JAM client as well. This relieves the user from the burden to specify the behavior of his or her avatar to the last detail. The JAM client is triggered by the natural-language utterances of the user which are analyzed by Spin, a Java-based template-matching tool developed within the SmartKom project [22].

5   Related Work

The Agneta and Frida system [8] incorporates narratives into a Web environment by placing two characters on the user's desktop. These characters watch the user during the browsing process and make comments on the visited Web pages. Unlike our approach, the system relies on pre-authored scripts, and no generative mechanism is employed. Consequently, the system operates on predefined Web pages only.

An earlier system by Cassell and colleagues automatically generates and animates dialogues between a bank teller and a bank employee with appropriate synchronized speech, intonation, facial expressions, and hand gestures [3]. However, their focus is on the communicative function of an utterance and not on the personality and the emotions of the single speakers. Furthermore, they do not aim to convey information from different points of view but restrict themselves to a question-answering dialogue between the two animated agents.

Walker and colleagues [23] concentrate on the linguistic capabilities of computer characters and examine how social factors influence the semantic content, the syntactic form and the acoustic realization of conversations. The generation of their dialogues is essentially influenced by the power the listener has on the speaker and the social distance between them. This approach has been later extended by Prendinger and colleagues to create animated dialogues for the Microsoft agents [18].

Our work was heavily inspired by research on interactive drama that aims at integrating a user in a scenario – either as an audience member or an active participant. To allow for user interaction, systems usually incorporate decision points in a narrative-style script [14] or model their characters as autonomous agents that select and instantiate actions under consideration of dramatic constraints, such as the plot of a story or the characters' role and personality [7]. The integration of dramaturgical elements has been proven useful for a large variety of applications. In particular, developers of educational software are increasingly employing narrative concepts to structure their pedagogical material. The spectrum ranges from virtual puppet theatres [11,12] for children to educational soap [13] and team training [20].

6   Conclusion

In this paper, we proposed performances given by a team of animated agents as a new presentation style. Infotainment and edutainment transmissions on TV as well as advertisement clips are examples that demonstrate how information can be conveyed in an appealing manner by multiple presenters with complementary characters and role castings. However, our approach distinguishes from conventional TV presentations by at least two features: *adaptivity* and *interactivity*. We demonstrated this by means of two subsequent versions of a test bed called the Inhabited Market Place.

In IMP I, we automatically generated scripts for sales dialogues depending on a number of character-related parameters to be specified prior to a presentation. The scripting approach bears the advantage that it enables the generation of coherent dialogues. It requires, however, that all the knowledge to be communicated to the audience is known in advance. Consequently, it is less suitable in situations where the agents have to immediately respond to events at presentation runtime, such as new incoming information to be presented or user interactions.

In IMP II, we moved to a character-centered approach. Instead of specifying the agents' behavior to the last detail, we just provide a character with a description of its role and profile according to which it has to behave at presentation runtime. Such an approach seems appropriate for scenarios that require immediate responses to external events, such as user interactions. It is, however, more difficult to ensure the coherence of a dialogue since no global organization of the information is possible.

In the future, we will make more extensive use of dramaturgical elements in order to achieve more interesting interactions. Inspired by our work on the Puppet project [11], we are currently investigating a dramaturgy framework which goes back to Greimer's ACTANT model [6]. A major element of the framework is that of an underlying conflict which is established by introducing a protagonist, that persecutes a certain goal, and a second character, the antagonist, that tries to accomplish a counter goal. Both the protagonist and the antagonist may be supported by one or more helpers. Once started, a certain "dramatic story" would unfold over time just by having the involved actors play their assigned roles. In the case of the Inhabited Market Place, we might model a buyer and a customer with conflicting interests. While the seller tries to present a car in a positive light, the customer persecutes the opposite goal – namely to point out the weaknesses of the car. In addition, we foresee a helper character who is to support the virtual customer and is played by the user. As a helper agent, the user may interact in the following ways: He or she may support the virtual customer directly by confirming its statements or expressing approval. In response to a seller's statement, he or she may utter disbelief or mention under-standing problems. The Inhabited Market Place II can be seen as a test bed which allows users to experiment with different dramaturgical elements in order to find out what kinds of setting tend to result into interesting improvisations.

Acknowledgements. The work described here has been partially funded by the BMBF project MIAU and the EU projects MagiCster and NECA. We are grateful to Peter Rist for the graphical design of Mr. Smith. We would also like to thank Bastian Blankenberg and Martin Klesen for the implementation of Jimpro and the interface for IMP I.

References

1. André E. (1999). Applied Artificial Intelligence Journal, Special Double Issue on Animated Interface Agents, Vol. 13, No. 4-5.
2. André, E., Rist, T. , van Mulken, S., Klesen, M. and Baldes, S. (2000). The Automated Design of Believable Dialogues for Animated Presentation Teams. In: Cassell, J., Sullivan, J., Prevost, S. and Churchill, E. (eds.): *Embodied Conversational Agents*, 220-255, Cambridge, MA: MIT Press.
3. Cassell, J., C. Pelachaud, N. I. Badler, M. Steedman, B. Achorn, T. Becket, B. Douville, S. Prevost, and M. Stone. (1994). Animated conversation: Rule-based generation of facial expression, gesture and spoken intonation for multiple conversational agents. *Computer Graphics* (SIGGRAPH '94 Proceedings), 28(4):413-420.
4. Cassell, J., Bickmore, T., Camphell, L., Vilhjalmsson, H. and Yan, H. (2000). The human conversation as a system framework: Designing embodied conversational agents. In: Cassell, J., Sullivan, J., Prevost, S. and Churchill, E. (eds.): *Embodied Conversational Agents*, 29-63, Cambridge, MA: MIT Press.

5. Craig, S. D, B. Gholson, M. H. Garzon, X. Hu, W. Marks, P. Wiemer-Hastings, and Z. Lu. 1999. Auto Tutor and Otto Tudor. In *AIED-Workshop on Animated and Personified Pedagogical Agents*, 25–30. Le Mans, France.
6. Greimers, A. and Courtes, J. (1982). *Semiotics and Language: An Analytical Dictionary.* Bloomington, IN: Indiana University Press.
7. Hayes-Roth, B., van Gent, R. and Huber, D. (1997). Acting in character. In: Trappl, R. and Petta, P. (eds.): *Creating personalities for synthetic actors,* 92–112. New York: Springer.
8. Höök, K., Persson, P. and Sjölinder, M. (2000). Evaluating Users' Experience of a Character-enhanced Information Space. Artificial Intelligence Communications, 13(3), 195-212.
9. Huber, M. (1999). JAM: A BDI-theoretic mobile agent architecture. Proc. of the Third Conference on *Autonomous Agents,* 236–243. New York: ACM Press.
10. Johnstone, K. (1989). *IMPRO: Improvisation and the Theatre.* Routledge: New York.
11. Klesen, M., Szatkowski, J. and Lehmann, N. (2001). A Dramatised Actant Model for Interactive Improvisational Plays. In: Proceedings of the Third International Workshop on Intelligent Virtual Agents, 181-194, New York: Springer.
12. Machado, I., Paiva, A. and Prada, R. (2001). Is the Wolf Angry or … Just Hungry? In: Proc. of the Fifth Conference on *Autonomous Agents,* 370–376. New York: ACM Press.
13. Marsella, S.C., Johnson, W.L. and LaBore, C. (2000). Interactive Pedagogical Drama. In: Proc. of the Fourth Conference on *Autonomous Agents,* 301–308. New York: ACM Press.
14. M. Mateas, M. (1997). An Oz-Centric Review of Interactive Drama and Believable Agents. Technical Report CMU-CS-97-156, School of Computer Science, Carnegie Mellon University, Pittsburgh, PA.
15. McCrae, R. R., and John, O. P. (1992). An introduction to the five-factor model and its applications. Special Issue: The five-factor model: Issues and applications. Journal of Personality 60: 175-215, 1992.
16. Mehlmann, O., Landvogt, L., Jameson, A., Rist, T. and Schäfer, R. (1998). Einsatz Bayes'scher Netze zur Identifikation von Kundenwünschen im Internet. *Künstliche Intelligenz* 3(98):43–48.
17. Microsoft Agent: Software Development Kit (1999). Microsoft Press, Redmond Washington.
18. Prendinger, H. and Ishizuka, M. (2001). Social Role Awareness in Animated Agents. In: Proc. of the Fifth Conference on *Autonomous Agents,* 270–377. New York: ACM Press.
19. Spiegel-Verlag. (1993). SPIEGEL-Dokumentation: Auto, Verkehr und Umwelt. Hamburg: Augstein.
20. Swartout, W., Hill, R., Gratch, J., Johnson, W.L., Kyriakakis, C., LaBore, C., Lindheim, R., Marsella, S., Miraglia, D., Moore, B., Morie, J., Rickel, J., Thiébaux, M., Tuch, L., Whitney, R. and Douglas, J. (2001). Toward the Holodeck: Integrating Graphics, Sound, Character and Story. In: Proc. of the Fifth Conference on *Autonomous Agents,* 409–416. New York: ACM Press.
21. Tulving, E. (1983). Elements of Episodic Memory. Oxford: Clarendon Press.
22. Wahlster, W., Reithinger, N. and Blocher, A. (2001). SmartKom: Multimodal Kommunikation with a Life-Like Character. In: Proceedings of *Eurospeech 2001*, Vol. 3, 1547-1550.
23. Walker, M., Cahn, J. and S. J. Whittaker, S.J. (1997). Improving linguistic style: Social and affective bases for agent personality. In *Proceedings of Autonomous Agents'97*, 96–105. Marina del Ray, Calif.: ACM Press.
24. von Winterfeldt, D., and W. Edwards. (1986). Decision analysis and behavioral research. Cambridge: Cambridge University Press.

Cooperating Agents for Holonic Manufacturing

S. Misbah Deen

DAKE Group
Department of Computer Science
University of Keele, England
deen@cs.keele.ac.uk

Abstract. In a Cooperating Knowledge Based System (CKBS) an agent is modelled as an autonomous and cooperative knowledge based system, capable of executing some tasks in the most effective way, using an engineering paradigm. The paper presents an abstract CKBS model, using Holonic Manufacturing Systems (HMS) as an application domain. HMS is a major international project on agent-based manufacturing, where a holon is a unit of production and is a type of agent, cooperating with other agents in task sharing. This paper describes a highly distributed architecture of the model (designed to provide systems robustness and fault-tolerance) and the necessary computational model required to ensure the correct systems behaviour.

Keywords. holonic manufacturing system, multi-agent system, cooperating knowledge based system, computational model, agent technology

1 Introduction

Holonic Manufacturing Systems (HMS) is an international project within the pre-competitive research initiative called Intelligent Manufacturing Systems (IMS) started in 1993 as a ten-year programme by Australia, Japan, Europe, Canada and the USA, supported by respective Governments. The HMS project is focused on what might be described as an agent-based manufacturing system, particularly suited to low-volume high-variety manufacturing. The term holon is defined as an autonomous and cooperative functional unit of a manufacturing system, and can be viewed as a kind of cooperative agent.

The ideas we employ are based on our work on Cooperating Knowledge Based Systems (CKBSs), carried out under the DREAM (Dake Research into an Engineering Approach to Multi-agents) programme, in which autonomous knowledge based systems (called agents) perform the dependent activities of a joint task (global task) using an engineering approach. The resultant DREAM model (also referred to as the CKBS model) forms an abstract model for the HMS applications. Its implementation version (the concrete model) is based on an extension of IEC Function Block (FB) [8] standard 61499 for distributed controller. We shall refer to this concrete model as the HMS/FB model. The differences will be outlined later.

The DREAM model (more general than HMS/FB model) is designed for distributed heterarchical task processing. This presentation will focus on the DREAM

V. Mařík et al. (Eds.): MASA 2001, LNAI 2322, pp. 119–133, 2002.
© Springer-Verlag Berlin Heidelberg 2002

model to explore ideas, rather than the implementation specifications in the HMS/FB model.

Engineering Paradigm

A Cooperating Knowledge Based System (CKBS) [1,2,10] seeks to develop a good formalised solution of the computational issues in distributed applications, using an *Engineering paradigm*. In this approach:

- An agent is an autonomous Knowledge Based System having a compulsory software component and an optional hardware component.
- Agents are endowed with computational (as against human behavioural) attributes. All agents are *implicitly* cooperative.
- Effectiveness, Robustness, Reliability, Stability, Performance. Multi-userness and user-friendliness are very important.
- The behaviour of an agent must be predictable and controllable.

Ideas from both distributed databases and the DAI multi-agent systems are blended together to build a CKBS.

Some Basic Concepts

A CKBS agent has a head responsible for social interactions and a body responsible for supporting its individuality. The body is made up of a heterarchy of functional components (*funcoms* for short) which could be pure software or software representing and interfacing hardware. Funcoms help in fault localisation

To accomplish a joint task one agent (usually the user-agent) acts as the coordinator and it select other agents, as cohorts, thus forming what we call a Cooperation Block (CB). A cohort in turn can form a lower-level CB, thus forming a hierarchy of Basic Cooperation Blocks (BCBs).

Three basic CKBS constructs are:

- An agent is an autonomous unit in a cooperative processing
- A funcom is a unit of execution within an agent, usually forming heterarchy
- A Basic Cooperation Block (BCB) is a unit for inter-agent cooperation

Equivalents in HMS/FB

A Function Block (FB) is the equivalent of a funcom. An FB is modelled as a C++ object with an added special public item for control flows (events flow). A holon is an agent. Instead of a CB, the HMS/FB model uses a concept of Cooperation Domain (CD) which includes a physical infrastructure for communications and facilities for coordination, such data storage and other communication facility. In the DREAM model, the CB is purely a logical structure, relegating all communication facilities to a lower layer, and leaving all coordination to the coordinator (an agent). The CD is not a holon and designed to support only the requirement of the IEC distributed controller (controller-level cooperation), it cannot support the higher-level inter-holon cooperation, such as for cooperative scheduling. In contrast, the CKBS concepts of CB and Coordinator are meant to support all inter-agent cooperation, and hence more powerful in their abilities.

A highly distributed system such as the one considered here is complex, prone to errors and higher maintenance cost. The reward of employing a high-level of distribution is the systems robustness, which is not feasible in a centralised system. We shall describe a fault tolerant architecture and outline how this can be achieved through our model. How can we show that such a highly distributed and error-prone system behaves correctly and offers stability? This is another essential requirement of the HMS applications, and will be addressed in this paper. We begin with a very brief description of the related work.

Related Work

Concepts of belief, desire and intention (BDI) as the basis of a single-agent architecture were introduced by Bratman et al [4,5] and developed further by Rao and Georgeff [6,7]. These concepts are also employed in many DAI/multi-agent architectures presrented in this ACAI-2001 workshop, and therefore will not be discussed here, except to mention that the BDI scheme defines the internal processing of an agent through a set of mental categories, within a control framework for rational selection of a course of action, often with the added concepts of goals and plans.

An IEC group has recently proposed a distributed architecture for manufacturing systems, based on what it calls Function Blocks, for distributed programmable controllers [8]. This architecture is being adapted for agent-based manufacturing by the HMS project, and can be viewed as an implementation instance of our more formalised model [9,10].

There are a number of research papers available that address the area of agent-based manufacturing. Parunak et al [11] addressed the issues in agent-based manufacturing, in which he offers an elaborate test environment for ideas, while Jarvis et al [12] investigated quality control issues in holonic manufacturing. P. Valckenaers et al [13] have developed an agent-based architecture called PROSA relates to manufacturing production but not to the controller issues. It uses three classes of holons: order, product, and resource holons, where the order holon represents the task in manufacturing, the product holon holds the product and process knowledge and the resource holon stands for physical production resource of the manufacturing system, which includes an information processing part that controls the resource.

A major difference between these approaches and ours, is that our model is highly distributed as it is based on the Function Block Architecture, which specifies detailed agent-components to meet the requirements of the distributed controller for manufacturing. However, none of the models we know of provide any computational model to ensure the correct dynamic behaviour of the agent-based system. There is a partial parallel between our concept of a coordinator and some of the activities of the order holon. Finally although FIPA [14] generally endorses the BDI approach, it is also currently developing a standard (in cooperation with the HMS project) for agent-based manufacturing, using the present HMS/FB approach.

2   A Fault-Tolerant Architecture

2.1 Service Classes

We group agents into five service categories:

> Coordinator Class
> Skill Class
> Provider Class
> Support Class
> Minder Class

The skill agents becomes cohorts in a CB. Strictly speaking coordination is also a type of skill, but we make a convenient distinction between the role of coordination and the other skills. The provider class includes Directory and Tool agents. A robot could be treated either as a skill agent or a provider agents as convenient. Support includes devices (e.g. computers) and communication networks as the potential source of faults and breakdown. Each class may have subclasses. Here we shall focuss only on skill classes. Each agent A providing a skill K belong to the skill class K and its instances are called twins. If a twin fails, it can be replaced by another of the same class. Associated with the skill class K, there will be a agent minder (Aminder) agent that looks after the instances of that class, such replacing one twin by another. The concept of twins and minders are used to provide fault tolerance and robustness.

Paralleling the concept of skill class, we also classify the funcoms, all funcoms providing the same subskill belonging to the same funcom class, serviced by a funcom minder (Fminder) for that funcom class. It permits a fault to be localised into a smaller replaceable unit under the control of the funcom minder.

Agent Minders (Aminders)
> To maintain the schedule and the operational status of each twin
> To schedule agents as requested by a coordinator
> To interact with coordinators, directory agent and other minders

Funcom Minders (Fminders) [including the kernel minder]
> To hold the diagnostics of each twin
> To provide replacement twins
> To construct the funcom instance via its next lower-level minder

The minders of software funcoms may act as holder (library) of those funcoms, possibly with many versions.

Failure Consequences:
- If the top-level funcom in the agent body (body kernel) fails, the agent fails, which is then replaced through the minder.
- If a lower funcom fails, it can be replaced, and hence the agent need not even fail, thus providing *fault-tolerance*.

It should be observed that in the event of failure the S/W funcoms can be restarted, but H/W funcoms must be replaced, requiring a physical transportation link.

Robustness

A system is robust if it is fault-tolerant and recovers quickly from failures. Funcoms help to achieve quicker fault localisation which in turn facilitates speedy re-allocation of work, and hence a quicker operational recovery. Therefore the system is *Operationally Robust*.

The highly distributed architecture outlined above has been for a simulation study to demonstrate its systems effectiveness in terms of handling delays and breakdown and reducing wasted production, without any global controller, using temperature as a metaphor to describe overloaded twins as hot and underloaded twins as cold. Earlier work on this appears in [15,16], and an updated paper is currently being written.

2.2 Task Representation

Let us assume a global task **T** is decomposed into:

$$\mathbf{T} = T_0, T_1, T_2, \dots T_n$$

where T_0 is the residual task for the coordinator and $\{T_1, \dots T_n\}$ are the other tasks for the skill agents $\{A_1, \dots A_n\}$.

Task T_f to be *any task* at *any level* decomposed into *r* lower-level tasks as:

$$T_f = T_{f0}, T_{f1}, T_{f2}, \dots T_{fr}$$

Tasks, Skill and Funcoms

Assume task T_f requires the skill K_f of the F_f:

$$K_f = K_{f0}, K_{f1}, K_{f2}, \dots K_{fr}$$

$$F_f = F_{f0}, F_{f1}, F_{f2}, \dots F_{fr}$$

Thus both skills and funcoms can form heterarchies corresponding to task heterarchies.

To describe task a T_f we need four elements:

1. *task scheme*, in which task T_f is described with its properties and constraints. The constraints will include pre, post and end conditions.

2. *trigger scheme,* in which triggers are specified to stipulate desired cohort be-haviour on various execution conditions, not discussed any further.

3. *dependency scheme*, in which relevant dependencies are described. The depen-dency rules will contribute to pre, post and end conditions.

4. *dependency satisfaction rule*, which must be satisfied in the execution of the task. The rule may permit choices.

We shall not elaborate these implementation-dependent representations any further except to state that a Postcondition is a quality check on the result while an EndCondition includes forwarding the result and the sending the completion messages to the appropriate destinations.

2.3 Operational Messages

In any distributed computer system, we can picture the following elements in operational cost:

CPU + I/O + Communication

In our case the communication cost is likely to be dominating and therefore worth investigating, as we do below. The coordinator decomposes the global task (using the implemented procedures) into several alternatives, chooses an alternative, determines the skills needed and then retrieves agent minders from the directory agent (Fig. 1).

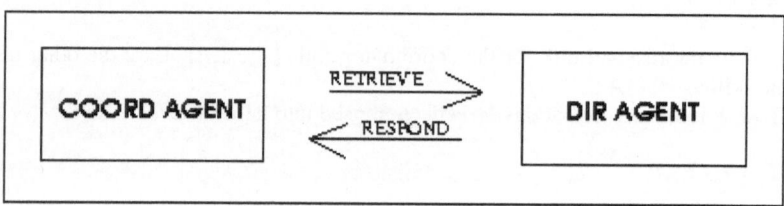

Fig. 1. Directory Search Agents

This takes 2 messages. The coordinator can find the Aminders for all the alternative decompositions. Now two cases.

Case I

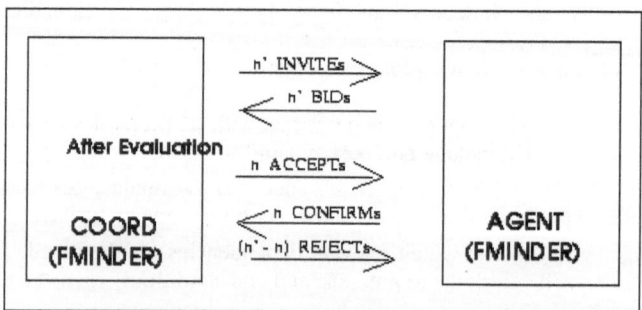

Fig. 2. ContractNet (CN) Protocol for Agent Selection from the Minders

If n out of n' agents (each of a different minder) is selected (by CN), then we have 3n' + n messages. Each of n minders must inform (and receive acknowledgment from) its successful twin. Thus the number of messages:

2 for Coordinator/Directory + (3n' + n) for CN + 2n for Aminder/Twin
= 2 + 3(n' + n) messages.

Case II

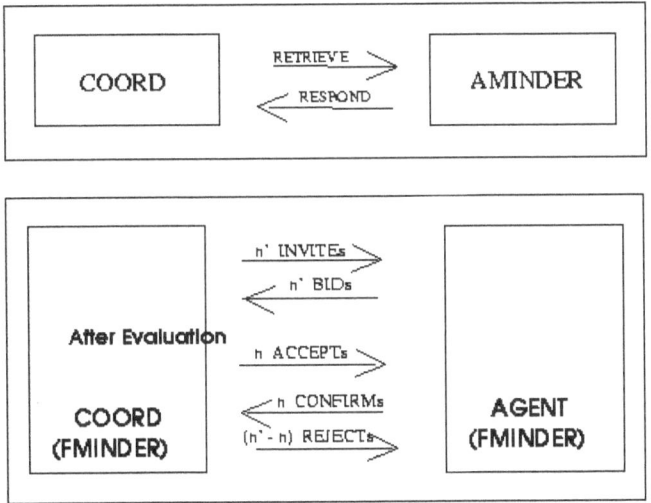

Fig. 3. Minders and Agent Selection by the Coordinator

The number of messages will remain the same, that is: (2 + 3n' + 3n).
[2 for the Coord/Dir, (3n'+ n) for CN and 2n for Coord/Aminders.]
Messages in the Body Construction
    Given there are on average r components at each level of d levels of an agent body tree, the number of Fminders involved: $m = (r^d - 1)/(r - 1)$, where $r > 1$.
    If only p funcoms (out of m) are physical then, we have

2 + 3 (n' + n + 2np) messages.
= 2 + 6 n (1 + 2p) messages, if n' = n.

If we assume a simple scenario in which there are only two runtime messages per funcom, one to send the task to solve from the parent (with all the necessary inputs) and the other to return all outputs to the parent, without any malfunctions and failures, then *we shall have 2m messages during runtime.*
    If we are dealing with a manufacturing system, or in general a system that involves hardware funcoms, the communication cost is likely to be negligible compared to the physical processing and transportation costs. However, if all funcoms are purely software, then one must consider the communication cost as the distri-

bution cost which increases with the granularity of agents. The more the number of funcoms, the higher is the granularity of the agent concerned. A higher granularity enhances fault-tolerance to be paid by a higher communication cost. The choices are design decision. Observe all communication messages could be intra-computer rather than inter-computer messages, depending on the application requirements.

Finally the costs given above are only the set up cost, not the runtime cost of operations, which will require a more elaborate modelling of the system behaviour on faults.

Fault Handling and Dynamic Reconfiguration: Hierarchical paths exists for fault reporting. Faulty funcoms are replaced/restarted dynamically.

Finally we close this section with a comparison between the DREAM and the HMS/FB models:

DREAM	*HMS/FB*
Funcom	FB
CB	CD*
Agent	Holon
Coordinator	CD* plus Holon
Service classes	Similar
Twins	Similar

(CD includes coordination and Communication infrastructure)

3   Computational Correctness in HMS

3.1 Requirements

Since the HMS environment is complex and highly distributed, the potential for something going wrong with wasted production is naturally high, and hence it is important to construct a computational model that specifies the correct system behaviour through all its operational states (including failure states) during execution. In constructing such a model we have borrowed ideas from the database transaction model, and have examined the following concepts:

- *Consistency*: It ensures that the final result produced in an error-prone environ-ment is equivalent to that produced in an error-free environment for the same inputs in spite of conflicts and possible systems malfunctions.

Task Completion (with Compensating Actions)
Serialisation (with Recovery Points)

Consistency will require (i) rollback to a recoverable point if the task is not completed successfully, and (ii) the observance of the serialisation rules by a holon during task execution.

- *Termination*: The execution must terminate in finite time. It demands convergence to a result (e.g. in a negotiation) and the absence of any loops. Time-outs can be used as the last resort.

A system must have structures and procedures that ensure these behaviours, as discussed here, drawing ideas from *distributed database transactions* We demonstrate these behaviours in terms of funcom below .

3.2 Inter-Funcom Interactions and Primitives

During the runtime a funcom, say serving two parents and two children will have the following interactions:

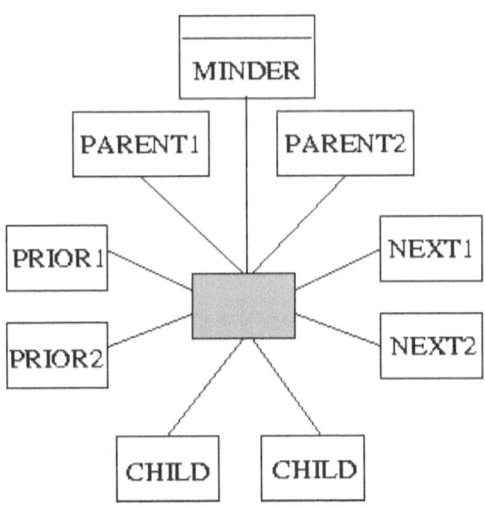

Fig. 4. Funcom Interactions. A physical funcom can be shared

We can model these interactions with the help of the following execution-time funcom primitives, where we shall use the term atomic primitive to imply a lowest (leaf) level primitive. Observe that each lower-level task T_{ij} will generally inherit dependencies from its parent T_i

Validation Primitives
   Pre-condition check (P) - a composite activity
   Post-condition check (P')
   End-condition check (E)

Do Primitives
   Do (D) - a composite with r lower-level tasks

Corrective Primitives
   Rollback (B)
   Quit (Q) - at a recoverable point
   Redo (R)

Message Primitives
   Processing of an input message (Ii)
   Generation of an output message (Io)

In addition we shall introduce two termination states:
   Successful termination (Ts)
   Termination at recoverable point (Tr).

We assume that this is the complete list of the primitives.

3.3 Consistency

We shall consider below both task completion and serialisation.

3.3.1 Task Completion

The system will have the following characteristics, as required for consistency:

(a) If the execution **E** is successfully completed without any malfunction, it will have proceeded in the following sequence as:

$$\mathbf{E} == \ <\text{P, D, P', E, Ts}>$$

(b) If the execution **E** fails in between two primitives, it must be rolled back to the end of the last successful primitive (recoverable point). We must assume this will be done using the other primitives defined, along with the logging and recovery facilities.

(c) If a failure occurs at the beginning, the execution **E** must be rolled back to the start, as if nothing has happened. This is a special case of (b).

Thus we can assert that a task ends successfully or ends at a recoverable point.

3.3.2 Serialisation

A schedule of activities (primitives) is correct, if it forms a valid execution order. A valid execution order will preserve consistency.
Serialisation rules produce a valid execution order, and if followed, then the execution will preserve consistency.

In contrast to DDB transactions, the execution order here changes dynamically in an error-prone environment. To determine dynamically the next correct primitive we require the following funcom internal logical structure:

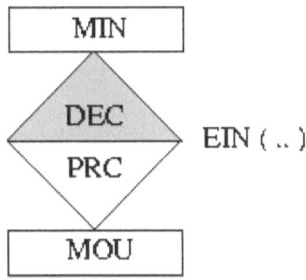

Fig. 5. Funcom Diagram

Its five elements are:

    EIN (parameters) - Event Indicator holding the execution status of each primitive
    MIN - Input messages
    MOU - Output messages
    DEC – Decider which determines the next correct action
    PRC - Processor

For serialisation, we assume:

    All illegal inputs will be rejected by DEC
    Quit never fails and can follow any primitive
    Quit must always be preceded by Rollback,
        but otherwise Quit can follow any primitive
    Any primitive after a specified number of Redo's must be
        rolled back to be followed by a Quit
    Any primitive after a specified time-out must be
        rolled back to be followed by a Quit
    Rollback (B) never fails
    All Redo (R) must be preceded by B
    Ii and Io never fail and can follow any primitive
    All communications (MOU/MIN) are ordered and failsafe.
    Quit from MIN may be followed by B, R or A.

Consider the execution of primitive W shown as :

W: $\{X \mid Y\}$,

If W succeeds, its next primitive is X,
If W fails, its next primitive is Y,

A sample of serialisation rules is shown below:

P: $\{D \mid R'\}$, R' = <B, R>
D: $\{P' \mid R'\}$
P': $\{E \mid R'\}$,
(D+P'): $\{E \mid R'\}$
E: $\{Ts \mid R\}$
R: $\{n \mid R\}$
B: $\{R \mid -\}$

where n is the next primitive in the correct sequence, n' is what would have been the next primitive, if the sequence was not interrupted by Io or Ii.

Some of these rules can be diagrammatically depicted as:

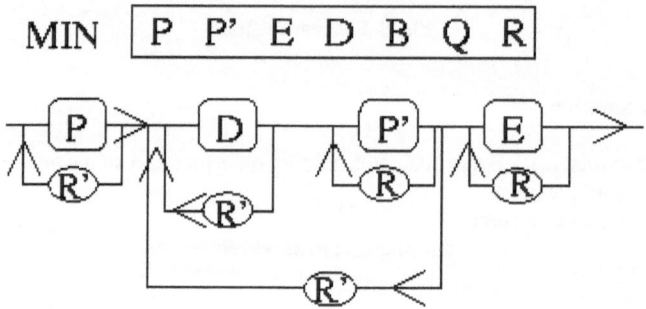

Fig. 6. An example of serialisation rules

These rules tell us that each functional component must be designed with

> a set of primitives
> a set of serialisation rules
> EIN, MIN, MOU, DEC and PRC
> backup facilities (logging, stable storage and software ...).

to ensure Consistency. The logical structure of a funcom shown in the diagram can be implemented differently.

3.4 Operational Stability and the Execution Features

Stability implies the absence of oscillations in the system. To control it one must have bounded input and bounded out. The computational model depicted above have the following characteristics:

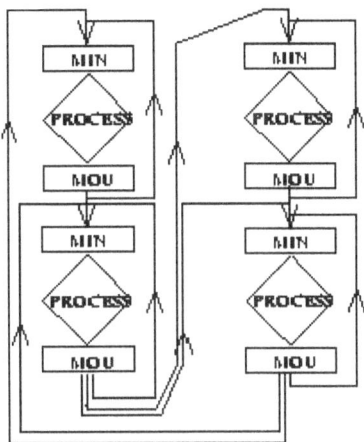

Fig. 7. Controlled Processing Funcom Network

Other Execution Features

1. Execution of an activity:

> During the execution of an activity, it may succeed or fail. In case of failure, it can be safely restarted or dropped (Quit) as desired.

2. Next Activity:

> The next activity is well-defined, and as long as the specification is correct, the system will behave correctly.

3. Denial of Services from MIN:

> MIN accepts only a limited volume of information (controlled by the buffer size), execution follows the correct Next activity, and hence no uncontrolled behaviour.

4. Idempotent Redo's:

> This problem can in principle arise only for the Do action, but since each redo is preceded by a rollback, *Redo (Redo ... Redo (x) ...))* becomes equivalent to *Redo (x)*.

4   Conclusion

- A highly distributed architecture supporting fault-tolerance and robustness
- A computational model that demonstrate the correctness of the execution system in spite of agent malfunctions.
- A system that guarantees stability in a complex and error-prone distributed environment.

The operational scenario depicted in this presentation is necessarily an abstract version of the reality. A real-world system will have more complex rules which must be investigated, analysed, formalised and implemented to ensure the correct operational behaviour. An implementation version of this abstract model is being defined as the HMS/FB by the HMS project.

Acknowledgement. Work presented here had been supported by EU grant BRPR-CT97-9000 for the IMS/HMS project. I would like thank all the partners of the project for their contributions which made it possible for me to write this paper, although the opinion expressed here is mine alone. Further thanks are due to the members of my own research group: Martyn Fletcher, Thomas Neligwa and Rashid Jayousi.

References

[1] S. M. Deen: "An architectural Framework for CKBS Applications", IEEE Transactions on Knowledge and Data Engineering, Vol (8:4), Aug 1996, pp 663-671.

[2] S. M. Deen: "A Database Perspective to a Cooperation Environment", Proc, CIA'97, edited by P. Kanzia and M. Klusch, Springer, 1997, pp 19-41.

[3] S. M. Deen: "A Fault-Tolerant Cooperative Distributed System", Proc. of the 9th IEEE DEXA Workshop, Vienna, Aug 1998, Edited by R. Wagner, pp508-513.

[4] M. E. Bratman: "Intentions, Plans and Practical Reason", Harvard University Press, 1987.

[5] M. E. Bratman, et al: "Plans and Resource Bounded Practical Reasoning", Computational Intelligence, Vol (4:4), pp349-355, Nov 1988.

[6] A. S. Rao and M. P. Georgeff: "Modeling Agents within a BDI architecture", KR'91, edited by R. Fikes and E. Sandewall, pp473-484, published by Morgan Kaufmann.

[7] A. S. Rao and M. P. Georgeff: " BDI agents - from theory to practice", Proc. of the 1st Int Confc on Multi-agent Systems, San Francisco, 1995.

[8] Function Blocks for Industrial Process-measurement and Control Systems, Part1: Architecture. Technical Report: International Electrotechnical Commission, TC65, WG6. ftp://ftp.ab.com/stds/iec/tc65wg6/document/pt1cd2.doc, 1997.

[9a] Martyn Fletcher (Ed):HMS Project, EU Brite-Euram [BPR-CT-97-9000], WP1/ Deliverables D1.1-1,and D1.1-2, Holonic Systems Architecture, Sept,1998, DAKE Group, Dept of Computer Science, University of Keele, Keele, England.

[9b] M. Fletcher, E. Garcia-Herreros, J.H. Christensen, S.M. Deen and R. Mittmann: "An Open Architecture for Holonic Cooperation and Autonomy", 11th Int. Conf on Database and Expert Systems Applications (DEXA'00), London, 2000, published by IEEE Computer Society.

[10] S. M. Deen and C. A. Johnson: "Formalising an Engineering Approach to Cooperating Knowledge Based Systems", IEEE Transactions on Knowledge and Data Engineering (to appear).

[11] H. Van Dyke Parunak et al: "The AARIA Agent Architecture":ICAA Workshop on Agent-Based Manufacturing, 1998

[12] D. Jarvis et al.: "Quality Control Holonic Manufacturing Systems", Technical Report, CSIRO, Australia, 1998.

[13] H. Van Brussels et al: "Reference Architecture for Holonic Manufacturing Systems: PROSA", Computers In Industry, Special Issue in

[14] FIPA Specifications: Foundation of Intelligent Physical Agents, home web-page: http://www.fipa.org

[15] S. M. Deen and M. Fletcher :"Temperature Equilibrium in Multi-Agent Manufacturing Systems", 11th Int. Conf on Database and Expert Systems Applications (DEXA'00), London, 2000, published by IEEE Computer Society.

[16] M. Fletcher and S.M. Deen: "Fault Tolerant Holonic Manufacturing Systems", Concurrency: and Computation: Practice and Experience, Vol (13:1), Jan 2001; John Wiley, pp. 43-70, ISSN: 1532-0626.

Multi-Agent Systems and Applications

ACAI 2001: Selected Student Papers

Self-Stabilizing Distributed Algorithms for Defeat Status Computation in Argumentation

Massimiliano Giacomin

Università di Brescia
Dipartimento di Elettronica per l'Automazione
Via Branze 38, I-25123 Brescia, Italy
giacomin@ing.unibs.it

Abstract. Argumentation is receiving an increasing attention as a technique for practical and uncertain reasoning underlying the realization of intelligent autonomous agents. In line with the evolution of agent architectures towards distribution, we propose a distributed approach to argumentation, where independent processes construct arguments and revise their defeat status by exploiting local information only. We present and compare two distributed self-stabilizing algorithms for defeat status computation, one specifically tailored to rebutting defeat, and the other able to handle any form of defeat. The property of self-stabilization is enforced to ensure a globally correct behavior of the system.

1 Introduction

Argumentation is receiving an increasing attention, among the techniques and methods underlying the realization of intelligent autonomous agents, as a flexible and computationally efficient framework for practical and uncertain reasoning. In a nutshell, reasoning is modeled as the process of constructing arguments for propositions from a given set of premises, by chaining rules of inference which may represent just provisional reasons for their conclusions. Since different arguments may contradict each other, the core problem is the computation of the "defeat status" of the arguments, namely determining which ones of them emerge undefeated from the conflict and which conclusions are the most credible ones. Besides providing an integrated model for belief revision and defeasible reasoning [4], argumentation takes into account the resource-bounded nature of a real agent, by providing the possibility of acting before the completion of the reasoning process on the basis of provisional conclusions, though some of them might be discarded at a later stage of the reasoning [16]. The relevant advantages are witnessed by the adoption of argumentation both at the level of multi-agent systems [15] and at the level of agent's internal reasoning [17].

In this paper, we focus on the use of argumentation at the single-agent level. We notice that while a decentralized organization has been widely recognized as an appropriate paradigm for autonomous agent architectural design, all the argumentation approaches we are aware of are based on centralized algorithms. As a consequence, the advantages of a distributed organization, which have been

V. Mařík et al. (Eds.): MASA 2001, LNAI 2322, pp. 137–147, 2002.
© Springer-Verlag Berlin Heidelberg 2002

recognized since the early DAI literature [6] and have biased the evolution of agent architectures towards decentralized control [7,1,5,10], can not be achieved. Therefore, it is interesting to explore the feasibility of a distributed approach to argumentation, by devising an argumentation system with a logically and computationally distributed architecture.

In the case of a real agent situated in a dynamic and uncertain world, it is reasonable to suppose that the agent will have to manage arguments generally based on multiple premises having different degrees of reliability. In order to carry out argumentation, the agent is engaged in two main activities:

1. Inferential activity, i.e. production of new arguments on the basis of premises continuously updated by perception and of previously drawn conclusions;
2. Computation of the defeat status of its conclusions (and premises), which may change because of new conflicting arguments produced by the inferential activity.

In our approach, we assume that inferential activity is carried out by several concurrent processes, which construct arguments independently of each other. For the sake of generality, we do not specify where or when information to make inferences is acquired, and we adopt the "finest grain model" concerning distribution of arguments, by assuming that each process puts forward exactly one argument. Since inferential activity may yield new conflicts among the generated arguments, each process has to revise its own defeat status, interacting with the other ones. More specifically, we assume that each process acquires information about the status assignment of its defeaters, namely arguments which are in conflict with it and are not weaker than it. The matter is that the defeat status assignment to the whole set of arguments, which emerges from the autonomous choices of single processes exploiting local information, has to satisfy a well founded semantics of argumentation, i.e. it must be the one which would be computed by a sound centralized algorithm exploiting global information. Since we do not assume any kind of synchronism, different processes can start their computation at different times, therefore the 'initial state' of the system cannot be determined in advance. Moreover, processes can be added or removed corresponding to the addition of arguments (inferential activity) and the addition or removal of premises (perceptual activity), and the processes have to react in such a way that the new correct status assignment is reached in a finite amount of time. We identify the class of distributed self-stabilizing algorithms as the most appropriate in order to satisfy the above requirements. In short, a self-stabilizing system is a network of processes, which, when started from an arbitrary (and possibly illegal) initial state, always returns to a legal state in a finite number of steps [8].

The rest of the paper is organized as follows. First, we describe the argumentation system underlying our approach (Sect. 2). Then, we develop two self-stabilizing algorithms for defeat status computation: we start with a tentative approach which fails in case of cyclic defeat graphs (Sect. 3), then we propose a specific algorithm able to handle a restricted form of defeat (Sect. 4), and finally we face the general case (Sect. 5). A comparison between these algorithms is provided in Sect. 6. Finally, Sect. 7 contains some conclusive remarks.

2   The Argumentation System

Specific argumentation systems (see [18] for a survey) differ in the adopted representation of arguments, in their form of conflict and in the semantics according to which they are considered "justified". For the sake of generality, we follow the approach adopted by Dung [9] which completely abstracts from both the internal structure of arguments and the specific notion of defeat between them. Arguments are simply conceived as the elements of a set, partially ordered by a binary relation of defeat. The primitive notion is that of argumentation framework:

Definition 1. *An* argumentation framework *is a pair*

$$AF = < \mathcal{A}, R >$$

where $\mathcal{A}$ is a set of arguments, and R is a binary relation on $\mathcal{A}$, i.e. $R \subseteq \mathcal{A} \times \mathcal{A}$.

In this paper, we will always suppose the set $\mathcal{A}$ to be finite. The meaning of the defeat relation R is the following: given two arguments α and β, $(\alpha, \beta) \in R$ if α *defeats* β, namely if accepting α as justified prevents accepting β. Note that this does not prevent β to defeat α too.

As far as the semantics is concerned, we adopt a "single status approach" [18], which defines the defeat status of the arguments in such a way that there is always exactly one possible way to assign them a status. In a distributed environment, this seems to be more viable than a multiple status approach, since it might be difficult for several asynchronous processes to consider different global status assignments and subsequently to evaluate the justification of their arguments on that basis. More specifically, we adopt the *grounded semantics* introduced in [9], and we define it inductively following Pollock's style [16] introducing the notion of level:

Definition 2. *Given an argumentation framework $AF = < \mathcal{A}, R >$*

- *All arguments of $\mathcal{A}$ are* in *at level 0.*
- *An argument of $\mathcal{A}$ is* in *at level $n + 1$ iff it is not defeated by any argument in* at level n.

Definition 3. *Given an argumentation framework $AF = < \mathcal{A}, R >$, the defeat status of the arguments of $\mathcal{A}$ is defined as follows:*

- *An argument is* undefeated *iff there is a level m such that for every $n \geq m$, the argument is* in *at level n.*
- *An argument is* defeated *iff there is a level m such that for every $n \geq m$, the argument is* out *at level n.*

– *An argument is* provisionally defeated *iff there is no level m such that the argument is* in *at all higher levels or* out *at all higher levels.*

The underlying idea is that an undefeated argument is one which the agent should believe given the current set of arguments, a defeated argument is one which it should disbelieve, while a provisionally defeated argument is controversial, for instance in the case in which there are two equally believable counter-arguments, it is not possible to prefer either of them. In this case, it is assumed that a skeptical attitude should be adopted: a provisionally defeated argument should not be believed but it should retain the potential to prevent other arguments to be justified.

An argumentation framework AF $=< \mathcal{A}, R >$ can be represented by means of a directed graph, called the *defeat graph* for AF, whose nodes are the arguments of $\mathcal{A}$ and whose edges represent the defeat relation. Moreover, we represent a status assignment to the arguments of $\mathcal{A}$ by means of a *labelled defeat graph* $< \mathcal{A}, R, L >$, where L is a function $L : \mathcal{A} \rightarrow \{\text{UNDEF}, \text{DEF}, \text{PROV}\}$. Since Definition 3 determines a univocal defeat status for every argument in $\mathcal{A}$, there is only one labelled defeat graph enforcing the status of defeat prescribed by the semantics: this graph is called the *right* labelled defeat graph.

Let us introduce the model of computation which will be adopted in the paper. Given an argumentation framework AF $=< \mathcal{A}, R >$, we consider the defeat graph $\mathcal{G}$ for $\mathcal{A}$ and we assume that each vertex of $\mathcal{G}$ is a sequential process or node. For each directed edge of R, we assume a unidirectional communication link. Each node has a set of local variables, including the representation of the status assignment of the associated argument, which can be updated by the node after evaluating its local variables and the local variables of its parents. Following the notation of [11], we will describe the program of each node as

$$ ^* [g\,[1] \longrightarrow a\,[1]_\square\, g\,[2] \longrightarrow a\,[2]_\square \ldots g\,[m] \longrightarrow a\,[m]] $$

where each *guard* $g[\ ]$ is a boolean function of the variables of process i and the variables of its parents, and each *action* (or *move*) $a[\ ]$ updates the variables of process i. At each iteration, one of the actions whose guards are true is selected for execution, and the algorithm terminates when all the guards are false.

In order to simplify the description, we assume that each node can examine the states of all its parents in a single atomic step, and that a central scheduler arbitrarily selects one of the enabled guards and allows the execution of the corresponding action to be completed before any guard is reevaluated. The results we obtain do not depend on these assumptions and can be easily extended to the case of distributed schedulers.

3   Developing a Self-Stabilizing Algorithm: A Tentative Approach

It can be proved that the right status assignment satisfies some constraints, that we call "coherence conditions":

Proposition 1. *A right labelled defeat graph* $< \mathcal{A}, R, L >$ *is* coherent, *i.e. every node* $\alpha \in \mathcal{A}$ *satisfies the following* coherence conditions:

- If $parents(\alpha) = \emptyset$ then $L(\alpha) = UNDEF$.
- If $\forall \beta \in parents(\alpha)$ $L(\beta) = DEF$ then $L(\alpha) = UNDEF$.
- If $\exists \beta \in parents(\alpha) \mid L(\beta) = UNDEF$ then $L(\alpha) = DEF$.
- If $\exists \beta \in parents(\alpha) \mid L(\beta) = PROV$ and $\forall \beta \in parents(\alpha)$ $L(\beta) \neq UNDEF$ then $L(\alpha) = PROV$.

A tentative approach might be arranged by simply letting the nodal processes react to the status of their defeaters according to the coherence conditions. However, a simple example shows that this approach does not work in case of a cyclic defeat graph. First, consider the case in which an argument without defeaters, say α, is constructed. Whatever its initial state is, α becomes undefeated according to the first coherence condition, as it should be. Then, suppose that an equally believable counter-argument, say β, is constructed, yielding the defeat graph of Fig. 1a. According to Definition 3, both arguments should be provisionally defeated. However, suppose that β, whose defeater α is undefeated, reacts according to the third coherence condition by changing its status to DEF. In this situation, the status assignments of both nodes satisfy the coherence conditions, but the global defeat status is not right.

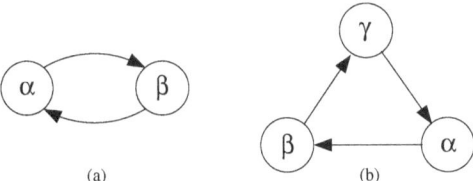

(a)   (b)

Fig. 1. Two problematic defeat graphs

As the example above has shown, the coherence conditions do not always enforce the right status assignment. Moreover, we will show in Sect. 5 that the system is not even stable, i.e. there are initial states and particularly "unlucky" process scheduling decisions, that prevent computation from terminating.

4   The Case of Rebutting Defeat: A Specific Algorithm

In this section, we describe a distributed self-stabilizing algorithm which can not be applied to the most general representation, but can handle a limited form of defeat [3]: we specify the form of the arguments of $\mathcal{A}$ and the defeat relationship R among them. We assume that arguments are constructed from a given set of premises by chaining rules of inference belonging to a given set IR. Each rule of inference I has the form $I = (\phi_1, \ldots, \phi_n \Rightarrow \phi, \nu)$, and represents a reason which creates a defeasible presumption of "strength" ν for the conclusion ϕ (we account for deductive reasons by letting $\nu = \infty$). We assume that all propositions belong to a language $\mathcal{L}$, that we don't specify. An argument θ is

1. A pair (ϕ, η), where $\phi \in \mathcal{L}$ and $\eta \in \Re^+$ (atomic argument made up of a premise with strength η); or
2. a formula of the form $\sigma_1, \ldots, \sigma_n \Rightarrow (\phi, \eta)$, where $\sigma_1, \ldots, \sigma_n$ is a finite sequence of arguments with conclusions $(\phi_1, \eta_1), \ldots, (\phi_n, \eta_n)$ corresponding to the reason $(\phi_1, \ldots, \phi_n \Rightarrow \phi, \nu)$ in IR, and $\eta = f_{\mathrm{str}}(\eta_1, \ldots, \eta_n, \nu)$.

In both cases, η is called the *strength* of the argument θ, denoted by strength(θ). Since f_{str} is a function that we do not specify, we do not commit to any particular criterion for the computation of the strength of arguments. We only constrain this function to satisfy two axioms, corresponding to those introduced in [19], which are sufficiently general to ensure that no interesting distribution of strength is excluded beforehand:

1. For any $\eta_1, \ldots, \eta_n, \nu$
   $f_{\mathrm{str}}(\eta_1, \ldots, \eta_n, \nu) \leq \min\{\eta_1, \ldots, \eta_n\}$
2. For any $\eta_1, \ldots, \eta_n$
   $f_{\mathrm{str}}(\eta_1, \ldots, \eta_n, \infty) \geq \min\{\eta_1, \ldots, \eta_n\}$.

The first condition ensures that any argument cannot be strictly stronger that any of its subarguments, while the second condition states that deductive reasons are conservative with respect to strength. For instance, a criterion for the computation of the strength satisfying the above axioms is the so called *weakest link principle* [16], which defines $f_{\mathrm{str}}(\eta_1, \ldots, \eta_n, \nu) = \min\{\eta_1, \ldots, \eta_n, \nu\}$.

As far as the adopted notion of defeat is concerned, an argument σ defeats another argument τ iff:

1. a subargument $\underline{\tau}$ of τ (possibly $\underline{\tau} = \tau$) has the conclusion (q, α); and
2. a subargument $\underline{\sigma}$ of σ (possibly $\underline{\sigma} = \sigma$) such that strength$(\underline{\sigma})$ = strength(σ) has the conclusion $(\neg q, \eta)$ and $\eta \geq \alpha$.

This definition is different from the one adopted in [16], but it can be proved to be equivalent as far as the defeat status assignment is concerned.

The basis of the algorithm, which is shown in Fig. 2, is as follows. Given a node α, its parents can be partitioned in two sets, namely contenders(α), such that $\forall \beta \in$ contenders(α) $(\alpha, \beta) \in R$ and $(\beta, \alpha) \in R$, and parents*(α) = parents$(\alpha) \setminus$ contenders(α). Starting from an arbitrary initial state, each node α continuously examines the assignments of its parents and revises its own status according to a modified version of the coherence conditions. In particular, the latter are modified in such a way that a contender parent of α can not bring about α to be defeated (this is entailed by Definition 3), thus enforcing the right labelled defeat graph.

The example of Fig. 1a, which is problematic for the tentative approach of the previous section, is handled correctly by the algorithm. In fact, the counter-argument β eventually recognizes α as its contender parent, with $L(\alpha) =$

{Program for node i}

M1: $^*[$ $(C_1[i]) \wedge (L(i) \neq \text{DEF}) \longrightarrow$
                    $L(i) := \text{DEF}$
M2: $\square$ $(C_2[i]) \wedge (L(i) \neq \text{PROV}) \longrightarrow$
                    $L(i) := \text{PROV}$
M3: $\square$ $(C_3[i]) \wedge (C_{3\alpha}[i]) \wedge (L(i) \neq \text{UNDEF}) \longrightarrow$
                    $L(i) := \text{UNDEF}$
M4: $\square$ $(C_3[i]) \wedge (\neg C_{3\alpha}[i]) \wedge (L(i) \neq \text{PROV}) \longrightarrow$
                    $L(i) := \text{PROV}$
        $]$

where

$C_1[i]$ $\equiv (\exists \beta \in \text{parents}^*(i) \mid L(\beta) = \text{UNDEF})$
$C_2[i]$ $\equiv (\exists \beta \in \text{parents}^*(i) \mid L(\beta) = \text{PROV}) \wedge (\forall \beta \in \text{parents}^*(i) \ L(\beta) \neq \text{UNDEF})$
$C_3[i]$ $\equiv (\text{parents}^*(i) = \emptyset) \vee (\forall \beta \in \text{parents}^*(i) \ L(\beta) = \text{DEF})$
$C_{3\alpha}[i]$ $\equiv (\forall \gamma \in \text{contenders}(i) \ L(\gamma) = \text{DEF}) \vee (\text{contenders}(i) = \emptyset)$

Fig. 2. The self-stabilizing algorithm to handle rebutting defeat

UNDEF, therefore it reacts by $M4$ changing its status to PROV. Then, also α, which has β as its unique contender parent, reacts by the same move yielding for both nodes the status of provisionally defeated. This is a stable state for the system, since both nodes have their guards false.

Apart from this particular example, the correctness of the algorithm can be proved in the general case, relying on the fact that, by the adopted definition of defeat, the topology of the defeat graph belongs to a restricted class, in that either the defeat graph is acyclic or for every cycle $< \alpha_1, \ldots, \alpha_n >$ (where $\alpha_n = \alpha_1$) we have that $\forall 1 \leq i \leq n \ (\alpha_{i+1}, \alpha_i) \in R$.

5   Handling the General Case

In the approach proposed in the previous section, defeaters attack other arguments by denying their (possible intermediate) conclusions: this corresponds to the so called *rebutting defeat* [16]. However, there is another class of defeaters, namely those which prevent the acceptance of other arguments by attacking the connection between premises and conclusion of a defeasible rule used by them. As an example, the fact that an object looks red is a defeasible reason to believe that the object is red, while the presence of red light is an *undercutting defeater* for any argument using this reason [16].

Encompassing undercutting defeaters invalidates any above constraint on the topology of the defeat graph, and this prevents the specific algorithm to work: the right status assignment is not always enforced, and the system is not even stable, i.e. there are initial states and particular "unlucky" process scheduling decisions,

{Program for node i}

M1: *[$(\text{parents}(i) = \emptyset) \wedge (\text{s}\,[i] \neq \text{UNDEF}\,(0)) \longrightarrow$
$$\text{s}\,[i] := \text{UNDEF}\,(0)$$

M2:   □ $(C_1\,[i]) \wedge (\min\,[\text{PU}_d\,(i)] < N) \wedge (\text{s}\,[i] \neq \text{DEF}\,(\min\,[\text{PU}_d\,(i)] + 1)) \longrightarrow$
$$\text{s}\,[i] := \text{DEF}\,(\min\,[\text{PU}_d\,(i)] + 1)$$

M3:   □ $(C_1\,[i]) \wedge (\min\,[\text{PU}_d\,(i)] \geq N) \wedge (\text{s}\,[i] \neq \text{PROV}) \longrightarrow$
$$\text{s}\,[i] := \text{PROV}$$

M4:   □ $(C_2\,[i]) \wedge (\text{s}\,[i] \neq \text{PROV}) \longrightarrow$
$$\text{s}\,[i] := \text{PROV}$$

M5:   □ $(C_3\,[i]) \wedge (\max\,[\text{PD}_d\,(i)] < N) \wedge (\text{s}\,[i] \neq \text{UNDEF}\,(\max\,[\text{PD}_d\,(i)] + 1)) \longrightarrow$
$$\text{s}\,[i] := \text{UNDEF}\,(\max\,[\text{PD}_d\,(i)] + 1)$$

M6:   □ $(C_3\,[i]) \wedge (\max\,[\text{PD}_d\,(i)] \geq N) \wedge (\text{s}\,[i] \neq \text{PROV}) \longrightarrow$
$$\text{s}\,[i] := \text{PROV}$$
]

where

$$C_1\,[i] \equiv (\text{PU}\,(i) \neq \emptyset)$$
$$C_2\,[i] \equiv (\text{PU}\,(i) = \emptyset) \wedge (\text{PP}\,(i) \neq \emptyset)$$
$$C_3\,[i] \equiv (\text{PU}\,(i) = \emptyset) \wedge (\text{PP}\,(i) = \emptyset) \wedge (\text{PD}\,(i) \neq \emptyset)$$

Fig. 3. The general self-stabilizing algorithm

that prevent computation from terminating. As an example, consider the defeat graph of Fig. 1b: in this case, since every node has no contender parents, it can be easily shown that the algorithm corresponds to the tentative approach of Sect. 3. Starting from the initial state $(\text{s}\,[\alpha], \text{s}\,[\beta], \text{s}\,[\gamma]) = (\text{UNDEF}, \text{DEF}, \text{UNDEF})$, if the scheduler selects the nodes in the order α, β, γ, it is easy to see that the system cycles indefinitely between the two states $(\text{UNDEF}, \text{DEF}, \text{UNDEF})$ and $(\text{DEF}, \text{UNDEF}, \text{DEF})$.

In order to enforce a correct behavior even in case of generic defeat graphs, we introduce for every node α an additional variable $\text{d}\,[\alpha]$, whose domain is the set of natural numbers; the state of α is indicated as $\text{s}\,[\alpha] = \text{DEF}\,(x) \mid \text{UNDEF}\,(x) \mid \text{PROV}$. The algorithm is presented in Fig. 3, where $N \geq 0$ is a constant and the following notations are used:

$$\text{PD}\,(\alpha) = \{\gamma \in \text{parents}(\alpha) \mid L(\gamma) = \text{DEF}\}$$
$$\text{PU}\,(\alpha) = \{\gamma \in \text{parents}(\alpha) \mid L(\gamma) = \text{UNDEF}\}$$
$$\text{PP}\,(\alpha) = \{\gamma \in \text{parents}(\alpha) \mid L(\gamma) = \text{PROV}\}$$
$$\text{PD}_d\,(\alpha) = \bigcup\nolimits_{\gamma \in \text{PD}(\alpha)} \{\text{d}\,[\gamma]\}$$
$$\text{PU}_d\,(\alpha) = \bigcup\nolimits_{\gamma \in \text{PU}(\alpha)} \{\text{d}\,[\gamma]\}$$

The underlying idea is the following. By Definition 3, if an argument α is defeated then there is a level k at which 'it becomes stably out', i.e. α is *in* at level $k - 1$ and *out* at all levels $m \geq k$. In this case, it can be proved that α has at least a defeater β, denoted as 'determinant node' for α, which 'becomes stably in' at level $k - 1$: in a sense, β is the 'cause' for α being defeated. In case an argument α is undefeated, by Definition 3 either it has no defeaters, or it becomes stably in at a level $k > 0$. In the latter case, it can be proved that all the defeaters of α become stably out at lower than k levels, and there is a defeater β which becomes stably out at level $k - 1$: again, β is the 'determinant node' for α. Basically, the algorithm works as follows: each node α updates its defeat status $L(\alpha)$ as it is prescribed by the coherence conditions, and it updates d $[\alpha]$ to the proper value d $[\beta] + 1$, where β is the node which α recognizes as its determinant node. The constant N represents the maximum level at which a generic node can become stably in or stably out, and plays a role when a node has to be provisionally defeated in the termination state. Let us refer to the aforementioned example, supposing $N = 6$ and d $[\ ] = 0$ for all nodes in the initial state. With the same scheduling order as above, after the 3rd round the state of the system is $(s [\alpha], s [\beta], s [\gamma]) = (\text{UNDEF} (4), \text{DEF} (5), \text{UNDEF} (6))$. During the 4th round, α changes its status to PROV by M3, as well as β and γ by M4. This is the right defeat status, and, since all the nodes have their guards false, the algorithm terminates.

Apart from this particular example, the correctness of the algorithm can be proved in the general case, provided that $N \geq n - 1$. In case the number of processes exceeds N, the algorithm does not assign the status of defeated or undefeated incautiously, but it assigns a 'cautious status' of provisionally defeated to those arguments it can not handle.

6 Comparison between the Proposed Algorithms

In order to compare the two proposed algorithms, we have to introduce a measure of the computational complexity of a self-stabilizing algorithm. As usual, we consider the round complexity, where a *round* refers to a minimum execution sequence in which each enabled action is taken at least once [12].

As far as the more specific algorithm is concerned, it turns out that it terminates after at most n rounds, where n is the number of processes. The more general algorithm instead terminates after at most $N + 1$ rounds, and since correctness is ensured if $N + 1 \geq n$, this yields a worst-case round complexity of n rounds *at least*.

We note that a more general underlying argumentation system yields an increased computational complexity, and requires a 'guess' on N, which must be high enough to always exceed the number of nodes of the dynamic defeat graph. Since the computational complexity increases with N, the latter represents a trade-off between efficiency and cautiousness. On the contrary, the specific algorithm does not require any guess of this kind.

7 Conclusions

We have presented two different self-stabilizing algorithms for defeat status computation, one specifically tailored to rebutting defeat, and the other able to handle any form of defeat. We believe that our proposal is a useful starting point to put argumentation in line with the evolution of agent architectures towards distribution. In a broader perspective, this effort is also related with the notion of 'emerging intelligence' advocated by Minsky [13], who conceives mental activity as the result of the cooperation and conflict between different mental entities.

Work is currently underway to implement these algorithms using "Actor Foundry", an actor based environment by the Open Systems Laboratory of University of Illinois [14], and to integrate them in a complete agent architecture based on the Active Mental Entities model [2].

References

1. P. E. Agre and D. Chapman. Pengi: An implementation of a theory of activity. In *Proceedings of AAAI-87*, pages 268–272, Seattle, WA, 1987.
2. P. Baroni and D. Fogli. Modeling robot cognitive activity through active mental entities. *Robotics and Autonomous Systems*, 30(4):325–349, 2000.
3. P. Baroni and M. Giacomin. A distributed self-stabilizing algorithm for argumentation. In *Proceedings of the 2001 International Parallel and Distributed Processing Symposium (IPDPS2001)*, San Francisco, CA, 2001. IEEE Press.
4. P. Baroni, M. Giacomin, and G. Guida. Extending abstract argumentation systems theory. *Artificial Intelligence*, 120(2):251–270, 2000.
5. R. P. Bonasso, D. Kortenkamp, D. P. Miller, and M. Slack. Experiences with an architecture for intelligent, reactive agents. In M. Wooldridge, J. P. Müller, and M. Tambe, editors, *Intelligent Agents II (LNAI 1037)*, pages 187–202. Springer-Verlag: Heidelberg, Germany, 1996.
6. A. H. Bond and L. Grasser. *Readings in Distributed Artificial Intelligence*. Morgan Kaufmann, San Mateo, 1988.
7. R. A. Brooks. A robust layered control system for a mobile robot. *IEEE Journal of Robotics and Automation*, 2(1):14–23, 1986.
8. S. Dolev. *Self-Stabilization*. MIT Press, Cambridge, MA, 2000.
9. P. M. Dung. On the acceptability of arguments and its fundamental role in nonmonotonic reasoning, logic programming, and n-person games. *Artificial Intelligence*, 77(2):321–357, 1995.
10. E. Gat. Integrating planning and reacting in a heterogeneous asynchronous architecture for controlling real-world mobile robots. In *Proceedings of AAAI-92*, pages 809–815, San Jose, CA, 1992.
11. S. Ghosh and M. H. Karaata. A self-stabilizing algorithm for coloring planar graphs. *Distributed Computing*, 7(1):55–59, 1993.
12. M. H. Karaata and F. Al-Anzi. A dynamic self-stabilizing algorithm for finding strongly connected components. In *Proceedings of the Eighteenth Annual ACM Symposium on Principles of Distributed Computing (PODC99)*, page 276, Atlanta, GA, 1999.
13. M. Minsky. *The Society of Mind*. Simon and Schuster, New York, 1986.
14. Open Systems Laboratory. The actor foundry: a java-based actor programming environment. Available for download at http://osl.cs.uiuc.edu/foundry/index.html.
15. S. Parsons, C. Sierra, and N. Jennings. Agents that reason and negotiate by arguing. *Journal of Logic and Computation*, 8(3):261–292, 1998.
16. J. L. Pollock. How to reason defeasibly. *Artificial Intelligence*, 57(1):1–42, 1992.
17. J. L. Pollock. *Cognitive Carpentry: A Blueprint for How to Build a Person*. The MIT Press, Cambridge, Massachusetts, 1995.

18. H. Prakken and G. A. W. Vreeswijk. Logics for defeasible argumentation. In D. Gabbay, editor, *Handbook of Philosophical Logic*. Kluwer Academic Publishers, Dordrecht, second edition. To appear.
19. G. A. W. Vreeswijk. Abstract argumentation systems. *Artificial Intelligence*, 90(1–2):225–279, 1997.

Replanning in a Resource-Based Framework

Roman van der Krogt, André Bos, and Cees Witteveen

Delft University of Technology
{R.P.J.vanderKrogt,A.Bos,C.Witteveen}@ITS.TUDelft.NL

Abstract. An important aspect of agents is how they construct a plan to reach their goals. Since most agents live in a dynamic environment, they also will often be confronted with situations in which the plans they constructed to reach their goals are no longer feasible. In such situations, agents have to change their plan to deal with the new environment. In this paper we describe such a replanning process using a computational framework, consisting of *resources* and *actions* to represent the planned activities of an agent.

1 Introduction

Often agents have to achieve a number of goals without a predefined way to accomplish them. Therefore, they have to make a plan that consists of a number of actions that, starting with the current situation, brings the agents to a desired state in which they have accomplished their goals. To assist an agent in such a planning task, a number of planning systems exists, e.g. Talplanner [4], Blackbox [9], FF [7] and many others. Most of such planning systems assume that the planning agent is the *sole cause of change* and that the actions have *deterministic effects*.[1] While these assumptions are necessary (but not sufficient) to make the planning process feasible, they usually no longer hold if an agent starts executing its plan in the real world. For instance, in a multi-agent environment, the agent will not likely be the only source of interactions with the world, violating the sole cause of change assumption. Moreover, in these situations, agents have to cope with unpredictable situations and actions. Hence, they are forced to adapt their original plan by *replanning* their actions.

A simple method of replanning is to give up the old plan and use a standard planning tool (such as mentioned before) to construct a new plan. This is, however, a rather inefficient approach: It will waste all the effort an agent has put in optimizing its current plan. Moreover, it might also violate agreements that have been made with other agents. Therefore, we propose a specialized plan revision method to adapt the current plan to a plan which takes into account the new situation. Unlike the approaches in [5] and [6] we do not need additional information gathered during the planning process itself, such as the reasons for adding certain steps, but we require the presence of a library of *plan schemes*, i.e. general plans that define the services an agent can provide. This library may

---

[1] See [14] for a discussion of planning systems and their assumptions.

V. Mařík et al. (Eds.): MASA 2001, LNAI 2322, pp. 148–158, 2002.
© Springer-Verlag Berlin Heidelberg 2002

contain a set of possible (pre-compiled) plan repairs, but can also come from other agents that "advertise" their services. Each such scheme can be used to adjust the plan by either *adding* a subplan to it or *removing* a subplan from it.

The replanning method discussed in this paper attempts to find a combination of such plan adjustments that transforms the current plan into a plan that can be used in the new state of the world. The paper is organized as follows: We first present the Actions and Resource Planning Formalism (ARPF) that is used to represent an agent's plan. We introduce two basic operations to adapt such plans to a new situation, and show a replanning algorithm that uses these operations. After giving some initial experimental results, we conclude by comparing our work to that of others and by sketching the future work.

2   The Action and Resource Planning Formalism

This section gives an overview of the framework that we will use to model the plan of an agent. This formalism is described in detail in [3]. We model a process, like a production or transportation, by an *action*. An application of an action consumes a set of (input) *resources* and produces a disjunct set of (output) resources. These actions can be combined to reach certain goals. Such a combination is called a *plan*.

Resources. Each resource is identified by its *type* (a predicate symbol) and the set of *values* for its *attributes*. For example, $truck(5 : id, \mathrm{StLouis} : loc, 15.^{00} : time)$ is the resource that describes truck number 5 being in St. Louis at $15.^{00}$.

A *resource scheme rs* is used to specify a set of resources sharing some attributes. Instead of ground values for attributes, a resource scheme may also contain variables specifying a set of values for an attribute.[2] For example, the resource scheme $truck(?i : id, \mathrm{StLouis} : loc, ?t : time)$ refers to the set of all trucks that are in St. Louis at some point in time.

A resource r is an *instance* of a resource scheme rs, if there exists a substitution θ of variables to values such that $rs\theta = r$. Similarly, a set of resources R satisfies a set of resource schemes Rs, denoted by $R \models_\theta Rs$, if there is a *resource-identity preserving substitution* θ such that $Rs\theta \subseteq R$.[3] Finally, we have an *extended resource scheme*, which is a tuple $\langle Rs, C \rangle$, where Rs is a set of resource schemes and C is a set of constraints that may restrict the possible resources in the extended resource scheme Rs . For example,

$$\langle \{ truck(?i_1 : id, \mathrm{StLouis} : loc, ?t_1 : time), load(?i_2 : id, \mathrm{StLouis} : loc, ?t_2 : time) \},$$
$$\{ t_1 = t_2 \} \rangle$$

denotes a truck and load in St. Louis at the same time.

---

[2] To distinguish between ground values and variables, a '?' is placed in front of a variable name, e.g., $?x$ denotes the variable x.

[3] A substitution θ is resource-identity preserving w.r.t. a set Rs of resource schemes if $\forall rs_1, rs_2 \in Rs \cdot rs_1 \neq rs_2 \rightarrow rs_1\theta \neq rs_2\theta$.

A resource set R *satisfies* an extended resource scheme $\langle Rs, C \rangle$, denoted by $R \models \langle Rs, C \rangle$ if for some resource-identity preserving substitution θ, $Rs\theta \subseteq R$ and $\models C\theta$, i.e. using θ all ground instances of constraints are valid. If the substitution θ has to be mentioned explicitly, we will also use $R \models_\theta \langle Rs, C \rangle$.

Actions. An action is a rule of the form $a : Rs_2 \leftarrow \langle Rs_1, C \rangle$. Here, a is the name of the action, Rs_2 is the set of resource schemes produced by a, Rs_1 is the set of resources schemes consumed by a and C the set constraints on Rs_1. For example,

$$driveStL : \{truck(?i : id, \mathrm{StLouis} : loc, ?t + d(?l, \mathrm{StLouis}) : time)\} \leftarrow$$
$$\langle\{truck(?i : id, ?l : loc, ?t : time)\}, \{?t > 7.^{00}, ?l \neq \mathrm{StLouis}\}\rangle$$

is an action to drive a truck to St. Louis. From a truck at some location $l \neq \mathrm{StLouis}$ at time $t > 7.^{00}$, it is possible to "produce" a truck in St. Louis at time $t + d(?l, \mathrm{StLouis})$. The set of input resources is denoted by $in(s) = Rs_1$, the output resources are denoted by $out(a) = Rs_2$. The application of an action transforms a set of resources R_1 into a set of resources R_2. Such an application is specified by a substitution θ changing each occurrence of a resource scheme in $in(a)$ and $out(a)$ to an occurrence of a fully specified resource. Let $a : Rs_2 \leftarrow \langle Rs_1, C \rangle$ be an action and let R_1 and R_2 be sets of resources. We say that R_2 can *immediately be produced from R_1 using a*, abbreviated by $R_1 \vdash_a R_2$, if there is a resource-identity preserving substitution θ such that (i) $R_1 \models_\theta Rs_1$, (ii) $\models_\theta C$ and (iii) $R_2 = (R_1 - Rs_1\theta) \cup Rs_2\theta$, i.e. all resources from $Rs_1\theta$ are removed from R_1 and the resources $Rs_2\theta$ are added. Generalising this production relation to a set of actions A, $R_1 \vdash_A R_2$ is said to hold iff there is some $a \in A$ such that $R_1 \vdash_a R_2$ holds. We will use $\vdash_A^*$ to denote the reflexive-transitive closure of $\vdash_A$.

Goals and Plans. A *goal* of an agent is a description of a resource the agent wishes to obtain. Therefore, goals will be described in terms of resource schemes. A goal g is a resource scheme. A *goal scheme* is an extended resource scheme $Gs = \langle G, C \rangle$, where G is a set of goals and C are constraints on G.

Let $\mathcal{R}$ be the set of resources and A the set of actions. Suppose that $R \vdash_A^* R'$, i.e., there exists some partially ordered set (poset) of instances of actions in A such that R' can be produced from R. This poset of instances of actions together with the ground instances of resources associated is called a *plan P*. Such a plan is a plan for a goal scheme Gs if, starting from the initial resources R, a set of R' resources is produced that satisfy Gs.

To represent a plan explicitly[4] , we use a (bi-partite) Directed Acyclic Graph $P = \langle N_\mathcal{R} \cup N_A, E \rangle$, where $N_\mathcal{R}$ is a set of *resource nodes* n_r with $r \in \mathcal{R}$, N_A a set of *action nodes* n_a where $a \in A$, and $E \subseteq (N_\mathcal{R} \times N_A) \cup (N_A \times N_\mathcal{R})$ is the set of arcs. For $n_r \in N_\mathcal{R}$ and $n_a \in N_A$, $(n_r, n_a) \in A$ means that resource r is used by an application of action a, and $(n_a, n_r) \in A$ means that resource r is

---

[4] Slightly abusing language, in the sequel we will use plans and plan graphs interchangeably.

produced by an application of a. A plan P consumes its set of *input* resources of P, denoted by $in(P)$, and produces its set of *output* resources, $out(P)$. Output resources that are not used to satisfy a goal are called *free resources*, denoted by $free(P, Gs)$, or just $free(P)$ if it is clear which goals Gs are to be satisfied. A plan P *realizes* a goal scheme Gs *using* a set of initial resources R and a substitution θ, denoted by $R \models_P Gs\theta$, if (i) $R \supseteq in(P)$ and (ii) $out(P) \cup (R - in(P)\theta) \models_\theta Gs$. If $R \models_P Gs\theta$, the triple (R, P, Gs) is called *adequate*.

Given a plan $P = (N_A \cup N_R, E)$ and a subset $N'_A \subseteq N_A$, the subplan P' *generated by* N'_A is the subgraph P' of P generated by the set of nodes $N' = N'_A \cup \bigcup_{a \in N'_A} out(a) \cup in(a)$.[5]

Plan schemes are used to denote the services an agent can provide, i.e. ways of organizing actions to obtain goals, specifying the input resources needed to obtain them by providing (extended) resource schemes. Hence, plan schemes contain resource schemes to label the resource nodes. They can be simply defined as follows: If Ps is a plan scheme, θ a ground substitution that assigns a value to every variable occurring in Ps and every ground instance of a constraint occurring in Ps is valid, $Ps\theta$ is a plan. Plans, therefore, also can be considered as special cases of plan schemes.

3   Plan Repair and Plan Operators

Suppose that an agent is able to achieve a goal scheme Gs using a plan P with initial resources R, i.e., the triple (R, P, Gs) is adequate. Since the agents operate in a dynamic environment, initial resources as well as the availability of actions and the goals to be achieved might change. So, after some time, the agent might discover that instead of the adequate triple (R, P, Gs), the actual set of available resources is R', the realizable part of his original plan is P', the actual goal scheme is Gs' and the triple (R', P', Gs') is no longer adequate.

Hence, his current plan P' has to be adapted. We thus concentrate on the following *replanning problem*:

> Given an adequate triple (R, P, Gs), an actual set of resources R', a realizable part P' of P and a goal scheme Gs', find a plan P'' such that (R', P'', Gs') is an adequate triple, i.e., there exists some substitution θ such that $R' \models_{P''} Gs'\theta$.

We will solve this problem by *changing* the plan P' to P''. Note that P' might fail for exactly one or both of the following reasons: (i) $out(P') \not\models Gs'$ i.e., P' is not able to satisfy the current goals; (ii) $in(P') - R' \neq \emptyset$, i.e., P' lacks some resources to satisfy the goals.

Note that both cases (and their combination) can be specified as a triple (R', P', Ers) where Ers is an extended resource scheme, specifying the (set of) resources needed in addition to P' and R' to satisfy all goals.[6]

---

[5] The subgraph of $G = (N, E)$ generated by a subset $N' \subseteq N$ equals $G' = (N', (N' \times N') \cap E)$.

[6] That is, there exists a substitution θ such that $(R' \cup Ers\theta, P', Gs')$ is adequate.

In order to obtain such a set of *missing resources* satisfying *Ers*, we might try to *add* a plan P_{add} to P' having *Ers* as its goal scheme such that the resulting plan can use R' to satisfy Gs'. Addition alone however might not suffice: sometimes we first have to *delete* some part of the existing plan and then add another plan to achieve the additional goals.[7]

We now describe these plan addition and deletion operators and then show that their combination is sufficient to guarantee a successful change whenever there exists a solution to the replanning problem.

Addition. The addition operator $\oplus$ adds two plans P and P' to form a larger plan $P'' = P \oplus P'$. Addition of plans, like deletion, however, is defined if they are *compatible* w.r.t. their resources and actions. Therefore, we will first define this compatibility relation:

Definition 1. *Let* $P = (N = N_{\mathcal{R}} \cup N_A, E)$ *and* $P' = (N' = N'_{\mathcal{R}} \cup N'_A, E')$ *be plans over a set of resources* $\mathcal{R}$ *and actions* A. *Then* P *and* P' *are said to be* compatible *if the following conditions hold:*

- *for every node* $n \in N_{\mathcal{R}} \cap N'_{\mathcal{R}}$, ($(n, a) \in E \wedge (n, a') \in E'$ *or* $(a, n) \in E \wedge (a', n) \in E'$) *implies* $a = a'$; *That is, if* P *and* P' *have common resources, then these resources are neither produced nor consumed by different actions.*
- *for every action* $a \in N_A \cap N'_A$, $out_P(a) = out_{P'}(a)$ *and* $in_P(a) = in_{P'}(a)$; *That is, if* P *and* P *have actions in common, then these actions consume and produce the same sets of resources.*
- $(N \cup N', E \cup E')$ *is an acyclic graph.*

Together these conditions guarantee that $P'' = (N \cup N', E \cup E')$ is a plan. Hence, for two compatible plans $P = (N, E)$ and $P' = (N', E')$, $P \oplus P'$ is simply defined as the plan $(N \cup N', E \cup E')$.

Example 1. Figure 1 shows an example use of the $\oplus$-operator. The different letters denote different resources, the numbered boxes represent actions. Action 2 is common to both plans, as are the resources C, D, E and F. The resulting plan has one new input resource, H, but does no longer require the resource D.

Deletion. Deleting a plan P' from a plan P is denoted as $P \ominus P'$, and is done by (i) removing the *common action part* of P and P' from P and generating the resulting plan from the remaining actions. So, for two compatible plans $P = (N_A \cup N_{\mathcal{R}}, E)$ and $P' = (N'_A \cup N'_{\mathcal{R}}, E')$, $P'' = P \ominus P'$ is defined as the subplan of $P \oplus P'$ generated by the set of remaining actions $N''_A = (N_A \cup N'_A) \setminus (N_A \cap N'_A)$.

Example 2. Referring to Fig. 1, if we would not add, but subtract the plan, the result would be the plan with actions 1 and 3, and resources A, B, C, E, G.

The following result can be easily proven:

---

[7] For example, if there are not enough input resources for the combined plan.

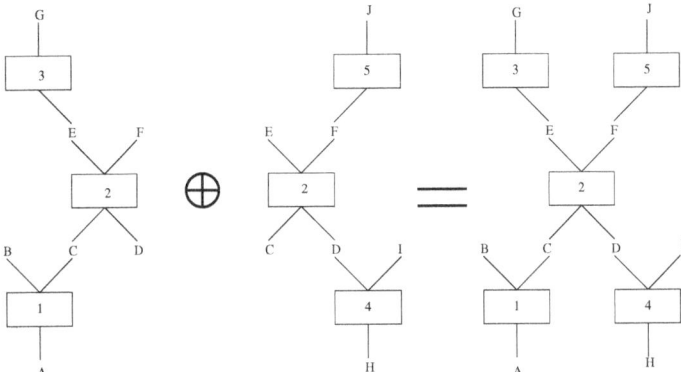

Fig. 1. Example use of the $\oplus$-operator. Here, a plan that produces resources B, F and G is shown on the left and we add to it and instantiated plan scheme that produces E, I and J.

Proposition 1. *Given an inadequate triple (R, P, Gs) and a plan P' be such that (R, P', Gs) is adequate. Then there always exist plans P_1 and P_2 such that $P" = (P \ominus P_1) \oplus P_2)$.*

Note that a sequence of a deletion followed by an addition also can be described by taking a replacement operator $\otimes$.

4   Replanning Using the Plan Operators

Although these operators are sufficient to describe all necessary changes, in real planning situations we will need a more refined approach. In this section we will describe how both addition and deletion can be described by iterative plan change processes using a library of plan schemes. This section will show how these operators can be combined in a replanning algorithm. Recall that our problem is to change a plan P in an inadequate triple (R, P, Gs) to a plan P' such that (R, P', Gs) is adequate. It can be proven that the three mentioned operators are sufficient to transform one plan into another, given a suitable plan scheme library. This section will show how these operators can be combined in a replanning algorithm. Recall that, initially, there is a plan P that satisfies certain goals Gs. Because of some events, this goal set Gs is changed to a goal set $Gs' = (Gs \setminus G_D) \cup G_A$, i.e. some of the goals are no longer needed and can be removed (G_D), while others must be newly satisfied (G_A). Proposition 1 states that we can transform the current plan P to the desired plan P' by using one addition and one deletion: $P' = (P \ominus Ps_1\sigma_1) \oplus Ps_2\sigma_2$. In practice however, it is very unlikely that the schemes Ps_1 and Ps_2 occur in our plan scheme library. Instead, we have to search for a sequence of smaller transformations, that together transform the plan completely. This leads to an iterative search procedure in which we, given the current situation (R, P, Ers), try to satisfy a

Algorithm 1. HOWTO

HOWTO(plan P, plan scheme Ps)
1. **if** all outputs of Ps are available in P **then**
       return$\langle\emptyset,\emptyset\rangle$
2. **let** $Ps' = Ps$
3. **let** $Ers = \emptyset$
4. **for** all skills $s \in Ps$ that produce outputs of Ps that are not available in P **do**
       4.1. **let** $\langle Ps', Ers'\rangle =$ CHECK_SKILL(s, P, Ps')
       4.2. **let** $Ers = Ers \cup Ers'$
5. **return**$\langle P \oplus Ps', Ers\rangle$

CHECK_SKILL (skill s, plan P, plan scheme Ps)
1. **if** s is marked **then**
       1.1. **return** $\langle Ps, \langle\emptyset,\emptyset\rangle\rangle$
2. **else**
       2.1. MARK(s)
3. **let** $\langle Rs, C\rangle =$GET_CONSTRAINTS(s)
4. **let** R be the set of resources r, such that $\exists rs \in Rs \cdot r \models rs \wedge C(r)$ is satisfiable

5. **let** $R' \subseteq R$ be the set of resources, such that $R' \models Rs' \wedge C(R')$ is satisfiable, where $R' \subseteq R$ is the largest subset of R that can be formed this way.
6. **let** $Rs^* = Rs - Rs'$
7. **let** $Ps' = Ps$, with all skills removed that are used solely for the production of resources from $Rs - Rs^*$
8. **if** $Rs^* = \emptyset$ **then**
       8.1. **return** $\langle Ps', \langle\emptyset,\emptyset\rangle\rangle$
9. **else**
       9.1. **let** $Ers = \langle\emptyset,\emptyset\rangle$
       9.2. **for** all skills s' that produce resource schemes of Rs^* **do**
           9.2.1. **let** $\langle Ps', Ers'\rangle =$ CHECK_SKILL(s', P, Ps')
           9.2.2. **let** $Ers = Ers \cup Ers'$
       9.3. **return**$\langle Ps', Ers\rangle$

---

subset Er of the needed resources Ers using a plan scheme Ps. As we have seen in Example 1, the addition of a plan scheme may introduce new input resources R_{req}. Therefore, during each iteration, the current situation is changed to the situation $(R, P \oplus Ps\sigma, Ers')$, where $Ers' = (Ers \setminus Er) \cup R_{req}$. After satisfying the new goals by adding plan schemes, the plan may contain actions that are not used for goal production. These have to be identified and removed using the $\ominus$-operator. The remainder of this section will discuss the functions to adapt the current plan using plan schemes in a library.

HOWTO: Adding Plan Schemes. In cases where removal of parts of the existing plan is not necessary, we may try to add plan schemes iteratively in order to satisfy one or more resources that are needed in the current situation. The plan schemes may be instantiated in different ways, affecting the way the plan is adapted. To perform an iteration step we introduce a function HOWTO to find out how to instantiate a given plan scheme Ps in a most efficient way, i.e. to find a substitution σ such that the number of new input resources to the plan is minimized. The HOWTO procedure (which is outlined in Algorithm 1) works as follows: Given the current plan P, satisfying goals Gs using initial resources R, i.e. $R \models_P G\theta$, it takes a goal g that is to be provided. HOWTO then computes an instantiation of Ps and an extended resource scheme Ers such that $R \cup Ers\tau \models_{P \oplus Ps\sigma} (G \cup g)\tau$, for some substitution τ. HOWTO then constructs the new plan $P' = P \oplus Ps\sigma$ and returns a tuple $\langle P', Ers\rangle$ consisting of the new plan and the missing resources Ers. Note that a new iteration step might consist in selecting some missing resource scheme from Ers as a goal and so on.

OVERLAP: Replacing Plan Schemes. Another function to obtain information about how to apply a single plan scheme during one iteration of the search is called OVERLAP and will be used to find a sub plan P' of P that can be removed in order to efficiently add an instantiated plan scheme $Ps\sigma$. This information is then used to implement the $\otimes$-operator, resulting in a plan $P'' = (P \ominus P') \oplus Ps\sigma$.

Like HOWTO, OVERLAP is given the current plan and a plan scheme Ps. It returns either *failure*, if it cannot find a suitable subplan of P to remove to make room for Ps, or a new plan in which Ps is applied to the plan using $\otimes$. The OVERLAP-procedure starts by locating which resources r_o are present in the plan that can also be provided by the plan scheme. These resources are the starting point for determining if part of the plan can be *replaced* by the plan scheme. From these resources, we search backwards in the plan to see if we can find resources r_i that correspond to input resource schemes of Ps. In short, the actions between r_i and r_o can be replaced by Ps.[8] If no such actions can be found, OVERLAP returns *failure*. After determining which subplan P' can be removed and which instantiation σ of the plan scheme to use, OVERLAP removes P' and uses the $\oplus$-operator on the plan $P \ominus P'$ and $Ps\sigma$ to obtain $P'' = P \otimes (P', Ps\sigma)$ i.e., the plan P where P' has been replaced by $\mathit{Ps\sigma}$. It also computes an extended resource scheme Ers that describes the new input resources that are to be provided. Then OVERLAP constructs a new plan $P'' = P \otimes (P', Ps\sigma)$ and returns the tuple $\langle P'', Ers \rangle$ consisting of the new plan P' and the missing resources Ers.

REMOVE_ACTIONS: Removing Obsolete Actions. After we have found a plan that satisfies the current set of goals, the plan still may contain actions that are used to produce actions that are not used to satisfy goals. These obsolete actions are removed by the function REMOVE_ACTIONS which will determine the actions of a plan P that can be removed. This is done by examining all actions a in the plan, and if $out(a) \subseteq free(P)$, then a can be removed using the $\ominus$-operator. Of course, removing a has implications for any actions a' for which $out(a') \cap in(a) \neq \emptyset$, i.e., actions that produce the resources that a consumed. An efficient scheme has to be developed for examining a plan for obsolete actions. Such scheme works as follows: We keep a list *obs* of resources that are not needed anymore. Initially, this list consists of the resources that satisfy the obsolete goals. One by one, the resources $r \in obs$ are removed from *obs* and examined: If the action a that produces r only produces unused resources, then a is removed and the resources $in(a)$ are added to *obs*. This continues until $obs = \emptyset$. The resulting plan has no actions of which products are not used. However, in some instances the plan can be further optimized by using some of the resources that have just become free. In these cases, plan merging techniques such as [3] can be used to optimize it.

Heuristic Search. We have combined the functions described above to implement a best-first search replanning algorithm to transform a plan into a plan

---

[8] Though this is quite a simplification of things, we omit the details for brevity.

that satisfies a new goal set G'. First, the current plan of the agent is expanded by using HOWTO and OVERLAP on all possible plan schemes. This produces a set of partial plans, from which we select a cheapest one. This plan is removed from the set and expanded. This produces a new set of partial plans, consisting of the partial plans of the first expansion, combined with those of the second expansion. Again, we select a cheapest partial plan and expand it. This continues until we have found a solution. When we have found a solution, we have found a solution, i.e. a plan satisfying G'. Finally, this plan is simplified by using REMOVE_ACTIONS.

5 Experimental Results

This section presents some preliminary results, as reported in [13]. The experiments were conducted as follows: First, we generated a plan with Blackbox for the four problems. Two of the problems (number 3 and 4) were from the AIPS planning competition, the two others were constructed by ourselves in ARPF. These consisted of a graph of 9 locations in which 2 trucks drive around, that can each move two loads simultaneously. A STRIPS translation of these plans was made to feed the Blackbox planner.

After making the initial plans, we randomly selected new goals for the AIPS problems and constructed a number of hard goals for our own problems. Then we ran Blackbox again for the new problems, and our own algorithm with the initial plan. Table 1 contains an overview of some running times for the four different problems. For different queuing strategies (different cost functions) we ran a series of 10 tests to see what the average time to complete was, and which size the resulting plans had. The *minimum* and *maximum* times in the table refer to the average time of the fastest and slowest strategy, the *average* time is the average of the average time for each strategy. As one can see, even in the worst cases, we performed better than Blackbox (whose time was also averaged over 10 runs). Note that the STRIPS translation of our framework contains a lot of overhead, which is why the difference is exceptionally large on these problems.

Table 1 also contains the results for the size of the solutions found. Again, the *minimum* and *maximum* sizes refer to the average size of the shortest and longest plans and the *average* size is the average of the average sizes. Here, we perform worse than Blackbox. In some cases, our solution is slightly better, but in general we do not find an optimal solution, considering the number of steps. One advantage we do have, however, is that we remain close to the original plan, where Blackbox sometimes finds a completely different plan.

6 Evaluation

We have remarked that a plan that is created under the assumptions of deterministic effects and sole cause of change may not remain valid in a dynamic environment. Other agents or failing actions may bring an agent into a situation where its plan becomes obsolete or inefficient. If this happens, the agent has to

Table 1. Time (in seconds) required to solve a problem and the size (in actions) of the resulting plan.

time	Prob 1	Prob 2	Prob 3	Prob 4
Minimum	0.35	1.58	0.10	0.20
Average	0.85	5.98	0.46	0.65
Maximum	1.73	9.47	0.73	0.98
Blackbox	233.36	508.30	2.53	43.93

size	Prob 1	Prob 2	Prob 3	Prob 4
Minimum	16.0	20.0	17.6	26.0
Average	18.7	22.5	18.2	26.5
Maximum	31.2	33.3	18.7	27.8
Blackbox	16.0	22.0	18.0	23.0

create a new plan. We proposed the use of generic plan-adjustment operators to adapt the current plan to the new situation. We showed how these operators are defined in the Action and Resource Planning Formalism and showed an iterative algorithm based on them and some initial experimental results with this algorithm

Future work includes a more efficient implementation and the incorporation of an interesting idea called *Sliding Scale of Commitment* (SSC) of Kott and Saks [10]. The principle underlying SSC is based on the observation that in general it is less worse to break a commitment far in the future than one whose deadline is soon. This heuristic adds extra costs to the plan changes the affect commitments in the near future. Furthermore, we are working on an *ordered plan scheme library*, to try more preferred plan schemes first.

Other approaches to plan modification have been proposed. Gerevini and Serina [5] have proposed a system that is based on Graphplan [2]. Their method requires that additional data structures that were used during the planning phase are still available during the replanning process. This also holds for the solution of Hanks and Weld [6], which records the *reasons* for each step that is taken during planning, and for the plan modification theory of Kambhampati [8], which relies on a *validation structure* that is computed during planning. An advantage of our method is that it does not require such additional data structures to remain available.

Ambite and Knoblock [1] also introduce the concept of plan operations. Their *plan rewriting rules* are domain-dependent however. Also, their system only considers complete plans, which greatly reduces the search space. This may mean that a large number of solutions cannot be found, and that the approach will not work once a plan is already broken. This makes it less suitable for use as a replanning method.

Another approach towards robust plan execution is to generate plans that already have measures to handle incidents. These plans have so-called conditional effects (see, e.g. [12]) depending on the actual situation of the world. The problem with this approach is that at forehand all possible contingencies must be enumerated together with the corresponding countermeasures (but see [11] for a discussion of selecting important contingencies).

References

1. J.L. Ambite and C.A. Knoblock. Planning by rewriting: Effiently generating high-quality plans. In *Proceedings of the 14th National Conference on Artificial Intelligence (AAAI-97)*, pages 706–713, Providence, Rhode Island, 1997. AAAI Press/MIT Press.
2. A.L. Blum and M.L. Furst. Fast planning through planning graph analysis. *Artificial Intelligence*, 90:281–300, 1997.
3. M.M. de Weerdt, A. Bos, H. Tonino, and C. Witteveen. A resource logic for multi-agent plan merging. *Submitted to the Annals of Mathematics and Artificial Intelligence*, 2001.
4. P. Doherty and J. Kvarnstrom. Talplanner: An empirical inverstigation of a temporal logicbased forward chaining planner, 1999.
5. A. Gerevini and I. Serina. Fast plan adaptation through planning graphs: Local and systematic search techniques. In *Proceedings of the Fifth International Conference on Artificial Intelligence Planning Systems (AIPS-00)*, pages 112–121, 2000.
6. S. Hanks and D.S. Weld. A domain-independent algorithm for plan adaptation. *Journal of AI Research*, 2:319–360, 1995.
7. J. Hoffmann and B. Nebel. Fast plan generation trough heuristic search, 2000.
8. S. Kambhampati. A theory of plan modification. In *Proceedings of the Eighth National Conference on Artificial Intelligence (AAAI-90)*, pages 176–182, Boston, Massachusetts, USA, 1990. AAAI Press/MIT Press.
9. H. Kautz and B. Selman. BLACKBOX: A new approach to the application of theorem proving to problem solving. In *Working notes of the workshop on planning as combinatorial search, held in conjunction with AIPS'98*, Pittsburgh, PA, 1998.
10. A. Kott and V. Saks. Continuity-guided regeneration: An approach to reactive replanning and rescheduling. In *Proceedings of the Florida AI Research Symposium*, 1996.
11. N. Onder. *Contingency Selection in Plan Generation*. PhD thesis, University of Pittsburgh, 1999.
12. L. Pryor and G. Collins. Planning for contingencies: A decision-based approach. *Journal of Artificial Intelligence Research*, 4:287–339, 1996.
13. R.P.J. van der Krogt. *Replanning methods in a skill-based framework*. Master's thesis, Delft University of Technology, Delft, August 2000.
14. D.S. Weld. Recent advances in AI planning. *AI Magazine*, 20(2):93–123, 1999.

Distributed Branch and Bound Algorithm in Coalition Planning

Jaroslav Bárta, Olga Štěpánková, and Michal Pěchouček

Gerstner Laboratory, Department of Cybernetics
Czech Technical University in Prague
Technická 2, 166 27 Prague, Czech Republic
{barta, step, pechouc}@labe.felk.cvut.cz

Abstract. We suggest the Distributed Branch and Bound Algorithm intended for solving problems with exponential complexity e.g. coalition planning. This technique consists of three parts: the state space distribution, effective search algorithm and partial solution expansion. We will describe CPlanT – an OOTW (operations other than war) coalition planning multi-agent system where this approach has been exploited.

1 Introduction

The main practical mission of Multi-Agent Systems and DPS (Distributed Problem Solvers) is behavioral representation of heterogeneous systems and planning their specific goal-oriented actions, e.g. the production planning [1]. An important research area of DAI has been coalition planning. We will introduce a novel approach (**anytime, decentralized, exhaustive** and **optimal algorithm**) to solving problems with exponential complexity like coalition planning. Our approach is different from coalition planning algorithms presented in [2,3,4], because we have replaced *coalition value* and *utility function* by *estimates of coalition price* (Sect. 1.1) and of *price evaluation function* F^* (Sect. 2.2). Distributed Branch and Bound Algorithm (Sect. 2) consists of three parts: the state space distribution (Sect. 2.1), effective search algorithm (Sects. 2.2 and 2.4) and partial solution expansion (Sect. 2.3). Properties of this algorithm will be presented in Sect. 2.5 and in Sect. 3 we will briefly describe CPlanT – coalition planning multi-agent system implementing specific modification of this approach.

1.1 Task Specification

Multi-Agent Systems and *Distributed Problem Solvers* are being developed for solving various tasks. Tasks are defined either by requirements for services or requirements for abilities of agents. It is necessary to find a group of agents (coalition), which can fulfill the task using cooperation and coordination methods. If we require intelligent

V. Mařík et al. (Eds.): MASA 2001, LNAI 2322, pp. 159–168, 2002.
© Springer-Verlag Berlin Heidelberg 2002

behavior from the system then we search for the coalition meeting specific criteria, for example price, utility, etc.

Let us consider a set of agents $A = \{A_1, A_2, ... A_N\}$ and a set $S = \{S_1, S_2, ... S_J\}$ of requirements the agents can be asked to meet. These requirements, called services, can be requested in certain amount of neccessary goods e.g. weight. Of course, each agent A_i is able to provide a part of these services (denoted as AS_i) only, namely the set $AS_i \subseteq S$. Moreover, each agent has limited capacity for any service. All this information is coded in the form of a matrix Ψ, its element Ψ_{ij} has the value 0 if the agent A_i is not equipped to provide the service S_j, else Ψ_{ij} is the capacity of the agent A_i to provide service S_j.

Let's define a *task* T and a *task structure* $T_{STR} = \{T_1, T_2,..... T_K\}$ consisting of a set of individual tasks T_i. Let the task T be described by a list of numbers corresponding to the requested amount of required services (requirements) $\{R_1, R_2,..... R_J\}$. We say that a set of agents $C \subseteq A = \{A_1, A_2, ... A_L\}$ satisfies the task T if C covers appropriate amount of all services S_i required in T, i.e. for any $i \leq J$ holds that the sum of services S_i of all agents in C is higher or equal to the amount R_i of service S_i required by the task T. A *task structure* $T_{STR} = \{T_1, T_2,..... T_K\}$ consists of a set of individual tasks T_i and a *coalition structure* $C_{STR} = \{C_1, C_2, ... C_K\}$ consists of mutually disjoint *coalitions*. Coalition structure C_{STR} solves T_{STR} if $\forall i$ $(C_i$ solves $T_i)$, where

$$\forall i \leq K : C_i \subseteq A, \tag{1a}$$

$$\forall i, j \leq K; i \neq j : C_i \bigcap C_j = \emptyset. \tag{1b}$$

The condition 1b has a simple consequence:

$$\bigcap_{i=1}^{K} C_i = \emptyset. \tag{2}$$

Let us consider task T and an agent A, who is able to contribute to solution of the task T. For each task T and each agent A there is fixed price $P(A,T) > 0$ for all services the agent A can contribute to the task (motivated by transport example, see Sect. 1.2).

Price of a coalition C, which has been formed in order to satisfy the task T, is the sum of prices of individual agents in C, formally:

$$P(C,T) = \sum_{A \in C} P(A_i,T). \tag{3}$$

When an agent joins a coalition, the resulting new coalition can resolve a broader set of tasks and new coalition price is higher than the original coalition price. An *optimal coalition* is any coalition satisfying the task T with the lowest coalition price compared to all possible ones.

Price of a coalition structure C_{STR}, which has been formed in order to satisfy the task structure T_{STR}, is the sum of coalition prices of individual coalitions in C_{STR}, formally:

$$P(C_{STR}, T_{STR}) = \sum_{i=1}^{K} P(C_i, T_i). \tag{4}$$

An *optimal coalition structure* is any coalition structure satisfying the task structure T_{STR} with the lowest coalition structure price compared to all possible ones.

To fulfill the task T, we have to identify such a set of agents, that its members can achieve the task T by applying cooperation methods. We can generate 2^N coalitions obviously. To find the optimal coalition it is impossible to use "generate and test" problem solving methodology in systems with high number of agents.

1.2   Brief Domain Description, Example

Our research has been motivated by coalition formation problems in planning the humanitarian relief operations. In this case, independent nongovernmental organizations (NGO) are ready to contribute to and participate in joint operations that provide humanitarian aid to the suffering regions. Let's have N cargo airplanes (agents). Each airplane A_i is defined by an airport where it is located and volume of its capacity. Each airport is defined by location (longitude and latitude) and list of available material with specific volume (content of its store). Applying formalism defined above we will have either

- task T : to deliver material R_i of volume R_{vi} to any place X, which is defined by longitude and latitude, or
- task structure T_{STR} consisting of the tasks T_1 and T_2:
  - T_1 to deliver material R_i of volume R_{vi} to any place X,
  - T_2 to deliver material R_j of volume R_{vj} to any place Y.

Let us define $P(A_i, T) = distance(location\ of\ A_i, X)$, provided A_i is situated at the airport which stores material R_i (or R_j). Then we have to find such C or $C_{STR} = \{C_1, C_2\}$; $C_1 \cap C_2 = \varnothing$ of airplanes, which satisfy T or T_{STR} and which minimize the price of coalition C or the price of coalition structure C_{STR} defined in (3) or (4). Moreover, the total sum of agents' capacities in C (or C_{STR}) has to be higher than R_{vi} (or R_{vi} plus R_{vj}).

2   Distributed Branch and Bound Algorithm

We have specified the task T in the previous section. An algorithm is denoted as *anytime* if it provides ever a solution – this solution need not to be an optimal one in the case the algorithm is interrupted before reaching its end. Now we present an anytime, decentralized and exhaustive coalition planning algorithm, which finds the optimal coalition [5]. The presented algorithm is divided into three parts: (i) state space distribution, (ii) search algorithm, (iii) partial solution expansion. All algorithm parts are explained more precisely below.

2.1   State Space Distribution

Let us assume we have a list (totally ordered set) of all agents, called the *agent-list*. We will search to find the optimal coalition C in the space of all possible coalitions (which is 2^N). Each coalition is presented in a unique way to that the original ordering of agent is preserved, this is ensured by agents ID introduced later in this paragraph. The root of the state space is equivalent to an *empty coalition* (consisting of no agent). The agent can be added to the coalition as the last member, if its position index in the *agent-list* is higher then position index of the last member in coalition. The full state space for 3 agents is shown at Fig. 1.

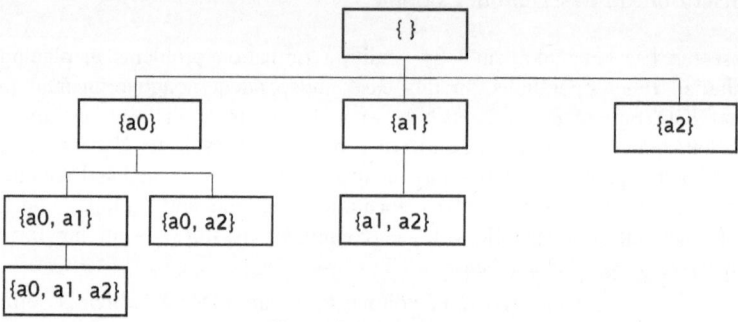

Fig. 1. Full state space

We will distribute the state space among available agents (computing units). The agents are sorted by their unique name in the *agent-list* and then identification number (ID) is assigned to each agent. The agent updates his *agent-list* if a new agent occurs in community or some agent is shut down. The agent considers coalition with agents of higher ID than its own ID (see Fig. 2). The agent has all necessary information about his potential partners in his social model [1] which is build as a result if initialization process. We will suggest three initialization processes: *a ring technology* [5], *a broadcast mechanism* and *a half broadcast mechanism*. While the first two initialization processes update service information of every agent about all agents in community then the last one updates service information of every agent about these agents only, which the agent considers as possible coalition members (see Fig. 2). We will use the following factors for initialization process description: the *number of messages* and the *number of time units*. For simplicity we suppose that each of the following steps can be done in a single time unit: encoding (or coding) information about any single agent from (or to) a message, removing the first part of information from a message, a message sending and receiving, all above with respect to possible parallelism. The ring technology requires *2*N-1* messages and it takes $N^2+3*N-1$ time units, the broadcast mechanism requires N^2-N messages and it takes *2*N-1* time units and the half broadcast mechanism requires $(N^2-N)/2$ messages and it takes *2*N-1* time units. A solution without using social model appears in [6].

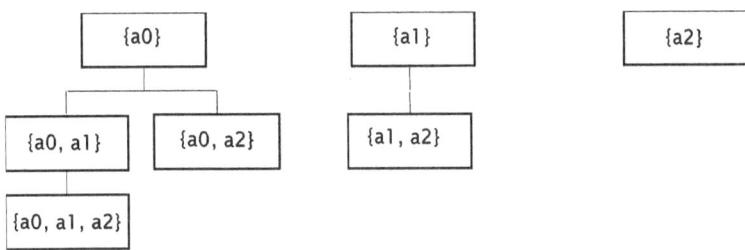

Fig. 2. State space distribution among three agents. Let us consider a system consisting of three agents. We will not consider state equivalent to the *empty coalition*. The state space on the left side is assigned to agent *A0* (ID=1, it is the first agent in *agent-list*), the state space in the middle of the figure is assigned to agent *A1* (ID=2, it is the second agent in *agent-list*) and the state space on the right side is assigned to agent *A2* (ID=3, it is the third agent in *agent-list*)

2.2 Search Algorithm

Each agent uses **Branch and Bound Algorithm** [7] for searching the part of state space that has been allocated to him according to the definitions given in 2.1. The transition between the states s_1 and s_2 corresponds to adding an agent to the present coalition (see Fig. 3). The boundary is determined as an estimate of the minimal coalition price for the actual coalition satisfying the task T, which agents have found since start up to this moment. This estimate for a state (coalition) evaluation is inspired by evaluation function used in A^* algorithm [7]. It consists of two parts [5]:

$$F^* = G + H^*, \tag{5}$$

where G is equivalent to the actual coalition price and H^* provides the admissible price estimate for all the agents, which will have to be added to the actual coalition to satisfy the task T. By using the combined function (5) we reduce the state space due to similar reasons as in A^* algorithm: F^* is better low estimate than in the case when H^* is equal to zero and we consider these states only from which we can generate some coalition which can satisfy the task T. Now we describe the algorithm for H^* specification more precisely.

Let us consider a *state* consisting of an *actual coalition* $C \subseteq A$, an *actual coalition price*, a non covered part T_u of the task T which the actual coalition C is not able to achieve and a *set* $S \subseteq A$ *of possible collaborators* (agents which can satisfy a nonempty part of requirements of the task T_u and which have ID higher than ID of the last member of the coalition C). The admissible price estimate (H^*) is defined with T_u and S:

```
min_number = 0
for every task service from Tᵤ do
        begin
        min_number_req = Determine minimal number of agents from S which
        will have to be added for satisfying the actual requirement
        if agents from S are not able to satisfy the actual requirement
        (min_number_req == NIL) then remove state from consideration
        else if min_number_req > min_number then
                min_number = min_number_req
        end.
H* = Sum of min_number agent prices from AGENT_price_list
```

The list of collaborators is defined for every task requirement sorted by specific task requirement from the highest to the lowest number before the search starts. There is a list of agents sorted by their price starting with the lowest price. The list is created before searching starts. It is clear that H^* is admissible, because we determine the minimal number of agents from the set S which will have to be added to the actual coalition for satisfying the task T and then we take the minimal agent prices from the set S (see Fig. 3).

Complexity of Specifying H^* Value. During `min_number_req` specification we have to search full list of all the agents. In the worst case we perform N operations. If we consider R requirements in the task T and the sum of `min_number` over all agents, then in the worst case we have to perform $(R+1)*N$ operations which is O(N). We have to store R agent lists sorted by requirement amount for H^* value specification. We have to update these lists for every expanded state then we have to perform $R*N$ operations in the worst case for every expanded state. In total we have to perform $(2*R+1)*N$ operations for every generated state, which is O(N).

These operations are performed once before searching starts: we have to sort R times agents by amount of their requirements – it is $R*N*log(N)$. We make $R*N*log(N) + (2*R+1)*N$ operations in the worst case for the first state, which is O(N*logN).

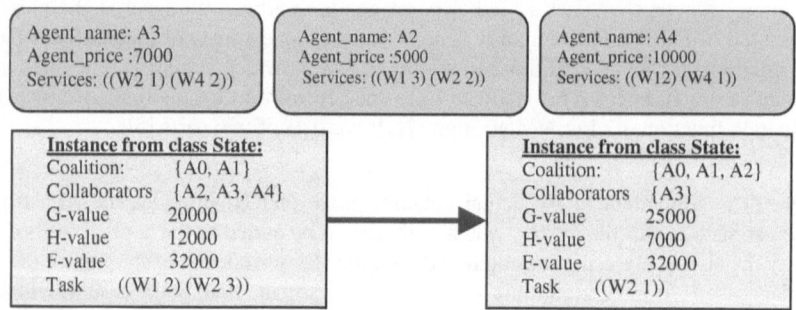

Fig.3. Generating a new state by joining the agent A2 to the coalition. The *Task* consists of two requirements (W_1 with required number 2 and W_2 with required number 3) in left placed instance from a class *State* (see Fig. 3). We need one agent for covering the requirement W_1 and two agents for covering the requirement W_2. *H-value* equals to the sum of two the lowest prices of agents (5000 + 7000 = 12000). Then we expand left placed state by joining agent A_2 to the *Coalition*, which results in right placed instance from a class *State*. The task consists of one requirement only, *G-value* has grown with price of agent A_2 and *H-value* is determined the same way as in the last step

2.3   Partial Solution Expansion

Each agent uses Branch and Bound Algorithm for searching the part of state space that has been allocated to him according to definitions given in 2.1. Let us define a set of coalitions SC_t, which satisfy all the requirements of task T and which have been found by the searching agent since searching started up to the time t. The actual boundary is equivalent to the coalition $C_t \in SC_t$ with the lowest price. For two different time samples C_i, C_j there holds:

$$\forall i, j; i \le j: P(Ci, T) \le P(Cj, T). \tag{6}$$

The boundary is shared among all agents. When the agent finds a coalition, which satisfies all the task T requirements, and its price is lower then a price of the actual coalition (actual boundary), then the agent updates the new coalition and informs the other searching agents (new boundary is found). Upon receiving this information, the agents update their lower bounds. After finishing the latest computation process, all agents are aware of the cheapest coalition, which satisfies the task T. We call this methodology Distributed Branch and Bound Algorithm (below only DB&B).

2.4   Fast Algorithm for Agents' State Space Search

We have designed and implemented coalition planning algorithm with very fast time responses (see Fig. 4), The main idea of the fast algorithm is based on utilization of parallel search [7] instead of simple Branch and Bound algorithm. We have used the state space distribution described in section 2.1, the solution expansion described in section 2.3 and the state space assigned to the agent is analyzed using parallel search limited by specific **branching factor** [5]. The number of expanded states is always equal or lower than the branching factor. For expanding process we choose the states with the lowest price estimate. The 'OPEN' list consists of the new generated states only, which are sorted by the price estimation (F*). The final algorithm is decentralized and exhaustive but it is neither optimal nor anytime. Experiments showed that algorithm does not find the optimal solution necessarily but results are very close to the optimal coalition (see Fig. 4). If we consider very fast time responses then anytime feature of algorithms is not important for us. We have performed several experiments to compare DB&B algorithm with the algorithm using fast search of the state space with the branching factor equal to two. It is clear that the higher branching factor the better solution is in the sense of coalition price and time requirements grow minimally.

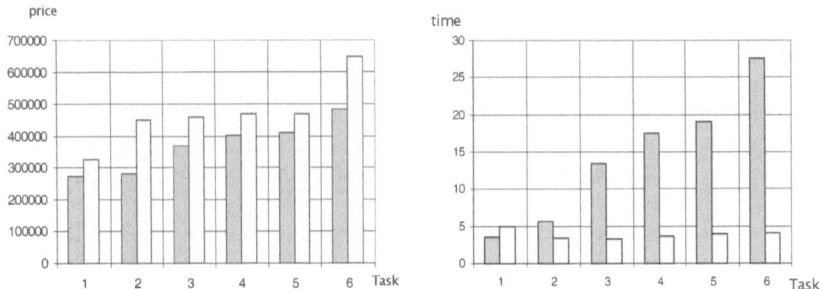

Fig. 4. Searching algorithm comparison: Branch and Bound algorithm (left columns, Sect. 2.2) and algorithm with fast search of the state space (right columns, Sect. 2.4). Left graph compares quality of algorithms, right graph compares time responses of algorithms

2.5 Properties of Both Described Algorithms

We distinguish among a number of expanded states, a number of generated states, a number of received messages and a number of performed operations. Now we will describe properties of DB&B algorithm in two cases, the first if agents use Branch and Bound (Sect. 2.2) searching algorithm and if agents use fast search algorithm (Sect. 2.4).

1. Let us consider the Branch and Bound algorithm. We have shown in [5] that it does not reduce original exponential complexity of generated states. The worst case complexity of the number of messages during computing process is exponential too. However our experimental results can be expressed using polynomials: the number of expanded states by all agents didn't exceed N^3 in most cases, then the number of generated states by all agents is not higher than N^4 and the number of operations performed by all agents is not higher than N^5. The number of messages received by all agents didn't exceed N^2.

2. Let us consider the fast search algorithm. We have proved in [5] $O(N)$ complexity of the number of expanded states, $O(N^2)$ complexity of the number of generated states and $O(N^3)$ complexity of the number of performed operations by an agent. Complexities for whole community we have proved too: $O(N^2)$ of the number of expanded states, $O(N^3)$ of the number of generated states and $O(N^4)$ of the number of performed operations. The number of received messages by all agents didn't exceed N^2.

3 CPlanT

Fast algorithm for agents' state space search has been applied in CPlanT (Coalition PLANning Tool) multi-agent system. CPlanT[1] (Coalition PLANning Tool) is a multi-agent system prototype for experimenting with collaborative operations planning, where each community member can equally initiate and coordinate the process of forming a coalition. There is no central facilitator or a yellow-pages component as the agents are reluctant to provide information about their services to any supervisory or coordinating agent. This is particularly the case of the humanitarian aid and other OOTW coalitions operations. The agents maintain social models of the collaborating agents and form alliances [9]. Within an alliance, the agents agree to share some type of semi-private information (such as services they provide, location of their troops, etc.). Across the alliances the agents collaborate using the classical contract-net-protocol mechanism.

The CPlanT architecture consists of several specific classes of agents: **Resource Agents** represent the in-place resources that are inevitable for delivering humanitarian aid, such as roads, airports, seaports but also subcontracted shipping agencies. **In-need Agents** are critical bodies in the entire simulation. They will represent the

---

[1] Implemented under support of the AFOSR/European Office of Aerospace Research and Development under contract number F61775-00-WE043

centres of conflict that call for help (e.g. cities, villages, etc.). **Resource Agents** and **In-need Agents** are implemented as one standalone application – **Map Agent**. **Humanitarian Agents** are computational representations of the participating humanitarian agencies.

The system is implemented in Allegro CLOS. Agents are utterly independent and communicate via TCP/IP protocol. Their content language and the ACL is fully FIPA-compliant. The functionality of the system is demonstrated by means of the specific observing agent (implemented in Java) who monitors and visualises dynamics of the community.

The operation of the CPlanT multi-agent has been tested on the Sufferterra humanitarian relief operations scenario that specifies physical arrangements of the objects and agents, their capabilities, and crisis description. For more information see cyber.felk.cvut.cz/gerstner/dai/cplant/.

4   Conclusion

We have designed and implemented a new **Distributed Branch and Bound Algorithm** for solving exponential problems like coalition planning. Original state space is distributed among computing units (agents). Agents use effective searching in assigned state space and they communicate their partial results. These facts result in significant the state space reduction. The number of generated states by whole community doesn't exceed N^4 in most cases. We have tested this approach in coalition structures planning too, and results prove to be even better here. We have described *fast algorithm for agents' state space search* for coalition planning with very fast time responses and the obtained results are close to the optimal coalition. Its number of generated states by whole community never exceeded N^3.

This concept has been exploited in the CPlanT multi-agent system for coalition planning in operations other then war and tested on Sufferterra [10] humanitarian relief scenario. Agents' reasoning has been implemented according to the *meta-reasoning social model* [11] in combination *with Contract Net Protocol* [12] and *teamwork theory* [13]. Coalition planning operations are performed with respect to private information of agents (humanitarian organizations).

Acknowledgements. This work is supported by the Ministry of Education of the Czech Republic within the Project No.LN00B096 as by AFOSR/European Office of Aerospace Research and Development under contract number F61775-00-WE043.

References

1. Pěchouček, M., Mařík, V., and Štěpánková, O.: Towards Reducing Communication Traffic. *Journal of Applied System Studies*, vol. 2, No. 1, UK, 2001, pp. 152-174.
2. Shehory, O., and Kraus, S.: Task Allocation via Coalition Formation Among Autonomous Agents. *IJCAI-95*, 1995.

3. Sandholm, T., Larson, K., Andersson, M., Shehory, O., and Tohmé, F.: Coalition Structure Generation with Worst Case Guarantees. *Artificial Intelligence*, 111(1-2), 209-238, 1999.
4. Contreras, J., Wu, F., Klusch, M., and Shehory, O.: Coalition Formation in a Power Transmission Planning Environment. In: *Proc of PAAM-97*, London, UK, April 1997.
5. Bárta, J., Pěchouček, M., and Štěpánková, O.: Object Oriented Approach to Coalition Forming. *GL 2000/100 - Technical Report of The Gerstner Lab CTU Prague & FAW Linz*, Hagenberg - Praha - Wien, 2000.
6. Shehory, O., Sycara, K., and Jha, S.: Multi-agent Coordination through Coalition Formation. *LNAI 1365, Intelligent Agents IV, A. Rao, M. Singh and M. Wooldridge (Eds.)*, Springer, Heidelberg, 1997, pp. 143-154.
7. Stubbefield, W., and Luger, G.: Artificial Intelligence, Structures and Strategies for Complex Problem Solving. *The Benjamin/Cummins Publishing Company*, 1993.
8. Finin, T., Labrou, Y., and Mayfield, J.: KQML as an agent communication language. In: *Software Agents (Jeff Bradshaw Ed.)*, MIT Press, Cambridge, MA, 1995.
9. Pěchouček, M., Mařík, V., and Bárta, J.: Acquaintance Models in Coalition Planning for Humanitarian Relief Operation. In: *The Second Asia-Pacific Conference on Intelligent Agent Technology (IAT-2001)*, Meabashi, Japan. October 2001, pp. 434-443.
10. Bárta, J., Pěchouček, M., and Mařík, V.: Sufferterra Humanitarian Crisis Scenario. *GL 2001/141 - Research Report of The Gerstner Lab CTU Prague & FAW Linz*, Hagenberg - Praha - Wien, 2001.
11. Pěchouček, M., and Norrie, D.: Knowledge Structures for Reflective Multi-Agent Systems: On reasoning about other agents. *Report Number 538*, Department of Mechanical and Manufacturing Engineering, University of Calgary, Alberta, Canada, December 2000.
12. Huhns, M., and Stephens, L.: Multiagent Systems and Societies of Agents. In: *Multi-Agent Systems: Modern Approach to Distributed Artificial Intelligence (Weiss G., ed.)*, The MIT Press, Cambridge, 1999.
13. Tambe M.: Towards flexible teamwork. *Journal of Artificial Intelligence Research*, 7:83–124, 1997.

Formal Conversations for the Contract Net Protocol

Roberto A. Flores and Robert C. Kremer*

Computer Science Department
University of Calgary
2500 University Dr., NW,
Calgary, Canada, T2N 1N4
{robertof, kremer}@cpsc.ucalgary.ca

Abstract. In this paper we present a fairly complex example of how the social model for agent conversations based on social commitments we have developed in the past formally supports the implementation of conversations for the Contract Net Protocol.

1 Introduction

In open environments such as the Internet agents from heterogeneous sources could exist and interact to accomplish joint activities. The common denominator for agents in these settings is not how they are built but how they *converse*. Furthermore, for conversations to be coherent, agents need the ability to understand messages (through *message semantics*) and their sequencing in time (through *compositional semantics*) [1].

In the landscape of current agent communication languages, most approaches specify messages as *speech acts* defined in terms of private states (such as beliefs and intentions), and whose sequencing is governed by conversation protocols. It has been argued that speech acts should be specified as a function of public events rather than private states [3;6;7;9], and that conversation policies should be favored over protocols to enable versatile and context-sensitive conversations [5].

To that end, we have specified a unified social model for conversations based on social commitments [4] in which speech act semantics is an emergent product of identity, conversational use, and expected accomplishments, and where conversational composition is guided by conversation policies.

In this paper we elaborate further on the application of our model to support conversations in the Contract Net Protocol.

The structure of this paper is as follows. In Sect. 2 we briefly describe the main elements and concepts in our social model for agent conversations. In Sect. 3, we describe in detail how our model supports the implementation of Contract Net Protocol conversations. Finally, in Sect. 4 we conclude this paper with an overview of future avenues of research.

---

* We thankfully acknowledge the support received from the Natural Sciences and Engineering Council of Canada (NSERC), Smart Technologies, Inc., and the Alberta Informatics Circle of Research Excellence (iCORE).

V. Mařík et al. (Eds.): MASA 2001, LNAI 2322, pp. 169-179, 2002.
© Springer-Verlag Berlin Heidelberg 2002

2   A Social Model for Agent Conversations

In this section, we briefly describe the basic definitions in our model, which we have specified using the Z formal notation [2]. In general, we see our model as being applied to guide the joint activities of autonomous agents whose interactions are primarily communicational.

We use illocutionary points, i.e., the publicly intended perlocutionary effects, as the basic compositional elements of speech acts. This view allows us to describe the meaning of a speech act as the emergent property of its enclosed illocutionary points.

As shown below, we define speech acts as structures composed of an illocutionary force and a set of illocutionary points.

```
_ SPEECH_ACT _____
 force: ILLOCUTIONARY_FORCE;
 points: P ILLOCUTIONARY_POINT;
```

We also specify that a speech act is a kind of action (where physical acts are other type of actions that could be included in this definition).

ACTION ::= SpeechAct 《SPEECH_ACT》

In addition, we specify that an utterance is an event that takes place at a certain moment in time, and which involves a speech act that is communicated from a speaker to an addressee.

EVENT ≅ [time:TIME; action: ACTION]
UTTERANCE ≅ [EVENT; speaker:AGENT; addressee:AGENT; speechAct:SPEECH_ACT |
(action ∈ ran SpeechAct) ∧ (speechAct = SpeechAct~ action)]

We define a social commitment as a structure where there is a debtor committed to an action relative to a creditor on whose behalf this action is done. Based on this definition, we then specify that a shared social commitment is a structure comprising a commitment being shared among agents.

Note that having speech acts been declared as actions allows us to have social commitments entailing a speech act.

```
_ SOCIAL_COMMITMENT _____       _ SHARED_SOCIAL_COMMITMENT ___
 debtor, creditor: AGENT;               SOCIAL_COMMITMENT;
 action: ACTION;                        among: P AGENT;
                                       _____
                                        among ≠ ∅
```

To denote that social commitments can be adopted or discharged we define the type OPERATION, which is defined in terms of a social commitment.

OPERATION ::= Add 《SOCIAL_COMMITMENT》 | Delete 《SOCIAL_COMMITMENT》

Succinctly, we conceptualize an agent in our model as an entity that maintains a set of shared social commitments and a history of the utterances it has witnessed. Agents autonomously decide whether other agents can affect their set of shared social commitments. This is supported by a negotiation process based on the utterance and sequencing of speech acts, as described next.

```
┌─ AGENT ──────────────────────────────────
│  commitments: P SHARED_SOCIAL_COMMITMENT;
│  utterances: P UTTERANCE;
│
└─
```

We define a basic protocol for the negotiation of social commitments, which we call the *Protocol for Proposals* (PFP). This protocol starts with a proposal from a sender to a receiver to concurrently adopt or discharge a social commitment. Either the receiver replies with an acceptance, rejection, or counteroffer, or the sender issues a withdrawal or counteroffer[1]. All utterances except a counteroffer terminate an instance of the protocol. A counteroffer is deemed as a proposal in the sense that its utterance is followed by any of the reply speech acts (but with speaker-addressee roles inverted if the original addressee is the speaker of the utterance). In theory, a counteroffer can follow another counteroffer *ad infinitum*; in practice, the number of successive counteroffers might be limited by the reasoning, competence, or endurance of interacting agents. Finally, it is expected that when an acceptance is issued both speaker and addressee will simultaneously apply the proposed commitments to their record of shared social commitments.

To model the PFP, we define five basic illocutionary points: PROPOSE, ACCEPT, REJECT, COUNTER, and INFORM. We define them as illocutionary points as follows:

ILLOCUTIONARY_POINT ::= Propose ⟪PROPOSE⟫ | Accept ⟪ACCEPT⟫ | Reject ⟪REJECT⟫ |
Counter ⟪COUNTER⟫ | Inform ⟪INFORM⟫

As shown in the definitions below, PROPOSE specifies the operation on commitment being proposed, and a time interval in which a reply is expected (we informally call this time the *window of interaction*). ACCEPT indicates the operation on commitment being accepted, and REJECT the operation on commitment being rejected. COUNTER is defined in terms of REJECT and PROPOSE, where the former indicates the commitment previously proposed and now being rejected, and the latter presents the new proposed commitment along with a new window of interaction. Finally, INFORM is specified as containing certain information being informed.

```
┌─ PROPOSE ──────────────────────         ┌─ COUNTER ──────────────────────
│  proposing: OPERATION;                  │  REJECT;
│  replyBy: TIME;                         │  PROPOSE;
│                                         │
└─                                        └─

┌─ ACCEPT ───────────────────────         ┌─ INFORM ───────────────────────
│  accepting: OPERATION;                  │  informing: INFORMATION;
│                                         │
└─                                        └─

┌─ REJECT ───────────────────────
│  rejecting: OPERATION;
│
└─
```

We specify three conversation policies that entail the adoption and discharge of commitments when the illocutionary points in the PFP are uttered. These policies are formally specified in terms of shared social commitments (see [4] for details). Informally, we describe them as follows:

---

[1] It is also possible that the addressee goes silent. In such cases, the elapsing of the expected reply time indicates to the speaker (or any observer) that the addressee either intentionally forfeited his obligation to reply or was unable to communicate as expected.

POLICY 1: For each PROPOSE or COUNTER illocutionary point in a just uttered speech act, add as a shared commitment between speaker and addressee that the addressee (the debtor) will do for the speaker (the creditor) a speech act (the action) containing an ACCEPT, REJECT or COUNTER illocutionary point with the same operation on commitment as that of the just uttered PROPOSE.

POLICY 2: For each ACCEPT, REJECT, or COUNTER illocutionary point in a just uttered speech act from speaker to addressee, such that there is a past utterance from addressee to speaker in which there is a PROPOSE or COUNTER illocutionary point with the same operation on commitment as that of the just uttered ACCEPT, REJECT, or COUNTER, and where the PROPOSE or COUNTER indicated a reply time that hasn't elapsed yet, then delete the shared commitment between speaker and addressee that the speaker (the debtor) is to do for the addressee (the creditor) a speech act (the action) containing an ACCEPT, REJECT or COUNTER with the same operation on commitment as that of the just uttered ACCEPT, REJECT, or COUNTER.

POLICY 3: For each ACCEPT illocutionary point in a just uttered speech act from speaker to addressee, such that there is a past utterance from addressee to speaker in which there is a PROPOSE or COUNTER with the same operation on commitment as that of the just uttered ACCEPT, and where the PROPOSE or COUNTER indicated the reply time that hasn't elapsed yet, then perform the operation on commitment that was proposed and is now accepted.

We define eight utterance definitions in terms of the relations between the speaker and addressee of an utterance, the creditor and debtor of a social commitment within such utterance, and the type of operation being applied to this social commitment.

The first four descriptions, which are based on PROPOSE, are: Request, Offer, Release, and Discharge. Informally, a Request is a proposal to adopt a social commitment for action in which the speaker is the creditor and the addressee is the debtor; an Offer is a proposal to adopt a commitment in which the speaker is the debtor and the addressee is the creditor; a Release is a proposal to discharge a commitment in which the speaker is the creditor and the addressee the debtor, and finally, a Discharge is a proposal to discharge a commitment in which the speaker is the debtor and the addressee the creditor.

The remaining four descriptions, which are based on ACCEPT, are: Accept, Grant, Comply, and Approve (which are the acceptance counterparts for Request, Offer, Release, and Discharge, respectively). Informally, an Accept is an acceptance to adopt a social commitment for action in which the speaker is the debtor and the addressee is the creditor of the commitment; a Grant is an acceptance to adopt a commitment in which the speaker is the creditor and the addressee the debtor; a Comply is an acceptance to discharge a commitment in which the speaker is the debtor and the addressee the creditor; and finally, an Approve is an acceptance to discharge a commitment in which the speaker is the creditor and the addressee the debtor.

3 Example: The Contract Net Protocol

In the dynamics of our model, agents will join societies where the description of activities is specified in terms of roles, sequencing of communicational actions, and the description of actions and their results.

Currently our model only accounts for the expected sequencing of communicative actions and roles in an activity. We acknowledge though the importance of action definitions, but their study will not be pursued here.

In this section, we present the application of our model to guide the evolution of a conversation in the Contract Net protocol (CNP) [8], which is a task allocation mechanism for requesting bids for a task and awarding its performance to the most suitable bidder. This protocol can be described as unfolding in five steps:

1. *Request for bids*: A manager requests a bidder to submit a bid.
2. *Submission of bids*: The bidder prepares a bid and submits it to the manager for evaluation.
3. *Awarding of contracts*: The manager evaluates the bid, which could (or not) be awarded as a contract to the bidder.
4. *Acceptance of contracts*: If awarded, the bidder is requested to accept (or decline) the execution of the contract.
5. *Submission of results*: The bidder submits the results of executing the contract.

We define three actions for this protocol: DoBid, EvaluateBid, and DoContract. We specify these as part of our the definition of action:

[DO_BID, EVALUATE_BID, DO_CONTRACT]
ACTION ::= SpeechAct ⟪SPEECH_ACT⟫ | DoBid ⟪DO_BID⟫ | EvaluateBid ⟪EVALUATE_BID⟫
          | DoContract ⟪DO_CONTRACT⟫

As previously mentioned we will not elaborate on the specification of these action definitions, and we only informally describe them as follows:

- DO_BID: described as "to produce a bid."
- EVALUATE_BID: described as "to assess the adequacy of a bid as a possible contract."
- DO_CONTRACT: described as "to perform a contract."

Under social models of agency, autonomous agents join normative societies through the adoption of roles defining their expected abilities and behavior. In the case of the CNP, we define the roles Manager and Bidder as follows:

MANAGER == AGENT
BIDDER == AGENT
ROLE ::= Manager ⟪MANAGER⟫ | Bidder ⟪BIDDER⟫

In the case of the interaction of purely communicational agents, all information that is shared is integrally passed among parties since there are no default settings through which results could be mutually accessed. In such circumstances, agents in a CNP conversation need to communicate three pieces of information: 1) the initial conditions to produce a bid (provided in the *Request for bids*); 2) the bid itself (in the *Submission of bids*); and 3) the results obtained from executing an awarded contract (in the *Submission of results*). We define these data as follows:

[CONDITIONS, BID, RESULTS]
INFORMATION ::= Conditions ⟪CONDITIONS⟫ | Bid ⟪BID⟫ | Results ⟪RESULTS⟫

As in the case of actions, we do not detail the definition of these data, but we acknowledge that complete implementations will include their concrete definitions as guidelines to justify the accomplishment of tasks (for example).

We define ten utterance names for the CNP (as with previous utterance definitions, that an utterance is equated to a name only implies that the utterance contains at least those illocutionary points given in the definition). These utterances are: RequestForBids, AcceptToBid, SubmitBid, AcceptSubmission, AwardContract, AcceptAwarding, RejectBid, AcceptRejection, SubmitResults, and ApproveResults.

Figure 1 shows these utterances as well as the illocutionary points they contain (shown in the shaded box next to the utterance). The utterance RequestForBids, for example, contains two illocutionary points: 1) a proposal to adopt a commitment in which the addressee (the debtor) is to do a bid for the speaker (the creditor), and 2) an inform containing the conditions over which the bid is to be produced. On the same lines, an AcceptToBid is an utterance in which the speaker accepts to adopt a commitment in which he is to do a bid for the addressee.

The remaining utterances are briefly described as follows:

- SubmitBid: utterance in which the speaker 1) proposes to the addressee the mutual discharge of the commitment that he (the speaker) does a bid for the addressee, 2) proposes to the addressee the mutual adoption of the commitment that she (the addressee) evaluates a bid, and 3) informs the addressee of a bid.
- AcceptSubmission: utterance in which the speaker accepts both the mutual discharge of the commitment that the addressee is to produce a bid, and the mutual adoption of the commitment that she evaluates the bid.
- AwardContract: utterance in which the speaker proposes 1) the mutual discharge of the commitment that she evaluates the bid, and 2) the mutual adoption of the commitment that the addressee commits to carry out the bid he proposed.
- AcceptAwarding: utterance in which the speaker accepts 1) the mutual discharge that the addressee evaluates the bid, and 2) the mutual adoption of the commitment that the speaker does the previously proposed bid and now awarded contract.
- RejectBid: utterance in which the speaker proposes the mutual discharge of the commitment that she evaluates the bid.
- AcceptRejection: utterance in which the speaker accepts the mutual discharge of the commitment that the addressee evaluates a bid.
- SubmitResults: utterance in which the speaker 1) proposes the mutual discharge of the commitment that he does the awarded contract, and 2) informs the addressee of the obtained results of doing the contract.
- ApproveResults: utterance in which the speaker accepts the mutual discharge of the commitment that the addressee does an awarded contract.

We define six conversation policies to describe the expected adoption and discharge of conversational commitments that advance the state of CNP conversations.

The first policy, which we identify here as Policy 4 (Fig. 2), indicates that the acceptance to a proposal for adopting the action DoBid causes the adoption of the shared commitment that the accepting agent will utter a speech act in which he proposes to discharge the commitment that he performs such action. This is, that an agent accepts to commit to do the action DoBid causes the adoption of another commitment in which he proposes to discharge that he does the action. Although this commitment could also be included in the proposing speech act RequestForBids, its definition as a policy in the public description of the CNP allows agents to know before hand how the interactions in this activity are expected to evolve.

Policy 5 (not shown) indicates that once the creditor agent has accepted the proposal to discharge the action DoBid, there is the automatic discharge of the shared commitment that the debtor has to propose discharging the commitment to do such action.

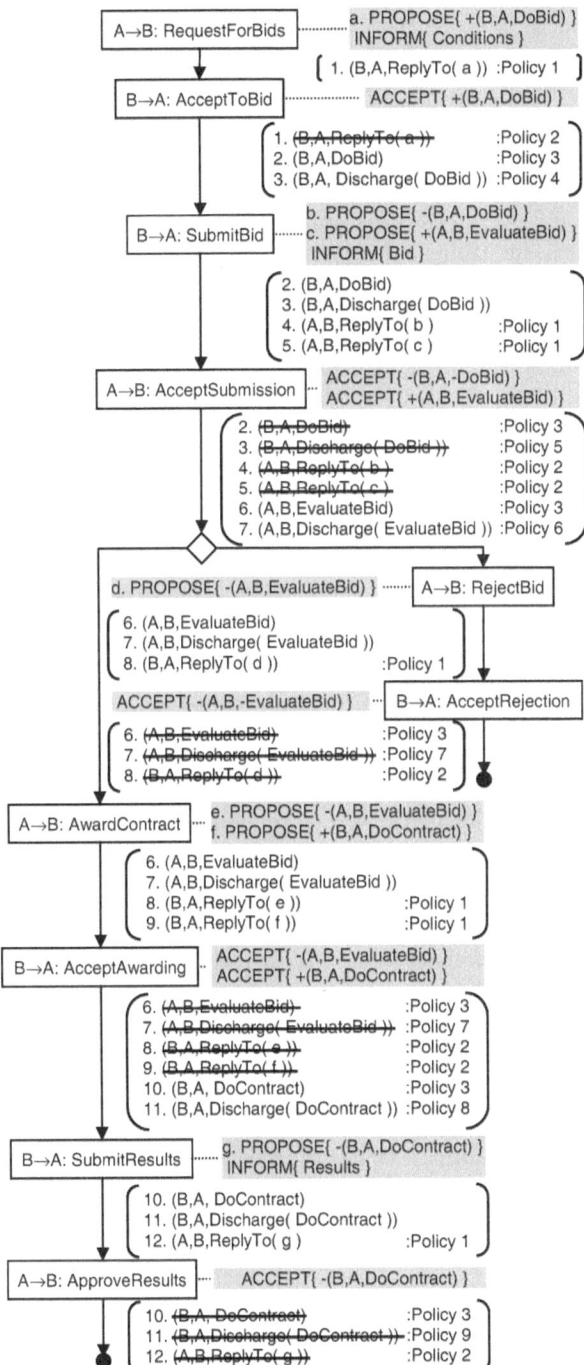

Fig. 1. Example utterances, sequencing, and state of social commitments for CNP conversations

Policies 6 and 7, and policies 8 and 9 (not shown) follow the same pattern of adoption and discharge of commitments that propose the discharge of commitments for the actions EvaluateBid and DoContract, respectively.

These policies, used in conjunction to those in the PFP, enable the coherent evolution of CNP conversations, as illustrated in Fig. 1.

Note that the diagram in this figure is an oversimplification of the possible conversations that are supported in our model. For simplicity and clarity of the example, we are only showing the sequence of proposals and acceptances that could occur using the PFP. This is the case, for example, of the utterance RequestForBids (a proposal from agent A) which is shown to be followed solely by an AcceptToBid (an acceptance from agent B). As mandated by the PFP, this proposal can also be followed by a rejection or counter from agent B, or a rejection or counter from agent A.

To illustrate the accumulation and discharge of shared commitments during this conversation example, we will track the evolution of the state of shared social commitments between agents A and B at all points in the conversation (this is shown in the round-bracketed areas located between the shadowed boxes in the figure). For the sake of the clarity of this example, the initial state of shared commitments is empty.

The conversation starts when agent A utters to agent B a RequestForBids speech act. As shown in the first bracketed area (from top to bottom), this utterance causes the application of Policy 1 (uttering a proposal causes the shared conversational commitment that this proposal will be replied) resulting in the addition of shared commitment number 1 to the state of shared social commitments.

Next is an utterance from agent B to agent A in which the former accepts committing to do the action DoBid. This acceptance triggers the following policies: Policy 2 (the reply to a proposal discharges the commitment to reply), which deletes commitment number 1; Policy 3 (the acceptance of a proposal causes the shared uptake of the proposed commitment, in this case that agent B will do a bid for agent A), which adds commitment number 2; and, Policy 4 (accepting to perform the action DoBid causes the shared commitment that the agent doing this action will propose the discharge of the commitment to do the action), which causes the adoption of shared commitment number 3.

This last utterance (AcceptToBid) indicates that the initial proposal (RequestForBids) has been accepted, thus signaling the termination of one instance of the PFP. At this point, two instances of the PFP could follow: 1) agent B can propose the discharge of the commitment that he produces a bid—presumably because he has produced one, or because he is polite enough to communicate that he will not produce one; or 2) agent A can propose to release agent B of this commitment[2]. From these options we only show the case in which agent B proposes the discharge of the commitment to do a bid given that he is submitting one (as defined in SubmitBid). In addition, this utterance proposes that the bid is evaluated for adequacy as a possible contract.

As shown, the uttering of a SubmitBid causes the application of Policy 1 (uttering a proposal causes the shared conversational commitment that it will be replied) twice, one per proposal in the utterance, resulting in the adoption of shared commitments 4 and 5 (indicating that the proposals in the utterance will be replied).

---

[2] We are yet to explore the effects that liability and compensation may exert in such circumstances, e.g., when an agent discharges a commitment without a reasonable justification (making her liable for breaking a commitment), or when an agent is released from a commitment (entailing a compensation for the efforts incurred).

```
┌─POLICY_4 ──────────────────────────────────────────────
│ Δ AGENT
│ utterance?: UTTERANCE;
│ set: P SHARED_SOCIAL_COMMITMENT;
│ manager, bidder: AGENT;
│ doBid: ACTION;
├─────────────────────────────────────────────────────────
│ utterance?.time = now;
│ #set = #(getallRequestForBidsforallAcceptToBid( utterances, utterance? ));
│ doBid ∈ ran ContractNet_DoBid;
│
│ ∃ role:ROLE | role ∈ ran Manager
│ • manager = Manager~ role ∧ manager = utterance?.addressee;
│ ∃ role:ROLE | role ∈ ran Bidder
│ • bidder = Bidder~ role ∧ bidder = utterance?.speaker;
│
│ ∀ accept:ACCEPT
│ | accept ∈ getACCEPTpoints utterance?.speechAct ∧
│ (∃ c:SOCIAL_COMMITMENT
│ | c.debtor = bidder ∧ c.creditor = manager ∧ c.action = doBid
│ • c = Add~ accept.accepting) ∧
│ (#{propose:PROPOSE | (∀ u:UTTERANCE
│ | u ∈ utterances ∧ u.time < now ∧
│ u.speaker = manager ∧ u.addressee = bidder
│ • propose ∈ getPROPOSEpoints u.speechAct ∧
│ propose.proposing = accept.accepting ∧
│ propose.replyBy > now)} > 0)
│ • ∃ sc:SHARED_SOCIAL_COMMITMENT; action:ACTION; s:SPEECH_ACT; p:PROPOSE;
│ c:SOCIAL_COMMITMENT
│ | sc.among = {manager, bidder} ∧ sc.debtor = bidder ∧ sc.creditor = manager ∧
│ action ∈ ran SpeechAct ∧ action = sc.action ∧ s = SpeechAct~ action ∧
│ p ∈ getPROPOSEpoints s ∧
│ c.debtor = bidder ∧ c.creditor = manager ∧ c.action = doBid ∧ c = Delete~ p.proposing)
│ • sc ∈ set;
│
│ commitments' = commitments ∪ set
└─────────────────────────────────────────────────────────
```

Fig. 2. Accepting to do the action DoBid commits to propose its discharge

This is followed by the utterance of AcceptSubmission, which triggers the following policies: Policy 3 (the acceptance of a proposal causes the shared uptake of the proposed commitment), which results in the discharge of commitment number 2 and the adoption of commitment number 6; Policy 5 (the acceptance of a proposal to discharge the action DoBid causes the discharge of the commitment to propose the discharge of the commitment to do this action), which discharges commitment number 3; Policy 2 (the reply to a proposal discharges the commitment to reply), which discharges commitments number 4 and 5; and Policy 6 (accepting to perform the action EvaluateBid causes the shared commitment that the agent doing this action will propose the discharge of the commitment to do the action), which causes the adoption of shared commitment number 7.

The pair of utterances SubmitBid and AcceptSubmission realizes another instance of the PFP. Again, two instances of the PFP could follow at this point: 1) agent A can propose to discharge the commitment that she evaluates the bid—because she has reached a decision, or because she will not reach one at all; or 2) agent B can propose to release agent A of her commitment to evaluate his bid, e.g., if he decides to withdraw his bid. The diagram shows the two cases in which agent A proposes to discharge the commitment that she evaluates the bid given that she is awarding the contract or rejecting the bid (as defined by AwardContract and RejectBid, respectively).

Uttering the latter (rejecting the proposed bid) causes the application of Policy 1 (uttering a proposal causes the shared conversational commitment that it will be replied), resulting in the adoption of commitment number 8. Accepting this rejection (through AcceptRejection) causes the application of policies 3, 7 and 2, which discharge the commitments 6, 7 and 8, respectively. At this point, all shared conversational commitments have been deleted, signaling the termination of the conversation.

As shown in the figure, this same pattern of proposals and acceptances develop for the execution of the contract (AwardContract and AcceptAwarding), and the submission of results (SubmitResults and ApproveResults).

4   Conclusions

In this paper we presented an implementation of the Contract Net Protocol for purely communicational agents based on our model of agent conversations and social commitments. With this example, we seek to demonstrate that our model can account rich and dynamic conversations

Currently we are working on an experimental engine that agents can use to support our model for conversations in an environment where agents could be engaged in multiple simultaneous conversations. Additionally, we are in the process of defining a set of theorems to prove the correctness of the theory in which our model is based.

References

1.   Craig, R.T. & Tracy K. (eds.) Conversational Coherence: Form, Structure, and Strategy, Sage Publications, 1983.
2.   Diller, A. Z: An Introduction to Formal Methods. John Willey & Sons, 1990.
3.   FIPA Agent Communication Language Specifications, Foundation for Intelligent Physical Agents, 1997, http://www.fipa.org/
4.   Flores, R.A. and Kremer, R.C. (2001) Bringing Coherence to Agent Conversations. Proceedings of the Second Workshop on Agent-Oriented Software Engineering, Fifth International Conference on Autonomous Agents (Agents'2001), M. Wooldridge, P. Ciancarini, and G. Weiss (Eds.), Montreal, Canada, May 28-June 1, 2001. (to appear)
5.   Greaves, M., Holmback, H. & Bradshaw, J. What is a Conversation Policy? Third International Conference in Autonomous Agents, Workshop on Specifying and Implementing Conversation Policies, M. Greaves & J. Bradshaw (eds.), Seattle, WA, 1999, pp. 1-9.

6. Huhns, M.N. & Singh, M.P. Agents and Multiagent Systems: Themes, Approaches, and Challenges. Readings in Agents, M.N. Huhns & M.P. Singh (eds.), Morgan Kaufmann Publishers, 1998, pp. 1-23.
7. Singh, M.P. Agent Communicational Languages: Rethinking the Principles. IEEE Computer, Volume 31, Number 12, 1998, pp. 40-47.
8. Smith, R.G. (1980) The Contract Net Protocol: High Level Communication and Control in a distributed Problem Solver. IEEE Transactions in Computers, Volume 29, Number 12, pp. 1104-1113.
9. Wooldridge, M. Verifiable Semantic for Agent Communication Languages. Third International Conference on Multi-Agent Systems, Y. Demazeau (ed.), IEEE Press, 1998.

Adaptive Agents in Argumentation-Based Negotiation

Cosmin Carabelea

"Politehnica" University of Bucharest
http://turing.cs.pub.ro/~cosminc
cosminc@turing.cs.pub.ro

Abstract. The paper presents a multi-agent system that comprises a society of self-interested agents that use argumentation-based negotiation to reach agreements regarding cooperation and goal satisfaction. The system is a generalization of some argumentation-based multi-agent systems proposed in the literature in which better cooperation agreements are reached through the use of human-like arguments. We then show how this type of negotiation can be adapted according to evolved models of other agents in the system. Negotiation is performed using different types of arguments varying from quantitative ones, such as money or trade objects, to qualitative arguments, such as promises, appeal to past promises, and past examples. The models of the other agents are built and refined incrementally during negotiation; these models are then used to adapt the negotiation strategy according to other agents' desires, preferences and behavioral characteristics during interactions.

1 Introduction

In a multi-agent system, an agent exists and performs its activity in a society in which other agents exist and act. Therefore, coordination among agents is essential for achieving their goals and acting in a coherent manner, for both self-interested and collectively motivated agents. The paper presents a multi-agent system in which self-interested agents are aiming to reach agreements through argumentation-based negotiation while developing models of the other agents in the system. In this way, agents will be able to evolve their negotiation strategy and adapt themselves according past negotiation experiences.

The paper is organized as follows. Section 2 presents the agent model and the architecture of the multi-agent system we propose. Section 3 describes the communication and negotiation mechanisms, and the types of arguments that are used in negotiations. Section 4 describes how agents can adapt themselves by evolving models of other agents in the system, while Sect. 5 describes experimental results, draws conclusions and traces directions for future work.

V. Mařík et al. (Eds.): MASA 2001, LNAI 2322, pp. 180-187, 2002.
© Springer-Verlag Berlin Heidelberg 2002

2   The Multi-Agent System

The system comprises a society of self-interested agents that use argumentation-based negotiation to reach agreements regarding cooperation and goal satisfaction. The system is a generalization of some argumentation-based multi-agent systems proposed in the literature [2],[4] in which better cooperation agreements are reached through the use of human-like arguments and considers how this type of negotiation can be adapted according to evolved models of other agents in the system. As opposed to the existing few such systems, our agents extend the possible types of argumentation so as to include both qualitative arguments, such as the ones proposed in [2] and arguments that are drawn from conventional negotiations based on costs and gain [1].

Each agent is endowed with a set of abilities or actions he is able to perform, has a set of desires, a set of beliefs about other agents (quite close to the BDI model), and has in its possession several physical objects and an amount of money. An agent's desire can be the execution of an action or the wish to posses a physical object. Each desire has its own preference, the main goal of an agent being to satisfy its most important desires. To satisfy its desires, an agent may need to persuade some other agents to give it an object or to perform an action on its behalf. Alternately, an agent may want to change the set of desires of some other agents in order to obtain the fulfillment of its own desires. Therefore, the agents can try to trade virtual objects which may be physical objects, actions performed on their behalf, desires of other agents, other agents' preferences, or money.

The system is open: an agent can enter or leave the system anytime and has no a priori information related to the state of other agents. A special agent, the facilitator, is responsible for keeping track of agents entering and leaving the system, of the public information that each agent declared about itself (some of the virtual objects it possesses), and of the market evolution, namely a history of the negotiated virtual objects and results of the corresponding negotiations (Fig. 1).

In each life cycle, an agent selects a desire to fulfil which represents its current goal. It may ask the facilitator about the agents able to satisfy its goal and then choose one of them to negotiate with, or it can make this decision based on its own beliefs about the other agents in the system. It then negotiates with the selected agent and the negotiation result is sent to the facilitator, along with an updated list of public virtual objects.

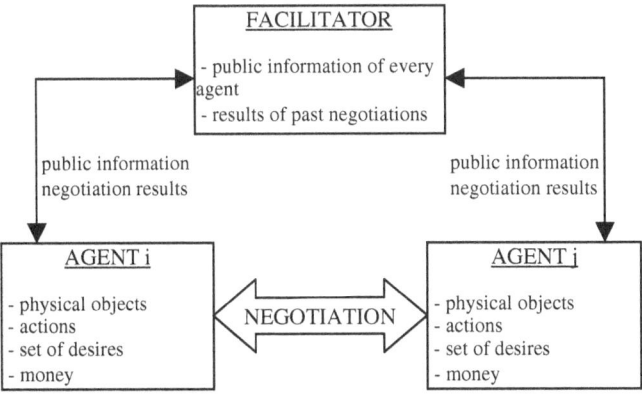

Fig. 1. The Multi Agent System

For the time being, all information known by the facilitator is free so that each agent in the system may use it at its convenience. In a future development of the system, some of the facilitator information, e.g. negotiation history, will have an associated cost and agents will have to trade this information with the facilitator. This implies to endow the facilitator with a subset of agent negotiation capabilities.

3   Communication and Negotiation

Negotiation is an iterative process between two agents called the persuader and the persuadee, the first trying to convince the second to do one of the following: give a physical object, change its desires (or the preferences of some of them), perform an action on its behalf. This can be generalized by saying that the negotiation's objects are virtual objects.

The agents have a planning module, which allows them to build negotiation plans by choosing the arguments to use in a negotiation. As a result of interactions, an agent builds models of the agents with which it has negotiated. These models are updated after each completion of a negotiation and, sometimes, depending on the relevance of gathered information, also during one negotiation. In the latter case, the agents need to enter a re-planning phase during which the negotiation plan is updated according to the modified model of the other.

3.1   Communication Language

In order to negotiate, an agent must be able to communicate with the other agents in the system. One of the most influential agent communication languages is KQML [3], as it has been used in many systems and it has served as a model for other many agent languages, like the one in [1]. Our proposed system uses a KQML-type of language, but modified to allow the use of different types of arguments. We have assumed that every agent understands this language and that all agents have access at common argument ontology, so that the semantics of a message is the same for all agents.

The agents communicate using the following communication primitives:

> *Request(Source, Destination, Item, Argument).*
> *Accept(Source, Destination).*
> *Reject(Source, Destination, Motivation).*
> *ModifyRequest(Source, Destination, Item, Argument, Motivation).*
> *CloseNegotiation(Source, Destination, Motivation).*

where:

- *Source* – is the agent sending the message;
- *Destination* – is the agent receiving the message;
- *Item* – is the virtual object of negotiation;
- *Argument* – is the argument proposed by an agent in exchange for *Item* (may be absent);
- *Motivation* is an optional explanation for a Reject or ModifyRequest message.

3.2 Argument Ontology

Negotiation is an intensively studied area in multi-agent systems, but most of the existing work focuses on cost-based negotiation, with little work emphasizing the use of arguments in negotiation. Several types of arguments have been proposed in [2], where argumentation is represented like an iterative process emerging from exchanges between agents to persuade each other and bring about changes in their intentions. The types of arguments used in [2] are the ones identified to be most commonly used in daily human interactions, like threats, promises, appeals to past promises, examples of similar situations or appeals to self-interest. We may call these arguments qualitative ones, to oppose them to what we consider being quantitative arguments, namely cost or money. In real life, good human negotiators may use both categories of arguments, qualitative and quantitative, as means to persuade or trade something with other humans. Our agents are using both categories of arguments, namely *Money* and *Trade*, and a subset of the qualitative arguments mentioned above: *Promises, Appeal to past promises* and *Past examples*, but in the future more arguments will be added.

For each of these types of arguments, there is a set of possible justifications to use in the *Reject* and *ModifyRequest* messages. For example, if the argument used by the persuader is a *Promise*, the persuadee can reply with a *Reject* message with no justification or a justification such as *don't trust you* or *not interested* (in the object of the promise).

If *Money* is used as an argument, the agent will propose to pay the negotiated virtual object with a certain the sum of money. The subject of the *Trade* argument is a physical object that the persuader offers for the required negotiation item or an action it is willing to perform provided it gets that item. The subject of a *Promise* argument is one of the persuadee's desires. The persuader "promises" that this desire will become one of its own. If an agent makes a promise to another agent, it is likely that the second agent will require the fulfillment of that promise, sometimes in the future. Therefore, the agents must have a memory of the past negotiations where to keep track their promises or to search past successful negotiations in order to use past examples as arguments.

An agent assigns a value to every physical object or action it cares about. This value is not measured in money, it represents instead how much that item worthies in the agent's opinion. For example, the value of an action represents how much it costs the agent to perform it. The agents are using the assigned values in order evaluate proposals received from other agents

3.3 Negotiation

The persuader chooses an argument by evaluating the presumed effect of that argument on the persuadee. The most accurate the model of the persuadee is, the most accurate is the evaluation. When receiving an argument, the persuadee has to evaluate it, considering both its current goal and its model of the persuader. If the evaluation results in a good enough value, the persuadee accepts the proposal, if not, it can make a counter-proposal or close the negotiation. The choice of arguments and responses to arguments is also affected by the agent desires to establish analogues of human notions such as credibility and reputation, during interactions with other agents in the system. Based on the ideas in [6], the negotiation protocol between two agents, the persuader and the persuadee, is represented as a finite state machine, as shown in Fig. 2.

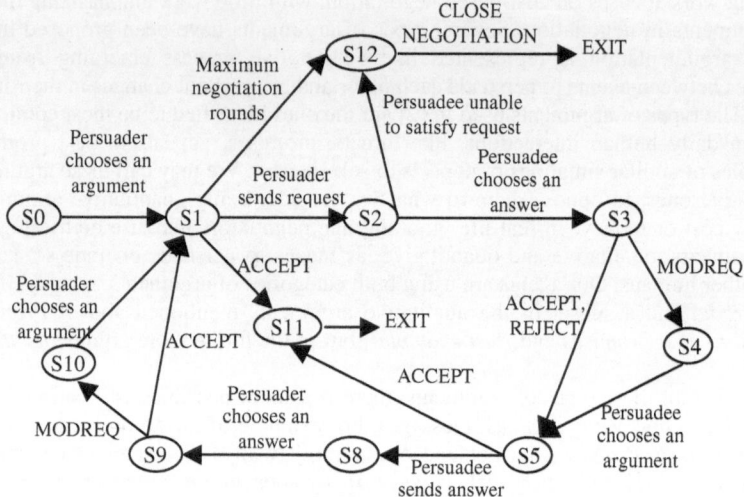

Fig. 2. The process of negotiation between two agents

In order to quantify the effect of a negotiation, we have introduced the notion of negotiation balance (NB), which is the ratio between the value of the item being negotiated and the value of the item being traded for it. Ideally, this rapport should be 1, meaning that the agent offers something with the same value in exchange, but in reality the persuader will try to raise the balance (the value of obtained item being bigger that the value of the given one), while the persuadee will try to lower it.

While evaluating an argument, the value of the NB is compared with some agent predefined values in order to make a decision. Examples of these values are the maximum limit of the NB for which the persuadee accepts the argument, the maximum limit of the NB for which the persuadee doesn't accept the argument but proposes a new one, the minimum limit of NB for which the persuader agrees with the argument, etc. These limits vary around 1 (the ideal value of the NB) depending on several parameters, e.g., how much an agent likes the other (LAg), how much an agent likes the type of the argument ($LArg$), or if there is a desire opposing that argument. The value of some limit also depends of the type of the virtual object being negotiated: physical object, action, change of desire.

When the persuader has to choose an argument, it creates a list of possible arguments from which it will choose the one that minimizes NB for the persuadee, keeping its NB greater that the lower acceptance limit. When the persuadee will face the same choice, the criteria should change so that the argument will be in its area of acceptance and will maximize the negotiation balance for the persuader.

As both agents must have the possibility to choose a response and an associated argument at different moments of negotiation process, a set of rules has been proposed for developing negotiation plans. This set of rules takes in consideration various aspects like negotiation balance, characteristics of other agents, convincing power of the argument (Fig. 3).

1. **if** it hasn't a desire for the object (action) offered
   then *Reject(Not_Interested)*
2. **if** its NB is less than the upper limit for acceptance
   and there is another object (action) X that would lower its
         NB, but it will not lower the persuader's NB
   then *ModifyRequest(X, More_interested)*
3. **if** its NB is less than the upper limit for acceptance
   then *Accept*
4. **if** its NB is less than the upper limit for new proposal
   and there is another object (action) X that would lower its
         NB
   then *ModifyRequest(X, No_justification)*
5. **if** its NB is less than the upper limit for new proposal
   then choose a new type of argument TA
   and *ModifyRequest(TA)*
6. **if** its NB is not less than the upper limit for new proposal
   then *Reject*.

Fig. 3. Rules used to choose the answer if the argument received by the persuadee is a trade

4 Adaptive Agents

An agent must build and refine models of other agents in order to obtain better results in negotiation. It can then use these models to adapt its negotiation to the other agent characteristics and to develop negotiation plans based on presumed reactions of these agents. The models are refined based on what the agent knows about past negotiations or on what it finds out during a particular negotiation. This includes the trace of its own previous negotiations or the results of negotiations performed by other agents in the past, which are accessible through the facilitator. The evolving models are based on the ideas of the "ideal modeling system" described in [5]. One important feature of the model is that it is built incrementally. Therefore, an agent doesn't always have to memorize all the acquired information about other agents, as this information will be used to refined the model only once. The proposed model an agent X develops to model an unknown agent Y includes several characteristics:

- how much X likes the other agent (Y);
- how much the agent Y likes different types of arguments;
- how much the agent Y wants/uses to keep its promises;
- the set of Y's desires.

One important characteristic is the "what are the arguments preferred by another agent". Although a persuader has a preference for a certain argument, it may change this argument with another one if it believes that the persuadee prefers this other type of argument. It is possible that an agent will believe another agent likes an argument only because that agent has used it or has accepted this type of argument many times before. But this acceptance may be triggered by the fact that the other agent is adapting to this one too, thus a convergence of the proposed arguments may occur. This convergence may be avoided by developing 2-level modeling agents [7] that are building models of other agents as agents building simple models of the others. In this way, an agent is able to distinguish if another agent is using an argument because it really likes it or because it just believes it will have a greater impact on it.

In order to learn how wilingful an agent is to keep its promises, an agent must monitor the answers given by that agent at requests for past promises. When an agent evaluates a proposal of a *promise* from another, its behavior is strongly related to how much it trusts the other. Because an agent knows about other agents only what they have declared as public virtual objects, it is very important that it has information on the desires of others, helping it to evaluate more accurate the arguments received from them. An agent may have beliefs based on the model he has previously built about some virtual objects of another agent, even if this information was not declared as public. Then, it will change its behavior, adapting to what the other desires, in order to fulfil its goal.

5   Conclusions and Future Work

We have presented a multi-agent system in which agents are able to negotiate in order to satisfy their goals and desires. The system is open, the agents in the system are self-interested and are using argument-based negotiation to reach agreements regarding cooperation and goal satisfaction. Negotiation is performed using different types of arguments varying from quantitative ones, such as money or trade objects, to qualitative arguments, such as promises, appeal to past promises and past examples.

The system has been developed in JADE, which is an open-source MAS platform that complies with FIPA standards. JADE is used here only as an environment that allows the agents to communicate using FIPA-compliant performatives. In order to permit the user to monitor the state of each agent and the negotiation process, a graphical user-interface has been developed.

The basic contributions of this paper are the following: the objects being negotiated are virtual objects which may represent physical objects, actions performed on their behalf, desires of other agents, other agents' preferences, or money; the argument-based negotiations are covering both economic type negotiations and symbolic daily life ones; the agents are adapting their negotiation plans according to an evolved model of the other agents in the system. The current set of arguments proposed in this paper include some of the most relevant and frequently used arguments in human interactions. More arguments are to be considered, among them being threats, counter-examples and appeal to common interest. Also, a combination of arguments will be allowed, an agent being able to use a cumulation of two or more basic arguments to persuade another.

Another future extension is the investigation of how different planning strategies influence the negotiation performances. In particular, we are aiming to construct agents that are building meta-negotiation plans based on the 2-level modeling. Alternately, an agent will be able to perform some fake negotiations to make the others evolve a false model of itself and then use this induced belief to obtain better results in future interactions. The 2-level modeling may detect such kind of false behavior.

Acknowledgements. This work has been supported by the National Council of Academic Research (CNCSIS) and the Ministry of National Education under Grant No.51, 1999-2001.

References

1. A. Florea, B. Panghe: Achieving Cooperation of Self-interested Agents Based on Cost. Proceedings of the 15th European Meeting on Cybernetics and System Research, Session: From Agent Theory to Agent Implementation, Vienna, 25-28 April 2000, pp. 591-596.
2. S. Kraus, K. Sycara, A. Evenchik: Reaching agreements through argumentation: a logical model and implementation, Artificial Intelligence, 104 (1998), pp. 1-69.
3. Y. Labrou, T. Finin: A Semantics approach for KQML – A General Purpose Communication Language for Software Agents. Proceedings of International Conference on Information and Knowledge Management, 1994.
4. S. Parsons, C. Sierra, N.R.Jennings: Agents that Reason and Negotiate by Arguing. Journal of Logic and Computation 8(3); 1998, pp. 261-292:
5. W. Pohl, A. Nick: Machine Learning and Knowledge Representation in the LaboUr Approach to User Modeling. Proceedings of the Seventh International Conference on User Modeling, UM99, Ed. J. Kay, Springer Wien New York, 1999, pp. 179-188.
6. K. Sycara: Multi-Agent Infrastructure, Agent Discovery, Middle Agents for Web Services and Interoperation, Multi-Agent Systems and Applications, editors: V. Marik, M. Luck, O. Stepankova & et al., Springer-Verlag, 2001.
7. J.M. Vidal, E.H. Durfee: The impact of nested agent models in an information economy. Proceedings of the Second International Conference on Multiagent Systems, Menlo Park, CA, 1996, AAAI Press, pp. 377-384.

Flexible Load Balancing in Distributed Information Agent Systems

Jacek Gomoluch and Michael Schroeder

Dept. of Computing, City University, London, UK
{j.m.gomoluch,msch}@soi.city.ac.uk

Abstract. One of the challenges in the design of information agent systems is how to provide flexible load balancing. In our work we aim to explore different market-based approaches to load-balancing. We give an outline of the scenario which we consider in our work. We also give a brief overview of different load balancing strategies. As a motivating example for load balancing we consider a distributed information processing application for biological data. We provide an abstraction of this system which covers its main characteristics in terms of load and profile. Next, we present the results of our first experiments where we implemented this abstraction on two platforms, RMI and Voyager, and compared their performance. We discuss the different design issues for employing a market-based load balancing policy in such a system. Finally, we draw conclusions and give the directions of our future work.

1   Introduction

Information agent systems are computational software systems that have access to multiple, heterogeneous and geographically distributed information sources. One of their main tasks is to perform active searches for relevant information in non-local domains on behalf of their users or other agents. Information from multiple autonomous sources is retrieved, analysed, manipulated and integrated to finally provide a high level access to information that is otherwise not efficiently usable.

Information agent systems usually comprise three types of agents:

- wrappers, which wrap up the information source and make it thus accessible in a standardised form,
- facilitators, which act as yellow-page service and know which wrappers provide what kind of information, and finally,
- mediators, which decompose a complex query into sub-queries, ask the facilitator for suitable wrappers, query these wrappers and finally integrate the partial results to an overall answer.

There are many open problems in designing the architecture of information agent systems. These include performance, scalability, adaptability and reliability. When dealing with these problems, an important question is how to allocate resources, i.e. how to balance the load in the system.

V. Mařík et al. (Eds.): MASA 2001, LNAI 2322, pp. 188–197, 2002.
© Springer-Verlag Berlin Heidelberg 2002

This problem is common for many applications. It can be very complex in large systems with geographically distributed computational resources, also referred to as *Computational Grids* [3]. The aim is to adapt the distribution of the work load to the utilisation and performance of the machines and to the requirements of the applications. We can distinguish load balancing strategies according to two criteria:

- Static vs mobile, i.e. are tasks assigned to hosts once and then stay there or can they migrate if it turns out at a later stage that it is advantageous to leave the machine;
- State-based vs model-based, i.e. is the load balanced according to a current snapshot of the system state, which is expensive to obtain, or according to a model, which predicts the system state but might be inaccurate.

The different strategies will be discussed in Sect. 3 in more detail. But first, we will describe the scenario which we examine as a load-balancing problem.

2   Scenario: A Market for Computational Resources

We study market mechanisms as a way of balancing the computational work load in distributed information processing applications. We use a model consisting of several clients, which try to access resources, and service providers, which 'sell' these resources. The resources can include CPU time, memory space or even more sophisticated services.

All participants in the system aim to maximise their gains: the clients try to access a given resource while paying as little as possible, whereas the service providers try to charge them as much as possible. Brokers or other intermediates may be employed to facilitate the process of resource allocation.

The system is assumed to be geographically distributed, and therefore network bandwidth and latency need to be taken into account. It is also an open system: the clients and service providers may join or leave it over time. We do not intend to model or build 'realistic' markets: we see the market mechanism as a vehicle to achieve allocation efficiency. This allows us to design policies and negotiation strategies as we consider them useful.

There are different degrees of complexity that our system can have – concerning its resources and the type of tasks to be carried out. We will distinguish the following cases:

Resources of the Same Type. In the simplest case the resources are of the same type and therefore more or less exchangeable. They are made available by one or more service providers and are demanded by several clients. The resources can have different properties, such as speed, location, response time, reliability, etc. POPCORN [16] and SPAWN [19] are examples of such computational markets, where the participants exchange CPU time. Such systems are very promising for so-called *parameter sweep applications* [5,6]. These consist of many independent tasks, which can be effectively executed, since the applications have no inter-task communication and no task precedences, thus resulting in a high computation to communication ratio.

Different Resources. In a more general system there exist different types of resources, and the clients are restricted to particular resource types – or at least have certain preferences. These could be a particular hardware platform, operating system, software package, etc. This scenario can be found not only in the domain of distributed computing [13], but also in various models of an 'information filtering economy' [12]. In [12] the resources are information goods such as articles or books which fall into different categories. The clients seek for articles of certain categories, and their preferences are modelled by utility functions.

Service Composition. In this case, the execution of the client's application requires a composition of resources which can be of different types. In [14] this problem class is referred to as *task mapping* in a heterogeneous computing environment. Again, there are analogies in other domains: In telecommunications it is the problem of virtual circuit routing [1], where a route is specified by a source and destination point, and the appropriate links need to be determined. Another example can be found in the freight domain [17]: Clients want their goods to be transported from one place to another and 'buy' this service from a broker. The service includes the purchase of all sub-services that are required for the transport, i.e. all the links of the route and all other services like insurance, temporary storage, etc. The aim of the brokers is to provide the cheapest possible service.

Service Composition with Task Precedences. A further degree of complexity is added when task precedences need to be taken into account in the service composition.

3   Load Balancing

In this section we will describe the different load balancing approaches and refer to some example systems. A more detailed survey can be found in [10].

3.1   Static, State-Based Load Balancing

Many systems employ static, state-based load balancing as it is easy to implement and can lead to good results. Basic middleware like PVM, CORBA, or Applets can be used to this end.

The message-passing library PVM can adapt to variations in the utilisation of machines and to reconfigurations of the network. In CORBA, load balancing can be achieved with a trader which recommends services on the least loaded machine. An even simpler approach uses Java Applets. Instead of having a central controller scheduling the tasks, the users can decide if they want to provide their resources by downloading an Applet, which communicates its results back to the server. With enough participants such a simple approach can scale up to form a massive machine. In fact, a similar approach, www.distributed.net, consists of more than 100.000 participants and claims to be the fastest computer on earth. There are a number of such systems. A good survey can be found in [3].

Market-Based Approaches. One way of representing the system state and balancing load uses a market mechanism to value resources and achieve a match of supply and demand for resources [9].

Different protocols for the transactions between clients and service providers can be employed. A very simple mechanism is dynamic pricing, where the sellers set their prices and may change them at any time, depending on the buyers' demand [12]. Another approach are auctions [18] where buyers bid for resources according to a particular auction protocol (English, Dutch, Sealed bid, etc.). An advantage of auctions is that they allow one to determine an unknown resource value in a group of agents. A disadvantage is that the communication cost is high. Also, auctions might not be appropriate for markets in which the demand for the resources is low.

Some systems like SPAWN [19] and POPCORN [16] use such auction protocols for the resource allocation. Others avoid the overhead of communication and use pricing mechanisms without negotiation. Dynasty employs a hierarchical brokering infrastructure where the price for resources is periodically fixed [2].

3.2 Mobile, State-Based Load Balancing

In static load balancing, tasks are stuck on one machine once launched. However, if the environment is very dynamic (e.g. changing demands of tasks, changing resources, network bandwidth, etc.) it may be advantageous for the tasks to migrate before completion. This can be achieved by mobile objects which can be implemented using Java RMI for example. Mobile agents, which have active threads and which can decide independently when and where to move to, add a further degree of flexibility in that scheduling can be handled locally. Rather than having a central scheduler which decides where tasks execute, the tasks become agents and can decide themselves locally with a global pattern of load-balancing emerging. There exist a number of systems which use a mobile agent based infrastructure. TRAVELER [21] makes specifically use of autonomous mobile agents roaming the net in search of the best host. In [4] a system is presented which provides market-based resource control for mobile agents. To allocate resources to the agents, the system uses electronic cash, a banking system and a set of resource managers.

3.3 Model-Based Load Balancing

Model-based approaches to load balancing are much rarer as they involve two challenging problems: How to obtain an initial model and how to adapt it as time passes. On the one hand the model can be inaccurate but on the other hand it can reduce the amount of communication. Since there are not too many systems using model-based load balancing, we will briefly describe both static and mobile strategies in this subsection.

A static approach can be found in the Challenger system [7]. It uses a market mechanism – however, without money. When a job is originated, a 'request for bids' containing its priority value and information which can be used to estimate its duration is sent to the agents in the network. These make bids giving the estimated time to complete that job on their machine. Important parameters, which have a major impact on the system performance, are the message delay and errors estimating the job's completion time. Learning behaviour has been introduced in order to deal with these problems.

In the area of operating systems model-based strategies have been explored to optimise load balancing by process migration [11]. The distributions of CPU load and process life-time have been used to decide if and when to migrate tasks from one machine to another. In comparison to static load balancing, a reduction of task delays (queuing and migration) was achieved with this approach.

4   Real-World Example: EDITtoTrEMBL

As a motivating example for load balancing we consider EDITtoTrEMBL [15], a distributed information processing system for biological data. It gathers and integrates information from a number of protein annotation tools and is implemented in Java and RMI. We used an abstraction of this system, which covers its main characteristics in terms of load and profile (i.e. the code size, data size, and itinerary of the information objects). In our first experiments we implemented this abstraction on two platforms, RMI and Voyager, in order to compare their performance.

4.1   Architecture

The EDITtoTrEMBL system consists of analysers, dispatchers and mobile information objects. The analysers act as wrappers of different protein analysis programmes by converting their in- and outputs to the required formats. The mobile information objects are generated by a creator agent and contain DNA sequence data. They have to travel to several analysers to be annotated with further data, before returning to the collector. The order in which the analysers are visited is partially determined by a set of pre-conditions for some analysers. The dispatchers are mediators which plan the itineraries of the information objects. At the same time they act as facilitators which register the analysers with their services.

EDITtoTrEMBL is an open system and allows new programmes to be easily integrated. As speed is of importance, and as there are many entries to be analysed, the system has to deal with load balancing.

For optimal route planning of the information objects, not only the pre-conditions but also some other parameters such as the location of the resources

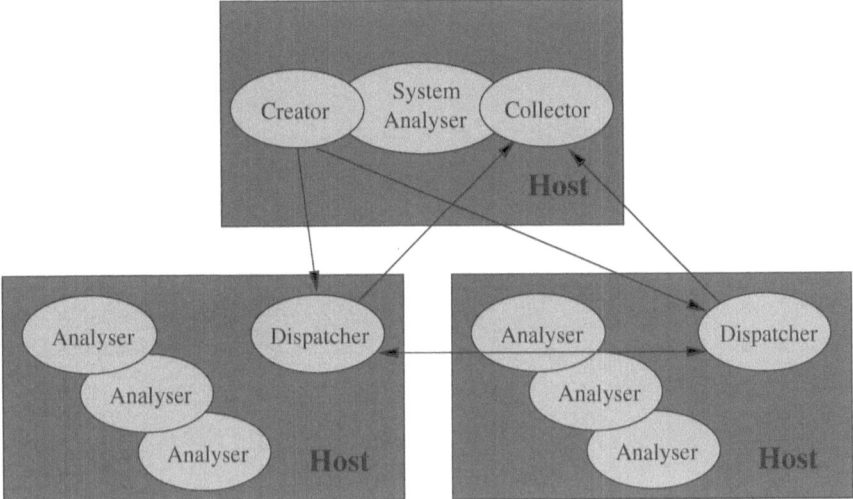

Fig. 1. Setup of the experiment

or the quality of service (e.g. speed) have to be considered. Thus, the problem to be solved with EDITtoTrEMBL can be classified as a service composition with task precedences (see Sect. 2).

4.2   First Experiments

In our experiments [8] we examined the performance of two platforms, RMI and Voyager, for EDITtoTrEMBL. We carried out simulations on three Linux PCs. The experimental setup is shown in Fig. 1. Two dispatchers are located on different hosts, and three analysers are attached to each of them. The creator, collector and system analyser are placed on a third host. The creator produces mobile information objects during a fixed period of time. On creation, each object is given the number of analysers it has to visit during its journey. This number is randomly generated. Like in the real system, the information objects' itinerary is not pre-defined. Instead, the information objects are given the next few, randomly generated destinations whenever they arrive at a dispatcher. The journey of the information objects terminates at the agent collector, and their data (travel time, number of analysers and dispatchers visited) is given to the system analyser for further processing.

4.3   Results

Figure 2 shows the results of an experiment, where mobile information objects were created over a period of 5 minutes, and where for each analyser visit an

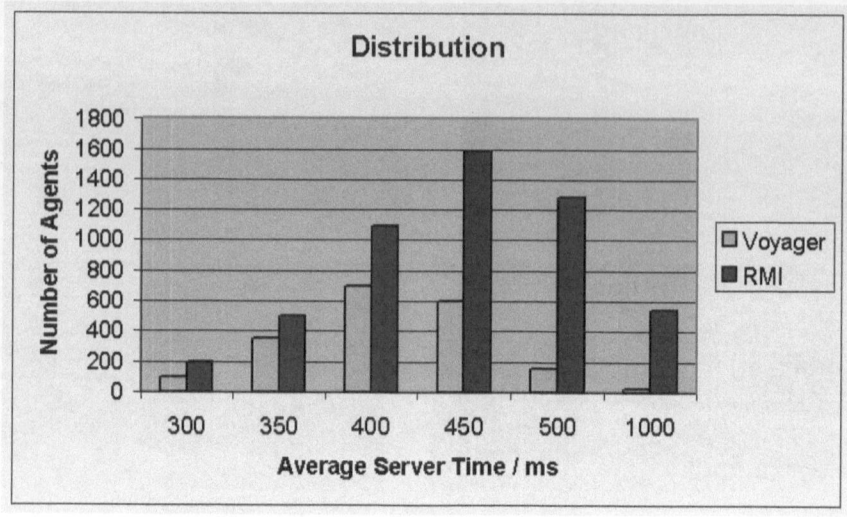

Fig. 2. Distribution of the average server time

additional delay of 500 ms was assumed. In the diagram the distributions of the average time per server (either analyser or dispatcher) for both, the Voyager and the RMI implementation, are shown. For RMI the average time per server tends to be slightly higher than for Voyager. However, the difference is not very large: The mean values for Voyager and RMI are 386.6 ms and 423 ms, respectively, and the standard deviations are 50.0 and 63.6. The figure also shows that with RMI about 2.5 times as many information objects are generated as with Voyager. This lower rate of object creation could be due to the platform itself or to our implementation of the objects as autonomous agents.

Similar observations have been made in other experiments where different delays where used for the analysers [8]. These experiments have also shown that Voyager was less reliable than RMI: some mobile objects simply got 'lost'. This problem occurred when the number of concurrent objects was high. The Voyager platform (we used version 3.3) did not provide any built-in recovery, and no exceptions have been thrown.

In summary, the differences between the two platforms are small: RMI is slightly slower than Voyager but it can handle higher loads. Thus, the Voyager platform will not improve EDITtoTrEMBL with its current architecture.

4.4 Design Issues for Load Balancing

After having evaluated the performance of the two platforms RMI and Voyager, we will examine whether performance improvements can be achieved by balancing the work load in the EDITtoTrEMBL system. As load balancing strategies we will employ market-based approaches. There are different design issues which have to be considered:

Pricing Policy. The main design parameter is the pricing policy that is used for the transactions between clients and service providers (see Sect. 3.1). Different policies may vary in the quality of the resource allocation, communication requirements, etc. for a given situation.

System Architecture. An important question is how to organise the system. In a large, geographically distributed system, a central marketplace may be a bottleneck [16]. As an alternative, a network of co-operating or competing markets can be employed. In such a system it will be difficult for the clients to have an overview of the resources (their price, location, quality, etc.). To deal with the loss of transparency in large systems, brokers or other intermediaries need to be introduced.

Negotiation Strategies. The quality of the resource allocation also depends on the negotiation strategies of the clients, service providers, and intermediates. A promising approach is to endow these agents with models of their environment. For instance, 'smart' brokers can be introduced which accumulate knowledge about the resources (e.g. price, distance, quality of service, reliability, etc.) and also learn the preferences of the clients.

4.5   Current Investigations

Before applying market-based strategies to EDITtoTrEMBL, we need to investigate them for less complex scenarios. We are currently using discrete-event simulation to study the performance of different protocols for the allocation of independent tasks with deadlines. The computational resources are traded at a central marketplace. As protocols we examine fixed pricing, dynamic (seller-adjusted) pricing, auctions and reverse auctions.

Objectives and Metrics. Our main objective is to optimise the system's performance in order to maximise the gains of the participants. From the clients' perspective, important metrics are the waiting and execution times of the tasks.

Other performance metrics include the throughput and the utilisation of the resources: From the system's point of view, one possible objective is to obtain even load in the system. Alternatively, the throughput can be maximised.

We also consider the stability and scalability of the system and the fairness in the resource allocation [20]. As the system is assumed to be geographically distributed, the communication costs are also taken into account.

5   Conclusions and Future Work

In our experiments we have evaluated the performance of two platforms, Voyager and RMI, for an abstraction of EDITtoTrEMBL, a distributed information processing application for biological data. Our results show that the performance of the platforms is similar. Voyager may not improve EDITtoTrEMBL with its current architecture. However, like other mobile agent platforms, it adds a new dimension of flexibility. It enables one to build a system, where mobile information objects can decide which resource to move to, and where they are also able to change their itineraries on the fly.

In our future work we will examine how to provide load balancing in EDITtoTrEMBL and other information processing applications. In particular, we will investigate market-based load balancing mechanisms which we are currently applying to less complex problems.

We will use discrete-event simulation which allows us to evaluate different scenarios and strategies without relying on a particular hardware infrastructure. This type of simulation also enables one to model communication delays in geographically distributed systems. To validate the simulations, we will carry out experiments such as those described in Sect. 4.

Acknowledgement. We would like to thank Patrick Cogan for creating the EDITtoTrEMBL abstraction and implementing it in Java RMI. We also would like to thank the anonymous reviewers for their helpful comments.

References

[1] Y. Azar. On-line load balancing. In *Online Algorithms - The State of the Art*, pages 178–195. Springer, 1998.

[2] M. Backschat, A. Pfaffinger, and C. Zenger. Economic-based dynamic load distribution in large workstation networks. In P. Fraigniaud et al., editor, *Proc. of the 2nd International Euro-Par Conference (in Lecture Notes in Computer Sciences)*, volume 2, pages 631–634, Lyon, France, August 1996. Springer-Verlag.

[3] M. Baker, R. Buyya, and D. Laforenza. The Grid: A Survey on Global Efforts in Grid Computing. Technical Report 2001/92, Monash University, Melbourne, Australia, May 2001.

[4] J. Bredin, D. Kotz, and D. Rus. Market-based resource control for mobile agents. In *Proc. of the Second International Conference on Autonomous Agents AA98*, Mineapolis, USA, May 1998. ACM Press.

[5] R. Buyya, J. Giddy, and D. Abramson. An Evaluation of Economy-based Resource Trading and Scheduling on Computational Power Grids for Parameter Sweep Applications. In *Proc. of the Second Workshop on Active Middleware Services (AMS 2000) in conjunction with the Ninth IEEE International Symposium on High Performance Distributed Computing (HPDC 2000)*, Pittsburgh, USA, August 2000. Kluwer Academic Press.

[6] H. Casanova, A. Legrand, D. Zagorodnov, and F. Berman. Heuristics for Scheduling Parameter Sweep Applications in Grid Environments. In *Proc. of the 9th Heterogeneous Computing Workshop (HCW'00)*, pages 349–363, May 2000.

[7] A. Chavez, A. Moukas, and P. Maes. Challenger: A multi-agent system for distributed resource allocation. In *Proc. of the First International Conference on Autonomous Agents AA97*, Marina del Ray, CA, USA, February 1997. ACM Press.

[8] P. Cogan, J. Gomoluch, and M. Schroeder. A quantitative and qualitative comparison of distributed information processing using mobile agents realised in RMI and Voyager. *To appear in the International Journal of Software Engineering and Knowledge Engineering (IJSEKE)*, 2001.

[9] D. F. Ferguson, C. Nikolaou, J. Sairamesh, and Y. Yemini. Economic models for allocating resources in computer systems. In *Market-Based Control: A Paradigm for Distributed Resources Allocation*. World Scientific, Hong Kong, 1996.

[10] J. Gomoluch and M. Schroeder. Information agents on the move: A survey on load-balancing with mobile agents. *Software Focus (Wiley)*, 2(2):31–36, 2001.

[11] M. Harchol-Balter and A. B. Downey. Exploiting process lifetime distributions for dynamic load-balancing. *ACM Transactions on Computer Systems*, 15(3):253–285, 1997.

[12] J. O. Kephart, J. E. Hanson, and A. R. Greenwald. Dynamic pricing by software agents. *Computer Networks (Amsterdam, Netherlands)*, 32(6):731–752, March 2001.

[13] L. Levy, L. Blumrosen, and N. Nisan. OnLine Markets for Distributed Object Services: the MAJIC system. In *Proc. of the 3rd USENIX Symposium on Internet Technologies and Systems (USITS 2001)*, San Francisco, CA, USA, March 2001.

[14] M. Maheswaran, T. D. Braun, and H. J. Siegel. Heterogeneous distributed computing. In J. G. Webster, editor, *Encyclopedia of Electrical and Electronics Engineering*, pages 679–690. John Wiley & Sons, New York, NY, 1999.

[15] S. Möller, U. Leser, W. Fleischmann, and R. Apweiler. EDITtoTrEMBL: A distributed approach to high-quality automated protein sequence annotation. *Journal of Bioinformatics*, 15(3):219–227, 1999.

[16] N. Nisan, S. London, O. Regev, and N. Camiel. Globally distributed computation over the Internet - the POPCORN project. In *Proc. of the 18th International Conference on Distributed Computing Systems (ICDCS'98)*, Amsterdam, Netherlands, 1998. IEEE.

[17] C. Preist, A. Byde, C. Bartolini, and G. Piccinelli. Towards agent-based service composition through negotiation in multiple auctions. In *Proc. of the AISB Symposium on Information Agents for E-Commerce (AISB'01 Convention)*, University of York, UK, March 2001.

[18] T. Sandholm. Distributed rational decision making. In G. Weiss, editor, *Multi-agent systems*. MIT Press, 2000.

[19] C. A. Waldspurger, T. Hogg, B. A. Huberman, J. O. Kephart, and W. S. Stornetta. Spawn: A distributed computational economy. *Transactions on Software Engineering*, 18(2):103–117, February 1992.

[20] P. De Wilde, H. S. Nwana, and L. C. Lee. Stability, fairness and scalability of multi-agent-systems. *International Journal of Knowledge-Based Intelligent Engineering Systems*, 3(2):84–91, 1999.

[21] C.-Z. Xu and B. Wims. A mobile agent based push methodology for global parallel computing. *Concurrency: Practice and Experience*, 14(8):705–726, 2000.

Autonomous Agents Applied to Manufacturing Scheduling Problems: A Negotiation-Based Heuristic Approach

Andrea Gozzi, Massimo Paolucci, and Antonio Boccalatte

LIDO Lab – Department of Communication, Computer and System Sciences (DIST)
University of Genoa
Via Opera Pia 13, 16145, Genova - Italy
{gozzi,paolucci,nino}@dist.unige.it

Abstract. In this paper, a heuristic approach to job scheduling, which is based on a multi-agent system model, is proposed. The class of scheduling problems considered is characterized by the presence of independent jobs and identical parallel machines, and by a non-regular objective, including both job earliness and tardiness penalties. The multi-agent scheduling system is composed by different classes of agents, and a schedule is progressively defined by a negotiation protocol among the agents associated with the jobs and the machines.

1 Introduction

In the recent years, an important factor speeding up the development and the exploitation of the new information technologies has been represented by the enlargement of the economic competition to the global market and the consequent need to integrate and accelerate the processes of the whole supply and production chain.

This trend has been witnessed by the introduction of the concept of "Agile Manufacturing" in production industries as an answer to the necessity of a more adaptability and flexibility to the changes in the market demand. Consequently, planning and operational decision activities relevant to logistics and production processes tend to be increasingly distributed among the various decision entities instead of being centralized. Integrated information systems, as Enterprise Resource Planning (ERP) systems, computer networks and, in general, the new communication technologies, represent the suitable framework for new methodologies and models to face decision and management problems in modern manufacturing. The research presented in this paper is focused on the possible application of multi-agent system paradigm to scheduling in manufacturing, which is usually considered one of the most challenging problems of production management. In the following, both the aspects of this research are briefly introduced.

The research on autonomous agent and Multi-Agent Systems (MAS) has received in the last years a growing interest from scientists and practitioners of various fields (a review can be found in [1]). The concepts of agent and MAS have been introduced from the Distributed Artificial Intelligent (DAI) and they can be applied to different contexts to provide distributed decision and control ability among the relevant system entities. Many definitions of agents have been given, and a quite general one by

V. Mařík et al. (Eds.): MASA 2001, LNAI 2322, pp. 198-207, 2002.
© Springer-Verlag Berlin Heidelberg 2002

Wooldridge and Jennings depicts an agent as "*a computer system that is situated in some environment, and that is capable of autonomous actions in this environment in order to meet its design objectives*" [2]. Common characteristics of agents are autonomy, reactivity (i.e., their ability to perceive changes in their environment and to act as a consequence), pro-activeness (i.e., their ability of taking the initiative to satisfy their objectives), social ability (i.e., their capability of interacting with other agents and humans) [3]. The scientific interest on MAS is also confirmed by the number of different applications of agent technology that have been recently investigated [4].

The work described in this paper deals with MASs devoted to manufacturing scheduling decisions, and, in particular a class of scheduling problem characterized by a non-regular objective has been considered. In general, the application of the autonomous agent paradigm to manufacturing is a quite extensively studied field (for a state of the art survey see [5]), especially after the introduction of the concepts of Intelligent Manufacturing and Holonic Manufacturing System (HMS) [6].

One of the most critical problems in manufacturing systems is represented by the scheduling of jobs on the available shop-floor resources. Such kind of problem is usually characterized by the presence of both dynamic and stochastic aspects that require the use of suitable on-line decision approaches. In addition, apart from very simple cases, the computational complexity of scheduling problem in manufacturing often suggests the use of heuristic decision models. Therefore, in Flexible Manufacturing Systems (FMS), where generally operational conditions are affected by random changes, simple scheduling rules are used to provide on-line schedules, or, alternatively, a set of on-line control rules is adopted to react to the variations possibly occurring with respect to a priori fixed nominal schedules.

The research presented in this paper is devoted to the definition of an approach based on a MAS architecture to face a class of scheduling problems that can arise in FMS contexts. The final objective is to provide a scheduling system, which can be effectively adapted to high dynamic manufacturing environments. The problem that has been considered to initially define the characteristics of the Multi-Agent Scheduling System (MASS) involves the scheduling of n independent job, characterized by release and due dates, on m identical machines with a non-regular objective, typical of Just-In-Time production, where both job earliness and tardiness costs are included. This problem, even if conceptually simple, belongs to the category of the computationally hard problems and actually does not present dynamic aspects. However, the architecture of the MASS that we are currently developing has been designed to face also the case of on-line job arrivals.

In the following section, the considered scheduling problem is formally defined and some literature references are reported. Then, the general components of a generic MAS model are described and the specific model adopted for the MASS facing the considered scheduling problem is detailed. Finally some computational results are reported and some conclusions are drawn.

2 The Scheduling Problem

We consider the problem of scheduling N independent jobs j=1,...,N, on M parallel identical machines i=1,...,M. The machines are always available, and can serve only one job at a time. The jobs cannot be preempted, and are characterized by a *processing time* p_j, a *ready time* r_j, representing the time instant at which the job is ready to start its execution, and a *due date* d_j, denoting the time instant at which the job should be completed without incurring penalties. Let us indicate with s_j the *starting time* of the process of the job j. Then the following quantities relevant to the job j can be defined: the *completion time*, $c_j = s_j + p_j$; the *earliness*, $e_j = \max [0, d_j - s_j - p_j] = \max [0, d_j - c_j]$; the *tardiness*, $t_j = \max [0, s_j + p_j - d_j] = \max [0, c_j - d_j]$.

The jobs have to be assigned and sequenced on the machines, fixing their starting time in order to minimize a weighted sum of their earliness and tardiness, that is

$$\sum_{j=1,\ldots N} (we_j \cdot e_j + wt_j \cdot t_j) \tag{1}$$

where we_j and wt_j, $j=1,\ldots,N$, respectively represent the weight associated with the earliness and the tardiness of the job j.

Most of the literature on scheduling is mainly focused on problems with regular objectives, i.e., that do not consider the possibility of earliness costs. However, problem with non-regular costs have recently received an increasing attention as they are clearly associated with the Just-In-Time production. The problem of single machine scheduling with earliness and tardiness (E/T) penalties has been first introduced by Kanet [7]. Since then, several E/T scheduling models have been presented and a reference survey can be found in [8]. Two different E/T scheduling problems have been proposed in the literature, namely, the ones considering the due dates as decision variables to be determined, and the others characterized by fixed due dates. For these latter, most of the studied models were focused on single machine problems; Emmons [9] and Hall [10] first extended the E/T scheduling to parallel machines, but even in the following works the case of a common due date was mainly taken into account. Optimal solutions for the common due date problems are provided by the so-called V-shaped schedules: the jobs are sorted in non decreasing order of their (weighted) processing times, that is in the Shortest Processing Time (SPT) first order, and are then assigned, starting from the first in the list, one to the set of the job completing before the due date and another to the set of job completing after the due date; the jobs completing before the due date are then sorted in non increasing order of their (weighted) processing times, that is in the Longest Processing Time (LPT) first order, and assigned so that the last job in the set completes just at the due date; differently, the jobs completing after the due date are sorted in the SPT order and are assigned so that the first job in the set starts exactly at the due date. This constructive procedure can be used only for problems with *un-restricted* due dates, i.e., due dates that are large enough to not influence the assignment of the jobs completing before it. On the other hand, problems with a *restricted* due date are computationally intractable even in the single machine case [11]. E/T problems with distinct due dates have not been largely investigated; the single machine case with symmetric E/T penalties is NP-hard [12], and the optimal solution may require idle times to be inserted with a not V-shaped structure. A recent work proposing a genetic approach for an E/T problem with distinct due dates and release times, but also sequence dependent setups and both uniform and identical machines, has been proposed in [13].

The class of E/T scheduling problems considered in this paper includes different due dates which can be generally restricted so that the solution provided by a V-shaped schedule may be not optimal. Such problems are static ones, but the MAS heuristics that we propose can be adopted even in dynamic and more realistic on-line contexts where the ready times correspond to the job arrival times.

3 The Multi-Agent System Model

In this section, we define the basic features of the general MAS model that has been used as a reference for the development of the proposed scheduling approach.

A MAS model corresponds to an environment where different classes of agents live, performing both autonomous and social activities. In order to specify a MAS model, two main components should be defined, namely, the description of the classes of agents populating the model, and the interaction protocol that is adopted among the agents. The general kind of agent that has been considered is characterized by four components: *private data*, *methods*, *knowledge* and *engine*. The *private data* are a collection of variables representing the current agent state and its perception of the environment state; the *methods* are a collection of functions that are used by the agent to perform some computations or actions; the *knowledge* is a set of rules which define the agent behavior. The agents can only communicate by exchanging messages. In general, whenever a message is received, an agent works out, based on its objective (specified in its *knowledge*), a decision (i.e., a behavior) and it sends some messages to other agents. The agent's knowledge is composed by a set of rules that includes a condition statement and a list of actions (computations or messages sending) that are performed in case of the rule firing. For each message received by an agent, at least one rule is defined; in general, more rules are introduced to specify different agent behaviors associated with particular message contents. Therefore, the agents represent the active decisional entities of the MAS model, and the set of rules qualifies the behavior of the agents. The *engine* behaves as an inferential engine and it is the responsible of the agent life process, which determines the sequence of computations on the basis of the available information. During its decision-making activity, an agent can use some *methods* to perform possible computations.

The social behavior of the agents is ruled by a social interaction protocol that is determined by the specific kinds of messages that can be exchanged and by the consequent agent actions. In the adopted MAS model, the interaction protocol is defined by specifying *agent communities*. A community is a set of classes of agents that can directly communicate for a given purpose by exchanging a particular set of messages; an *ontology* is associated with each community, which includes the set of messages that can be exchanged among the involved classes of agents. In general, agents can belong to more communities and a community could even be composed by agents of the same class.

In order to make the agents of a MAS communicate with external entities, such as, the user or any kind of information sources, some special classes of interface agents can be introduced. The methods of interface agents allow exchanging information with external information systems (i.e., reading and writing data in databases or sending and receiving messages with external software process and GUI dialog). Such interface agents communicate with the other model agents being included in appropriate agent communities.

4 The Multi-Agent Scheduling System

In the proposed MAS approach to scheduling, we define a model in which the following agents have been introduced:
- a set of job-agents, including a job-agent JA_j for each job j;
- a set of machine-agents, including a machine-agent, MA_i, for each machine i;
- one job-agent generator agent (JGA);
- one machine-agent generator agent (MGA);
- one contract coordinator agent (CCA).

At the system start-up, only the JGA, the MGA and the CCA are active. When the scheduling process starts, the JGA creates a new JA_j for each job j already arrived, whereas the MGA a new MA_i for each machine i available in the shop-floor. A JA_j agent knows in its private data, the r_j, p_j, d_j of the associated job, and the weights we_j and wt_j, that are used to determine the priority of the job. A MA_i knows the list of assigned jobs, and a list describing its available slots of time. The objective of a JA_j is to obtain service for the job j by a machine so that the job completes as close as possible at its due date. Each JA_j has a virtual budget that is used to bid for the service of the MAs. On the other hand, each MA_i tries to maximize both the number of served jobs and the amount of virtual money received from the job-agents. After the agents creation, the CCA signals to all the JA_j to start negotiating in order to receive service from the machines. The CCA manages the evolution of the time in the MASS, periodically calling the agents for contracting cycles; in the current version of our scheduling system the time evolution is only fictitious and it should be synchronized with the real time for a future use of the MASS as on-line scheduler. A JA_j, according with the current time and its d_j, decides whether send a service request message to the MAs, specifying the bid and the information about the job, or delay it. The MAs must reply to the JA requests and possibly contract with them. If a MA_i accepts to serve a JA_j, it sends a proposal message specifying the best service time available for the job schedule; otherwise, it sends a refuse message. Then, the JA_j selects the best among the possible proposals and sends an acceptance message to the MA. The contract among the job and the machine is finally committed by an acknowledge from the MA, which also causes the CCA to update the partial schedule. Figure 1 reports the interaction diagram among the different agents in the MASS, even showing the communication of information about jobs and machines between the MASS and the ERP system; in particular, the clouds in the figure indicate the sets of JAs and MAs, the boxes linked to the different agents include the main data and parameters of the agents' private data, the solid arrows denote the agent generation processes, and finally the directed links represent the exchanges of messages.

Let now us consider some more details about the behavior of the most relevant types of agents in the MASS, that is, JAs, MAs and CCA. JAs could be generated by the JGA all at once when the scheduling starts, or progressively in correspondence of their release date. This latter behavior is suitable with the scheduling of dynamic job arrivals in a real time context. A JA_j aims at finding a machine which serves the job j minimizing $V_j(s)$, specified in (2), which is the weighted sum of e_j and t_j as a function of the job starting time s, and it represents the contribution of job j to the global scheduling cost.

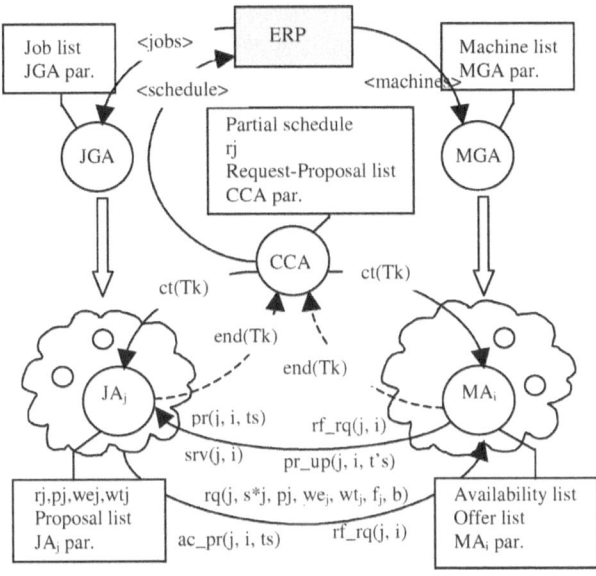

Fig. 1. The interaction among the agents in the MASS

$$V_j(s) = we_j \cdot max[0,d_j-s-p_j]+wt_j \cdot max[0,s+p_j-d_j] \tag{2}$$

Then, the optimal starting time for the execution of job j, s^*_j, is computed as in (3).

$$s^*_j = \min_{s:s \geq r_j} V_j(s) \tag{3}$$

Clearly, the optimal value, corresponding to $V_j(s^*_j)=0$, is given by $s^*_j = d_j - p_j$, if $s^*_j \geq r_j$ or by $s^*_j = r_j$ with $V_j(s^*_j) = wt_j \cdot (r_j + p_j - d_j)$. The JA$_j$ then computes the ideal starting time s^*_j and $f^*_j = s^*_j - r_j$, the job float to s^*_j from r_j. The budget of each JA$_j$ is initially fixed by the JGA depending on the weights we$_j$ and wt$_j$. Each time a JA sends a message asking for service, a fixed request cost has to be paid. Therefore, the JAs use a strategy to decide, on the basis of their floats, budgets and the current time, whether send a service request and the amount of its possible bid. This strategy is based on two distributions of probability, whose parameters are fixed by the JGA, and which characterize the different attitudes of the JAs in anticipating or delaying a request for service and in spending for being served. A JA$_j$ service request corresponds to a rq(j, s^*_j, p$_j$, we$_j$, wt$_j$, f$_j$, b) message to the MAs; with such a message the JA$_j$ declares the amount of process requested, the ideal starting time, the earliness and tardiness weights, the float f$_j$ computed at the current time τ, that is, f$_j$=min[f$^*_j$, s$^*_j$-τ], and b, the bid offered. Note that the presence of a bid leads to a competition among the JAs rather than a collaboration; such a behavior seems appropriate as it reflects the actual competition of jobs for shared resources.

The MAs, aiming at both maximizing the number of served jobs and their profits, tend to accept the higher job bids, but mitigate such a behavior taking into account the job floats. A MA_i, when receiving a service request, first determines if it can be accepted or refused by means of a criterion based on a stochastic acceptance distribution, which, as in the case of the JA decisions, is characterized by parameters fixed by the MGA. Briefly, on the basis of such a criterion, the requests from jobs with a float greater than a upper threshold are always refused and the ones with a float lesser than lower threshold are always accepted; the probability to accept the requests with a float included in those bounds decreases from the lower to the upper threshold and it is also proportional to the bid offered. In case the request for service is rejected, the MA_j sends a refusal message rf_rq(j, i) to the JA_j. If the request is accepted, the MA_j searches its list of available time slots for an interval to start the job service as close as possible to the ideal s^*_j. In case the job execution could not start at s^*_j, the MA_i determines a suitable alternative taking into account we_j and wt_j, and replies with a proposal message pr(j, i, ts), where ts is the proposed starting time. The JA_j can then accept the proposal, answering an ac_pr(j, i, ts) message or in turn refuse them. After receiving one or more acceptance messages, the MAs sort them according to associated bids, and serve as agreed the first JA, updating the time availability list and sending a conclusive srv(j, i) message. The MAs then consider the following JAs as sorted and give them service if the agreed time intervals result still available; otherwise, they reply with an updated proposal pr_up((j, i, t's), starting in such cases a new iteration of negotiation.

A JA_j receiving the original proposals from the MAs, evaluates them by computing $V_j(ts)$, and accepts the best one. If this proposal is successively updated by the MA_i, the JA_j evaluates again the updated and the old proposals and selects the new best candidate until it manages to be served by a MA. This negotiation process terminates after a finite number of steps as, at each iteration, at least one JA certainly obtains the service and leaves the competition. Note that even JAs exhausting their budget are finally served whenever their float exceeds the lower float threshold of MAs.

The schedule is progressively defined by following the above described negotiation protocol between JAs and MAs and is coordinated by the CCA. The CCA records all the successful contracts and updates the partial schedule, but its main role is that of time manager. In the off-line use of the MASS, a cycle time interval is a priori fixed, and, after the completion of a negotiation session, the CCA moves forward the current fictitious time, calling the agents for a new contracting cycle.

It should be observed that the role of the JGA and the MGA will turn out to be essential to face dynamic scheduling contexts: the JGA generates a job-agent on the occurrence of a new arrival of a job; the MGA both generates a machine-agent whenever a new machine becomes available and modifies the machine-agent state according to possible changes with respect to the nominal behavior of associated machine (e.g., breakdowns). A final remark regards the CCA that could be considered a bottleneck in the MASS as it centralizes the definition of the schedules, especially in case of on-line scheduling applications; however, in such cases the CCA could be removed by adopting a fully distributed negotiation protocol. This latter point will be the subject of future developments.

5 Experimental Results

In this section, some experimental results obtained testing our MASS on a set of randomly generated problems are reported. It should be observed that appropriate benchmarks do not seem to be available in the literature for the considered class of problems, as only recently they have received an increasing attention and they have not been largely investigated so far.

Our analysis aims at verifying the behaviour of the scheduling system facing several sets of problems that are characterized by different difficulty levels. In particular, the problem difficulty has been considered as depending on the number of jobs and machines, and on the spread of the jobs on the time, which is an index of how the requests for service of the jobs are in conflict. Such a kind of tests provides useful hints to verify the suitability and the effectiveness of the MASS applied to actual manufacturing contexts. Finally, the tests have been used to lead the tuning of the parameters that affect the behaviour of the agents. Such parameters, in particular, influence the time instants at which job-agents send their requests for service, and the decisions of machine-agents to accept or not the service requests. As different parameter values, which yield different agent behaviours, lead to different scheduling solutions, a self–tuning system could be developed in order to optimise the MASS performances.

Let us describe now the procedure used to produce the test problems. The job processing times have been randomly generated with a uniform distribution between a minimum and a maximum value, U[40, 200]. The job release times have been randomly generated following a uniform distribution, $U[0, \bar{p} \cdot n/m]$, where $\bar{p}$ is the mean job processing time, n is the number of jobs, and m is the number of machines. The job due date has been calculated as the sum of ready time, processing time plus a slack value; such a slack value has been defined as $\bar{p} \cdot k$, being k a given positive constant which has been used to set the spread of the jobs on the time and hence the problem difficulty. A quite similar problem generator procedure has been used in [13].

Table 1. The data used to generate the tests

n	m	k
10		
20	4	10
30	2	2

The values of the number of jobs, the number of machines, and k which have been used for the test problems are listed in the table 1.

For each configuration of the above three parameters, 10 problems have been generated and tested. Fig. 2 reports the trend of the cost of the solutions obtained for the different configurations (indicated in the three abscissa axes). Noting that the ideal (even not feasible) cost for the problems is zero, the curve in fig.1 shows the trend of the problem difficulty that increases by increasing values of n and decreasing values of m and k.

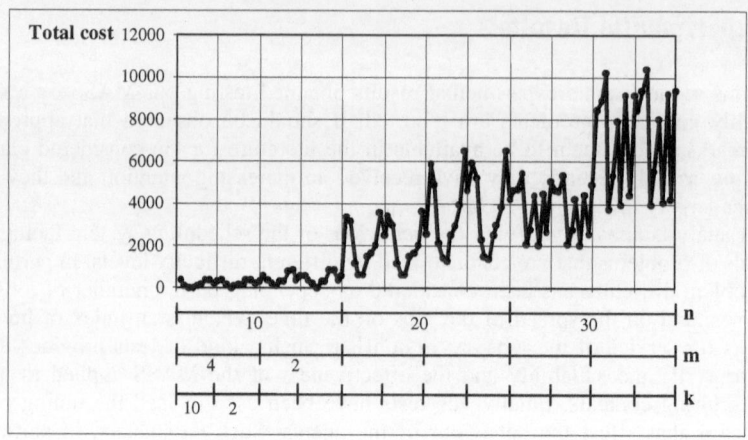

Fig. 2. The trend of cost for the scheduling test problems

The execution of the tests put into evidence the ability of the MASS to provide, with short computational time, scheduling solutions characterized by a good load balance among the machines, suggesting the suitability of the MASS even in presence of large number of jobs and machines.

The MASS has been tested with different values for the parameters that character-ize the behaviour of the agents. Two different configurations have been used for job-agents and machine-agents; in particular, job-agents that tend to send requests for service early (EJ) and late (LJ), and machine-agents that tend to satisfy the requests easily (EM) or difficultly (MD), have been considered. For each of the test problems the four possible configurations of the above behaviours have been compared, and the percentages of the difference of the costs obtained with respect to the best solution have been computed. Table 2 shows the average of the percent difference over all the tests executed.

Table 2. The average relative cost difference for the tested agent behaviours

EJ-EM	EJ-DM	LJ-DM	LJ-EM
22.5%	0.6%	14.6%	37.2%

6 Conclusion and Future Research

Introduced in the DAI, the multi-agent modeling paradigm is currently the object of many research efforts in different fields of the information technology and decision sciences. A multi-agent model can also represent a heuristic decision approach to optimization problems, where the optimization of a global objective derives from the autonomous behavior of single decision entities. This paper proposes an approach, that we are currently investigating, based on a MAS model to the scheduling of jobs in a manufacturing context. A MASS exploiting such a heuristic approach is being developed and tested by means of a software tool, named AgentLab, for the design and analysis of MAS models.

A future improvement of this approach could consist in including a learning behavior for the agents, in order to automate the fitting of the model parameters, providing adaptability to the scheduling system. In this connection, the MGA and JGA could track both the job arrivals, and the JA and MA activities in order to select the best configuration of the agents according with the current market demand. With this feature, the agents could adapt dynamically their behavior to the market changes.

References

1. Oliveira E., Fischer K. and Stepankova O.: Multi-agent systems: which research for which applications. Robotics and Autonomous Systems 27 (1999) 91-106.
2. Wooldridge, M. and Jennings N.R.: Intelligent agents: Theory and practise. The Knowledge Engineering Review 10, 2 (1995) 115-152.
3. Wooldridge, M.: Intelligent Agents. In Multiagent Systems: A Modern Approach to Distributed Artificial Intelligence G. Weiss (Ed.), MIT Press, Cambridge, MA. (1999).
4. Jennings, N.R. and Wooldridge M.J.: Applications of Intelligent Agents. In Agent Technology: Foundations, Applications, and Markets N.R. Jennings and M.J Wooldridge (Eds.), Springer. (1998).
5. Shen, W. and Norrie D.H.: Agent-Based Systems for Intelligent Manufacturing: A State-of-the-Art Survey. Knowledge and Information Systems, an Int. Jour. 1, 2, (1999) 129-156.
6. Van Leeuwen, E.H. and Norrie D.H.: Intelligent manufacturing: holons and holarchies. Manufacturing Engineer 76, 2 (1997) 86-88.
7. Kanet J.J.: Minimizing the average deviation of job completion times about a common due date. Naval Research Logistics Quarterly, 28 (1981) 643-651.
8. Baker K.H. and Scudder G.D.: Sequencing with earliness and tardiness penalties: a review. Operations Research, 30 (1990) 22-36.
9. Emmons H.: Scheduling to a common due date on parallel uniform processors. Naval Research Logistics, 34 (1987) 803-810.
10. Hall N.G.: Single and multiple-processor models for minimizing completion time variance. Naval Research Logistics Quarterly, 33 (1986) 49-54.
11. Hall N.G., Kubiak W., Sethi S.P.: Earliness and tardiness scheduling problems, II: deviation of completion time about a restrictive common due date. Operations Research, 39 (1991) 847-856.
12. Garey M.R., Tarjan R.E., Wilfong G.T.: One-processor scheduling with symmetric earliness and tardiness penalties. Mathematics of Operations Research, 13 (1988) 330-348.
13. Sivrikaya-Serifoglu F., and Ulusoy G.: Parallel machine scheduling with earliness and tardiness penalties. Computers and Operations Research, 26 (1999) 773-787.

International Workshop
on Adaptability and Embodiment
Using Multi-Agent Systems

AEMAS 2001: Selected Papers

Adaptability and Embodiment Using Multi-Agent Systems

Jean-Pierre Briot[1], Angélica Muñoz-Meléndez[1], and Alain Cardon[1,2]

[1] Laboratoire d'Informatique de Paris 6
UPMC Case 169, 4 Place Jussieu
75252 Paris Cedex 05
[2] LIH, Faculté des Sciences
Université du Havre, 76057 Le Havre Cedex
{Jean-Pierre.Briot,Angelica.Munoz,Alain.Cardon}@lip6.fr

1 The Embodiment and the Adaptability

What does *embodiment* mean? Is it a running process? Is it required in order to be adaptive? Is it important to distinguish between high-level and low-level cognition processing in order to talk about embodiment and adaptability? Is there a distinction between social embodiment and self-embodiment? What are the best models for behaviour and embodiment? Those questions have been wandering in our minds for a long time, and they have encouraged us to organise a forum to discuss about the meaning and the role of adaptability and embodiment in Multi-Agent Systems (MAS), our subject of research.

Adaptability and embodiment are key concepts of living systems. These notions are very important when designing adaptive MAS, systems composed of multiple autonomous entities that inhabit a dynamic and unpredictable environment, and usually have goals.

> We define **adaptability** as the property of a MAS of improving its competence based on its experience. **Embodiment** denotes, for us, the ability of such a system to set-up a self-representation in the environment.

The problem of generation and maintenance of an *image* of itself is a deep question in the system design. A large and diverse community in the fields of Artificial Intelligence, Artificial Life and Robotics is concerned with this problem. We consider that the MAS approach is very appropriate for studying the notions of adaptability and embodiment, due to the need of flexible systems, which are able to modify the relationships between their components and determine their behaviour in an emergent, bottom-up way.

2 The Workshop

We have selected two papers presented during the AEMAS Workshop, an affiliated event of the Advanced Course on Artificial Intelligence, ACAI 2001, celebrated in Prague in July 2001. These papers reflect the diversity of the subjects treated during AEMAS.

V. Mařík et al. (Eds.): MASA 2001, LNAI 2322, pp. 211–212, 2002.
© Springer-Verlag Berlin Heidelberg 2002

- The first paper is signed by Frances Brazier, Maarten van Steen and Niek Wijngaards and treats the problem of distributed shared agents. They consider the notion of embodiment from the point of view of representation of agents. Their paper addresses important issues involved in the replication of software agents.
- Samuel Landau and Sebastien Picault are the authors of the second paper. They are concerned with the adaptiveness of MAS. Their paper describes a model to develop adaptive multi-agent systems, based on an evolutionary approach.

We would like to thank the members of our programme committee: Kerstin Dautenhahn, Toru Ishida and Alexis Drogoul, for reviewing of the submitted papers, and for their valuable suggestions on the organisation of the workshop. Les Gasser, invited speaker of the workshop, presented an excellent review of the adaptive dimensions of MAS and we are very grateful for his participation. Finally, we also thank Hana Krautwurmova and the members of the local committee, who gave us a great support on the organisation of AEMAS.

Distributed Shared Agent Representations

Frances Brazier[1], Maarten van Steen[2], and Niek Wijngaards[1]

[1] Vrije Universiteit Amsterdam, Faculty of Sciences
Department of Artificial Intelligence
Intelligent Interactive Distributed Systems Group
de Boelelaan 1081a, 1081 HV Amsterdam, The Netherlands
{frances niek}@cs.vu.nl
http://www.iids.org
[2] Vrije Universiteit Amsterdam, Faculty of Sciences
Department of Computer Science, Computer Systems Group
de Boelelaan 1081a, 1081 HV Amsterdam, The Netherlands
steen@cs.vu.nl
http://www.cs.vu.nl/vakgroepen/cs

Abstract. The external representation of an agent is (part of) the embodiment of an agent: other agents may observe this information. The public representation of an agent usually contains at least the identity of an agent, and may include profiles of the agent, profiles of the user of an agent, an avatar, etc. In large-scale agent systems, scalability is an important issue. Replication is a scaling technique for distributing information over a number of locations. Replication of the external representation of an agent results in distributed shared agent representations. This paper addresses a number of issues involved in the realisation of such distributed shared agent representations, and briefly discusses middleware that is being devised to support such developments.

1 Introduction

Different definitions of agents [1,12,20,26,32] use concepts such as autonomy, pro-activity, reactivity, social abilities, and intentional models [2,5]. Very few (if any), however, refer to an agent's external representation: the part of an agent that can be observed.

This representation is the visible part of an agent: (part of) its embodiment. This external representation may be limited to an agent's identity (e.g. name of owner or an IP address of the host on which it resides). It may also contain extensive public information about an agent (e.g. its profile), or it may even be a graphical figure (e.g. an avatar) representing an agent. An agent's external representation is not necessarily a representation of the agent's internal processes. The environment of an agent includes objects, and representations of itself and other agents. It's obvious that an agent's environment influences the thoughts and actions of an agent [9,14], but it may also influence its own representation.

The distinction between an agent's external representation and an agent's internal processes and knowledge makes it possible to consider new ways to im-

V. Mařík et al. (Eds.): MASA 2001, LNAI 2322, pp. 213–220, 2002.
© Springer-Verlag Berlin Heidelberg 2002

plement large scale systems. Section 2 discusses the problem of scalability. Section 3 addresses the option of agent replication in this context. Section 4 presents a short overview of middleware that is currently being designed to support such replication. Section 5 summarizes the new areas of research involved.

2   The Problem of Scalability

In the multi-agent system community, large multi-agent systems are considered to consist of hundreds of agents, not thousands nor millions. As an example, consider the claim that Auctionbot is scalable, which is supported by an experiment with only 90 agents [33]. In the near future, however, we expect that multi-agent systems will need to be able to scale (in terms of the number of agents and available resources) to much larger populations. This almost immediately without noticeable loss of performance, or considerable increase in administrative complexity [18].

The current support for scalability in multi-agent frameworks is discussed in Sect. 2.1. A number of scaling techniques are described in Sect. 2.2.

2.1   Scalability in Multi-Agent Frameworks

The term *scalability* is not always used to refer to architecture, services and performance of systems. In some cases it is used to refer to scalable functionality. For example, the SAIRE approach [21], claims to be scalable because it supports heterogeneous agents. Shopbot [6] claims to be scalable because its agents can adapt to understand new websites. In both cases, the term *extensibile functionality* would seem to be more appropriate.

Researchers and developers of multi-agent frameworks are beginning to realise that scalability in the sense of architecture, services and performance is an issue. Most multi-agent frameworks (e.g. DECAF [13], InfoSleuth [19], April [17], AgentTcl [10], JAFMAS [4], Plangent [22], DESIRE [3]) do not seem to address the problem of scalability at all.

Other multi-agent frameworks rely on another framework to solve the problem of scalability. For example, scalablity in the CoABS (DARPA Control of Agent Based Systems) approach [29] is based on adequate support from computational grids in providing a plug-in backplane for agents [8].

There are, however, frameworks that clearly address one or more aspects of scalability. In ZEUS [31] scalability is defined to be the growth rate of the maximum communication load (as a function of the number of agents). Their conclusions are that the maximum communication load grows at worst linearly with the number of agents. This addresses a loss of performance problem, and is a step towards developing scalable multi-agent frameworks. In OAA (Open Agent Architecture) [16] matchmaking agents are described which can handle larger number of agents. The RETSINA MAS infrastructure [28] is designed to support multi-agent systems that run on a number of LANs and to avoid single-point of failures (e.g., in agent name services). The DARX framework [15] aims for fault-tolerance in distributed multi-agent systems by incorporating replication of (tasks of) agents.

Turner and Jennings [30] propose to (automatically) change the organization of agents in the multi-agent system to handle an increase in the population of a multi-agent system. For example, more middle agents or matchmakers are introduced to reduce overhead. Their approach is a possible step towards addressing administrative problems related to scalability.

None of the aforementioned approaches addresses minimizing the loss of performance as well as minimizing administrative overhead.

Research on specific services in multi-agent systems such as directory services also address scalability. The approach taken by Shehory [25] is an example in which agents locate agents based on each agent's own caching lists of agents they know. The theoretical analysis is based on a population of size 10,000; no experiments have yet been conducted.

Although agents have an identity in all of these multi-agent frameworks, none have explicitly distinguished explicit agent representations. Some multi-agent frameworks offer matchmaking services – in which information about agents is made public to some extent. None have considered using agent-based replication: replication of agents' external representation.

2.2   Scaling Techniques

Three scaling techniques can be distinguished to minimise loss of performance: (1) hiding communication latencies, (2) distribution, and (3) replication.

Hiding communication latencies is applicable in the case of geographical scalability, that is, when an agent system needs to span a wide-area network. To avoid waiting for responses to requests that have been issued to remote agents or services the requesting agent is programmed to do other useful work. This approach does require that an agent can be interrupted when the expected response (if any) is to be delivered.

Distribution generally involves partitioning a (large) set of data into parts that can be handled by separate servers. A well-known example of distribution is the natural partitioning of the set of Web pages across the approximately 25 million Web servers that are currently connected through the Internet. Other examples of distribution include the vertical or horizontal partitioning of tables in distributed databases [23].

When considering large-scale networks like the Internet it becomes crucial to combine distribution with latency hiding. Unfortunately, this is not always possible, for example when an agent simply needs an immediate response.

A third, and widely applied technique is to place multiple copies of data sets across a network, also referred to as *replication*. The underlying idea is that by placing data close to where they are used, communication latency is no longer an issue, so that agent-perceived performance is high. Having multiple copies means that such performance is good for all agents, no matter where they are located.

Keeping replicas consistent introduces a consistency problem that can be solved only by means of global synchronization. However, global synchronization in a multi-agent system is not a realistic option. Scalable multi-agent systems will need to support configurable and perhaps even adaptive replication strategies. No single strategy will show to be optimal under all conditions. Even for relatively simple systems such as the Web, differentiating strategies can make a lot of difference [24].

3   Replicating Agents

As stated above: one approach to handling scalability in a multi-agent system is to replicate agents. The distinction between an agent's external representation and an agent's internal representation makes replication possible. Section 3.1 discusses what is to be replicated of an agent, Sect. 3.2 discusses issues that play a role in distributed shared agent representations.

3.1   Replicating Agents or Public Representations

An agent can be seen as a a (multi-threaded) process with internal knowledge, and an external representation. Replication of an entire agent is not an obvious option for the realisation of scalable systems (running processes in parallel on different machines will seldom be synchronous, e.g., see [11] for an approach on replicating entire agents). In some cases cloning an agent may be a viable alternative to replication, but this is clearly application dependent and outside the scope of this paper.

Replicating an agent on a number of hosts makes it possible to decrease the load on each of the individual hosts. Consider, for example, an auction room. Having an auction hall replicated on different hosts, makes it possible to decrease the load on each individual machine. Instead of having any number of agents having to reside on the same machine in order to participate in a given auction, each agent's internal state and processes need only to reside on one of the hosts on which the auction room is replicated. Each agent's external representation is, however, replicated on each of the machines individually: this representation becomes a *distributed shared agent representation*. The internal process and data (or knowledge) of each agent resides on one machine, their public information is replicated. The agents do not need to know the location of the other agents: their presence is obvious, as is the information which needs to be shared.

Another example is that of information acquisition. An agent may wish to be informed of interesting publications by a number of bookstores at a time: as if it were actually in each of these bookstores at the same time. One way to accomplish this is to replicate the agent's external representation on each of the bookshops sites. This representation would include a profile of an agent's interests, book collection, and any other relevant information. If an agent's state changes, e.g. new books have been acquired, the agent's profile changes thus changing the profile in the agent's external representation It is as if the agent was actually residing on each of the bookstores sites.

3.2   Issues in Distributed Shared Agent Representations

Replication of public representations of agents, i.e. distributed shared agent representations, raises a number of issues regarding agents, and supportive middleware. These issues are related to policies (and/or strategies) for replication, accessibility, authority, and awareness.

- A number of issues concern *replication strategies*. The first issue is whether the middleware enforces a specific replication strategy, or whether each agent or system is able to specify its own replication strategy.
- A number of issues concern *accessibility policies*. Which agent may access which part of a public representation?
- A number of issues concern *authorisation policies*. Which agents are allowed to change part of the public representation of an agent? Only the agent itself? Other (authorized) agents? All agents? A human agent?
- A number of issues concern *awareness policies*. Does an agent notice modifications to its public representation? Does the agent know that replicas exist? Their location? Which agent observes its replica?

By combining choices, more and more complex situations may arise. Consider for example the combination of:

- public representation is replicated as soon as another agent wishes to observe it (i.e., many replicas)
- all agents may change a specific part of the public information of an agent
- an agent is aware of all changes to its public information.

The middleware needed to support this combination of policies, involves more expensive mechanisms (in terms of communication between entities in the multi-agent system) than a situation in which only the agent itself may modify its public representation. The question may even arise whether the more complex case scales well.

4   AgentScape: A Scalable Agent Framework

AgentScape is a currently being designed to support the design and development of worldwide distributed, scalable, secure, and extensible agent systems. It aims to provide support in two ways. First, support is provided on the level of a basic agent operating system. Second, support is provided by services, such as location and directory services, automated creation of agents, and management of agents, objects, locations and groups. AgentScape provides basic building blocks needed to build such systems.

AgentScape is a basic agent middleware system, intended to be usable for a wide range of multi-agent applications. As middleware, it offers primitives on the level of agents, shielding application developers from details at lower levels. In a sense, AgentScape is similar to UNIX. Within UNIX, everything is a file, on which operations are defined. Within AgentScape, two main concepts are distinguished: agents and objects. An agent is an active process, while an object is passive. Operations are defined on agents, akin to file operations in UNIX: move (mv), change owner (chown), change group (chgrp), change security modus (chmod), create, remove (rm), etc. Similar operations are defined on objects. Unique to AgentScape is the use of objects that are physically distributed across multiple machines, and that encapsulate their own distribution strategy. These objects are adopted from the Globe wide-area distributed system [27].

An important issue for AgentScape is that its model of agents and objects enable scalable solutions. In our approach, agents are expected to be mobile and can be implemented in different ways. This approach allows for implementing applications that require a high degree of interoperability across heterogeneous platforms. For a similar reason, our objects have self-managing capabilities. In contrast, most distributed-object models are based on remote objects in which the object state is not distributed, and is managed by the server the object is located [7]. Clients are only provided transparent access to an object through a proxy.

An agent in AgentScape consists of an external, visible part and and an internal, invisible part. The external visible part of an agent may be observed by other agents, and contains the public representation of the agent. The internal (invisible) part of an agent includes local information, its process, data and/or knowledge. The visible part of an agent may be replicated, the invisible part of an agent is not replicated. The visible part of an agent may be (nearly) empty. Any amount of information may be included in the public representation of an agent. The public representation of an agent is implemented as a distributed shared GLOBE object [27].

An agent operating system intended to be used in a worldwide setting needs services to enable retrieval of, for example, agents. Specific directory services are being developed, with which agents, distributed (and possibly replicated) objects, and groups of agents or objects can be found. Another service is a multi-agent factory with makes automated agent creation and modification possible. Finally, management services are being developed to reactively and pro-actively control agents, objects, locations, and groups in AgentScape. The challenge for these services is that they too need to be scalable across a worldwide network and they need to be able to support vast numbers of agents and objects.

5   Discussion

Distinguishing an external representation of an agent from its internal processes and knowledge, makes it possible to consider replication as an option with which large scale multi-agent systems can be devised. The challenge is to design an enviroment in which replication of an agent's public information is possible and effective. Which replication strategies are most useful and applicable, which accessibility, authorisation and awareness policies are needed, are clearly, as yet, unanswered. Scalable services to support such environments, is another challenge. These services address the notion of finding "agents" without necessarily having to contact a home address (not all agents necessarily have a home address), and finding objects, building new agents and adapting existing agents. Further research is clearly required!

Acknowledgements. This work was supported in part by NLnet Foundation. The authors wish to thank Guido van 't Noordende and Andy Tanenbaum for discussions on agents and agent platforms.

References

1. J.M. Bradshaw, (ed). "Software Agents." AAAI Press / MIT Press, 1997.
2. F.M.T. Brazier, B. Dunin-Keplicz, J. Treur and L.C. Verbrugge. "Modelling Internal Dynamic Behaviour of BDI agents." In: J-J. Meyer and P. Schobbes, (eds.), *Formal Models of Agents, Selected papers from final ModelAge Workshop*, Springer Verlag, Lecture Notes in AI, Vol. 1760, pp. 36–56, 1996.
3. F.M.T. Brazier, B. Dunin-Keplicz, N. Jennings, and J. Treur. "DESIRE: Modelling Multi-Agent Systems in a Compositional Formal Framework.." *International Journal of Cooperative Information Systems, special issue on Formal Methods in Cooperative Information Systems*, 6:67–94, 1997.
4. D. Chauhan. "Developing coherent multiagent systems using jafmas." In *Proc. International Conference on Multi Agent Systems, ICMAS98*, Cite des Sciences - La Villette, Paris, France, July 1998.
5. D.C. Dennett. "The Intentional Stance." Cambridge: MIT Press (1987).
6. R. B. Doorenbos, O. Etzioni, and D. S. Weld. "A Scalable Comparison-Shopping Agent for the World-Wide Web." In W. L. Johnson and B. Hayes-Roth, (eds.), *Proc. Proceedings of the First International Conference on Autonomous Agents (Agents'97)*, pp. 39–48, Marina del Rey, CA, USA, 1997. ACM Press.
7. W. Emmerich. *Engineering Distributed Objects*. John Wiley, New York, 2000.
8. I. Foster and C. Kesselman, (eds.). *Computational Grids: The Future of High Performance Distributed Computing*. Morgan Kaufman, San Mateo, CA., 1998.
9. J.S. Gero. "Conceptual Designing as a Sequence of Situated Acts." In: I. Smith, (ed.), *Artificial Intelligence in Structural Engineering*. Berlin: Springer, pp. 165–177, 1998.
10. R. Gray, D. Kotz, G. Cybenko, and D. Rus. "Agent Tcl." In W. Cockayne and M. Zyda, (eds.), *Proc. Mobile Agents: Explanations and Examples*. Manning Publishing, 1997.
11. Z. Guessoum, M. Quenault, and R. Durand. "An Adaptive Agent Model." In *Proc. AISB-2001*, pp. 100-116, York, 20-24 mar, 2001, ISBN 1 902956 17 0.
12. N.R. Jennings and M.J. Wooldridge, (eds.). "Agent Technology; Foundations, Application, and Markets." Springer Verlag, Berlin (1998).
13. J. G. Keith. "Towards a Distributed, Environment-Centered Agent Framework."
14. M.L. Maher, S. Simoff and A. Cicognani. "Understanding Virtual Design Studios." London: Springer-Verlag, 2000.
15. O. Marin, P. Sens, J-P. Briot, and Z. Guessoum. "Towards Adaptive Fault Tolerance for Distributed Multi-Agent Systems." In: *Proceedings of ERSADS'2001*, Bertinoro, Italy, May 14-18, 2001.

16. D. Martin, A. Cheyer, and D. Moran. "The Open Agent Architecture: a framework for building distributed software systems." *Applied Artificial Intelligence*, 13(1/2):91–128, 1999.
17. F. McCabe and K. Clark. "April: Agent Process Interaction Language." In N. Jennings and M. Wooldridge, (eds.), *Proc. Intelligent Agents*, volume 890 of *Lecture Notes in Computer Science*. Springer-Verlag, 1995.
18. B. Neuman. "Scale in Distributed Systems." In T. Casavant and M. Singhal, (eds.), *Readings in Distributed Computing Systems*, pp. 463–489. IEEE Computer Society Press, Los Alamitos, CA., 1994.
19. M. Nodine, B. Perry, and A. Unruh. "Experience with the InfoSleuth agent architecture." In *Proc. Proceedings of the AAAI-98 Workshop on Software Tools for Developing Agents*, 1998.
20. HS. Nwana. "Software agents: an overview." *The Knowledge Engineering Review*, 11(3):205–244, 1996.
21. J. B. Odubiyi, D. J. Kocur, S. M. Weinstein, N. Wakim, S. Srivastava, C. Gokey, and J. Graham. "SAIRE–a scalable agent-based information retrieval engine." In *Proc. Proceedings of the first international conference on Autonomous agents*, pp. 292–299, Marina del Rey, CA USA, Feb. 1997.
22. A. Ohsuga, Y. Nagai, Y. Irie, M. Hattori, and S. Honiden. "Plangent: An Approach to Making Mobile Agents Intelligent." *IEEE Internet Computing*, 1(4), July 1997.
23. T. Özsu and P. Valduriez. *Principles of Distributed Database Systems*. Prentice Hall, Upper Saddle River, N.J., 2nd edition, 1999.
24. G. Pierre, I. Kuz, M. van Steen, and A. Tanenbaum. "Differentiated Strategies for Replicating Web Documents." *Comp. Comm.*, 24(2):232–240, Feb. 2001.
25. O. Shehory. "A Scalable Agent Location Mechanism." In *Proc. Lecture Notes in Artificial Intelligence, Intelligent Agents VI*, 1999.
26. Y. Shoham. "Agent-oriented programming." *Artificial Intelligence*,60:51–92, 1993.
27. M. van Steen, P. Homburg, and A. Tanenbaum. "Globe: A Wide-Area Distributed System." *IEEE Concurrency*, 7(1):70–78, Jan. 1999.
28. K. Sycara, M. Paolucci, M. van Velsen, and J. Giampapa. "The RETSINA MAS Infrastructure." Technical Report CMU-RI-TR-01-05, Robotics Institute Technical Report, Carnegie Mellon, 2001.
29. C. Thompson, T. Bannon, P. Pazandak, and V. Vasudevan. "Agents for the Masses." In *Proc. Agent-Based High Performance Computing - Problem Solving Applications and Practical Deployment at Autonomous Agents 1999*, Seattle, Washington, USA, May 1999.
30. P. J. Turner and N. R. Jennings. "Improving the Scalability of Multi-Agent Systems." In *Proc. 1st International Workshop on Infrastructure for Scalable Multi-Agent Systems*, 2000.
31. P.D. Wilde. "Stability, Fairness and Scalability of Multi-Agent Systems."
32. M. Wooldridge and N. Jennings. "Intelligent agents: theory and practice." *The Knowledge Engineering Review*, 10(2):115–152, 1995.
33. P. R. Wurman, M. P. Wellman, and W. E. Walsh. "The Michigan Internet AuctionBot: A configurable auction server for human and software agents." In K. P. Sycara and M. Wooldridge, (eds.), *Proc. Proceedings of the 2nd International Conference on Autonomous Agents (Agents'98)*, pp. 301–308, New York, 9–13, 1998. ACM Press.

Modeling Adaptive Multi-Agent Systems Inspired by Developmental Biology

Samuel Landau and Sébastien Picault

LIP6, Université Pierre et Marie Curie
case 169, 4 place Jussieu, 75 252 Paris CEDEX 05, FRANCE
{Samuel.Landau,Sebastien.Picault}@lip6.fr
http://www-poleia.lip6.fr/{landau,picault}

Abstract. This paper addresses the issue of adaptive multi-agent systems and their design based on living systems features such as phylogeny and ontogeny. We argue that the evolutionary design of agents behaviors implies several specific features that are missing in classical evolutionary approaches. Therefore we propose a new approach that would be more adequate to MAS, and present a model for building MAS as the result of evolving, interacting, self-organizing agents. We finally mention a use of such an approach for the embodiment of robots.

Keywords. adaptive multi-agent architecture, agent behavior evolution, development, body image

1 Introduction

Adaptability is a property of living organisms that not only relies on learning, but also on the ability to reorganize themselves, for instance to reshape parts of their body or of their cognitive structures, to give adequate responses to environmental changes. In addition, living organisms have a body image (a representation of their physical body) that is built by and during their development. This body image is the result of a coupling process between the growth of the physical body in an unpredictable and highly dynamical environment and the reorganization of cognitive structures.

We would like to investigate the problem of designing individuals that can exhibit similar properties: their development can indeed be modeled with an ecosystem (actually a MAS). This especially implies an evolutive approach, either to have such individuals gradually evolve (phylogeny) or to build them through an ontogenetic process (the whole system being organized by a selection of available agents behaviors).

In that context, the key problem is the ability to really have *agents behaviors* evolve, rather than just parameters in prior designed behaviors. To our point of view, existing evolutionary approaches, which aim at *solving problems*, are not completely adequate for that purpose. We will discuss in the next section the limitations of classical evolutionary approaches and present the requirements of a model allowing the evolution of agents behaviors. Section 3 will then describe

V. Mařík et al. (Eds.): MASA 2001, LNAI 2322, pp. 221–229, 2002.
© Springer-Verlag Berlin Heidelberg 2002

such a model, *ATNoSFERES*, with which we are currently working. Finally, we will deal with the issue of using this approach for embodiment in robots.

2   Towards *Ethogenetics*

The general principle of evolutionary algorithms involves the following steps:

1. "individuals" representing potential solutions for the problem are built *from a hereditary substratum* (the *genotype*)
2. these individuals belong to a population
3. their adequation to the problem is evaluated (either explicitly through a "fitness" function, or implicitly through survival criteria for instance)
4. some of them (mainly the most adapted) are selected to produce offspring (by mixing their genotypes) ; others are removed from the population
5. the process cycles with the new population.

We would like to adapt this general paradigm to the evolution of developing multi-agent systems in place of individuals, in order to get the adaptive properties mentioned in the introduction. The reorganization of the MAS relies on a collective behavior resulting from the behaviors exhibited by each agent in the system. In addition, it can be useful (for instance to bootstrap the system with prior knowledge, or to specify a behavioral constraint) to keep the possibility to explicitly design parts of the system. Thus we assume that a convenient evolutionary algorithm should have the following properties:

– There should be a quite good continuity between the genotype and the behaviors built from it: small variations in the genotype should induce in general only slight variations in the resulting behaviors, or else the evolutionary process gets closer to a pure random search.
– There should be a large expressive power in the behaviors built from the genotype. The behavior of an agent is actually not a succession of independent actions, but a consistent structured sequence of actions.
– The behavior design process should be incremental, i.e. adding a selective constraint on the system (e.g. a new collective goal to achieve) should not force the algorithm to restart from scratch, but reuse the existing behaviors and slightly modify them.

Unfortunately, the existing evolutionary computing paradigms are inadequate for this purpose:

– on the one hand, **Genetic Algorithms** [1,2,3] and **Evolutionary Strategies** [4,5] have a very poor expressive power, since their purpose is the optimization of a set of parameters [6] in behaviors which *have to be given a priori*. However, they allow fine-grain encoding, so that small variations in the genotype generally induce small variations in the phenotype (in our case, the resulting behavior).

- on the other hand, the Genetic Programming paradigm [7], which is based on the evolution of *programs* (i.e. instruction trees), has a much higher expressive power. But in such a tree structure, genetic variations most of the time have a strong impact on behaviors (not only parameters, but also instructions are subject to modifications), all of the more since the impact of variations tightly depends on the location in the tree hierarchy. Additionally, the issue of incremental design of behaviors with instruction trees is still a difficulty [8].

Therefore, we propose a specific evolutionary approach, that we call *Ethogenetics*, the purpose of which is to provide general principles to the design of evolutive agent behaviors – the ability to *build* agent behaviors (with a large expressive power) from a meaningless genetic substratum. In addition to the properties required for this purpose, the Ethogenetics approach advocates the following features:

- *The structure describing the behaviors should be understandable.* It may be useful to provide the agents with *explicit understandable behaviors* : some control architectures such as artificial neural networks might be very efficient, but the resulting behavior cannot be clearly described. The ability to easily interpret the behaviors would allow on the one hand to understand *what* has been selected, and on the other hand, to explicitly specify some of the behaviors using this same structure, allowing to set *a priori* the behaviors of some agents.
- *Behaviors should be situated.* Since the system will have to operate in a given environment, it should be able to adapt itself, to reconfigure according to environmental constraints. Thus the semantic structure representing behaviors should avoid using explicit parameters : parameters are a kind of shortcut, they reflect prior knowledge about the environment. The building of *situated behaviors* has to be independent from any parameters, in order to keep more flexibility.

In the next section, we present ATNoSFERES[1], a model aimed at implementing those properties.

3   Description of the **ATNoSFERES** Model

3.1   General Principles

The ATNoSFERES model [9,10] is a specific implementation of the Ethogenetics principles. It uses the SFERES framework [11] as a tool for modelling the agents classes, integrating those classes to the system, designing an environmental simulator and providing classical evolutionary techniques.

In particular, ATNoSFERES provides a general class, the ATNAgent, the behavior of which is produced from a bitstring (the genetic substratum) through the following steps:

---

[1] see http://miriad.lip6.fr/atnosferes

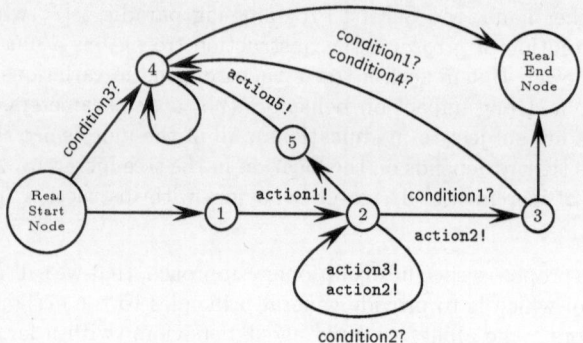

Fig. 1. An example of ATN

1. a translator produces *tokens* from the string,
2. an interpreter uses these tokens as instructions to *build a graph* (an ATN[2]),
3. finally, the graph is expressed to produce the behavior of the agent.

The translator and the interpreter themselves are agents; in the following lines, we will consider that their behavior is given, but it could evolve as well to provide the system with higher autonomy.

3.2   The ATN Graph and the `ATNAgent`

The `ATNAgent` class is intended to behave according to an ATN graph [12]. ATN have previously been used by Z. Guessoum [13] for designing agent behaviors. Each subclass of `ATNAgent` is associated with two collections of tokens: condition ones and action ones. The actions are behavioral "primitives" that can be performed by the agent, the conditions are perceptions or stimuli that induce action selection. The edges of the graph are labeled with a set of conditions and a sequence of actions (see Fig. 1).

The ATN built by adding nodes and edges to a basic structure containing two nodes: a "Real Start Node" and a "Real End Node". At each time step, the agent (initially in the "Real Start Node" state) randomly chooses an edge among those having either *no condition* in their label, or *all conditions simultaneously true*. It performs the actions associated with this edge and jumps to the destination node. It stops working when its state is the "Real End Node".

3.3   The Interpreter

The purpose of the interpreter is to build an ATN from tokens. Some of these tokens will be action or condition ones that are used to label edges between nodes

---

[2] ATN stands for Augmented Transition Network

Table 1. The ATN-building language

token (initial list state) $\longrightarrow$ (resulting list)
condition? $(x\ ...)$ $\longrightarrow$ (condition? $x\ ...$)
action! $(x\ ...)$ $\longrightarrow$ (action! $x\ ...$)
node $(x\ ...)$ $\longrightarrow$ $(N_i\ x\ ...)^a$
startNode $(x\ ...)$ $\longrightarrow$ $(N_i\ x\ ...)^b$
endNode $(x\ ...)$ $\longrightarrow$ $(N_i\ x\ ...)^c$
connect (c2? $x\ N_i\ y$ c1? z a2! a1! $t\ N_j\ u\ ...$) $\longrightarrow$ $(x\ N_i\ y\ z\ t\ N_j\ u\ ...)^d$
dup $(x\ y\ ...)$ $\longrightarrow$ $(x\ x\ y\ ...)$
dupObject $(x\ y\ N_i\ z\ ...)$ $\longrightarrow$ $(N_i\ x\ y\ N_i\ z\ ...)$
popRoll $(x\ y\ ...\ z)$ $\longrightarrow$ $(y\ ...\ z\ x)$
pushRoll $(x\ ...\ y\ z)$ $\longrightarrow$ $(z\ x\ ...\ y)$
swap $(x\ y\ ...)$ $\longrightarrow$ $(y\ x\ ...)$
forget $(x\ y\ ...) + [z\ ...]$ $\longrightarrow$ $(y\ ...) + [x\ z\ ...]^e$
recall $(x\ ...) + [y\ z\ ...]$ $\longrightarrow$ $(y\ x\ ...) + [z\ ...]^e$

[a] creates a node N_i
[b] creates a node N_i and connects "RealStartNode" to it
[c] creates a node N_i and connects it to "RealEndNode"
[d] creates an edge between N_j and N_i, with (c1?& c2?) as condition label and the list {a1!,a2!} as action label
[e] with an auxiliary stack

in the ATN. The other ones are interpreted as instructions, either to create nodes or connect them, or to manipulate the structure under construction.

As we mentioned above, the structure built by the tokens sequence has to be robust towards variations in the genotype. For instance, the replacement of one token by another, or its deletion, should have only a *local impact*, rather than transforming the whole graph. Therefore, we use a "top-level" programming language operating on a list (see Table 1).

If an instruction cannot execute successfully, it is simply ignored, except instructions operating on nodes (i.e. *connect* and *dupObject*) which are "pushed" in the list until new nodes are produced; then they try to execute again with the new data. Finally, when the interpreter does not receive tokens any more, it terminates the ATN: actions and conditions tokens still present between nodes are treated as *implicit connections* (so that new edges are created) and the consistency of the ATN is checked ("Real Start Node" is linked to nodes having no incoming edges, except from themselves; in the same way, nodes having no outgoing edges are linked to "Real End Node").

3.4   The Translator

The translator has a very simple behavior. It reads the genotype (a string of bits) and decodes it into a sequence of tokens. It uses a *genetic code*, i.e. a function

$$\mathcal{G} : \{0,1\}^n \longrightarrow \mathcal{T} \quad (|\mathcal{T}| \leq 2^n)$$

where $\mathcal{T}$ is a set of tokens, which includes both action and condition ones (specific to the agent to build) and those understood by the interpreter (see Table 1).

Depending on the number of tokens available, the genetic code might be more or less redundant. If necessary, it can be designed in order to resist mutations, but we will not discuss this issue in this paper.

4   Features of the **ATNoSFERES** Model

4.1   Evolutionary Computation Considerations

As an evolutive approach, the **ATNoSFERES** model provides three main features. First, it separates the genetic information structure (plain bit string, the lexical structure) from its interpretation (ATN, the semantic structure). Thus, thanks to the interpreter language, the semantic structure that is built is *always correct*. The behavior described by the ATN always has a meaning – even if it is not adequate.

The second main evolutive feature is related to the genetic operators. The level of influence of the classical genetic operators – mutation and crossover – does not depend on the parts of the bit string they involve (neither on their location in the bit string nor on their size). This is also a main advantage over many evolutive approaches. As a matter of fact, mutations only have a local impact in the expression of the genetic information, and crossovers involve bit substrings which carry locally functional genetic code. We might also consider more exotic genetic operators, such as deletions/insertions in the bit string. These operators in particular permit to smoothly manage string resizing, since they only have a local impact in the **ATNoSFERES** model.

The third feature is that the model does not use any parameter to build behaviors. The behaviors execution only depends on environmental conditions, thus hard-coded genetic parameters are not even needed. Apart from behaviors design, parameters encoding is a problem in many evolutive approaches, (see for example discussion on epistasis in [14]), but as long as building behaviors is concerned, we think it should be considered not to rely on fixed parameters in order to produce situated, adaptive behaviors.

4.2   MAS Design Considerations

As a model for designing multi-agent systems, the **ATNoSFERES** model does not set any restriction neither on the agent level specification nor on the choice of the agents. The granularity of the system modelisation is free ; furthermore, agents can be introduced later on at a lower organization level (for instance inside an agent), keeping the latter structure, if a finer-grain agent specification is needed.

If the designer has prior knowledge about the system structure, he can specify and fix some agents behaviors, and use them as a constraint to drive the evolution of the system organization. On the other hand, the only specification that must be given for the evolving agents of the system is their sets of actions and perceptions, and consequently the micro-environment in which they operate. Not only can this micro-environment be a part of the system environment, but it can also for instance be the inside of an upper-level agent.

4.3   Agents Behaviors Design Considerations

As a model for automatic behavior design (as part of ATNoSFERES), ATNs use a simplified framework, where only the conditions and actions of the agents have to be specified. With an ATN as the structure for behavior description, it is possible to directly describe the behavior of any agent : this is an interesting perspective for behavior explanation.

4.4   The ATNoSFERES Model with Regard to Ethogenetics

The ATNoSFERES model fulfills the Ethogenetics requirements expressed in section 2. Preliminary experiments [10] have validated the use of ATNoSFERES regarding the following aspects:

- the ability to evolve *adequate* agents behaviors in a simple situation, from *random graphs*;
- the consistency of the ATN-building evolutionary language.

The experimental results have also confirmed that the generation of behaviors do not rely on a precise structure in the genotype: various adequate solutions have been found, based either on different graph-building strategies, or on the use of properties of the graphs (more details can be found in [10], and genetic related issues have been discussed in [15]).

5   ATNoSFERES and Embodiment for Robots

ATNoSFERES should allow to incrementally build multi-agent systems able to reorganize and develop, by evolving agent behaviors that can be previously partly specified. The system and the agents have to face internal and external constraints that induce selective pressure. Throughout evolution, the selective process shapes the organization of the system and its collective behavior, including the capacity to reorganize.

The reorganization and adaptation take place during the system lifetime and while it is acting. These processes reflects the movement of the system towards adequation to the changing environment – be it inner environment, that is the environment of the agents inside the system, or outer environment, that is the "real-world" environment in which the system is immersed. When they take place in a multi-agent system that is put into a robot that the system must control and that shapes the system, we think that these reorganization and adaptive processes are a distributed representation of the robot body. This is a weaker distributed conception of embodiment for robots than the one that can be found of others works involving, in particular, a body consciousness [16].

6 Conclusions and Perspectives

We have presented Ethogenetics, an approach for evolving adaptive multi-agent systems, and discussed its specific features. To summarize, interesting agents behaviors can be built through an evolutionary approach that is able to ensure *continuity* between the genetic substratum and the phenotypic behavior, and a *high expressive power* in the behavior produced. We propose therefore a two-step building that leads to graph-based behaviors (the ATNoSFERES model).

We assume that a multi-agent system, whose agents behaviors have been evolved that way, exhibit organizational features as a consequence of the selection pressure that shaped individual behaviors. When implemented on a robot, the organization of the system is able to constitute a representation of the robotic body.

In order to more precisely investigate the organizational features of the AT-NoSFERES model, further experiments regarding collective strategies (especially predator-prey simulations) are currently ongoing. The embodiment issues will be studied through real-robots applications, as part of the MICRobES Project[3] [17,18] will be led in the following months.

References

1. J. H. Holland, *Adaptation in natural and artificial systems: an introductory analysis with applications to biology, control, and artificial intelligence.* Ann Arbor: University of Michigan Press, 1975.
2. K. A. De Jong, *An analysis of the behavior of a class of genetic adaptive systems.* PhD thesis, Dept. of Computer and Communication Sciences, University of Michigan, 1975.
3. D. E. Goldberg, *Genetic algorithms in search, optimization, and machine learning.* Addison-Wesley Pub. Co., 1989.
4. I. Rechenberg, *Evolutionsstrategie: Optimierung technischer Systeme nach Prinzi pien der biologischen Evolution.* Stuttgart: Frommann–Holzboog, 1973.
5. H.-P. Schwefel, *Evolutionsstrategie und numerische Optimierung.* Dr.-Ing. Thesis, Technical University of Berlin, Department of Process Engineering, 1975.
6. T. Bäck and H.-P. Schwefel, "An overview of evolutionary algorithms for parameter optimization," *Evolutionary Computation*, vol. 1, no. 1, pp. 1–23, 1993.
7. J. R. Koza, *Genetic Programming: On the Programming of Computers by Means of Natural Selection.* 1992.

---

[3] See http://miriad.lip6.fr/microbes

8. S. Perkins, *Incremental Acquisition of Complex Visual Behaviour using Genetic Programming and Shaping*. PhD thesis, University of Edinburgh, 1998.
9. S. Picault and S. Landau, "Ethogenetics - A Darwinian Approach towards Individual and Collective Agents Behavior," technical report (in press), LIP6, Paris, 2001.
10. S. Landau, S. Picault, and A. Drogoul, "ATNoSFERES: a Model for Evolutive Agent Behaviors," in *Proc. of AISB'01 symposium on Adaptive Agents and Multiagent systems*, pp. 95–99, 2001.
11. S. Landau, S. Doncieux, A. Drogoul, and J.-A. Meyer, "SFERES, a Framework for Designing Adaptive Multi-Agent Systems," technical report, LIP6, Paris, 2001.
12. W. A. Woods, "Transition networks grammars for natural language analysis," *Communications of the Association for the Computational Machinery*, vol. 13, no. 10, pp. 591–606, 1970.
13. Z. Guessoum, *Un environnement opérationnel de conception et de réalisation de systèmes multi-agents*. PhD thesis, LIP6 – Université Paris VI, may 1996.
14. R. Salomon, "Increasing Adaptivity through Evolution Strategies," in *From animals to animats 4, Proc. of the fourth international conference on simulation of adaptive behaviour* (P. Maes, M. J. Mataric, J.-A. Meyer, J. Pollack, and S. W. Wilson, eds.), pp. 411–420, MIT Press, 1996.
15. S. Picault and S. Landau, "Ethogenetics and the Evolutionary Design of Agent Behaviors," in *Proc. of the 5th World Multi-Conference on Systemics, Cybernetics and Informatics (SCI 2001)* (N. Callaos, S. Esquivel, and J. Burge, eds.), vol. 3, pp. 528–533, 2001.
16. A. Cardon, "The approaches of the Concept of Embodiment for an Autonomous Robot," in *Proc. of the Adaptive and Embodiment using Multi-Agent Systems workshop (AEMAS) of ACAI'01*, 2001.
17. S. Picault and A. Drogoul, "The MICRobES Project, an Experimental Approach towards "Open Collective Robotics"," *Proceedings of DARS'2000*, 2000.
18. S. Picault and A. Drogoul, "Robots as a Social Species: the MICRobES Project," *Proceedings of SIA'2000, AAAI Fall Symposium Series*, 2000.

International Workshop on Industrial Applications of Holonic and Multi-Agent Systems

HoloMAS 2001: Selected Papers

Holons & Agents: Recent Developments and Mutual Impacts

Vladimir Mařík[1,2], Martyn Fletcher[3], and Michal Pěchouček[1]

[1]Gerstner Laboratory, Department of Cybernetics, Czech Technical University in Prague
{marik,pechouc}@labe.felk.cvut.cz
[2]Rockwell Automation Research Center, Prague
vmarik@ra.rockwell.com
[3]Agent Oriented Software, Cambridge, UK
martyn.fletcher@agent-oriented.co.uk

Abstract. This position paper briefly gathers together the recent trends in the related aras of holonic systems and multi-agent systems with the main goal to present the Holonic Manufacturing Systems area to the MAS community. The vision of a Holonic Factory is very near to being realized, and draws a number of its concepts from the world of multi-agent systems. That is why many similarities can be identified between these two areas, and many opportunities exist for the crossover of research results. The IEC 61499 standard for real-time function-block oriented holonic control was completed recently. It has been recognized by the holonic manufacturing system community that this standard is able to help in solving low-level control tasks only. That is, where the time horizon of decisions made by holons (e.g. concerning stopping the physical movement of robots, or executing safety-critical tasks) is in the range of microseconds to seconds. Yet this standard does not address all the topics needed to construct an intelligent agile factory. The MAS area can significantly help to avoid the current deadlocks in HMS research. In terms of mutual impacts, holonic systems are based on pragmatic manufacturing control requirements, and so they can offer a wealth of attractive opportunities for deploying agent-based ideas into real industrial settings. And vice versa, the application of agents into manufacturing domains, connected with physical production, should motivate a MAS community that has (until now) concentrated on just information agents.

1 Introduction

The increasing complexity of intelligent manufacturing systems as well as the overall demands of flexible and fault-tolerant control on production processes has stimulated development of two emerging technologies. They will soon make an important breakthrough in the field of intelligent manufacturing and control. These two paradigms are the event-driven control strategy, typical for **holonic systems**, and the distributed information processing resulting in **multi-agent systems.**

The research communities working in both fields approach the problem of intelligent manufacturing from different viewpoints and nearly independently. They use their specific terminology and techniques. The holonic system (HS) community is rooted in the concept of holons as presented by Koestler [42] and is strongly influenced by the requirements of industrial control. In truth, holonic systems have only

V. Mařík et al. (Eds.): MASA 2001, LNAI 2322, pp. 233-267, 2002.
© Springer-Verlag Berlin Heidelberg 2002

really been applied to manufacturing domains, and that has been done mainly in order to make the factories more agile. The community is well organized around the international HMS (Holonic Manufacturing Systems) consortium [38]. This consortium is within the framework of the Intelligent Manufacturing Systems (IMS) program, and was started in early 1990's as "an international industrially-driven project to address systemization, standardization, research, pre-competitive development, deployment and support of HMS architectures and technologies for open, distributed, intelligent, autonomous and cooperating systems through a global partnership" [31]. Results from phase 1 of this consortium, though limited in their extent, have made a significant impact on the ideas presented here. Interested readers are referred to workshops [8] and [50] and papers in [10] and [45] for an overview of HMS applications.

On the other hand, a comparatively much larger and more diverse community of researchers and developers working in the multi-agent system (MAS) area, are influenced by the ideas of highly distributed computing in computer networks as well as by the ideas of distributed artificial intelligence. As the community is much more heterogeneous and agents have been applied to a wider spectrum of problems, there are different organizational frameworks where the researchers are grouped. The European MAS researchers are organized into the AgentLink consortium [2]. Meanwhile, on the worldwide stage, they participate in IFMAS (International Foundation for MAS), Agent Society, Agentcities [1] and, with an emphasis on setting industrial standards, in FIPA (Foundation for Intelligent Physical Agents) [27]. Though the general paradigms of autonomous intelligent software agents and multi-agent systems have been documented over some considerable time, only recently have unifying principles been clearly specified.

Both the holonic system and multi-agent system metaphors share some ideas and they differ in the other issues. In general, the research topics of HMS and MAS are strongly overlapping in the areas of communication protocols, reasoning, coordination and cooperation strategies, and planning and scheduling. Both research communities respect the same, very fundamental attributes of holons and agents, e.g. they are *autonomous, cooperative and open*. Furthermore, the architectures of either holons or agents are multi-layered: a standardized head/kernel architecture in the case of holons and a body/wrapper architecture as in agents being the most popular at present. Both approaches use similar communication mechanisms such as blackboards, matchmakers, brokers, or mediators. There are similar trends in standardization (the IEC 61499 standard in the case of holonic systems, and the FIPA standards in the area of multi-agent systems).

The dual progress achieved by holonic systems and multi-agent systems, as well as the mutual convergence of these areas during the last several years has been really significant. The researchers in these areas clearly identified the role each other can play in manufacturing and industrial control, and have recognized the weak and strong points of each other's approaches. This paper critiques these recent developments and mutual impacts.

The structure of this paper is as follows: Section 2 outlines the key contributions made by researchers and developers from the HMS community. Section 3 outlines how some HMS technology has been deployed (though to a limited extent) in commercial manufacturing and control systems. Section 4 highlights the research contributions from the world of MAS with particular emphasis on those topics that can benefit HMS. Section 5 presents some topics where HMS has started to adopt technology and ideas from MAS. Section 7 discusses the critical topic of holonic planning and scheduling; this topic offers probably one of the best opportunities for exchanging ideas between the two communities. Section 8 presents some concluding remarks.

2 Holonic Manufacturing Systems Research

2.1 Rational for Holonic Manufacturing Systems

The rational for needing holonic manufacturing system technology is that it represents a novel paradigm for addressing some of the most critical manufacturing problems encountered as businesses come to grips with the 21st century market. These problems include:

- The need to support *mass customization*, i.e. 'make-to-order' rather than 'make-to-stock'. This helps the business to regularly react to rush orders and new product specifications from customers.
- The requirement to cope with a hybrid combination of production *variety* and *volume* within a single shop floor. Businesses are discovering that there is a need to manufacture 1,000,000 orders of item A and 1 order of item B simultaneously. Traditional manufacturing thinking is not geared to this imbalance.
- The demand from people to have their customer-specific products presented into the market with *short* 'order-to-delivery' times.
- The need to have *tightly integrated* supply chains and hold minimal reserve stocks. Being idle while waiting for a supplier to deliver component parts costs money; so does holding large inventories of stock.

Holons are autonomous, cooperative, open, and (to some degree) intelligent building blocks, within a decentralized manufacturing system [13]. The manufacturing system composed of several or many holons (a holonic manufacturing system) is used for transforming, transporting, storing and/or validating of information as well as of physical objects. The linkage between holons and the physical elements of the manufacturing and material-handling infrastructure is stressed: a holonic manufacturing system *must* have a direct interface to the shop floor.

In the other words: Holons are autonomous, cooperative units which can be considered as elementary building blocks of manufacturing systems with decentralized control. Holons as the building blocks can be organized in a hierarchical or heterarchical structures. Each holon usually contains: (i) a **hardware/equipment part** able to physically influence the real world (e.g. a device, tool, or other manufacturing unit, or a transportation belt, or a storage manipulator etc.) and (ii) a **control part** responsible for both the hardware/equipment part control and communication with the rest of the holonic community.

Holons for real-time control are expected to provide reactive behavior rather than being able of deliberative behavior based on complex "mental states" and strongly pro-active strategies. Holons are expected mainly to react to changes in the manufacturing environment (e.g. when a device failure or a change in the global plan occurs). Under "stable circumstances", during a routine operation, they are not required to change the environment pro-actively. The reason for prevalence of reactive behavior of the real-time control holons is given namely by the fact that each holon is linked to a physical manufacturing facility/environment, the changes of which are not very simple, cheap and desirable in a comparatively "stable" manufacturing facility. The physical linkage to physical equipment seems to be a strong limiting factor of the holons' freedom in decision making.

In holonic systems, the data flow is clearly separated from the control information flow. Two or more similar holons being linked appropriately together can create another, "bigger" holon. In this case, the elementary holons react to the same control events, and their data processing parts are linked together in order to achieve a higher processing capability.

The term *holon,* in the sense which it is currently used in the manufacturing area, was firstly used by A. Koestler [42] who studied a dichotomy of wholeness and partness in living organisms and social organizations. He stated that – in principle – wholes and parts in the absolute sense do not exist anywhere. To emphasise this point, he suggested a new term holon as a fusion of the Greek word *holos* meaning the "whole" and the suffix "on" denoting a particle (as in neutron). A very important feature of holons resulting from their definition is their recursion. A holon, unlike an agent, can contain other holons of the same architecture or structure.

As a matter of fact, the extension of the holonic visions towards (production) planning and scheduling and supply chain management issues covers exactly the same area as the MAS research. The same ideas, but different terminological terms are used. On this higher level of the manufacturing business, the holonic community currently stays with the general ideas (fully compliant or even identical with the MAS ideas), whereas the MAS research provides already theoretical background and particular technical solutions. It seems to be quite natural that the holonic visions should be implemented through exploring the MAS technology.

The application of such holonic ideas was first applied to manufacturing by [68] to represent a more flexible alternative to computer integrated manufacturing (CIM), and provides principles to ensure a higher echelon of responsiveness and handling of system complexity. **Holonics is not a new technology, but it is a system-wide philosophy for developing, configuring, running and managing a manufacturing business. Multi-agent system area is a promising technology provider to accomplish the ambitious holonic visions.**

This is especially true in the tasks of (ontology) knowledge representation, communication architecture, negotiation, coordination and cooperation principles and algorithms as well as in the corresponding standardisation.

In contrast to traditional CIM approaches, a holonic manufacturing system is constructed in a bottom-up fashion by integrating holons in such a way that they collaborate to provide an array of system-wide characteristics. These behavioral attributes include flexibility, robustness, self-similarity, openness and so forth. The appearance and the whole existence of holons are tightly connected with the requirement of system reconfigurability to support the aforementioned manufacturing agility, and holons are considered as the lowest level of granularity in the reconfiguration tasks.

These holonic ideas have lead to the vision of a "Holonic Factory" (see Fig. 1) [12]. Here all the operations (starting from product ordering, planning, scheduling, manufacturing, till invoicing the customer) are based entirely on holonic principles. A

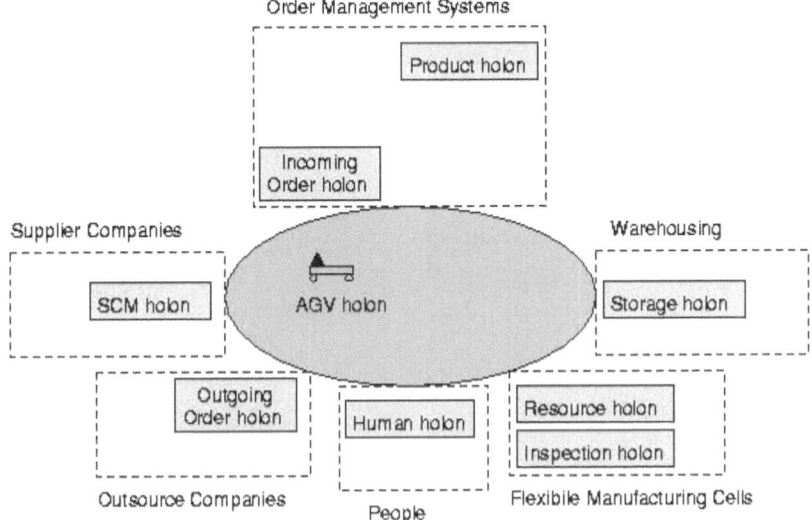

Fig. 1. The holonic factory

holonic factory contains a group of principal system components (holons) that represent physical manufacturing entities such as machines, products, and orders. The holons work autonomously and cooperate together in order to achieve the global goals of the factory. Thus, the factory can be managed towards global goals by activities of individual autonomous holons operating locally.

The holonic terminology has been used mainly in the engineering of control systems for a varied set of diverse manufacturing domains. Several industrial holonic-based solutions have been already proposed [34], [40]. Yet special products to support holonic manufacturing are still missing from the commercial automation and control marketplace. The only standard developed in the holonic manufacturing area is the IEC 61499 standard aimed at the low-level real-time function-block-oriented control accomplished by PLCs. But the importance and applicability of this standard is very often overestimated by the holonic manufacturing community.

2.2 Architectural Issues of Holonic Manufacturing Systems

With respect to their structure, a number of architectures have been proposed to describe the relationship among entities within a holon. For our purposes in this paper, we propose that a holon has three basic entities:

- A compulsory software entity for non-real-time decision-making. It is now widely accepted that this entity will be implemented using an intelligent software agent[1].
- An optional hardware entity together with the necessary software capabilities to control, in real-time, the operations associated with this resource/machine.
- A suitable set of interfaces to the environment in which the holon operates (e.g. to other holons, the manufacturing machinery, humans, supply chain management systems and so forth).

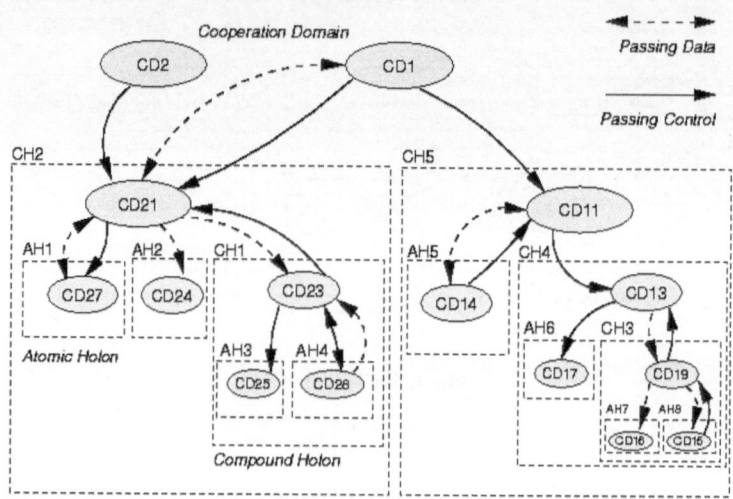

Fig. 2. An example of a holarchy

Using this structure, multiple holons can dynamically aggregate themselves to form a recursive heterarchy (also called a *holarchy*) that doesn't necessarily mean a hierarchical arrangement of holons. See Fig. 2.

It has been proposed that the interactions among holons within a holarchy are facilitated by a logical structure named a *cooperation domain* [25], which enables holons to: (i) locate, advertise their services and contact each other; and (ii) collaborate with each other to plan, schedule and execute manufacturing tasks.

A cooperation domain is a structure consisting of a set of holons which have to cooperate together to carry out a specific complex functionality. The cooperation within the frame of the cooperation domain is usually strictly pre-programmed, and thus, the holons engaged in the cooperation domain create a "hard-wired" structure with pre-defined reactions to alternative situations. The ambitious and idealistic visions of having the cooperation domain structure evolutionary and self-organizing is very, very far from the current implementations. But more and more often, one of the holons in the domain is dedicated just to solve the managerial tasks within this coop-

---

[1] However, in this case we lose the capability of a holon to decompose into a group of other holons. An agent, by definition, cannot by composed by other agents.

eration domain. Here we can find a certain potential for increasing the self-organizing capability inside the cooperation domain.

Holons are able to communicate via information exchange mechanisms, and cooperate via participation in one or more cooperation domains. In each cooperation domain, holons are able to perform certain group- or team-based decision-making. In principle, holons are expected to explore opportunities for interacting in the most coherent fashion via simple negotiations. The key aspect of a general holonic system architecture is that it integrates all levels of the manufacturing business (i.e. devices, work cells, workshops, factories, enterprises and entire supply chains) to provide a highly distributed, very flexible system that supports a modern global business. A common description of the manufacturing processes operating within such a business and complying with these holonic principles is the widely accepted PROSA (Product, Resource, Order and Staff Architecture) model (for details see [72] and [73]). The PROSA reference architecture consists of the following holon types:

- **Product holon** – a unit comprising the physical product being produced, and any human/computer support needed to initiate and monitor the act of producing it.
- **Resource holon** – a single unit representing one or more physical processes to transform, transport and validate artifacts. This holon type also comprises the resources' control system and specifications of any human-based operations needed.
- **Order holon** – a unit representing the requirements of a particular order. This holon type includes information such as product qualities, due dates, priorities, costs etc. It may also contain the information on the state of processing (finished, unfinished) or information about the order status.
- **Staff holon** – an optional support unit providing coordination among the holons, and ensuring that the global goals of the factory are achieved. The holon type compromises the pure vision of a heterarchical control by providing services, arranged in a hierarchical fashion, on issues like transport times, best ways to schedule tasks etc. The advice given by the staff holon can be rejected by the other (basic) holon types.

Each of these holons – once created – are expected to be able to accomplish autonomously certain local reasoning and decision-making tasks, as well as to mutually communicate and negotiate in a peer-to-peer or master-slave manner. Thus, the PROSA architecture can be considered as a specific holonic system reference architecture that exploits many relevant results from multi-agent research. This is another reason for the HMS community to have a look at the MAS achievements.

2.3 Challenges and Milestones for Holonic Manufacturing Systems

The main challenges for the holonic-based solutions are:
- The architectures must be simple, and use plug-and-play components, which when aggregated together create complex control solutions.
- The system must be unified, have interoperable building blocks, and operate in a distributed way.

- Both reactive and proactive features in holons' behavior must be supported in order to respond equally well to unexpected short-term changes and long-term disturbances.
- The HMS must be able to anticipate critical situations and prepare itself for them. In other words the holonic system, and each holon contained therein, must treat changes as 'business as usual' [51].
- The system must be able to handle reconfiguration (self-organizing) tasks efficiently.
- The HMS must potentially have a higher degree of reliability and fault-tolerance than existing complex control solutions. In other words, the system must degrade gracefully in the face of failures/catastrophes.

The challenges mentioned above helped to formulate the global and partial milestones for the HMS research. As one of its key milestones, the HMS project consortium made significant progress in defining the first set of standards for holonic systems. The IEC 61499 standard builds on the function block part of the IEC 61131-3 standard for languages in programmable logic controllers (PLCs) and significantly extends the function block language in the direction needed for holonic control.

When considering a holon as an aggregation of a set of function blocks, some of the major advantages of using this IEC 61499 standard are:

- The factory control system is viewed as a collection of devices linked by communication networks (using either wireless LAN, DeviceNet, TCP/IP and so on). Each device contains several resources, which in turn can execute one function block at a time. See Fig. 3 for an illustration of the system and its encapsulation of devices and resources.

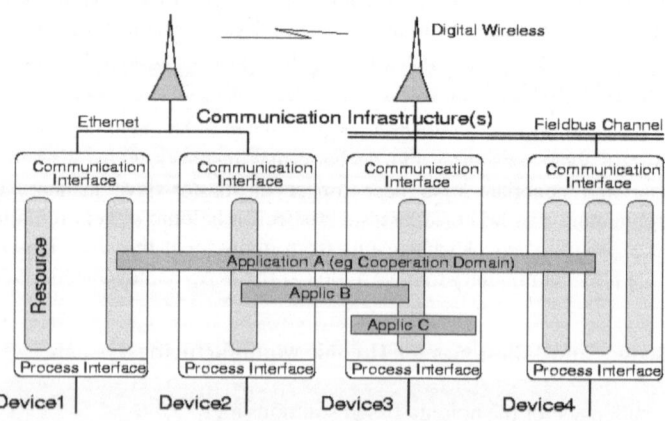

Fig. 3. The IEC 61499 system model

- There is a clear separation between the data flow and the event flow amongst various function blocks. These multiple function blocks would be logically grouped together, across multiple devices into an application, to perform some process control (see e.g. Fig. 8).

– The function block concept is enhanced through: (i) encapsulating the algorithm and private data variables; and (ii) having an execution control facility, based on state transition diagrams, for each function block. See Fig. 4 for an overview of the function block interfaces.

– Suitable system development and engineering facilities have been incorporated to perform a number of useful tasks, e.g. explode a compound function block into its component parts, move function blocks between resources and/or devices, and use management services to alter data/event connections at runtime.

Thus, holons satisfying this standard are suitable for event-driven, real-time control. Quite specific operating systems (for instance the FBOS – Function Block Operating System) have been designed recently to handle the event control of the IEC 61499 function blocks [24]. This event-driven control is a new paradigm that is in its infancy. Moreover it is, in principle in many aspects, contradictory with today's ladder-logic-oriented PLC-instrumented control philosophy. The scan-based approach used in "classical" PLCs does not enable the required flexibility with respect to scheduling of events, especially in the case of hard real-time control. This makes the exploration of this new control approach, in combination with the "old automation machinery", more difficult. Furthermore it incurs the so-called *migration problem*, as mentioned in [11]. It looks like the migration problem is one of the main obstacles (besides others including the failure-protection and re-setting mechanisms) in embedding holonic ideas into the present generation of manufacturing automation and control products.

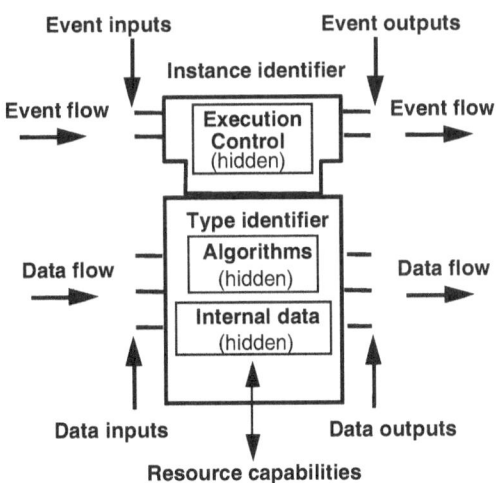

Fig. 4. The IEC 61499 function block model

Another very important milestone in the development of holonic devices was presented at the HMS-16 consortium meeting held in Kitakyushu (October 2000). That is the interoperability of IEC 61499-based solutions developed by three different companies, namely by Rockwell Automation (USA), Profactor (Austria) and Softing (Germany) was successfully demonstrated. On the other hand, it was recognized in parallel that the applicability of the IEC 61499 approach to distributed control tasks suffers from significant limitations as well. This type of control is suitable for hard real-time control tasks that do not require very complicated knowledge exchanges or negotiations among the control units. The information about particular events is used just for switching from one set of function blocks to another pre-programmed set. It has been clearly recognized that more intelligent solutions can be achieved by encapsulating the function block solutions into a certain kind of higher-level software. This principle enables more sophisticated, more intelligent negotiation processes (based on a richer knowledge representation schemas) to be utilized in realizing the agile holonic factory. Thus, the holonic systems researchers have started to look for suitable agent-based software solutions to complement the aforementioned real-time solutions. We will continue the overview of that investigation later in the paper, but first let us see where function blocks have been deployed.

3   Deployment of HMS Technology

We now illustrate how function blocks can be used as a foundation for designing the holonic control system for a real-world application scenario, and make some conclusions concerning IEC 61499's suitability.

3.1   Application Scenario

The Holonic Assembly System is inspired by one of DaimlerChrysler's engine assembly plants. This plant is a pragmatic industrial setting where distributed control is being experimented with to provide increased productivity with respect to both system flexibility (i.e. to support robustness) and operational flexibility (e.g. to maximize throughput). Such flexibility can be provided by the installation of holonic (IEC 61499) or agent-based concepts. The agent-based approach is discussed in [9] while here we narrate the function block viewpoint. We have abstracted the key features of this plant and extended it to provide additional opportunities to illustrate greater flexibility in planning, scheduling and routing, as well as to show how holonic features could work in practice. This holonic assembly system model is a generic infrastructure suitable for designing a wide variety of holonic manufacturing systems and is shown in Fig. 5. This sketch of the manufacturing facility and the subsequent description of the controlled processes, i.e. how the workpiece travels through the factory (see Fig. 8) correspond to step 1 of the methodology outlined in Sect. 6.

Key features of the infrastructure are:
- The layout tries to minimize any impact of logistical disturbances at assembly stations and encourages agile part flow to increase productivity.

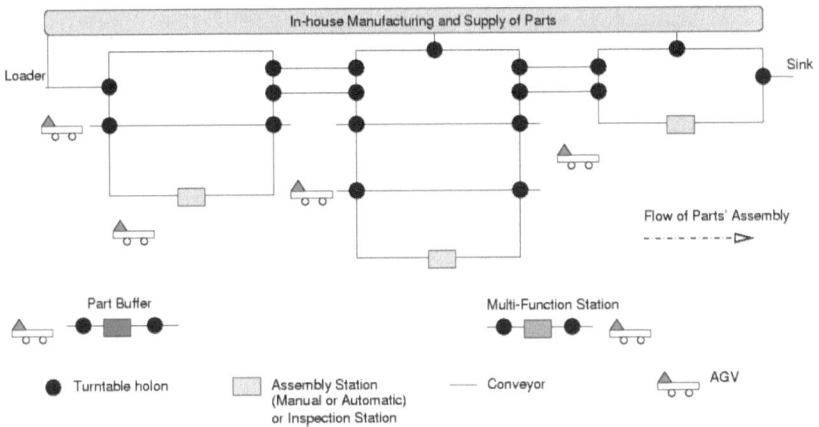

Fig. 5. Layout of the holonic assembly system

– The holonic assembly system has a simple structure that can be overlooked by various classes of user and incurs a start-up investment that is not prohibitive.

Having dedicated assembly stations that are either automated or manual, as well as having multi-function (MF) stations that can perform the processes associated with several assembly station holons, alternative assembly capacity is provided. Thus a part can be either processed at the designated assembly station or at a multi-function station holon. To better use this capacity, flexible part flow mechanisms are provided by a combination of conveyors and Automated Guided Vehicle (AGV) holons. Conveyors cover some aspects of part transportation, for instance inside the configuration of stations representing a manufacturing cell, or between such cells. Meanwhile transport to part buffer holons or multi-function stations is supported by AGVs. Within the infrastructure, there exist a number of turntable holons at every intersection of conveyors and/or AGV docking stations. If we focus our modeling on such turntables (see Fig. 6) then we can identify how they monitor and direct the flow of parts.

Multi-function stations and part buffers have two connected docking stations, each managed by an independent turntable. These docking stations are responsible for the input and output of parts. We make this proposition in order to let turntables exclusively manage the arrival/dispatch of parts through the associated docking stations. Therefore multi-function stations and part buffers do not control the loading of parts or direct parts within the factory network. Observe that parts advance through inspection processes as well as assembly processes to ensure manufacturing is to a high quality. In our model, assembly and inspection station holons have similar functionality and hence here we use the term assembly to cover both assembly and inspection stations. The proposed layout can reroute parts that arrive at a disturbed assembly station so that starvation and blockades can be avoided. Therefore the options for where a part can be routed to or stored include:

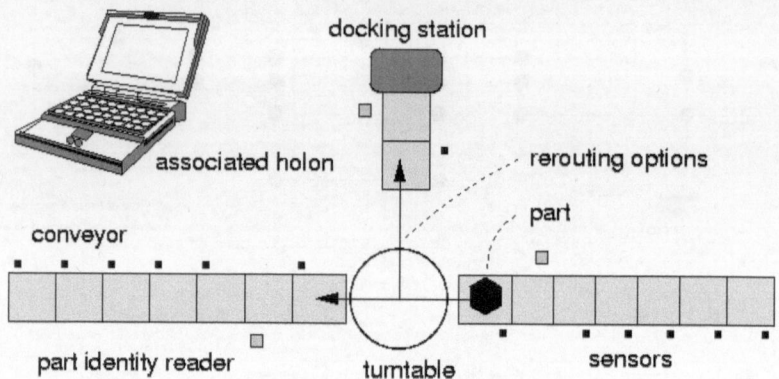

Fig. 6. Model of a turntable and holon

– Transfer the part (via a series of one or more conveyors) to the next designated assembly station on the main assembly line.
– Move the part (using an AGV) to a multi-function station that can perform the same activities as those in the disturbed assembly station.
– Temporarily store the part on conveyors within the factory network.
– Use an AGV to transfer the part to a part buffer for longer-term storage.

The carrying capacity of conveyors and the dimension of part buffers provide dynamic holding capacity and help the system cope with disturbances without loss of productivity. Such buffering is defined when the factory is set up because additional conveyors and warehouses cost money and space is limited. Conveyors and part buffers must be managed so that assembly stations are not starved or blocked. Assembly could be affected due to the station not having all the necessary subsidiary parts to fix together when the major sub-assembly arrives at the station. For example a crankshaft has progressed through the factory network and arrives at a station for insertion into the crankcase housing (manufactured separately) that has *not* been delivered. Sub-assemblies affected by their missing subordinate parts should have their delay managed so they do not block the overall material flow.

A loader holon introducing a part (e.g. a raw engine block) into the assembly system initiates the HMS. The loader may determine a route, based on its current knowledge of the factory network, which the part will try to follow. The loader may also generate a provisional schedule by negotiating with the assembly holons along that route. This path and schedule also contain a set of conveyors and AGVs to reach stations at scheduled times. As the part travels along its approved path, it passes from one manufacturing cell to the next and hence from the jurisdiction of one sub-group of turntables to another. During their progress, parts are subjected to variation in their route and schedule parameters due to *contentions*.

A contention occurs mostly when there is a high density of parts in a particular manufacturing cell, when high priority 'rush' parts are introduced or when stations breakdown. In this situation, parts are stored either upon the conveyor for the short term or within the part buffer for longer periods. Contentions cause a reduction in productivity and so must be resolved as quickly as possible. Contentions can be resolved by a turntable holon, in consultation with other holons, causing an alteration to the route/schedule parameter(s) of one or more parts. The scope of our holonic IEC 61499 approach to the distributed control system modeling can resolve contentions and handle coordination based on the holons' autonomy, cooperation and openness [76].

3.2 Scope of Approach

If we focus on the turntable holon then its behavior generates the following sequence of operations:
1.   workpiece either reaches sensor on in-belt (1a), or it reaches sensor from docking station after being delivered by the AGV holon (1b), which is not shown here,
2.   workpiece is transferred onto turntable,
3.   workpiece directed onto out-belt (3a), and removed from out-belt by next machining station holon (3b),
4.   workpiece directed to docking station (4a), and removed from docking station by the AGV holon (4b).

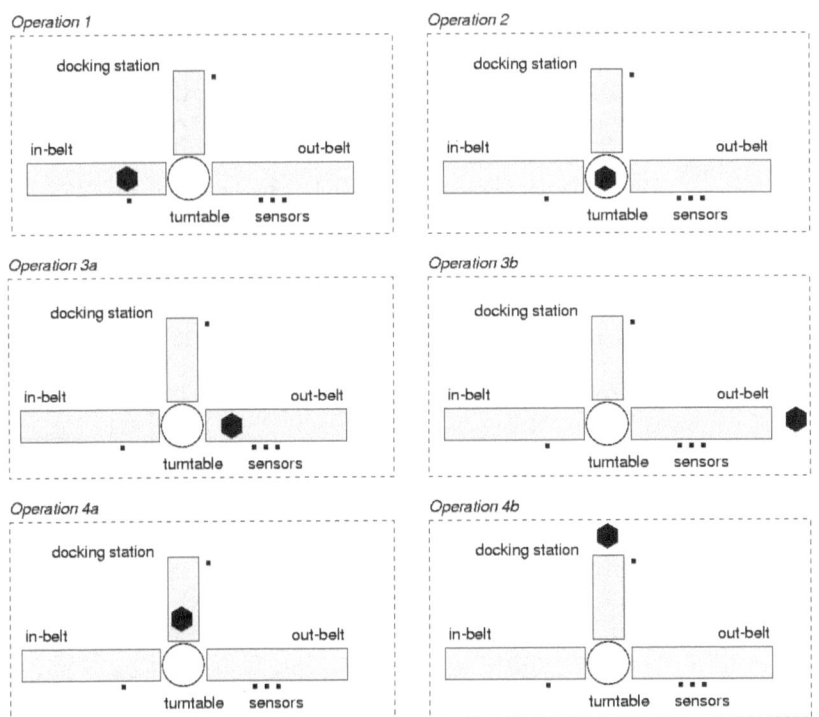

Fig. 7. Flow of parts through a turntable

If we continue our modeling of the holonic control system in the turntable holon then we can identify how these holons: (i) interact via their process interface, namely execute their algorithms to re-direct the flow of workpieces onto and away from the assembly line; and (ii) interact via their communications interface, namely send/receive messages amongst each other as part of a suitable cooperation protocol. Step 2 of our later methodology is to instantiate holon instances from the generic classes, and so here we organize the various holons using IEC 61499 concepts. The interconnection of function blocks to control the turntable holon is shown in Fig. 8.

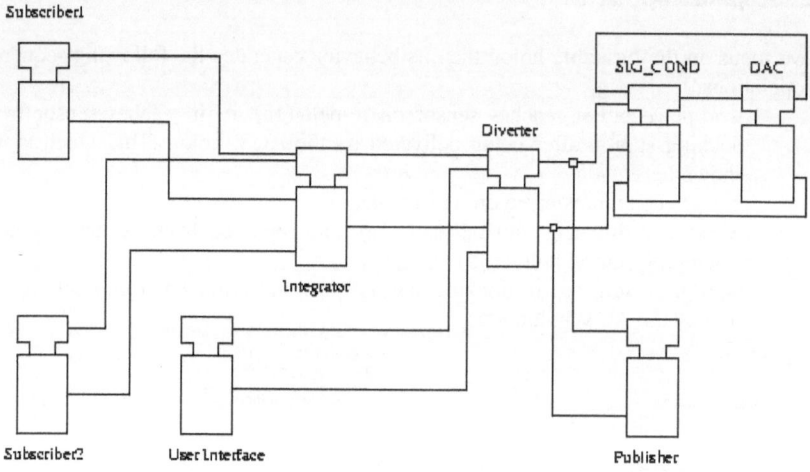

Fig. 8. Function blocks used to control a turntable holon

The turntable holon uses the publisher-subscriber model of communication. Subscriber1 receives data from sensors on the conveyors throughout the holonic assembly system. It also gathers information from the part identity readers in the vicinity of that turntable. Subscriber2 receives data from related holons. For example, the length of conveyor queues maybe acquired from neighboring turntable holons, the availability to transfer a workpiece might be gained from nearby AGV holons. The Integrator decides how to combine this information through suitable reasoning techniques, and the User Interface gains the human expert's parameters. The conclusions are passed to the Diverter to select where the arriving workpiece should go. The control output is disseminated to other holons through the Publisher. Moreover, SIG COND and DAC convert the digital signal into an equivalent analog one to drive actuators at the turntable to physically shift the workpieces' flow. The turntable holon contains examples of all four function block classes as described in the IEC 61499 standard: *basic, compound, adapter* and *service interface*.

3.3 Summary of Deployment and Problems

Firstly, function blocks are suitable for developing distributed control systems where real-time decision-making plays a critical role, such as the one required for the above DaimlerChrysler engine assembly line. This is because IEC 61499 provides modern software engineering facilities to encapsulate, execute and reuse software within a decentralized architecture. Existing control environments do not allow such engineering. Moreover, function blocks can be aggregated in many ways to form agile applications.

Secondly, a drawback of our approach is that the methodology to apply function blocks in realistic manufacturing settings demands additional development as few full-scale implementations have been attempted, and few experiences have been detailed. More work is needed to define the stages and dependencies in such a methodology.

Thirdly, both agents and the function blocks can be used to model the aforementioned holon control activities. In DaimlerChrysler's multi-agent implementation of the control system, each holon is represented as a single agent with one module. IEC 61499 offers more flexibility and control on the hard real-time level than a MAS approach because:

–   The sources of data and events into and out of a function block are decoupled. This means that data values can be sampled one source (e.g. a sensor function block) while events indicating when to take such samples can originate from a distinct source (e.g. a clock function block). Such a division of information flow is not easily implemented using the current agent technologies.
–   A function block can receive events from parallel sources at different times. The function blocks can process them to reflect these timing constraints before the next event is received. As suggested earlier, if these real-time constraints (e.g. algorithm X must be started in 50 microseconds from now and must be completed in 75 microseconds) are not critical then an agent-based solution will suffice.
–   Autonomous software agents adopt a top-down *intelligent* approach while function blocks apply a bottom-up real-time paradigm to control physical machinery.

Fourthly, a benefit of the function block oriented approach is that the various activities of a holon (e.g. sensing, actuation, control, inter-holon communication and interacting with users) can be independently developed and physically distributed over several resources, and even across multiple devices. Even though CORBA provides facilities for remote execution calls among dispersed objects, it is unclear whether you can break apart an agent and have its elements running concurrently over several hardware platforms. Let us now return to multi-agent systems to see how their recent progress could help the HMS community.

4 Multi-Agent Systems Research

Unlike the holon, that is rather a methodological, design and organisational concept, an agent is an independent and autonomous computational (or physical to the extent needed) unit. Either hierarchical, heterarchical or partially structured communities of agents perform joint decision making by means of communication, collaboration, negotiation, and responsibility delegation that are based on agents' individual rationality and social intelligence. Even though a single agent may be implemented internally by the multi-agent technology, an agent cannot be composed of other agents. In rare cases, when an agent is implemented as a lower-level multi-agent system, we do not allow these lower-level agents to interact autonomously with the higher-level agent. Agents group themselves into teams [70], coalitions [62], alliances [56], platforms, organisations etc. Unlike the "hard-wired" cooperation domains, the coalition and teams are very flexible and allow agents to autonomously join and leave the coalition, or the team respectively.

In the area of MAS, the agent architectures have been studied from many different perspectives. While the HMS function blocks contain the execution control part and the data processing part that interact, the basic integration architecture of an agent consists of **agent's body** and the **agent's wrapper** [48]. The wrapper accounts for the inter-agent communication and real-time reactivity. The body is an agent's reasoning component. It very often happens that the agent's body is a pre-existing piece of software/hardware that is integrated by the agent's wrapper into the agent structure. From the outside such a software system cannot be distinguished from an "ordinary" agent. This integration activity is called **agentification** and provides an elegant mechanism for solving the migration problem, where new pieces of automation machinery must be integrated with the currently running information system. Recently, the agent integration architecture has been improved by formalising the concept of social intelligence [47], [48] that is represented by an *acquaintance model* which becomes a part of the agent wrapper.

The MAS research community provides various techniques and components for the architecture of an agent community. The crucial categories of agents according to their intra- and inter-community functionalities (e.g. resource agents, order or customer agents, information agents) have been identified. Services have been defined for specific categories of agents (for example white pages, yellow pages, brokerage etc). In some of the architectures, the agents do not communicate directly among themselves. They send messages via facilitators which play the role of communication interfaces among collaborating agents [52]. Other architectures are based on utilisation of matchmakers which proactively try to find the best possible collaborator, brokers which act on behalf of the agent [15], or mediators which coordinate the agents by suggesting and promoting new cooperation patterns among them [63]. An increasing attention within the multi-agent community has been recently drawn to the concept of the meta-agent which independently observes the inter-agent communication and suggests possible operation improvements [18], [47], [57]. Message-exchange, interaction and negotiation scenarios are now widely accepted by organizations interested in the agent technology. An important contribution of the agent community is their research work in the area of ontologies – definition of the domain specific formal semantics of the inter-agent communication [21].

There are several standardisation efforts in the community. The FIPA (Foundation for Intelligent Physical Agents) consortium [27] has brought several **normative specifications**: FIPA's agent communication, agent management, agent message transport, abstract architecture and **informative specifications** (application-specific standards) such as nomadic application support, agent software integration, personal travel assistance and others. There are several open source platforms for implementing FIPA-compliant systems, e.g. FIPA-OS [58], ZEUS [54], JADE [5], and APRIL [4]. The former two provide the developers with a powerful environment for building FIPA-compliant multi-agent systems. Suitable knowledge ontologies for specific problem domains have been also being defined within the FIPA effort.

In the past few years, the multi-agent research community has been much more focused on the investigation of the specific models for representing knowledge about cooperating agents (acquaintance or social models) [48] as well as on various negotiation scenarios, usually based on the contract-net-protocol [65], auctions and market economies. Modal logic has also been widely applied not only to represent the semantics of FIPA-compliant messages (often called performatives after the Speech Act theory of Searle [61]), but also to express and model agents' beliefs, desires, and intentions, and other generic MAS aspects [75]. The JACK development environment [39] from Agent Oriented Software (AOS) [3] is a realization of the belief-desire-intention model of agency with its applications in the area of defence, air traffic control, telecommunication, network management and, most importantly here, manufacturing [41].

Meta-reasoning and (self-) reflectivity of a multi-agent system are other issues being intensively studied [57]. The coalition formation problem [70] and teamwork coordination [67] became hot topics. In specific application domains, such as humanitarian relief operation planning [56] separation of the private, semi-private and public knowledge owned by the agents has been required.

Besides the track record in application fields of multi-agent systems in production planning, scheduling, or routing assistance, the theoretical backgrounds of multi-agency have penetrated to new application fields relevant to HMS. This is the case of the Internet business (especially the B2B area), various military applications (command support, coalition formation, intrusion detection in information systems etc.). The integration methodology to "glue" sub-systems of diverse nature into a complex system (e.g. for diagnostics) has been explored more and more often.

The area of manufacturing and industrial control, especially when now connected with the ambitious holonic visions, seems to be a very attractive and high-priority application field for the MAS research.

5 HMS Trends Influenced by MAS

5.1 Real-Time Control

The HMS community has fully realized that the function block based technology is mature for only very limited control tasks and that it is necessary to leverage the results achieved in the MAS field. Several general architectures for combining both the function block and MAS technologies have been designed. For instance, the most popular new holon model encapsulates one or more function block oriented devices into a *wrapper* containing a higher-level software component (see Fig. 9).

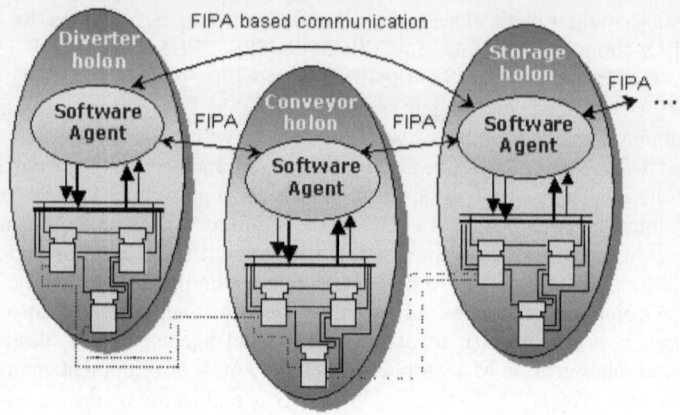

Fig. 9. The wrapper model

In such a holon, equipped with a higher-level software component, three communication channels should be considered:

–   **intra-holon** communication among the function block part and the software agent component,
–   **inter-holon** communication that is aimed at communication among the agent-based parts of multiple holons – FIPA standards are used more and more often for this purpose,
–   a **direct** communication channel among function block parts of the neighboring holons. If we are prepared to break the autonomy of an independent holon then this communication is standardized by IEC 61499 already, otherwise a new type of real-time coordination technology is needed to ensure real-time coordination. Such a model is presented in [22].

As a matter of fact, the holons defined in this way behave – on the level of inter-holon communication – like standard software agents. They can widely communicate among themselves, carry out complex negotiations, develop manufacturing scenarios, etc. We can call them *holonic agents* (agentified holons) as they consist of both the holonic part connected with the physical layer of the manufacturing system (operating in hard real-time) and the software agent for higher-level, soft real-time or non-real-time intelligent decision making. It was already mentioned that the inter-holon communication is usually standardized by the FIPA approach, and direct communication could be achieved by IEC standards (not necessarily 61499). Therefore the attention of system developers is aimed mainly at the intra-holon communication that is usually both application- and company-specific and it is usually connected with the solution of the migration problem. McFarlane [51] and others (see articles reviewed in [12]) introduced a blackboard system for accomplishing the intra-holon communication. To support the solution of the migration problem, Rockwell Automation developed JDL (Job Description Language) as a language specified in the XML format aimed to play the role of a content language of the FIPA-ACL [70]; while other HMS partners proposed using a special management service interface function block [23].

The software components of holons help to solve the migration problem as well, e.g. it is possible to locate several software components on one PLC (Programmable Logic Controller) and thus to create several holons. The software component can be even located on two or more PCs and transferred to the PLC when necessary. The "boundary" among holons running on the same platform or several platforms is mainly given by the particular organization of the intra-holon and inter-holon communication channels [6]. One approach, as detailed in [12], to achieve such migration is shown in Fig. 10. The encapsulation approach can be viewed just as a bottom-up attempt to extend the capabilities of the low-level, hard real-time control elements by adding some higher-level software components. This might help in solving certain categories of tasks where the groups of cooperating holons (interacting via the *cooperation domains* in HMS terminology) are not too complex and are clearly separated. For more complicated tasks, a more general, top-down analysis of the control and decision-making specifications was required.

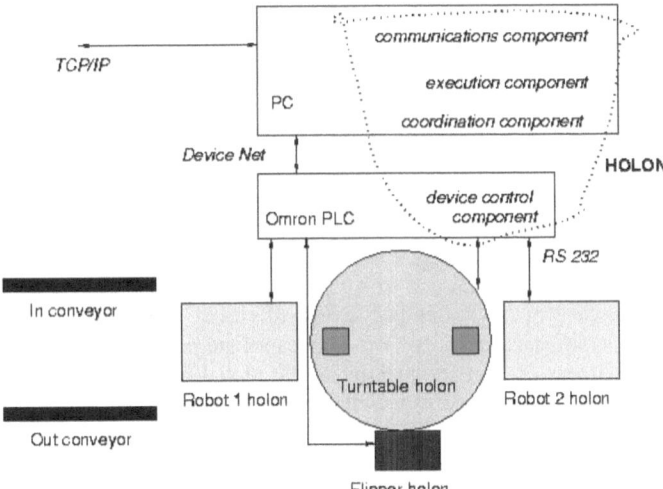

Fig. 10. Migrating holons onto control technology

The real-time control requirements combined with the expectations of global and intelligent decision-making are reflected in the multi-layered architecture of holonic agents proposed in [26]. The architecture consists of four layers, namely

- *execution layer* (E) which is directly connected with physical control of the hardware/equipment part,
- *control execution layer* (CE) which contains and executes control instructions in a low, elementary machine code,
- *execution control layer* (EC) which contains the appropriate control algorithms – these are not represented in a real-time form (usually written in a higher language). The EC layer is responsible for translating the control algorithms into the CE real-time code,

- *planning & scheduling layer* (PS) covering the tasks of long-term activities planning and scheduling.

The algorithms located at higher levels cannot be accomplished in real-time. Thus, it is expected to carry out the low level real-time control tasks just on the E or CE level (such a solution can be called "light-weight agents"), while the CE and PS layer algorithms can be slower, dedicated to more sophisticated decision-making. A similar multi-layered architecture needed for real-time control and decision-making has been proposed in [18]. Five layers are considered, namely physical part (PP), control (C), execution (E), scheduling (S), and planning (P). These echelons aim to break down the rigid layering of traditional computer integrated manufacturing. In CIM, an order arrives at the factory and a corresponding plan for its manufacture is generated. The plan is then given to the scheduling function that assigns timings to actions within the scope of the plan. The schedule is finally presented to the machines that execute them, monitor status values and report any irregularities up through these unbending operational layers. This method works well in factories where hierarchical control is dominant. But in manufacturing shop floors where heterarchical control is needed (such as those where the holonic vision is to be realized), having inflexible organizational layers does not work. By a detailed analysis it can be recognized that PP and C levels in [49] represent E and CE levels in [26], E and EC are identical. Furthermore PS in [26] is split into two separate levels in [49]. Let us make a general remark: The higher the level in the hierarchy, the less critical the response time is and the requirements of the algorithms are for greater intelligence. As a result, the more complex tasks can be solved at the higher levels, so long as the greater computing power required is available.

It would be ideal for each holon to have a chance to be directly involved in decision-making on each of the mentioned levels; this ideal architecture can be seen in Fig. 11a. Such well-furnished holons would encapsulate modules for taking part in all the phases and levels of decision-making in the global holonic control system. But both the migration problem and especially different computing requirements on different information processing levels do not currently allow designers to build such well-furnished holons. In reality, there are currently available planning and scheduling holons (we can call them agents as they are not physically connected with the manufacturing process) that communicate with the execution control agents and the low-level holons for real-time control (see Fig. 11b).

The ideal mapping of holonic components onto the classical CIM hierarchical control architecture was presented in [12] (see Fig. 12a for a representation of how a 'resource' holon can be mapped; a different structure maybe needed for 'product' or other types of holons). The mapping is usually achieved in experimental studies. Reality is much more modest, usually just the cell and machine level integration is achieved within a holon framework (see Fig. 12b).

There are several agent-based manufacturing systems that that bear a resemblance to the HMS concept. Rockwell Automation designed one of *industrial solution* of the agent-based control that solves the above specified migration problem. This three-layered architecture, offered for use by the HMS consortium [33], was presented at the HMS-18 meeting (Prague, October 2001) and consists of:

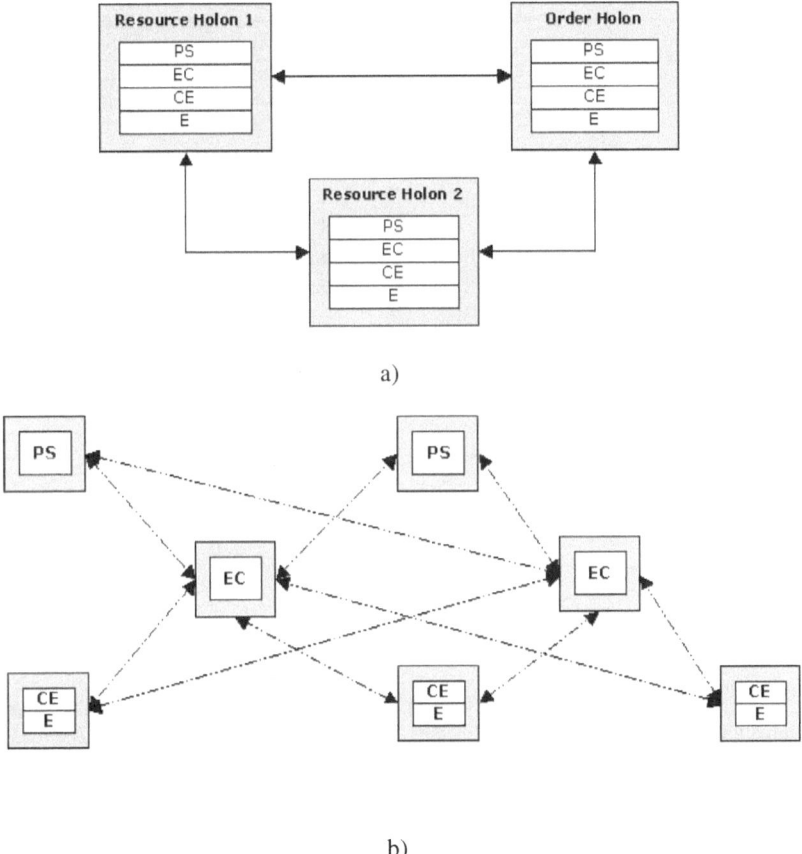

a)

b)

Fig. 11. Different holonic architectures: a) an ideal architecture where each holon is equipped with all four layers, b) currently more obvious architecture with specialized holons on both the EC and PS levels

- **Information Agents (IA)** on the top of the hierarchy. They represent part of the manufacturing information data system with the reaction time of between sub-seconds to minutes. These agents are responsible for strategic planning and scheduling.
- **Distributed Control Agents (DCA)** represent physical resources such as processes or pieces of equipment. They are responsible for operational planning and scheduling and for control execution with the reaction time of between 50 milli-seconds to 1 second. These run the ControlLogix platform (i.e. the successor of PLC technology) and represent an extension of the so-called Autonomous Cooperative Units (ACUs) [71]. More agents can run using the same ControlLogix platform [14].

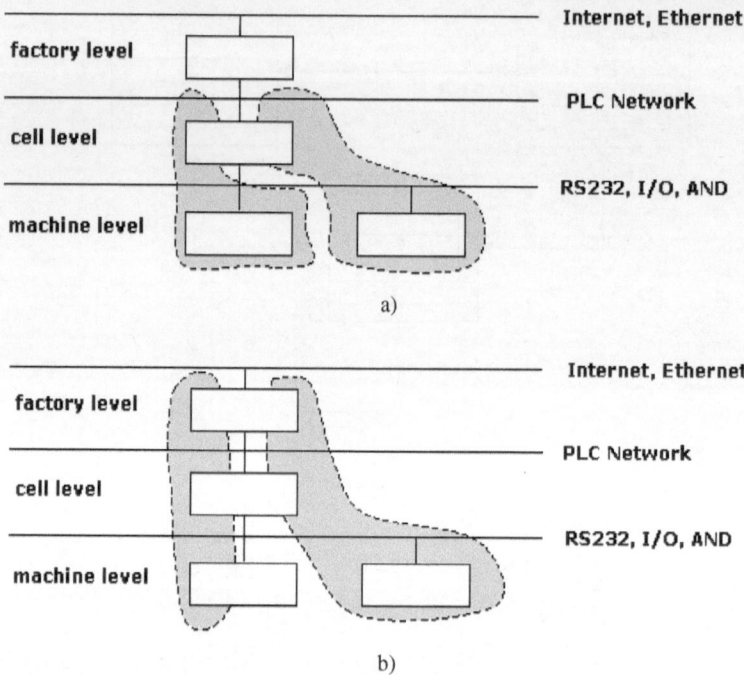

Fig. 12. Mapping Holonics to CIM Layers: a) an ideal mapping where each holons covers all the three levels of a classical CIM architecture, b) more obvious solution: a holon is spread just across the cell and machine levels

– **Control Units (CU)** represent the physical controllers, operating within hard real-time constraints.

The information agents will be implemented in JAVA on Windows CE platforms and are expected to communicate with the distributed control agents using FIPA-compliant messages. DCAs are programmed in C++ (for the future, an implementation in JAVA is considered as well) with communication between the DCAs and CUs being carried out by means of the JDL (Job Description Language) [71]. DCAs can negotiate cooperatively to achieve mission or process objectives. The Rockwell architecture represents just the necessary shift from classical hierarchical control towards agent-based control in order to realize holonic systems. This shift is within the framework of the classical scan-based software and hardware platforms. The mapping of agents to the hierarchical control architectures is shown in Fig. 14b. This small, but important technological step is just the first movement in the direction towards more agile manufacturing automation and control systems. These future directions can be seen from the advanced research activities reported in [49].

5.2 Communication Standards

It is expected that the communication among holonic agents will be standardized for many reasons. One reason is that these holonic agents should be involved in global communities of company agents where they can directly participate in supply chain management negotiations or contribute to virtual enterprise simulation games etc. The FIPA communication standards are considered preferable for implementing the inter-holon communication. To develop these standards, the HMS community must declare message specification as combinations of the already defined standard performatives, in order to define their semantics and to develop the appropriate knowledge ontologies. This seems to be quite a demanding task as manufacturing, material handling, production planning or supply chain management requirements significantly differ in different industries and between different types of production.

6 Design, Simulation, and Virtual Holonic Environments

The process of developing and implementing a holonic system relies on several phases:

1. **Identification of holons**: The design of each holonic system starts from a thorough analysis of:
   - The system to be controlled or manufacturing facility to be deployed.
   - The control/manufacturing requirements, constraints, and hardware/software available.
   - The result of this analysis is the first specification of holons to be introduced. This specification is based on the application and its ontology knowledge.

2. **Implementation/Instantiation** of holon classes from the holon type library. The holon type library is either developed, or re-used (if already available). Particular holons are created as instances of the holonic definitions in the holon type library. Furthermore the implementation of communication links among these holon instances is established within the framework of initialization from these generic holon classes. In such a way, the first prototype of holonic control/manufacturing system is designed.

3. **Simulation:** The behaviour of a holonic system is not deterministic. Yet the direct experimental testing of it with the physical manufacturing/control environment being involved is not only extremely expensive, but non-realistic as well. Simulation is the only way out. For this purpose, it is necessary to have:
   - A good model of the controlled process or the manufacturing facility. This model must depict all the entities with the holonic factory and their interfaces to the external world.
   - A good simulation tool for running the 'controlled process or manufacturing facility' model. Standard discrete event simulation tools like e.g. Arena, Grasp or Silk are adequate and are usually used for this purpose.
   - A good simulation environment for modeling the holonic agent parts interacting within the system. This environment can be provided in at least two

ways [21]. Firstly using commercial software like JACK. Secondly using
JADE, ZEUS or other open source FIPA platforms; this is the most used way.

- A suitable simulation environment to model the real-time parts of multiple
  holons. There are function block emulation tools from Rockwell Automation
  (holobloc [37]) and the modified 4-control platform from Softing [77]. Yet
  these tools do not adequately generate and handle real-time control problems.
  A more sophisticated real-time solution would be to use embedded firmware
  systems like JBED, with its time-based scheduler, to run JAVA objects (that
  simulate function blocks) and manage events in realistic manner. Another approach to such low-level simulation is to encode the necessary function blocks
  as UML capsules and then execute them with Rational RealTime [59]. This
  solution allows the capsules to be downloaded on specific hardware and run
  using real-time operating systems like VxWorks.
- System integration strategies developed and implemented in the form of subsystem interfaces. Of particular concern are the interfaces that "glue" together
  diverse simulation tools and enable the designer to switch from simulation
  tools to physical manufacturing/control systems as appropriate.
- HMI (human-machine interfaces) for all the phases of the system design and
  simulation.

4. **Implementation of the target control/manufacturing system**: In this stage, the
   target holonic control or manufacturing system is re-implemented into the (real-
   time) running code. This implementation usually relies on ladder logic, structured
   text or function blocks at the lowest level of control. However, some parts of the
   targeted manufacturing systems (such as resource or operation planning subsystems) are often reused as in the phase 3. In the eXPlanTech production planning
   multi-agent system [60] there was 70% of the real code reused from the simulation
   prototype. Therefore, the choice of the multi-agent platform in the phases 3 and 4
   is critical (it has been advised to operate with one platform only).

The simulation phase is much more crucial for the development process of holonic
systems than it has been for the development of "classical" control/manufacturing
systems. That is why significant attention must now be paid to the use of suitable
simulation techniques, tools, and environments. One of the most important work-
packages of the HMS Phase 2 consortium, called HOMES (Holonic Man-Machine
and Emulation Systems), is aimed at developing a complex virtual holonic environment that would solve all the issues connected with the above simulation phase.

HOMES will also provide multi-user man-machine interfaces and information systems integration [31].

7   HMS Planning and Scheduling

In this section, we review holonic planning and scheduling based on some of: (i) the
current thinking; and (ii) the background literature. Such planning and scheduling is
one of the largest topics for immediate exchange of ideas between the MAS and the
HMS research communities.

7.1 Current Thinking on HMS Planning and Scheduling

Both planning and scheduling in the holonic manufacturing system environment are naturally organized as physically distributed processes that involve localized decision-making. Using the context proposed in [49], we take *holonic planning* to mean:

– Decomposition of an order by a product holon into a causal sequence of manufacturing operations.
– Allocation of these operations to resource types (but not to quite assigning them to particular resource holons).

The main advantage of this holonic planning method is that it is an iterative nego-tiation process involving both resource and product holons, where the product holons represent the request to manufacture a specific order and have the knowledge relating to how it should be made. The processes of task decomposition, operation iden-tification and selection are also carried out in a distributed way. In [49], these mech-anisms are founded on a **resource-driven** approach designed to maximize the re-source utilization by each machine selecting what task to do next based on the physi-cal part at the head of its input buffer. This philosophy contrasts with **order-driven** approaches (like PROSA) that ensure the order to be decomposed and all constituent tasks to be assigned to machines. Each philosophy has its merits and drawbacks as outlined in [22]. However, this two level order-resource architecture is not sufficient enough in some cases. In the ProPlanT system [46] the architecture consist of the **project planning agents**, who represented an order, **production agents** representing resources. In between of these layers, there is a community of **project managing agents**, who took responsibility for a part of a project.

As a rule in the resource-driven philosophy, the planning process is led by re-source holons that inform and iteratively consult the corresponding product holon or other resource holon(s) as needed [36]. The final plan is stored by the product holon. Distributed AI and MAS methods are broadly explored for the negotiation purposes. In [46] social knowledge owned by individual holons (agents) was applied to speed-up the planning process and to make it more efficient. Within the same context as above, *holonic scheduling* means:

– Allocation of production operations to specific instances of resource holon types.
– Specification of the timing (starting time, duration, due time) for the given opera-tion.

The scheduling process can again be seen as an iterative negotiation process, and is initiated by:

– An order holon seeking assistance from resource holons and taking care of the most important constraints (due time, costs). This is the order-driven philosophy.
– A resource holon seeking for tasks to utilize the resource in an optimal (maxi-mum) way. This is the resource-driven philosophy.
– A combination of both approaches can be considered as well.

The holonic scheduling processes have a very similar nature to those of holonic planning and are based on distributed-problem solving and exploitation of MAS ap-proaches [19], [20], [55]. In general, these MAS technologies appear to be nearly compatible with software requirements for holonic systems. There are, in principle, no differences in requirements put on holonic and MAS planning and scheduling. The background for the negotiation process is most frequently provided by the contract-net-protocol metaphor [63], auctioning mechanisms [54], acquaintance model based contraction [48], and many modifications of cooperative interaction strategies can be found in the literature [16]. The interaction strategy is used either to adjust local processing parameters (e.g. starting time, batch size, processing speed etc.) or to re-calculate the local costs. In the latter case, local cost functions constrained by global production requirements are used by individual holons (for further details see [30]).

The ideas of holonic activities do not assume any central decision-making element in the community of holons. On the other hand, in practical applications of scheduling systems, we generally can find that a certain degree of central co-ordination exists. This ensures the decisions done locally (i.e. within the scope of a flexible manufacturing cell) are aligned in order to achieve the global goals of the entire enterprise. In other words, individual holons' decisions are orchestrated to maintain system-level coherence. The key point of having a (more or less strong) central holon represents a significant constraint to the autonomy and agility of the holons' behavior. Therefore decentralized planning and scheduling are demanded in a HMS.

Furthermore, the establishment of suitable plans and schedules cannot be considered as one-shot processes. They are invoked repeatedly, nearly permanently, at least after any change in the orders, in the capabilities or capacities of elements of the production facility, resources, technical faults of equipment etc. They occur after any type of system reconfiguration that is often done on the fly or in an adaptive way. One of the important issues that should be always handled carefully is the maintenance of a *clear separation* between planning and scheduling activities from execution and device/machine control activities. The transition or switching from the current schedule to a new schedule that was pre-prepared in the meantime (when the first part of original schedule was being run) can be carried out just at certain moments [47] when the original plans are "frozen". Note however that for finer-grained forms of reconfiguration (e.g. changing a robot's fault diagnosis algorithm from a rule-based model to a fuzzy-logic model while the robot is moving) demands the next generation of change management. This requirement is also going to be demanded by holonic systems, and so there will be many sophisticated interactions between the modules for planning, scheduling, execution, control, diagnostics and so on within a holon.

The holonic planning and scheduling approaches are still under-developed (see the background material in 7). That is why, the HMS consortium announced in 2000 a special work-package called HOPES (Holonic Production Execution Systems) for the Phase 2 of its activities with the stress on the following objectives [31]:

- To develop adaptive methods to support decentralized decision-making processes.
- To develop, implement and test methodologies for decentralized, agent-based scheduling.
- To integrate scheduling and process planning.
- To develop, implement and test concepts and models for agent-based supply chain management.

The HOPES work-package focuses on the transfer of methods and principles from Holonic Manufacturing Systems into the higher levels of company planning and production execution. This new vision will work both within single company (i.e. the holonic factory) and crossover several companies (inside a suitable multi-link supply chain management framework).

7.2 Existing Literature on HMS Planning and Scheduling

Note that for the economy of the paper, this review is not comprehensive, but rather it provides an outline and representative sample of the key approaches typically adopted so far. The computational problem of determining the optimal plan or schedule, when there are multiple resources that a manufacturing task can run on, is NP-hard. Therefore in conventional manufacturing control, methods for planning and scheduling use centralized *a priori* approaches like Enterprise Resource Planning (ERP) and Program Evaluation and Review Technique (PERT) respectively to reduce the complexity of these NP-hard computations. However these technologies often do not take into account problems that regularly arise in a holonic environment, including:

– The changeable nature and number of manufacturing resources on the shop floor.
– The dynamic nature of orders' arrival.
– The precedence constraints among tasks in order to manufacture highly variable products.
– Decisions to reconfigure the control system must often be made in real-time.

To manage the first issue, research has focused on developing heuristics that the holons can use for searching and collaborating in order to determine a satisfactory solution [64]. To manage the second issue, order holons have been introduced into the software infrastructure [7]. These are dedicated to monitoring and ensuring that the production of each order is completed in a timely manner. To tackle the third issue, [44] proposes that the Lagrangian Relaxation (LR) method, similar to the pricing concept of a market economy, replaces sub-project precedence constraints by 'soft' prices to identify any violations. The cost and benefit of violating a constraint can then be judged and paid for, if necessary [29]. To handle the fourth issue, researchers have studied the use of rules and model-based reasoning [74] as part of a *design-to-control* infrastructure to quickly determine the 'best' course of action to take in order to compensate for any observed anomalies.

One of the major papers on holonic planning and scheduling technique, and its application to a robotic assembly cell is [28]. The authors present two methodologies and two methods (one each for planning and scheduling). In summary, the planning method works as follows. First, determine parts and assembly operations by identifying all permutations of how parts can be combined, and then eliminate permutations that do not satisfy all constraints on how to combine the parts until a consistent product specification exists. Second, determine an assembly sequence and their machine types by applying the necessary precedence constraints and constraints set by the capabilities of each available machine. In other words, the approach is the resolution of a constraint satisfaction problem. The chief criticism that can be leveled at this approach is that is not backed up with a sufficiently complex implementation in the real world, and so any results are obtained from a simulation with limited relevance to pragmatic manufacturing systems. This complaint will be directed at many of the holonic approaches until full-scale demonstrators can be used as an experimental testbed.

The dynamic establishment of an initial schedule for the holons to execute (with respect to what job that is to be done, at what time, and by what machine) is also discussed in [66]. Here an order scheduling holon (using the PROSA architecture principles discussed earlier) with explicit schedule management knowledge initiates a negotiation with a group of resource holons to determine a feasible job assignment and avoid any conflicts. Though their protocol is easy to comprehend, it is unclear whether the exchange of messages will always result in a convergence to a mutually acceptable solution within some time limit, or how close this solution is to the optimal. This criticism can be targeted at many of the protocols proposed for a HMS. The approach presented in [53] is from a more economic viewpoint and concerns the impact of the planning process on inventory throughput and other commercial metrics regularly applied by manufacturing business.

A distinct perspective on the operations of a HMS is presented in [69] where the focus is on real-time scheduling using an existing plan. The authors hypothesize that two keys to using such a real-time rescheduling mechanism are that it is object-oriented and is driven by simple events and rules. The events used include the breakdown of a machine or the changing of a job's status to being high-priority. While the rules for determining the new machine to run a job on include using the machine with lowest efficiency. Such reactive approaches are often simple to build and generate good, if not optimal, results. Yet as no searching of a solution space is involved, various sub-optimal behaviors can emerge, e.g. bouncing a job between machines and having some jobs with such a low priority that they will never be executed.

A similar approach to dynamic re-distribution of work was proposed in [17] and is shown in Fig. 13. Here holons use the concept of heat to perform reactive re-distribution of manufacturing tasks among cells with equivalent skills. Each holonic cell determines how heavily loaded it is both now and it expects to be at some time in the future. Thus through some algorithm, each cell can calculate its temperature. At regular time intervals, the hottest cell uses the classic contract net protocol [65] to negotiate with the cooler cells to re-assign to them one or more of its tasks.

These algorithms can operate either with or without pre-knowing additional constraints on the future manufacturing of the workpiece, thus producing a 'look before you leap' or a 'hot potato' approach respectively. As a result, overall the heat of each cell (i.e. a function of their workload) will become balanced evenly, and so improving reaction to unforeseen circumstances. The approach is also scaleable, in that as cells are added or removed the method still operates in the same way. On the downside, the approach does not consider adopting alternative plans to manufacture the part or take in account putting the parts into storage (and so re-scheduling when the part is to be manufactured). Moreover, if there are no cool holons that can perform the same skills as the hottest holon then the approach fails to migrate tasks away (and thus cooling) from a heavily loaded cell.

Another interesting contribution to this topic is [43] that discusses how the schedule and machine configurations must adapt to the materials being processed. The scenario used is that of lumber dissection. Here, upon cutting a tree trunk along the X dimension reveals a group of defects in the wood, that mean the subsequent cuts of the lumber (along the Y and Z dimensions) must be modified to avoid any knots, stains, splits and so forth. This type of problem will be typical in the disassembly of raw material where the objective is to maximize the volume of highest value material, satisfy all orders and minimize storage requirements.

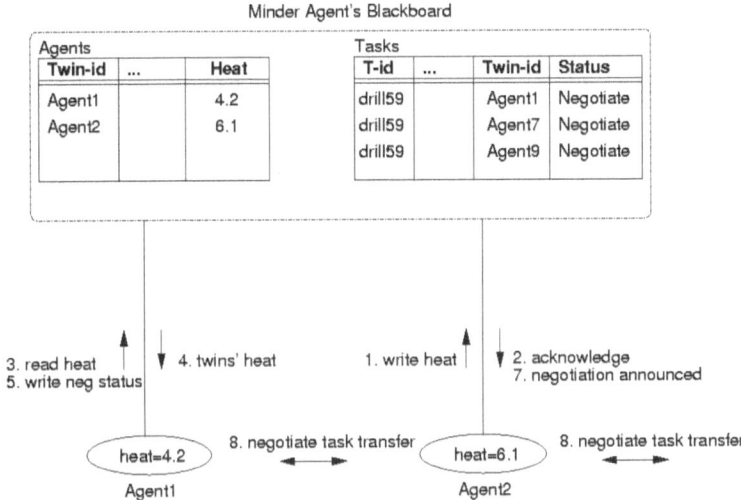

Fig. 13. An Example of holonic re-planning and re-scheduling

As multi-agent systems provide a suitable technology for implementing the 'smart' aspects of a holon, planning and scheduling approaches based on classic distributed artificial intelligence (DAI) metaphors offer some opportunities. For instance, [32] uses the contract net protocol as a foundation for agent-based holons to bid (to some controller) relating to how well they could plan or schedule the operations needed to manufacture the product. Each holon has knowledge about the geometric features that it can produce, e.g. a slot, rectangular projection and so on. The controller issues a description of the product. Then each holon offers a bid to perform the work needed to create the features in their repertoire, so that eventually the controller determines a coherent picture of which holon should do what feature and issues contracts to these holons to execute the work. When the work is to be done is also assigned through a similar round of bids and contract offers.

The aforementioned body of literature originates from the academic community. A specific example of planning in an industrial system is [9] where the authors have applied agent technology to an engine assembly line at DaimlerChrysler. They conjecture that "While in the classical assembly an engine has no choice but to move from one station to the next, in holonic assembly an engine may either be processed at the next station, at one of the multi-function stations, or it can be stored in a flexible buffer. Because of these processing alternatives, system control (and in particular the holon to task assignment made as part of the planning process) must take into account global aspects during the operation". Meanwhile the application of holonic control in a robot cell to isolate some scheduling features is narrated in [36]. The authors discuss how the scheduling aspects of control, which can be distributed throughout the system, are also based on a contemporary implementation of the contract net negotiation scheme.

8 Conclusions

We have tried to describe briefly the current situation in both the fields of HMS and MAS, mainly with the goal to present the HMS research results/problems to the community investigating multi-agent systems. Both areas have been developing in an insulated way for many years. However the common features of holons and agents (like autonomy, cooperativeness, intelligence and openness) are being recognized just recently. The differences between these approaches are mainly owing to motivation, to specific features of technical solutions as well as to historical reasons. Let us mention some of these distinctions:

– **Motivation:** The HMS research is motivated by problems encountered when trying to realize the vision of the holonic factory. In other words, achieving flexible manufacturing. On the opposite side, the MAS research is motivated by implementation of distributed computational systems, decentralized decision-making and, to a lesser extent, imitation of how groups of people act and interact.

– **Subject of Research**: The HMS community has (where possible) oriented its research towards the real-time end of the manufacturing process. Here low-level communication, behavioral standards, integration methodologies, etc are critical. Unlike the HMS people, the MAS researchers aim at implementing social behavior of intelligent entities, cooperation and coordination strategies, intelligent brokerage, learning from own experience, teamwork and coalition formation etc. From a very simple viewpoint, we can see the HMS research stream providing platforms/frameworks for implementation of knowledge-driven higher-level coordination and communication strategies based on the MAS research results.

– **Holarchy**: The holarchy principle allows the dynamic creation of a holon as a recursive set of more holons integrated together to solve a manufacturing problem and once resolved will disband. Furthermore it has been proposed that these holons (supplied by distinct vendors) must adopt the same architecture in order to be efficiently aggregated into this hierarchy. This is not the case in the MAS field where autonomy and functional differences of individual agents are rather preferred. Moreover their linkage into a self-similar structure is not demanded. However, agents very often group themselves hierarchically into teams to solve a specific problem. A perfect example of this principle is JACK with its Team Oriented Programming [41].

– **Human Interface**: Each holon is usually equipped with interfaces to the physical environment, other holons and humans. Moreover every holarchy is a holon and so it must also provide these essential interfaces. In contrast, human interfaces in MASs are very often implemented as separate agents providing services to the community as a whole.

The **HMS researchers** model distributed control from the *bottom-up*, i.e. from the real-time control of physical entities. Rather quickly, they have recognized the limits of their approach with respect to controlling more complex agile manufacturing tasks. In comparison, the **MAS researchers** are focused mainly on a *top-down* approach. They concentrate on the decomposition of a global system into functionalities that can be encapsulated as individual agents. Therefore we can put forward the following conclusions:

–   **The MAS area helps to avoid the dead-locks in HMS**: The exploitation of results from the MAS community will help the HMS researchers to solve the dead-locks in holonic real-time control. MAS research also offers a rich variety of methods, concepts, standards and techniques (all with well-defined semantics) that can assist in the building of a HMS. In particular, MAS ideas are also becoming dominant in decentralized planning, scheduling, simulation, virtual environments, and system diagnostics; these areas are of particular interest to the HMS community.

–   **Attractive HMS applications motivate the MAS area:** The MAS area has been aimed at information processing. It suffers from the lack of access to control of physical entities in which many new aspects should be considered. For instance problems relating to real-time control, imposition of manufacturing and transportation constraints, limited and changing capacity of resources etc. These problems, new to the MAS community, require the development of novel information processing techniques, knowledge ontologies, communication standards, and negotiation protocols to name but a few. Thus the HMS area plays the motivation role. The potential application fields in different industries are very broad and economically extremely attractive.

–   **MAS provides technology for HMS:** From the more general point of view, holonics provides a system-wide philosophy, and a general framework for developing flexible and intelligent complex manufacturing systems. The current holonic technology itself is limited, and not mature enough for immediate deployment. While MAS researchers do not have in the most cases a unified vision of the global enterprise-wide multi-agent manufacturing system, they can provide the HMS people with available experimental but also implemented technology.

The research in both fields must inevitably converge. It is time to systematically bridge the gap, reuse similarities and capitalize on differences.

References

1. Agentcities - a new initiative aiming to build a worldwide, publicly accessible, testbed for the deployment of dynamic, composed, agent-based services, http://www.agentcities.org/
2. AgentLink, Europe's network of excellence for agent-based computing, http://www.agentlink.org/
3. Agent Oriented Software Pty, http://www.agent-oriented.co.uk
4. April Agent Platform, http://sourceforge.net/projects/networkagent/

5. Bellifemine, F., Rimassa, G., and Poggi, A., JADE – A FIPA-compliant Agent Framework. In: *Proceedings of 4th International Conference on the Practical Applications of Intelligent Agents and Multi-Agent Technology*, London, (1999)

6. Bochmann, O.,Valckenaers, P., and Van Brussel, H., Negotiation-based Manufacturing Control in Holonic Manufacturing Systems. In: *Proceedings of the ASI'2000 Conference*, Bordeaux, (2000)

7. Bongaerts, L., van Brussel, H., and Valckenaers, P., Interaction Mechanisms in Holonic Manufacturing Systems. In: *Proceedings of the 32nd CIRP International Seminar on Manufacturing Systems*, (1999)

8. Brennan, R.W., Workshop on Agent-based Manufacturing. In: *Proceedings of the 5th ACM International Conference on Autonomous Agents*, Montreal, (2001)

9. Bussmann, S., and Sieverding, J., Holonic Control of an Engine Assembly Plant: An Industrial Evaluation. In: *Proceedings of the IEEE International Conference on Systems, Man and Cybernetics*, Tuscon, (2001)

10. Camarinha-Matos, L., Afsarmanesh, H., and Mařík, V. (eds), *Intelligent Systems for Manufacturing: Multi-Agent Systems and Virtual Organisations*. Kluwer Academic Publishers, Boston, (1998)

11. Chirn, J.-L., and McFarlane, D.C., A Holonic Component-Based Approach to Reconfigurable Manufacturing Control Architecture. In: *Proceedings of 11th IEEE International Conference on Database and Expert System Applications*, London, (2000), pp. 219-223

12. Chirn, J.-L., and McFarlane, D.C., Building Holonic Systems in Today's Factories: A Migration Strategy. *Journal of Applied Systems Studies*, vol. 2, no.1, Cambridge International Science Publishing, (2001)

13. Christensen, J.H., Holonic Manufacturing Systems: Initial Architecture and Standards Directions. In: *Proceedings of 1st European Conference on Holonic Manufacturing Systems*, Hannover, (1994), pp. 1-20

14. ControlLogix, http://www.ab.com/plclogic/clogix/controllogix.html

15. Decker, K., Sycara, K., and Williamson, M., Middle Agents for Internet, In *Proceedings of International Joint Conference on Artificial Intelligence* 97, Japan, (1997)

16. Deen, S.M., A Co-operation Framework for Holonic Interactions in Manufacturing. In: *Proceedings of the 2nd International Conference on Cooperating Knowledge Based Systems*, Keele, (1994), pp. 103-124

17. Deen, S.M., and Fletcher, M., Temperature Equilibrium in Multi-Agent Manufacturing Systems. In: *Proceedings of the 11th IEEE International Conference on Database and Expert System Applications*, London, (2000)

18. Dix, J., Subrahmanian, V.S., and Pick, G., Meta Agent Programs. *Journal of Logic Programming*, 46(1-2): 1-60, (2000)

19. Durfee, E.H.: Distributed Problem Solving and Planning. In: *Multi-Agent Systems and Applications*, LNAI No. 2086, Springer Verlag, Heidelberg, (2001), pp.118-149

20. Durfee, E.H., Lesser, V.R., and Corkill, D.G., Trends in Co-operative Distributed Problem Solving. *IEEE Transactions on Knowledge and Data Engineering*, vol.11, no. 1, (1989), pp. 63-83

21. FIPA's Working Group on Product Design and Manufacturing http://www.fipa.org/activities/groups.html

22. Fletcher, M., Designing a Holonic System Architecture and Coordination Domains with JACK. Submitted to the *International Conference on Artificial Intelligence*, Las Vegas, (2002)

23. Fletcher, M., and Brennan, R.W., Designing a Holonic Control System with IEC 61499 Function Blocks. In: *Proceedings of the International Conference on Intelligent Modeling and Control*, Las Vegas, (2001)

24. Fletcher, M., Garcia-Herroros, E., Christensen, J.H., Deen, S.M., and Mittmann, R., An Open Architecture for Holonic Cooperation and Autonomy. In: *Proceedings of 11th IEEE International Conference on Database and Expert System Applications*, London, (2000)

25. Fletcher, M., McFarlane, D.C., and Chirn, J.-L., A State of the Art Report on Holonic Manufacturing Systems. *Technical Report of the Institute for Manufacturing*, University of Cambridge, 2001

26. Fletcher, M., Norrie, D.H., and Christensen, J.H., A Foundation for Realtime Holonic Control Systems. *Journal of Applied Systems Studies*, vol. 2, no.1, Cambridge International Science Publishing, (2001)

27. Foundation for Intelligent Physical Agents (FIPA) organization, http://www.fipa.org/

28. Gou, L., Hasegawa, T., Luh, P.B., Tamura, S., and Oblak, J.M., Holonic Planning and Scheduling for a Robotic Assembly Testbed. In: *Proceedings of the 4th International Conference on Computer Integrated Manufacturing and Automation Technology*, (1994)

29. Gou, L., Luh, P.B., and Kyoya, Y., Holonic Manufacturing Scheduling: Architecture, Cooperation Mechanism, and Implementation. In: *Proceedings of IEEE/ASME International Conference on Advanced Intelligent Mechatronics*, (1997)

30. Gou, L., Luh, P., and Kyoya, Y., Holonic Manufacturing Scheduling: Architecture, Co-operation, Mechanism, and Implementation. *Computers in Industry*, vol. 37, (1998), pp. 213-233

31. Gruver, W.A., Kotak, D.B., van Leeuwen, E.H., and Norrie, D.H., Holonic Manufacturing Systems Phase 2. In: *Proceedings of 18th International Meeting of the Holonic Manufacturing System Consortium*, Prague, (2001) – will appear in the *Manufacturing Engineering Journ.*

32. Gu, P., Balasubramanian, S., and Norrie, D.H., Bidding-Based Process Planning and Scheduling in a Multi-Agent System. *Computers and Engineering Journal*, vol. 32, no. 2, (1997)

33. Hall, K., Agent Infrastructure for use by HMS Consortium, *Technical Report of Rockwell Automation*, (2001), http://www.rockwell.com/

34. Hasegawa, T. Gou, L., Tamura, S., Luh, P.B., and Oblak, J.M., Holonic Planning and Scheduling Architecture for Manufacturing. In: *Proceedings of the 2nd International Conference on Cooperating Knowledge Based Systems*, Keele, (1994)

35. Heikkila, T., Jarviluoma, M, and Hasemann, J.M., Holonic Control of a Manufacturing Robot Cell. *Technical report of VTT Automation*, (1994) http://www.vtt.fi

36. Heikkila, T., Jarviluoma, M., and Juntunen, T., Holonic Control for Manufacturing Systems: Design of a Manufacturing Robot Cell. *Integrated Computer Aided Engineering*, vol. 4, (1997), pp. 202-218

37. Holobloc from Rockwell Automation. http://www.holobloc.com

38. Holonic Manufacturing Systems (HMS) consortium, http://hms.ifw.uni-hannover.de/

39. Howden, N., et al, JACK Intelligent Agents – Summary of an Agent Infrastructure. In: *Proceedings of the 5th ACM International Conference on Autonomous Agents*, Montreal, (2001)

40. Institute for Manufacturing, University of Cambridge, http://www-mmd.eng.cam.ac.uk/automation/

41. Jarvis, D., Jarvis, J., Lucas, A., Ronnquist, R., and McFarlane, D.C., Implementing a Multi-Agent Systems Approach to Collaborative Autonomous Manufacturing Operations. In: *Proceedings of IEEE International Conference on Systems, Man and Cybernetics*, Tuscon, (2001)

42. Koestler, A., *The Ghost in the Machine*, Arkana, London, (1967)

43. Kotak, D.B., Fleetwood, M., Tamoto, H., and Gruver, W., Operational Scheduling for Rough Mills Using a Virtual Manufacturing Environment. In: *Proceedings of IEEE International Conference on Systems, Man and Cybernetics*, Tuscon, (2001)

44. Liu, F., and Luh, P.B., Scheduling and Coordination of Distributed Design Projects. *Annals of the CIRP*, vol. 47, no. 1, (1998)

45. Luck, M., Mařík, V., Štěpánková, O., and Trappl, R. (eds), Multi-Agent Systems and Applications. *Proceedings of the 9th ECCAI Advanced Course and AgentLink's 3rd European Agent Systems Summer School*, LNAI NO. 2086, Springer Verlag, (2001)

46. Mařík, V., Pěchouček, M., Štěpánková, O., and Lažanský, J., ProPlanT: Multi-Agent System for Production Planning. *Applied Artificial Intelligence*, vol. 14, no.7, (2000), pp. 727-762

47. Mařík, V., Pěchouček, M., and Štěpánková, O., Acquaintance Models in Replanning and Reconfiguration. In: *Advances in Networked Enterprises*, Boston, Kluwer Academic Publishers, (2000), pp.175-186

48. Mařík, V., Štěpánková, O., and Pěchouček, M., Social Knowledge in Multi-Agent Systems. *Multi-Agent Systems and Applications*. LNAI No. 2086, Springer Verlag, Heidelberg, (2001), pp. 211-245

49. McFarlane, D.C., and Bussmann, S., Developments in Holonic Production Planning and Control. *Production Planning and Control*, (2000)

50. McFarlane, D.C., and Gruver, W., Workshop on Intelligent Distributed Manufacturing Management and Control. In: *Proceedings of IEEE International Conference on Systems, Man and Cybernetics*, Tuscon, (2001)

51. McFarlane, D.C., Kollingbaum, M., Matson, J., and Valckenaers, P., Development of Algorithms for Agent-Based Control of Manufacturing Flow Shops. In: *Proceedings of IEEE International Conference on Systems, Man and Cybernetics*, Tuscon, (2001)

52. McGuire, J., Kuokka, D., Weber, J., Tenebaum, J., Gruber, T., and Olsen, G., SHADE: Technology for Knowledge-Based Collaborative Engineering. *Concurrent Engineering: Research and Applications*, 1(3), (1993)

53. Mezgar, I., Kovacs, G.L., and Paganelli, P., Co-operative Production Planning for Small- and Medium Sized Enterprises. *International Journal of Production Economics*, vol. 64, (2000)

54. Nwana, H., Ndumu, D., Lee, L., and Collis, J., ZEUS: A Tool-Kit for Building Distributed Multi-Agent Systems. *Applied Artificial Intelligence Journal*, vol. 13, no.1, (1999), pp. 129-186

55. Parunak, H.: Industrial and Practical Applications of Agent-based Systems. In: *Multiagent Systems: A Modern Approach to Distributed Artificial Intelligence*. MIT Press, Cambridge, MA, (1998), pp. 377-424

56. Pěchouček, M., Mařík, V., Bárta, J., Acquaintance Models in Coalition Planning. In: *Intelligent Agent Technology - Research and Development*, World Scientific, Singapore, (2001), pp. 434-443

57. Pěchouček, M., and Norrie, D., Knowledge Structures for Reflective Multi-Agent Systems: On Reasoning about Other Agents. *Research Report 538*, Department of Mechanical and Manufacturing Engineering, University of Calgary, Canada, (2001)

58. Poslad, S., Buckle, P., and Hadingham, R., The FIPA-OS Agent Platform: Open Source for Open Standards. In: *Proceedings of 5th International Conference on the Practical Applications of Intelligent Agents and Multi-Agent Technology*, Manchester, (2000), pp. 355-368

59. Rational RealTime from Rational for developing UML capsules and deploying them in embedded real-time environments, http://www.rational.com

60. Říha, A., Pěchouček, M., Krautwurmová, H., Charvát, P., Koumpis, A.: Adoption of an Agent-Based Production Planning Technology in the Manufacturing Industry. In: *Database and Expert Systems Applications*. New York : IEEE Computer Society Press, 2001, vol. 1, pp. 640-646.

61. Searle, J.R., *Speech Acts*, Cambridge University Press, (1969)

62. Shehory, O., and Kraus S., Methods for Task Allocation via Agent Coalition Formation. *Artificial Intelligence Journal*, vol. 101 (1–2), (1998), pp. 165–200
63. Shen, W., Norrie, D.H., and Barthes, J.A., *Multi-Agent Systems for Concurrent Intelligent Design and Manufacturing*, Taylor and Francis, London, (2001)
64. Shin, J., and Cho, H., Planning and Sequence Heuristics for Feature-Based Control of Holonic Machining Equipment. *International Journal of Flexible Manufacturing Systems*, vol. 13, (2001)
65. Smith, R.G., and Davis, R., Negotiation as a Metaphor for Distributed Problem Solving. *Artificial Intelligence*, vol. 20, (1983), pp. 63-109
66. Sousa, P., and Ramos, C., A Dynamic Scheduling Holon for Manufacturing Orders. *Journal of Intelligent Manufacturing*, vol. 9, (1998)
67. Stone, P., and Veloso, M., Task Decomposition, Dynamic Role Assignement and Low Bandwidth Communication for Real Time Strategic Teamwork. *Artificial Intelligence*, vol. 110 no. 2, (1999), pp. 241-273
68. Suda, H., Future Factory System Formulated in Japan. *Japanese Journal of Advanced Automation Technology*, vol. 1, (1989)
69. Sugimura, N., Tanimizu, Y., and Ae, S., Object-Oriented Simulation of Real-time Scheduling in Holonic Manufacturing Systems. In: *Proceedings of the International Conference on Advances in Production Management Systems*, (1999)
70. Tambe, M., Towards Flexible Teamwork. *Journal of Artificial Intelligence Research*, vol. 7, (1997), pp. 83-124
71. Tichy, P., Slechta, P., and Maturana, F.., Job Description Language (JDL), *Technical Report of Rockwell Automation*, (2001)
72. Valckenaers, P., Van Brussel, H., Kollingbaum, M., and Bochmann, O., Multi-agent Co-ordination and Control Using Stigmergy Applied to Manufacturing Control. In: *Multi-Agent Systems and Applications*, LNAI No. 2086, Springer Verlag, Heidelberg, (2001), pp. 317-334
73. Van Brussel, H., Valckenaers, P., Bongaerts, L., and Peters, P., PROSA: A Reference Architecture for Holonic Manufacturing Systems. *Computers in Industry*, vol. 37, (1998), pp. 155-274
74. Wang, L., Integrated Design-to-Control Approach for Holonic Manufacturing Systems. *Robotics and Computer Integrated Manufacturing*, vol. 17, (2001)
75. Wooldridge, M., *Reasoning about Rational Agents*. MIT Press, Cambridge, MA, (2000)
76. Zhang, X., Norrie, D.H., Christensen, J.H., and Brennan, R.W., Performance Analysis Model of HMS Real-Time Controller. In:§ *Proceedings of IEEE International Conference on Systems, Man and Cybernetics*, Tuscon, (2001).
77. 4-Control from Softing AG, http://www.softing.com

Material Handling Problem:
FIPA Compliant Agent Implementation

Pavel Vrba and Václav Hrdonka

Rockwell Automation Research Center, Americka 22, 120 00 Prague, Czech Republic
{pVrba,vHrdonka}@ra.rockwell.com

Abstract. This paper describes a proposal of a multi-agent FIPA-compliant solution of a general material handling system problem. Simple knowledge ontology for material handling and basic classes of FIPA-compliant agents/messages
for this kind of systems are presented in this paper. The abilities to solve reconfiguration problems either in the case of failure detection or within the framework of a physical reconstruction of the whole system are outlined.

1 Introduction

Growing customer requirements for rapid dynamic changes in production styles in the
manufacturing area today together with the increasing complexity of problems to be
solved are forcing major changes in the traditional software approaches. Sequential
and centralized solutions used so far are being found insufficiently powerful to meet
the requirements for robustness, flexibility and dynamic reconfiguration capabilities.
Using traditional centralized hierarchical approaches can result in almost the whole
system being shut down by an insignificant failure of its single component.

The manufacturing strategies in the 21st century will need to satisfy the demands
for (i) open and dynamic structure to allow the on-line integration of new subsystems
or removal of existing subsystems from the system without the need to stop and reini-
tialize the working environment, (ii) agility to adapt quickly to continuous and unanticipated changes in the manufacturing environment and (iii) fault tolerance to be
capable to detect and recover the failure of a system part by minimizing its impact on
the whole system [1].

To meet these requirements, the need for distributed intelligent manufacturing systems has become inevitable. Recently, the agent technology has been recognized as an
important approach for designing these kinds of systems [2]. In the past ten years
many researches have attempted to apply the agent technology to various manufacturing areas such as supply chain management, manufacturing planning, scheduling and
execution control or even developing new concepts of manufacturing systems.

Under the international Intelligent Manufacturing Systems (IMS) Research Program one of such a new concepts of so-called *Holonic Manufacturing Systems* (HMS)
has been proposed in 1994. A holon as a combination of Greek words *holos* (meaning
the whole) and *on* (part) following Koestler [3] is defined by the HMS consortium as
an autonomous and cooperative building block of a manufacturing system for transporting, transforming, storing and/or validating information and physical objects [4].
These units should be *autonomous* in the sense of ability to manage their own, "local"

V. Mařík et al. (Eds.): MASA 2001, LNAI 2322, pp. 268-279, 2002.
© Springer-Verlag Berlin Heidelberg 2002

behavior and *cooperative* in the sense of mutual collaboration with each other via negotiation in order to solve global level tasks [5].

According to HMS specifications, the structure of holon is basically composed of two parts: (i) the low-level control part which is physically connected to the hardware (sensors and actuators) and (ii) high-level software agent part responsible for the inter-holon communication, negotiation and decision making. Its obvious that this part of a holon is a key mechanism which ensures the cooperative character of holon.

Let us mention that substantial part of the effort in HMS group has been so far oriented towards the low-level control part of holons. It utilizes recently emerged IEC 61499 control standard known as *function blocks*, bringing undoubted benefits for the RT control resulting from the separation of the data-flow and event-flow [4]. Unfortunately, not too much attention was paid to the higher-level aspects in which holons should behave as cooperative units, in other words *agents*. Simply said, the benefits of agent technology, which seem to be powerful to satisfy the demands of next-generation manufacturing systems, has not as yet been fully utilized in the HMS community.

The higher-level agent-oriented extension of holonic control systems represents the main content of this paper. It includes the initial visions about how the basic agents, messages and a simple ontology for the manufacturing area should look like while focusing primarily on the material handling problem of manufacturing.

Take note that the success of penetration of the holonic concepts into industry depends on the availability of development tools and platforms which protect the developers from the need of developing basic functionality within each system from the scratch. Moreover, such tools presume the existence of publicly recognized standards defining precisely what that basic functionality should be and how it should be presented [1].

For purposes of the agent-oriented extensions of holonic systems mentioned previously, we found it reasonable to follow the specifications of the Foundation for Intelligent Physical Agents (FIPA) consortium [9]. This organization provides widely accepted standards for agent-based systems development and recently, number of agent-development open-source platforms compliant with the FIPA standards have emerged, such as the FIPA-OS, JADE, ZEUS or APRIL (see [9], link *Resources/ publicly available agent platform implementations*).

In our research we have primarily focused our attention on the first two, i.e. the FIPA-OS developed at Nortell Networks and the JADE platform developed at CSELT in order to evaluate at least two different JAVA-based agent toolkits and reveal their possible advantages or weaknesses. It means that the environment we have developed for agent-based simulation of a material handling systems (see later) is available and fully functional in both the FIPA-OS and JADE platforms.

2   Material Handling Problem Specification

As already mentioned, our first attention was paid to the material handling problem, especially to the transportation subtask of it. As shown in Fig. 1, we treat this problem as a graph, where each node and arc represents a particular component of a material handling system (MHS), such as a storage, diverter, conveyor belt, etc.

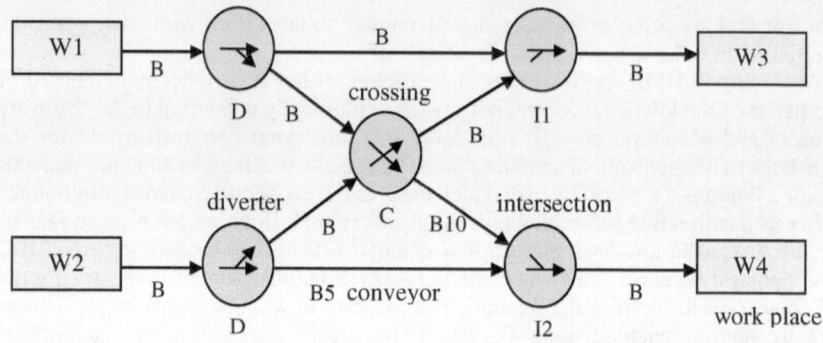

Fig. 1. Transport problem of a material handling system treated as graph

From the nature of a graph we can distinguish two main types of components: *node components* representing the nodes of a graph and *transport components* representing its arcs.

Basically, the *node components* constitute (static) places in a material handling system between which the *workpieces* are transported, where by *workpieces* we mean the subjects of a transport, such as pallets, semi-products, parcels, pieces of raw material and so forth. As depicted in Fig. 1, the node components could be further separated into two different classes. The former one we call ***workplace*** (the rectangles W1, ..., W4) which could be e.g. a storage/retrieval system, CNC machine or any other component in an MHS able to receive, store/process and resend workpieces. The latter is the node component we call ***crossing*** (circles in Fig. 1) which function is to receive workpieces coming from several input transport components (see below) and reroute them (according to their destination) to several different output transport components.

As Fig. 1 shows, we further distinguish two specialized subtypes of crossing, (i) the ***diverter*** which receives workpieces from one input and reroutes them to two outputs (D1 and D2 in Fig. 1) and (ii) the ***intersection*** which merges workpieces coming from 2 inputs into one output (I1 and I2).

The transport components, i.e. the arcs of a graph, are those capable of the physical transport of workpieces between node components. At this point we consider only *conveyor belts* (B1, ..., B10) capable of one or bi-directional transportation between one input and one output node component. However, the proposed structure can easily be extended by other transportation facilities, such as an AGV (automated guided vehicle), robot arm, etc. In any case, we presume each of them transports for prespecified *cost* (where less means better), which is then used as a criterion in finding of optimal routes between workplaces (see Sect. 5).

In such a discrete system we assume, that the basic transportation task is the delivery of a workpiece from *start* to *destination* workplace via transport and crossing components. If there are several possible routes how to make the delivery, the optimal one must be found, which should be done during the transportation by on-line minimalization of a criterion computed as a sum of transport components costs.

Note that at this point we don't consider complex transportation tasks (i.e. to deliver some workpiece from a storage to some machine, then, after processing, to another machine and than back to storage e.g.). For these situations a division of such a complex task into a series of basic transportation tasks can be done using e.g. holonic paradigms [4]. Note again that it is not the subject of our interest now.

3 Agent Implementation

In the multi-agent implementation of a material handling problem specified in the previous section, or more precisely in the contribution to the agent-oriented extension of manufacturing-oriented holonic systems, an agent part of each material handling component mentioned earlier was necessary to be introduced. Then, each of these components will be an autonomous unit able to solve local tasks (e.g. to reroute transported items and maintain the list of reachable destinations in the case of a crossing) and also cooperative ones via message passing between each other in order to solve global level tasks, e.g. to deliver items between workplaces.

As already mentioned we decided to follow the specifications provided by the FIPA organization and to use two different JAVA-based FIPA-compliant open source platforms, the FIPA-OS and JADE. Not only for the content language [10] of the FIPA-compliant messages sent among agents but also as a general format for the knowledge representation, we decided to use the Extensible Markup Language XML to be consistent with the current industrial trends.

3.1 Workplace Agent

This agent represents a node component, e.g. a storage or CNC machine, i.e. the place in an MHS capable of receiving, storing and/or processing and sending out the workpieces. From the transport problem point of view the workplace plays a role of a starting and destination place in the system between which the workpieces are transported.

For these purposes we suppose, that the workplace has one transport component connected to it as an input (i.e. one input conveyor belt in this stage) with the sensor which detects the workpieces arriving to it and one output conveyor by which the workpieces can be sent out to next wokplaces. Moreover, it is supposed that the input sensor is equipped with the bar code reader of workpiece's ID (see below) so that the workplace knows which item is currently arriving to it.

In the previous section we mentioned that the agents communicate together via message passing. The FIPA standard defines the message to consist of the *performative* describing the type of the message (e.g. REQUEST, INFORM, AGREE, REFUSE etc. – see [11]), the *sender* and the *receiver* of the message and finally the *content* of the message together with the *ontology* identifier.

One of the messages the workplace agent can receive is the REQUEST message to send a specified workpiece which is supposed to be present in it (particularly in the case of a storage). Let us assume that the workplace W3 from the example in Fig. 1 requires the workplace W2 to send it a workpiece with the ID 'wp1245'. The message sent to W2 looks as follows:

```
(REQUEST
    :sender W3 :receiver W2
    :content (<sendWorkPiece>workPieceInXML</sendWorkPiece>)
    :language XML :ontology material-handling
)
```

where workPieceInXML specifies the item to be sent using this format:

<workPiece ID = "wp1245" **destinationWorkPlace** = "W3" **/>**.

Take note of the attribute destinationWorkPlace, which indicates the final destination to which the workpiece should be delivered (workplace W3 in this case). This information is used during the transportation of the workpiece through the whole system, especially when the workpiece passes crossings, which have to switch it to the appropriate direction in order to reach the supposed destination.

When the workplace W2 receives the message mentioned above it looks whether the item with ID "wp1245" is really stored in it. On one hand if there is no such item available it replies to W3 with the REFUSE message. On the other hand if the required workpiece is present in W2, it takes the following sequence of actions: first, replies AGREE to W3 and second, it sends the workpiece to its output conveyor (b4 in this example), i.e. it sends the INFORM message to the conveyor b4 with content **<workPieceSent>**workPieceInXML**</workPieceSent>**.

Let us now describe how we cope with the situation when the workplace receives a workpiece coming from the input conveyor. As noted above we suppose that the workplace will be equipped with the input sensor capable to read workpiece's ID. When a signal from this sensor is indicated by the low-level control code of a holon (such as the ladder logic or the function blocks in PLC or another control platform), the software agent part have to be informed about it. For these purposes we have introduced a method **inSensor**(String receivedParcelID) to the workplace agent. At this point, where only a software simulation without a connection to the real hardware exists, this method is triggered by "virtual workpieces" running in the simulation whenever they arrive to the workplace. Then the workplace stores the workpiece (or starts to process it somehow) and alternatively informs other necessary agents that the workpiece has arrived.

3.2 Crossing Agent

The crossing agent is one of the "smartest" agents in our system. Each crossing maintains knowledge about which destination workplaces are reachable by each of its output conveyors together with the delivery costs. Whenever a workpiece comes to the crossing from some of its input conveyors (indicated by the input sensor as in the case of a workplace), the knowledge base is sought by this crossing through in order to find out the appropriate output conveyor, to wich the workpiece should be switched so that it finally reaches its required destination for the minimal cost.

Should be noted that we found this solution to be similar to the ideas in [7] to apply *stigmergy* (the techniques inspired by the behavior of social insects) to the manufacturing control. The important capability of this approach is that the global information (i.e. how to reach the destination workplace in the case of material handling problem) is made available locally (i.e. in crossings, which know to what direction the workpiece should be switched). Let us note that this distributed knowledge is kept up-to-date by the material handling environment itself, i.e. is dynamically changed as various workplaces are becoming unreachable when failures of system components, e.g. conveyors, are detected (see Sect. 5).

4 Proposal of the Material Handling Ontology

One of the most important contribution of our research is the proposal of an *ontology* specialized to the material handling domain.

The ontology plays a significant role in the inter-agent communication because it represents a structure providing agents with the semantic of terms (or symbols) used in the messages [12]. Thus, if an agent sends a message to another agent using specified ontology it can be sure that the other agent (of course if it shares the same ontology) will understand the message.

The key ingredients that make up an ontology are a vocabulary of basic terms and a precise specification what those terms mean and what is their relationship to other terms. Let us note that our choice for XML as a main data format simplifies the definition and further utilization of the knowledge ontology. The XML enables to define custom tags with desired syntactic structure via its DTD (Document Type Definition) which can be according to [12] viewed as an ontology specification.

Some of the ontology elements have already been shown in this article, e.g. the specification of the transported item which we call a ***workpiece***. Its XML description for the transportation purposes looks e.g. as follows:

The ID attribute is used for the unique identification of the workpiece or the class of workpieces (e.g. ZIP codes of parcels in a parcel distribution center) in the material handling system whereas the destinationWorkPlace attribute denotes the destination workplace to which this workpiece should be delivered.

Another important ontology element was introduced for the description of a material handling system components such as already mentioned crossings, conveyor

belts, wokplaces and so on. The XML description we propose looks like:

<component type = "WorkPlace" **name** = "W1" />

The type attribute denotes the type of a component (one of WorkPlace, Crossing, Diverter, Intersection or ConveyorBelt) and the name attribute is used to uniquely identify the appropriate agent in the multi-agent community.

If we look at the Fig. 1, we can see that the workplace component W1 (described earlier) is connected with the diverter component D1 by the conveyor belt B1. Let us suppose that the cost for which this conveyor delivers is 12. Then the XML specification of it will look as follows:

```
<component type = "ConveyorBelt" name = "B1">
    <connection from = "W1" to = "D1" defaultCost = "12" />
</component>
```

It is obvious that this approach makes our solution open for the future introduction of new material handling components, such as AGVs, robots, CNC machines etc. In the simulation tool for a material handling system (see section 6), when an XML file including the description of a system (using previous ontology terms) is being read, the appropriate JAVA class of the name specified by the type attribute of each component is dynamically loaded (ConveyorBelt.class file e.g.). Then its method createInstance, which is supposed to be defined in this class, is called. In this method other necessary attributes are obtained (i.e. from, to and defaultCost attributes in this case) and according to them new instance of such a class, i.e. a new FIPA agent is automatically created. The introduction of the new component is simplified to such an extent that only a new JAVA class file has to be added to appropriate package without the need to modify other JAVA classes (especially that one which reads the configuration file) or rebuild the whole JAVA project.

Last ontology term we would like to mention here we call **reachableWorkPlaces**. This one is used by agents while looking for the optimal routes through the system during initial configuration and within the reconfiguration as a consequence of a failure detection as well. The use of this ontology term will be described in the following section.

5   Dynamic Reconfiguration Capabilities

In Sect. 2 we have defined the basic transportation task the agents should be capable to solve (delivery of a single workpiece from a start to the destination workplace via transport and crossing components). It is obvious, that in a particular system there can be more than one possible route from the start to the destination and that the crucial components which have to contribute to the optimal-delivery solution are the crossings. As mentioned in Sect. 3.2, the crossing component has more than one output conveyors and therefore must decide to which of them to send the arriving workpiece out so that it finally reaches its destination. Moreover, this decision must be optimal, i.e. if more output conveyors can be used for this delivery, the "best one" has to be chosen so that the delivery cost of the remaining route (i.e. from this crossing to the destination workplace) is minimal.

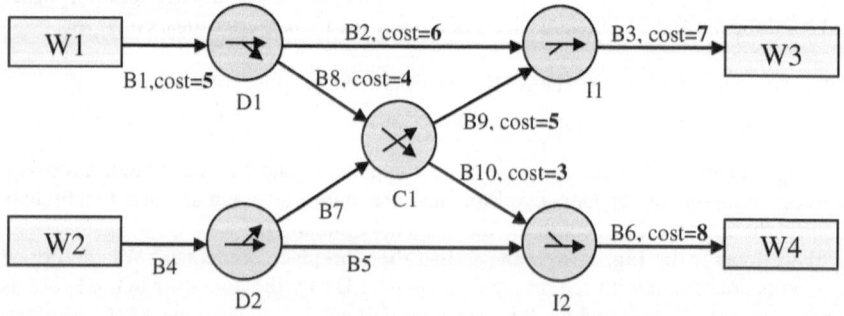

Fig. 2. Material handling system example. Each conveyor belt delivers for a certain cost, where "less means better". Crossing components (D1, D2, C1) maintain knowledge about optimal routes to the destination workplaces (W3, W4) using reachableWorkPlaces ontology term

In the example of a system mentioned in Sect. 2 (depicted once more in Fig. 2), the diverter D1 e.g. can use both the B2 and B8 output conveyors in order to reach the destination W3. Thus if the cost of the route to W3 using conveyor B2 is less then the cost using B8, the diverter should prefer B2 to B8.

To solve such a tasks, each crossing agent holds for each output conveyor the list of names of all the reachable destination workplaces together with the costs of the delivery. Whenever some workpiece enters the crossing, the agent searches through these lists and finds which one contains the workpiece's destination for the lower cost; finally the workpiece is sent out to the appropriate output conveyor.

In this example, the diverter D1 maintains the knowledge (using **reachableWork-Places** ontology term mentioned in the previous section) which looks like follows:

For output conveyor **B2**:

```
<reachableWorkPlaces>
    <workPlace name="W3" cost="13" />
</reachableWorkPlaces>
```

For output conveyor **B8**:

```
<reachableWorkPlaces>
    <workPlace name="W3" cost="16" />
    <workPlace name="W4" cost="15" />
</reachableWorkPlaces>
```

Whenever a workpiece with the destination W3 enters D1, this diverter knows that using output conveyor B2, the cost of the remaining route to W3 will be **13** whereas using B8 the cost is **16**. Its obvious that it sends this workpiece out to B2.

The information about the accessible destinations through a particular output conveyor obtains the crossing agent from this conveyor which propagates such a list received from its output node backward to its input node while adding its cost to the costs of all destinations in the list.

As the crossing receives such a list, it stores it for the purposes mentioned above and then merges it with the other lists received from other output conveyors. The result is then sent by the crossing back to all of its input conveyors (they propagate it back again in the same way) so that even other components in the system would be informed about the accessibility of destinations. Its obvious, that such a cascade of messages is originally triggered by the destination workplaces themselves as each of it sends a list (including itself as a reachable workplace) to its input conveyor. In other words, for optimal route finding the agents use a **backward** propagation algorithm, i.e. from destinations to sources.

In the example from Fig. 2, the destination workplaces W3 and W4 send messages to their input conveyors (B3 and B6). Then they hold following knowledge:

B3:
```
<reachableWorkPlaces>
    <workPlace name="W3" cost="0" />
</reachableWorkPlaces>
```

B6:
```
<reachableWorkPlaces>
    <workPlace name="W4" cost="0" />
</reachableWorkPlaces>
```

These conveyors add their costs (7 and 8 respectively) and send these lists to their input nodes, i.e. to intersections I1 and I2. Thus, they hold another piece of knowledge:

I1:
```
<reachableWorkPlaces>
    <workPlace name="W3" cost="7" />
</reachableWorkPlaces>
```

I2:
```
<reachableWorkPlaces>
    <workPlace name="W4" cost="8" />
</reachableWorkPlaces>
```

Both intersections propagate their knowledge back to all of their input conveyors, i.e. I1 to B2 and B9 and I2 to B5 and B10; they add their costs and propagate the knowledge again. Then the crossing agent C1 e.g. receives and stores this knowledge:

C1 for output **B9**:
```
<reachableWorkPlaces>
    <workPlace name="W3" cost="12" />
</reachableWorkPlaces>
```

C1 for output **B10**:
```
<reachableWorkPlaces>
    <workPlace name="W4" cost="11" />
</reachableWorkPlaces>
```

As already said, the crossing C1 merges these lists and sends them to all of its intput conveyors. When the B8 receives it, adds its cost (4) and sends it to the diverter D1, its clear, that the knowledge of reachable destinations hold by this diverter will be as shown earlier in this section, i.e.

D1 for output conveyor B2:
```
<reachableWorkPlaces>
    <workPlace name="W3" cost="13" />
</reachableWorkPlaces>
```

D1 for output conveyor B8:
```
<reachableWorkPlaces>
    <workPlace name="W3" cost="16" />
    <workPlace name="W4" cost="15" />
</reachableWorkPlaces>
```

Even the diverter D1 combines this knowledge and sends result to its input conveyor. Eventually, B1 propagates it back to the workplace W1 which is then equipped with such a knowledge base:

W1:
```
<reachableWorkPlaces>
    <workPlace name="W3" cost="18" />
    <workPlace name="W4" cost="20" />
</reachableWorkPlaces>
```

The key benefit of this solution is the capability of the system to safely react to the failures of any of its components, i.e. what we call the *light-weight* dynamic reconfiguration. In a situation when a low-level control code of some component detects a physical failure (e.g. conveyor belt stops for some reason), the failure method we have introduced to the agent part of a holon is called up. It causes that the agent sends an **empty** list of reachable destinations, because none of the destination is reachable now through this component. This information is propagated backwards to the other agents in the same way as shown above so that even other agents, especially crossing ones, know that the routes to some destinations doesn't exist or have changed.

Another benefit of the same importance is the capability of what we call *heavy-weight* dynamic reconfiguration. It allows the physical reconstruction of the system "on the fly", i.e. to remove any components from the system and/or incorporate new components to it during the run-time without the need to stop the system or to make changes to the software. Considering the proposed architecture, such a capability was easy to implement. Whenever a component is removed from the system, it sends a <disconnected/> message to its neighbors. These react to it as they would receive an empty list of reachable destinations. If a new component is added to the system, it sends a <connected> message to its neighbors and, as a consequence, receives the reachableWorkPlaces list which propagates further in the same manner.

6 Simulation Tool

In order to demonstrate the functionality of the proposed solution and to show the benefits araising from the use of agent technology in particular, we have developed a graphical simulation tool in the JAVA language using both FIPA-OS and JADE agent development kits. Its screenshot can be seen in Fig. 3.

The tool can be used mainly for two purposes. First, a material handling system composed of various components, like workplaces, crossings (of various kinds) and conveyor belts can be designed in a graphical manner. Second, a user-defined software simulation (without a physical hardware) of a designed system can be run.

In such a simulation, for each component on the screen appropriate FIPA-compliant agent is running behind in the agent environment (both FIPA-OS and JADE can be used) and communicates with each other via FIPA-compliant messages as the system transport workpieces to their destinations. Then during the simulation, without stopping it, the user is allowed to "generate" a failure of any component (or "repair" faulty ones) and see how the workpieces are transported using alternative routes. Even more, the user can remove any of the components in run-time and/or add new ones – these are incorporated in the existing system and started to be utilized.

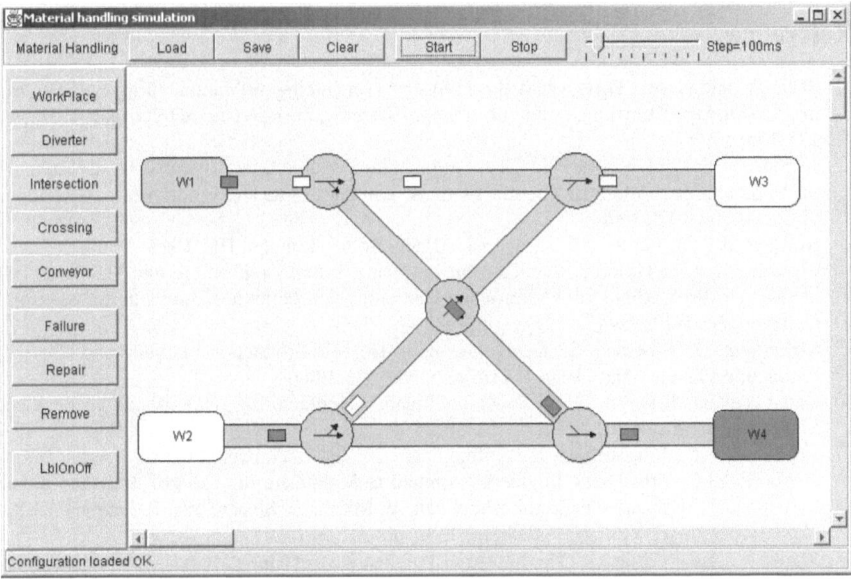

Fig. 3. Material handling simulation tool screenshot

7 Conclusion

This paper describes the first achievements in the effort to proceed in the development of the agent level of the holonic control systems.

It is namely the multi-agent approach which can prove this novel technology to be a competitive alternative to the classical control solutions by promoting its advantages as the robustness, particularly in the cases of a failure detection, ability to react to changes in the manufacturing environment, reconfigurability and so forth.

We have focused primarily on the material handling area for which we have proposed a general classes of agents and the types of FIPA-compliant messages and introduced a prototype of an ontology. Moreover, we have developed a graphical simulation tool using both FIPA-OS and JADE FIPA-compliant open sources to demonstrate the functionality of the system, particularly in the reconfiguration tasks.

Practical testing of both FIPA-OS and JADE versions revealed an interesting fact that the JADE one is much more faster in the message delivery and requires far less memory and computation power than the FIPA-OS version. Particularly in the cases of larger systems (50 agents and more) the FIPA-OS powered simulation was incredibly slow on PIII 600MHz (in some cases the message delivery between the sender and the receiver took up to 5 seconds).

Acknowledgement. We would like to express thanks to our fellow-workers Pavel Tichý and Petr Šlechta for enriching discussions regarding multi-agent area and especially to Vladimír Mařík for guidance and help in the preparation of this paper.

References

1. Shen, W. and Norrie, D.H: Agent-Based Systems for Intelligent Manufacturing: A State-of-the-Art Survey. Knowledge and Information Systems, an International Journal, 1(2), pp. 129-156, 1999
2. Jennings, N.R. and Wooldridge, M.J.: Applications of Intelligent Agents, Agent Technology: Foundations, Applications, and Markets. Jennings, N.R. and Wooldridge, M.J (Eds.), Springer, pp. 3-28, 1998
3. Koestler, A.: The Ghost in the Machine. Arkana Books, London, UK, 1967
4. Christensen, J.H.: Holonic Manufacturing Systems: Initial Architecture and Standards Directions. In Proceedings of 1st European Conference on Holonic Manufacturing Systems, Germany, pp. 1-20, 1994
5. McFarlane, D., Bussman, S.: Developments in Holonic Production Planning and Control. Production Planning and Control, 11(6), pp. 522-536, 2000
6. Van Leeuwen, E.H. and Norrie, D.: Intelligent Manufacturing: Holons and Holarchies. Manufacturing Engineer, 76(2), pp. 86-88, 1997
7. Valckenaers, P., Van Brussel, H., Kollingbaum, M. and Bochmann, O.: Multi-Agent Coordination and Control Using Stigmergy Applied to Manufacturing Control. In Multi-Agent Systems and Applications (Editors: M. Luck, V. Marik, O. Stepankova, R. Trappl), LNAI No. 2086, Springer Verlag, Heidelberg, 2001, pp. 317-334
8. Mařík, V. and Pěchouček, M.: Industrial Applications of Holonic and Multi-Agent Systems. In Proceedings of 11th DEXA International Workshop, Greenwich, UK, 2000, pp. 212-213
9. Foundation for Intelligent Physical Agents (FIPA) website: *http://www.fipa.org*

10. FIPA Content Languages Specifications (document identifier XC00007),
    http://www.fipa.org/specs/fipa00007
11. FIPA ACL Message Structure Specification (document identifier XC00061),
    http://www.fipa.org/specs/fipa00061
12. Obitko, M.: Ontologies:Description and Applications. Report No. GL 126/01, Gerstner
    Laboratory for Intelligent Decision Making and Control, Czech Technical University in
    Prague, 2001, *http://cyber.felk.cvut.cz/gerstner/reports/GL126.pdf*

Industrial MAS for Planning and Control

Pavel Tichý[1], Petr Šlechta[1], Francisco Maturana[2], and Sivaram Balasubramanian[2]

[1]Rockwell Automation Research Center, Americka 22, 120 00 Prague 2, Czech Republic
{ptichy, pslechta}@ra.rockwell.com
[2]Rockwell Automation, Cleveland, Ohio, USA
{fpmaturana,sbalasubramanian}@ra.rockwell.com

Abstract: In this paper, we summarize advantages of using agent technology in the design and operation of industrial control systems. To support appropriate responses to dynamically generated events, we divided the agent operation into two main levels: planning and real-time control. A higher-level software agent covers the planning phase and low-level distributed control agent provides the real-time control. The proposed architecture is targeted on applications where real-time response is essential but also more sophisticated higher-level control mechanisms are needed for efficient control. An implementation of such system is briefly described.

1   Introduction

In the last decades, a lot of theoretical and practical work has been done in the area of multi-agent systems. The research came from an idea of distributed control and migrated into development of intelligent agents that express autonomous and cooperative behavior. The multi-agent systems are very efficiently applied to areas where control is distributed physically and logically. Key features of these systems are flexibility, survivability, real-time behavior, safety, and stability. The Main restrictions are limited memory and computing power of logical controllers. From the intelligent agent point of view not only social and responsive behavior is needed, but also proactive behavior mainly in cases of equipment failure is expected.

In this paper, we describe the architecture of a multi-agent system for automation of complex industrial systems. Our goal is to improve the degree of survivability, readiness, global sustainability, and ability to automatically reconfigure the system. In areas, where logical controllers are used for automation, our approach is to distribute the controllers around the system. Each controller hosts several intelligent agents that deal with planning, communication, diagnostics, and control. This task imposes interesting challenges to the software architecture, since the distribution of control requires a clever decoupling of control supervision among the controlling devices. We explain a methodology how to move the control supervision into the agent level and the control ownership into the device level. In conventional control, these two activities are part of the same execution control object.

In recent work, our primary focus of research has been on the aggregation of autonomous behaviors and coordinated decision making coalition of smart resources. An important result of this work is a general architecture to deploy information agents for resource discovery in a highly distributed system. The architecture is now ready to

V. Mařík et al. (Eds.): MASA 2001, LNAI 2322, pp. 280-295, 2002.
© Springer-Verlag Berlin Heidelberg 2002

be merged with agent standards to rationally move from high-level information processing into the time critical operations and vice versa. Moreover, in our previous research and pilot testing of intelligent systems, we have experimented with autonomous cooperative architecture for real-time control systems [9, 6]. In this paper, we make reference to the next step concerning the evolution of intelligent units architecture and its language.

Let us consider, in this paper, a multi-agent system for automation of HVAC (Heating Ventilating and Air Conditioning) system of a large building. This type of distributed system to be controlled is used as a typical example for the explanation of the multi-agent system design.

We identified three basic types of equipment agents (see section on Logical Structure of Agents) in the HVAC example: suppliers, consumers, and transportation agents. Chiller agents represent the suppliers and they can be viewed as a source of a cold water or a source of a pressure in the system. Air-cooled rooms and water-cooled equipment are represented by Load agents and they are consumers of the cold water. Valves and pipe segments are transportation type of agents and they can be used for cold or hot water transportation purposes.

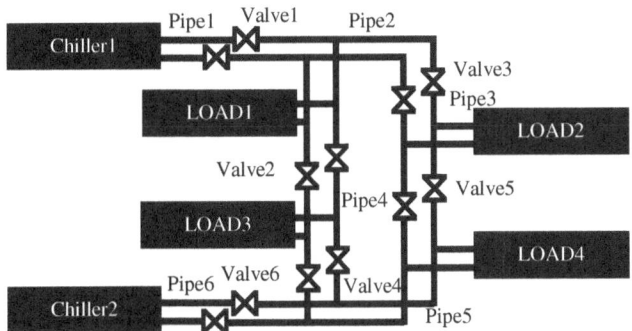

Fig. 1. Example of the simple HVAC system

Furthermore, the presented multi-agent system platform can be applied also to other types of complex distributed automation systems (sorting stations, steel mills, etc.), because we have developed a generic platform with no hard-wired behavior.

2   Approach

There are important restrictions in implementing agents inside logical controllers. This implies that for an agent implementation in the control domain we need to consider programming languages that are fast, stable and very close to device hardware. A present choice is to use C++ language due to its execution speed and reliability.Although a C++ implementation of agents in the control domain solves an important aspect of the system, we still have memory restrictions that limit an expanded coding of agent functionality. In our approach, we reduced the size of agents by making agent code generic. Also, we created agent development tools to simplify programming effort during the agent creation.

The multi-agent system platform resides in the controllers' firmware. In this manner, the platform can be used to design and implement different multi-agent systems. The separation of general multi-agent system parts from application specific parts simplifies the customization of application specific behavior as user-level programs, which are embedded in the controller at runtime. In this direction, we emphasize on a greater involvement of application designers to enter application specific information into the system. The application specific information also includes control algorithms and planning strategies. In the high-level information layers, there are development tools to automatically generate agent code for all parts of the multi-agent system. The parts of the system that are application independent are generated automatically without assistance of the application designer.

The Foundation for Intelligent Physical Agents (FIPA) provides well-defined and accepted standards for multi-agent systems development [1]. There are several implementations of the FIPA compliant systems available as JAVA [4] open sources - for instance JADE [3], FIPA-OS [2], and ZEUS [12]. These open implementations can be used to speed-up development of new multi-agent systems. There are predefined components dealing with communication, negotiation, agent creation, white and yellow pages support. FIPA standard provides a good definition of information level functionality that can be combined with the distributed-control to support the discovery of resources and capabilities.

With regards to the FIPA compliance, we met FIPA communication specifications by implementing Directory Facilitator (DF) and Agent Management System (AMS) as described in the subsequent sections. To be fully compliant with the FIPA standards, we need to develop also Agent Communication Channel (ACC).

We are inspecting possibility to use JAVA language to program the controller. This can open a possibility to use already developed JAVA implementation the FIPA compliant systems and also to use JAVA open source implementations of DF, AMS, and ACC agents.

In following sections, we describe the logical and physical structures of the multi-agent system platform. We also explain the architecture of an agent, the inter-agent communication, planning and scheduling methods, and plan execution runtime phases.

2.1   Multi-Agent System Structure

The multi-agent system can be structured in two ways. One of them is represented by a physical structure, where an application designer can decide on a physical location of an agent in the distributed system. Second way how to structure agents in the system is their centralized, decentralized, hierarchical, or mediated logical distribution across the whole system as described in following section.

Logical Structure of Agents

The multi-agent system architecture can be either static or dynamic. The static architecture corresponds to the design time, in which permanent connections and relationships among agents are established. The dynamic architecture is based on agent capabilities, which are used to dynamically discover agent relationships. In both architectural views, the multi-agent system contains multiple hierarchical structures that express structured functionality.

The basic paradigm is that there are no pre-established hierarchies. On the contrary, there are necessary functional hierarchies to be created by the system designers during the mapping of the system. In order to complete the functional structure for run-time, the dynamic approach is used. This concept enables the creation of flexible organizations that can conform to a hierarchical or a heterarchical structure. This evolution of hierarchies depends on the nature of the problem. In the case of a dynamic architecture, the structured functionality is formed on-the-fly. Other considerations that need to be considered when deciding about the functional structure are:

- A flat architecture is very autonomous, but hard to create and maintain, since this needs to maintain several associations among agents.
- An n-hierarchical architecture is modular, but introduces more single points of potential global failure and more communication.

In the multi-agent architecture proposed, we have chosen a 3-tier modified hierarchical structure for the static functionality. The functionality of these layers is shown in Fig. 2.

- System-wide layer: The top most level is an entry point to the multi-agent system. It maintains overall system goals and provides strategic decisions.
- Process-wide layer: The middle level is used to logically split the whole system into smaller groups of agents and usually logically follows a natural system functionality structure.
- Equipment-level layer: The bottom most level has physical connection to the hardware (see Fig. 1 for an example of the equipment-level layer). It is responsible for local real-time control, maintains state of the equipment, and provides local planning and constraint evaluation.

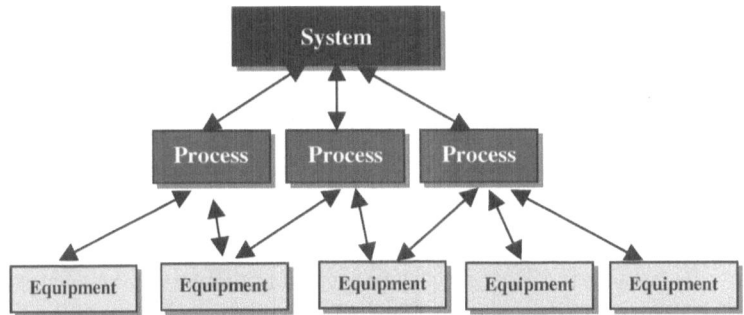

Fig. 2. Functional structure

The separation of the top and the middle levels depends on the application specific information. These two layers should combine their behavior to satisfy application specific goals. There is not a specific guideline to organize these layers. The application designer has to make sure that the agents in these layers are properly backed up, either by software or hardware means, because an agent failure in these layers can impact the whole multi-agent system.

For the bottom level, there are clear procedures how to program control intelligence for equipment. The agent portion of the bottom level relates to the following decomposition rules.

The concept of an Agent Element is used to express the smallest possible area of the system that can be controlled by an agent, e.g., the Agent Element can be a valve or a motor. First, the system designer has to identify all the Agent Elements that can be possible candidates for 'agentification'. If it is feasible to have one agent representing only one Agent Element then the decomposition is simple. Usually the Agent Elements are too small units. Thus, there is a need to group the Agent Elements to obtain higher complexity and efficient distribution of reasoning resources. The following rules can be considered as a simple grouping methodology:

- Rule 1: Group Agent Elements if an output from the first Agent Element is an input exclusively to the next Agent Element (Group neighbor serial Agent Elements).
- Rule 2: Group Agent Elements if two Agent Elements have the same connection to the equipment (Group double controlled Agent Elements).
- Rule 3: Do not group Agent Elements if they have the same input or output (Do not group neighbor redundant parallel Agent Elements).

Rule 1 means that if the first Agent Element is physically connected by its output only to the next Agent Element's input, then we should consider grouping these two Agent Elements together. Rule 2 means that when two Agent Elements are connected to the same equipment, we should consider grouping these two Agent Elements so there would be no conflicts caused by controlling the same equipment from two different points. Rule 3 is to prevent the grouping of parallel Agent Elements. This last rule increases the level of survivability.

The next level of agent organization is to establish dynamic hierarchies. Initially, at the startup the agents are not organized. Using capability discovery behavior via Directory Facilitators, agents establish functional hierarchies. Agents form and dissolve functional hierarchies as they monitor the status of their equipment. The functional hierarchy is a virtual organization of agents that provides plans to execute operations. Each operation is planned according to the equipment constraints and logic behaviors. The logic behaviors are reactive executing programs that operate on behalf of actuators and sensors. In essence, when agents form a virtual organization, they use a federated-based approach to organize the system in aggregated capabilities.

To accomplish capability search services, the agent infrastructure has been built based on mediation agents [8]. The mediation agents correspond to the FIPA standard Directory Facilitator. These are mandatory agents in order to be compliant with the FIPA standardization effort. Another important aspect of the Directory Facilitators is that their behavior can be expanded to handle complicated capability search. Fig. 3 shows a capability match pattern. On each capability request, the Directory Facilitator agent provides a list of agents that have the requested capability.

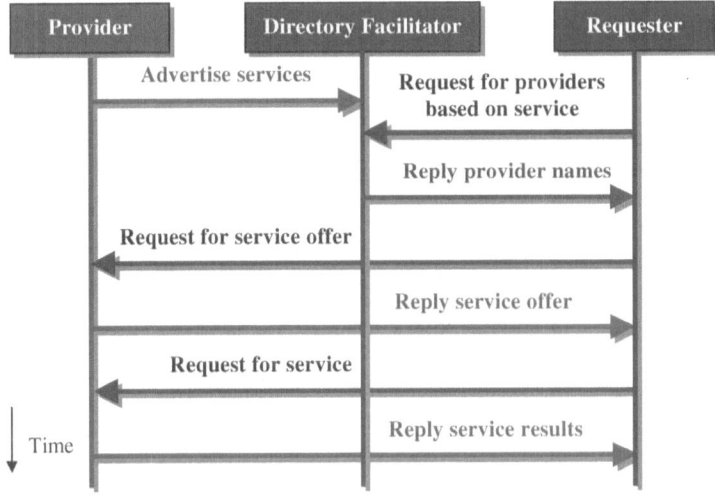

Fig. 3. Directory facilitator functionality

There are several options to design the Directory Facilitators. A first option is to create one Directory Facilitator for the whole system. Obvious problems of this approach are that this one agent represents communication bottleneck and single point of failure. Other possibility is to have several Directory Facilitators with local knowledge, or with redundant global knowledge (see Fig. 4).

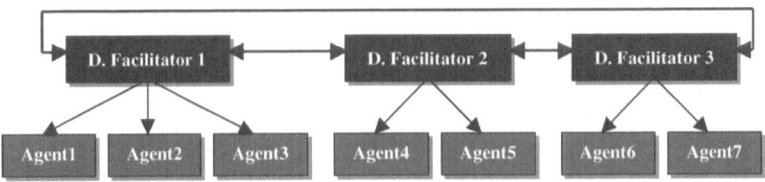

Fig. 4. Distributed structure of directory facilitators

It is also possible to design hierarchical structure of the Directory Facilitators, where each of them maintains local knowledge and some of them are designed to maintain global knowledge about the agent capabilities. In an automation system, it is advantageous to use local Directory Facilitators and one global Directory Facilitator for the whole system (see Fig. 5). If the system detects that global Directory Facilitator is not available, then new global Directory Facilitator is chosen from existing ones.

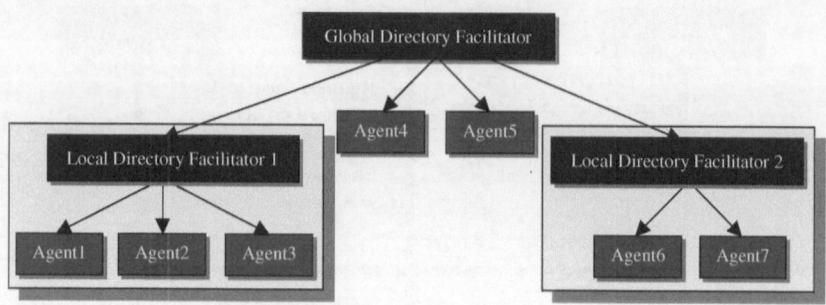

Fig. 5. Hierarchical structure of directory facilitators

When an agent registers capability by the local Directory Facilitator then there are two main approaches how to deal with this new information. First approach is that this information is automatically propagated through hierarchical structure of the Directory Facilitators. In this case, it becomes global knowledge in the system and this information is searched locally. Second approach is not to propagate this information, only remember it locally. To search for this information, agents need to contact the local Directory Facilitator.

In the first approach, capability information is propagated automatically. The advantage of using this approach is that at time of search the information is immediately available. The disadvantage relates to the communication overhead during the agent registration, but in control domain it is usually done once during the system startup.

The social knowledge can be also stored locally within each agent to decrease communication traffic in the system. Using subscribe/advertise approach in the tribase acquaintance model (3bA) [5] the agent is notified about changes in the system. The Directory Facilitator in this case is enhanced with ability to send updates to the subscribed agents. The 3bA model has been successfully used in ProPlanT system [7] and can be potentially explored in our approach as well.

Physical Structure of Agents

In this section we will focus on physical distribution of agents and hardware limitations. In the area of industrial control it is usually not possible to use conventional PC due to environment issues. That is why the logical controllers are used as control hardware and our development focuses on this case. The controllers have to provide multitasking environment, which is essential for the multi-agent systems. If the environment does not provide multitasking, then each controller is limited to contain just one agent.

Usually, it is possible to use classical languages for control as ladder logic, structured text, or block diagrams. In this case, the agent functionality cannot be very sophisticated. It is desirable to use C++ language when more complicated agent behavior is required. With the present hardware architecture (ARM 6 processors with 2 Mbytes RAM), it is possible to host several agents in one controller. This is also simplified by the software architecture, in which we generalized the agent infrastructure.

The multi agent system deals with an environment where any part of the hardware can fail. The system has to ensure not only safety, but reconfiguration to make the whole system survivable. An ideal multi-agent system design uses physical redundancy of the system to reconfigure the equipment when failures occur. Any part of the system that is redundant and physically distributed requires a logical separation in the agent organization. In this way, it is ensured that when a part of the redundant hardware is not operational, the agents still have an excess resources to reconfigure system. This follows rule 2 that specifies segmentation of redundant parallel elements.

Each controller has a local Directory Facilitator and a unique controller is selected to host a global Directory Facilitator. In this manner, the number of Directory Facilitators is optimized while offering an intelligence grid for survivability and reduced communication bandwidth. In cases when a controller fails, not only the local Directory Facilitator fails but also local agents that may provoke a catastrophic event for a small domain. If only the global Directory Facilitator controller fails, a local Directory Facilitator is promoted to act as a Global Directory Facilitator.

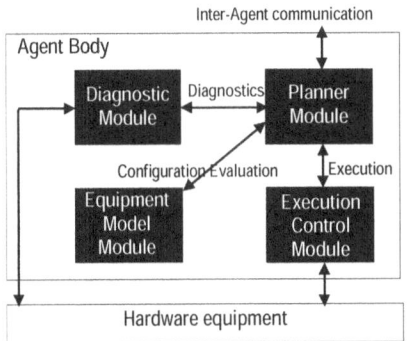

Fig. 6. Agent structure

2.2   Internal Agent Structure

In the previous section we described structure of the whole multi-agent system. In this section we would like to study the architecture of an agent. The agent is composed of four basic modules (see Fig. 6):

- Planner Module
- Diagnostic Module
- Equipment Module
- Execution Control Module

Each of these modules has specific functionality (e.g. the Planner can design a plan). Each module has defined interface, so other modules can access it. In following text, we briefly describe the functionality of these modules.

Planner Module

The Planner Module is responsible for:
- planning and scheduling activities
- allocation of resources, which were attached to a plan
- execution of prepared plans

The functionality of this module is described in more detail in Sect. 2.4.

Diagnostic Module

The Diagnostic Module provides:
- diagnostics of the hardware represented by an agent
- support to Planner Module with diagnostic results

The Diagnostic Module has access to hardware I/O points attached to the agent and provides information about the equipment health. The user is able to decide what diagnostic algorithm will be used and what diagnostic results are needed. The Diagnostic Module notifies the Planner Module about changes of the hardware equipment health. This information affects planning, scheduling and execution of prepared plans.

Equipment Module

The Equipment Module serves for:
- simulation of hardware attached to an agent
- computation of control efficiency

The Equipment Module simulates behavior of the hardware attached to the agent. This module is used by the Planner Module to optimize hardware control. The Planner Module specifies input values and range of output values and the Equipment Module computes values of outputs and control efficiency. The Planner Module calls the Equipment Module inside a loop that is influenced by heuristics until both returned outputs and control efficiency are acceptable.

Execution Control Module

The Execution Control Module is responsible for:
- physical execution of plans prepared by the Planner Module
- emitting control events back to the Planner Module

When a plan is prepared to be executed, the Planner Module calls the Execution Control Module to start the execution of the plan. The Execution Control Module passes the plan parameters to the control code and starts to run this code. The control code physically controls the hardware equipment attached to the agent. It runs in a high priority thread. Its goal is to control hardware using parameters emitted by all executed plans.

2.3   Communication among Agents

In the previous section we described structure of the agent. The agent is not an island in the system and to give it possibility to interact with other agents in the system it is necessary to establish communication among agents.

Communication in the multi-agent system is in most cases based on a message passing technique. In our system, based on the logical controllers, we are able to use the asynchronous message passing that allows pure parallel computation. The message passing is done behind the scenes so that sending message locally within one controller or to another controller is transparent to the agents. The physical message passing among the logical controllers is based on the TCP/IP protocol.

Several types of multi-agent systems can talk to each other on a standardized basis. The FIPA compatibility requires the use the IIOP protocol (which is based on the TCP/IP and the GIOP protocols). To accomplish this level of communication, the following agent services have to be implemented:

- Directory Facilitator (DF) agent that provides white pages services
- Agent Management System (AMS) agent that provides yellow pages services
- Agent Communication Channel (ACC) agent that provides message routing within or over the borders of an agent platform

We are presently considering to extend the agent services to an external PC on the same Ethernet line to contain DF, AMS, and ACC agents to provide additional compatibility with the FIPA standard. A Job Description Language (JDL) based on the XML format was built as a content language. The XML format has been selected because it is designed to serve for data exchange among heterogeneous components and it is widely used. Moreover, the XML format is supported by FIPA as a content language. The JDL language is still work in progress. The ontology construction is defined according to the Document Type Definition (DTD) format, which is a standard format for the description of the XML structures [11]. Along with the definition of the language, a JDL Parser has been built for two purposes:

1) It can take a JDL string written in the XML format and parse it to create an Object Model. The JDL Object Model then can be used to work efficiently on message data in structured manner using object-oriented approach. Also other XML parsers can be used for JDL parsing for instance Xerces [10];

2) It is possible to serialize the JDL Object Model to the JDL message in the XML format.

The JDL language was designed for the inter-agent messaging. It can also be used by the planning module to create plans. In JDL, the agents encode sequence of actions and hierarchy of actions that are streamed into JDL scripts. The planning engine uses the JDL scripts to select and process local actions. The parts of the script that can not be done locally are extracted from the main script to build sub-scripts. The planning engine uses the sub-script to initiate Contract-Net subcontracting. The sub-scripts are then processed according to the capability discovery protocol and emitted to recruited agents.

There are several advantages to use the JDL Parser and its Object Model. First, it is a generic component that can be shared among agents within the same controller and it is fully reusable. Second, the JDL Parser can be used in visualization components that work with textual messages to present them to the user in a structured way. Third, the JDL Parser can be used in development tools, where message creation works with the JDL Object Model to store information from the user.

2.4   Planning and Scheduling

As we already described the agent architecture and communication among agents, we can now focus more closely to the agent behavior. The most interesting part of agent behavior can be found in planning and scheduling techniques followed by plan execution. Planning and scheduling activities are part of the Planner Module. All requests for planning (e.g. "create plan how to move 50 gallons of water from point A to point B") are passed to this module.

When the Planning Module receives a request for planning, it searches for a script associated with the incoming request. The system designer can define a set of scripts, which are associated with a specific request for planning. Each script has defined a firing condition; the script, which satisfies its firing condition in the best way, is selected. For illustration, see Table 1.

Table 1. Example of scripts associated with request for planning

Type of request for planning	Associated script(s)	Firing condition of script
CoolWater	Script1	Amount < 5 gpm
	Script2	(Amount >= 5 gpm) & (Amount < 20 gpm)
	Script3	Amount >= 20 gpm
CoolAir	Script4	Destination = Room13
	Script5	Destination ≠ Room13

If no script has been found, the Planning Module replies with the Fail Message (this message informs the plan requester that the plan creation failed). Otherwise, the found script becomes a plan template. The plan template is a semi-plan, which describes how to solve incoming requests. To clarify, what a plan template is, see the following example:

Table 2. Plan template request for cooling

Incoming request:	(cool-room (location room_101))
Template for this request:	1. (cool-water (agent UNKNOWN) (water-in ?X1) (water-out ?X2)) 2. (move-water (agent UNKNOWN) (water-in ?X2) (water-out ?X3)) 3. (cool-air (agent UNKNOWN) (water-in ?X3) (water-out ?X4)) 4. (move-water (agent UNKNOWN) (water-in ?X4) (water-out ?X1))

To start air-conditioning in the room number 101, some agent has to cool the water (step 1), some agent has to move this cold water to other agent that can cool the air (step 2), some agent has to use the cold water for the air cooling (step 3), and finally another agent has to return the hot water back (step 4).

The structure of scripts is more complicated than in the example above. The script can contain information about dependencies between steps, it can contain some recommendations (e.g. which agent should solve the step), and other information.

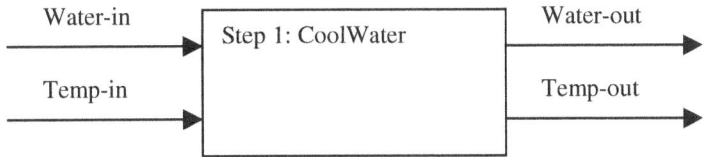

Fig. 7. Step of script as a function block

The script contains various steps. Each step of the script can be drawn as a function block (see Fig. 7) with a collection of inputs and outputs. At that figure, a step with the name "CoolWater" represents a chiller that can cool the water. The step has two inputs: (a) Water-in, which represents a connection point where the chiller water inlet is connected to, and (b) Temp-in, which corresponds to temperature of the incoming water. Two outputs of the step are: (a) Water-out, which corresponds to a connection point where the outlet of the chiller is connected, and (b) Temp-out, which represents temperature of the outgoing water.

Also, the script has its own inputs and outputs. The script consists of steps, which can be represented by function blocks. Each function block is processed either locally (by an agent that is processing the script), or remotely by another agent (a request is sent to this agent by the agent, which is processing the script). An example of a script shown in form of interconnected function blocks is shown in Fig. 8.

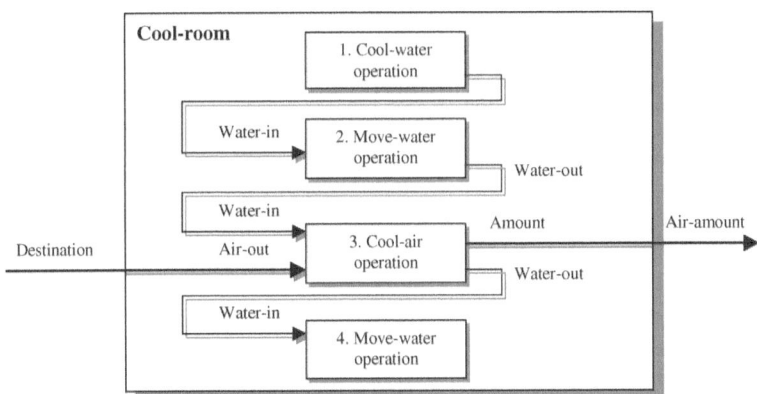

Fig. 8. Script as connected function blocks

As described above, each agent owns a set of scripts and each script has a firing condition. The firing condition describes when to use this script and this decision is based on an agent status. When the agent has found the script, how to solve a particular request, it processes the script. The algorithm that was used for script processing is described as follows.

```
For each step do
        If the step name corresponds to one of agent's service
                Find local solution for this step
        Otherwise
                Find who is able to solve this step via yellow pages
                Send request to all of found agents
        End if
End for each
```

Fig. 9. Script processing algorithm

After the script is processed, the agent waits for responses to its requests. When a response comes, the agent stores the response to the corresponding step as one solution. If all responses for the step have been received (or time-out for response was reached), the agent selects the best bid from the received responses. We call this selection process 'concentration of the step'. When all steps are concentrated, the agent concentrates the whole script and sends the result back to the requester (to the agent that sent the request).

The mechanism described above allows the agents to use the same format for messages and for storing of scripts. The system designer defines scripts, which contain application specific knowledge and is not required to program the communication and negotiation details (this is done by the Planner Module).

The whole communication is based on the JDL messages (see Sect. 2.3). Different negotiation mechanisms can be implemented – subcontracting and counter-bidding are also considered in the implementation. The subcontracting negotiation is used when an agent is not able to solve the whole step alone. In this case, the agent solves only part of the step and subcontracts the rest of the step with other agents (see Fig. 10).

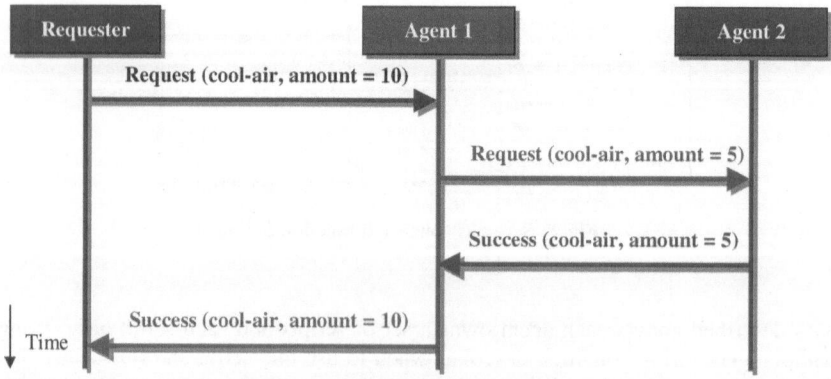

Fig. 10. Subcontracting mechanism example

Negotiation based on the counter-bidding is used in situations similar to that of subcontracting. The difference is that if an agent can not solve the whole step by it-self, it sends a counter-bid back to the requester. The counter-bid contains information about 'maximal' part of the step, which the agent is capable to solve. The requester needs to relax the parameters in the original request and re-send the new request to the agent to continue the planning process. For illustration, see Fig. 11.

Agent plans are distributed in the system. When the planning phase has been com-pleted, each agent owns information how to solve a portion of the overall plan. Also, each agent knows associations with other agents that should be contacted during the process of commitment and execution.

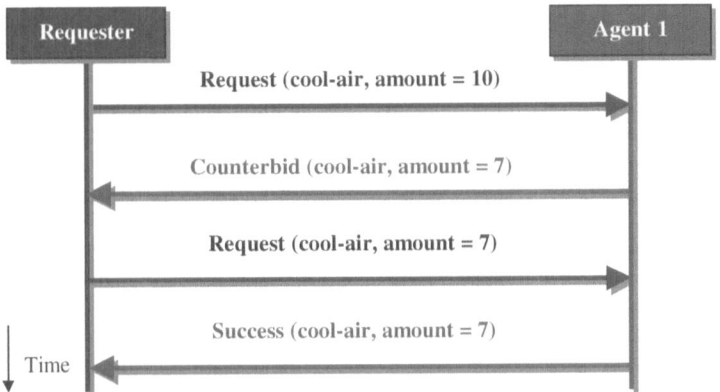

Fig. 11. Counter-bidding mechanism example

2.5   Plan Execution

When the planning phase has been completed, the plan requesters initiate a commit-ment communication. Upon receiving a request for commit, each agent tries to re-serve all resources, which are needed for successful plan execution. After allocating all needed resources, each agent replies with success to its requester. If the agent can not reserve all required resources, it replies with a failure message. When all agents have committed to some plan, the plan is prepared for execution. At proper time, the request for plan execution is sent and each agent, who participates in this plan, exe-cutes its portion using the Execution Control Module.

In the systems for real-time control we have to face issues connected with speed of execution and execution synchronization. In these systems we cannot purely rely on execution synchronization via agent communication, because of speed restrictions. In the real-time systems, a faster way of synchronization is needed. Also we need differ-ent protocol than TCP/IP, because it does not guarantee real-time delivery of the mes-sages.

We can solve this problem by creating a real-time control agent portion called Execution Control Module. This module provides a real-time control of the local equipment and synchronization with distant equipment (controlled by other agents). The software agent controls this module. The Execution Control Module can trigger some events back to the software agent - it can for instance send a message with a description of the event. This way we can separate slower negotiation, planing, and decision-making activities from the faster real-time control of the equipment.

3 Summary

In our approach we explain how to move the control supervision into the agent level and the real-time control into the equipment level. In conventional control systems, these two activities are part of the same execution control object.

Our system is planned to be the FIPA compliant, even if we cannot use the JAVA open implementations of the FIPA standards for several reasons. We have created guidelines for system partitioning to help multi-agent system designers in the design of highly flexible control systems that encapsulate system survivability, and diagnostics behaviors.

In our approach we used the multi-agent architecture based on 3-levels of the hierarchy. Our goal is to move the system intelligence to the equipment, so that the overall system survivability can be increased.

We described usage of hierarchical structure of Directory Facilitators that are distributed in the system to increase communication efficiency and survivability of the system. We presented the overall agent architecture and functionality of individual agent modules, where we mainly focused on planning and scheduling problems. In the last section we have described the plan execution phase that, for real-time systems, should be located in a separate module offering fast control of the equipment, where the software agent changes parameters of the real-time control.

Our main goal throughout the design of the system was to create generic infrastructure of the multi-agent system for real-time control. To help the system designer in development, we simplified the creation of an agent as much as possible, so only an application specific information needs to be entered to the system. The application engineer can easily use this infrastructure to develop agents along with their behavior, diagnostic, and real-time control to design specific solutions for particular applications.

Acknowledgements. We would like to thank to Vladimír Mařík, Dave Vasko, and Raymond Staron from the Rockwell Automation Comp., Pavel Dražan visiting professor at Czech Technical University, and Martyn Fletcher from the Agent Oriented Software Comp. for help and valuable advice that helped us to complete this development. The research was also supported by the Multi-agent System group of the Gerstner Laboratory for Intelligent Decision Making, Czech Technical University in Prague.

References

[1]   FIPA (The Foundation for Intelligent Physical Agents): www.fipa.org
[2]   FIPA-OS (Open Source), Emorphia: fipa-os.sourceforge.net
[3]   JADE (Java Agent Development Environment), CSELT S.p.A & University of Parma: sharon.cselt.it/projects/jade
[4]   JAVA - The Source for JAVA Technology, Sun Microsystems: java.sun.com

[5]   Mařík V., Pěchouček M., and Štěpánková O.: *Social Knowledge in Multi-Agent Systems.* In: Multi-agent Systems and Applications (Luck M., Mařík V., Štěpánková O., Trappl R. eds.) LNAI 2086, Springer-Verlag, Heidelberg, 211-245, 2001.

[6]   Maturana F., Balasubramanian S., and Vasko D.: *An Autonomous Cooperative Systems for Material Handling Applications.* ECAI2000, Berlin, Germany, 2000.

[7]   ProPlanT (Production Planning Tool), the Gerstner Laboratory, Czech Technical University in Prague: cyber.felk.cvut.cz/gerstner

[8]   Shen W., Norrie D., and Barthès J.-P.: *Multi-agent Systems for Concurrent Intelligent Design and Manufacturing.* Taylor & Francis, London, 2001.

[9]   Vasko D., Maturana F., Bowles A., and Vandenberg S.: *Autonomous Cooperative Systems Factory Control.* PRIMA 2000, Australia, 2000.

[10] Xerces XML parser, part of Apache XML Project: xml.apache.org

[11] XML & DTD specification, World Wide Web Consortium: www.w3.org/XML

[12] ZEUS, British Telecommunications: 193.113.209.147/projects/agents/zeus

An Integral Implementation of a Machine-Holon Applying the ZEUS Agent Framework

Klaus Glanzer[1], Alexander Hämmerle[2], and Ralf Geurts[2]

[1]Vienna University of Technology – INFA 361, 1040 Wien, Austria
kg@infa.tuwien.ac.at
[2] Profactor Productionresearch GmbH, Wehrgrabengasse 1-5, 4400 Steyr, Austria
{ahaemm,rgeurt}@profactor.at

Abstract. The concept of Holonic Manufacturing Systems (HMS) is the key to meet future demands of highly dynamic production environments. A hierarchy of holons, which are autonomous entities, represents the internal structure of a HMS, where intelligent software agents embody the intelligent nuclei of complex holons. This paper deals with the implementation of a multi-agent system with ZEUS, an open source, JAVA™-based, Agent Building Toolkit from British Telecom. Our application is based on a job shop scheduling problem, where task allocation is achieved through negotiation between cooperating agents. The second focus is laid on the interaction with legacy software, in this case low-level control systems.

1 Introduction

What is the relationship between intelligent agents and holons?
It is not possible to describe the nature of holons only by defining the term. We have to describe the context in which holons are embedded. Holons are bricks of a holarchy, a hierarchy of holons, where holons act as closed wholes relating to subordinated entities and as parts of a whole to superordinated entities of the hierarchy. A fundamental characteristic of a holon is its autonomy.

Autonomy is here understood as representing a sub-functionality of a system by a closed sub-system, whose space of possible actions constitutes in a high variety of flexible strategies restricted by a set of fixed rules to pursue a fundamental goal.

Transferring this paradigm to speech, simply a word is a sub-holon of a sentence and letters are sub-holons of words but words are 'autonomous' entities in sentences.

The other elementary paradigm in HMS are intelligent software agents. Similar to holons one fundamental characteristic of agents is its autonomy. The notion of holons and holarchies yield a methodology for analyzing really complex systems, e.g. manufacturing systems, to identify autonomous sub-systems. Current manufacturing systems are built out of 'passive' holons structured in a static hierarchy. On a proper level of hierarchy it is reasonable to extend these existing holons with the functionalities of intelligent software agents, cf. Fig. 1. Now, e.g. machines exhibit reactive, pro-active and social behaviors, which are the foundation for cooperation and dynamic team formation.

V. Mařík et al. (Eds.): MASA 2001, LNAI 2322, pp. 296-307, 2002.
© Springer-Verlag Berlin Heidelberg 2002

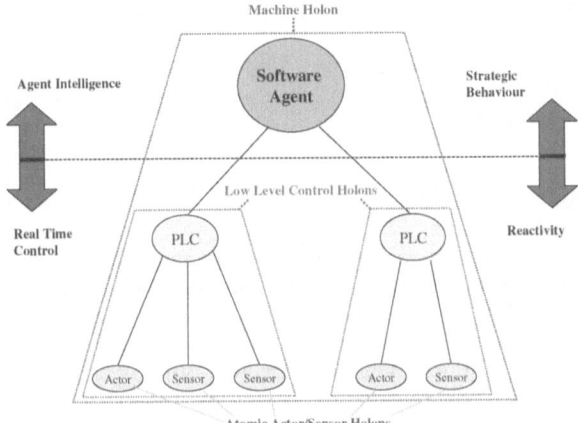

Fig. 1. Machine holarchy

Figure 1 shows an example for a holarchy in the manufacturing domain, namely a machine holon. The atomic holons on the lowest level of the holarchy are actors and sensors, being subordinate holons to the PLC (programmable logic controller) holons, which in turn are subordinates to the intelligent software agent. The figure indicates that moving towards higher holarchic levels the holons are more involved in strategic behaviour, whereas lower level holons show time-critical, reactive behaviour. This implies that from a certain point upward it makes sense to use agent technology to implement holonic behaviour, in Fig. 1 indicated by the dashed horizontal line.

What are the axiomatic/self-evident advantages of this paradigm?
The characteristic of emerging markets caused by increasing global networking is the growth of the variety of products, not the growth of quantity. Thisclaims highly sophisticated control architectures. Manufacturing systems of the future need to be agile, robust and smart. Robustness means the degree of stability against internal or external disturbances of the system. In a job shop organization proper reconfiguration keeps the system in an optimal state related to the current system'sboundary conditions in cases of varying orders or disturbances. Reconfiguration of functionalities, capabilities, relationships and acquaintances is in line with the idea of dynamic holarchies. Holons can concurrently belong to several holarchies and these assignments can change dynamically.

Implementing Holons with Agent Building Tools
Implementing a multiagent system from scratch requires a vast amount of time and thus high developing costs. For this reason we searched for an agent building tool allowing rapid development of multiagent systems. One hurdle for a broad application of multiagent systems is the lack of standards in the domain of agent technologies. Therefore a criterion for choosing an agent building tool was compliance to the emerging agent standards from FIPA (Foundation for Intelligent Physical Agents www.fipa.org). On the one hand agent building tools speed up the implementation phase but on the other hand the functionalities provided to the developer can yield strong restrictions to the application. An open source tool tackles this problem in the

way that developers are able to modify given functionalities and gain their understanding how agents work. These two major criteria are met by ZEUS (www.labs.bt.com/ projects/agents.htm). Other related agent building tools e.g. are JADE from CSELT S.p.A. and FIPA-OS from Emorphia's former Nortel Networks Agent Technology Group.

2 Experimental Setup

In this section we outline the scenario for our agent application. The scenario is focussed on job shop manufacturing, assuming a shop floor with three similar high-speed cutting machines (HSC1..3). Each of these machines is capable of a set of milling or cutting tasks. Some tasks are available on more than one machine, thus these tasks are redundant on the shop floor. When a production order is committed from a higher enterprise level to the shop floor, the manufacturing system has to figure out the set of tasks to achieve the given order and to allocate tasks to machines in an optimal manner with respect to costs, due dates, workloads etc. The results are local schedules specifying when each machine performs the tasks needed for production. The problem domain described above is known as a finite capacity scheduling problem 1.

The application scenario is based on following assumptions:

- Production plans with sequential/parallel branches are given, consisting of linked production steps.
- The scheduling algorithm uses a short-term strategy, i.e. if a production step for an order is about to be finished, the next step in the production plan is scheduled. This minimizes the effort of re-scheduling complete schedules where large sets of production steps are allocated.
- Machines have input queues, where physical workpieces are stored. The queue somewhat decouples transport from machining, relieving the constraints of timely delivery of workpieces. As soon as a workpiece arrives in the input queue for a machine, no re-scheduling of the workpiece on this machine is possible.

3 ZEUS Components and Their Application

ZEUS combines two major emphases in agent development namely communication facilities and internal infrastructure. ZEUS comprises a set of components, which are running concurrently in separated threads. These components are Mailbox, Message Handler, Co-ordination Engine, Execution Monitor and the Planner and Scheduler. Facilitating the implementation of agents, ZEUS provides comprehensive graphical user interfaces including a multiagent system project editor, an ontology editor, an agent editor and a task editor. The ZEUS Agent Generator produces Java source code from the specification that have be done in the editors. That code can be directly adapted by the developer and have to be compiled. These tools decrease the effort of programming directly in Java source code and therefore speed up the development of the multiagent systems.

The following chapters discuss benefits and drawbacks of particular components of ZEUS with respect to manufacturing environments and our implementation.

3.1   ZEUS Agent Platform Architecture

An agent platform provides the infrastructure in which agents can be deployed, including operating systems, agent support software and multiagent system managing components.

The ZEUS agent platform comprises two utility agents, the Agent Name Server (ANS) and the Directory Facilitator (DF). The ANSs maintains a registry of known agents, enabling to map agent identities to logical network locations. The DF's responsibility is managing the system's yellow pages, which map the agents' abilities to the according agent names. These two utility agents can support a highly agile and robust shop floor control. It is mandatory to deploy at least one ANS but we have to prevent being dependent to a single agent.

Processing machines are equipped with a local machine control and a local intelligence, the high-level control. So the machine and the belonging control units together are an autonomous entity, a holon. Which machines, or of more interest, which processing tasks are currently available to the system are automatically managed by the ANS and the DF agents. ANS and DF agents periodically inquire all agents about their capabilities and update their registries. If a machine changes its possessed tasks due to system reconfigurations, these tasks are announced through the DF to the others. In our special shop floor scenario all tasks offered by the three HSCs are redundant. This allows soft degradation of the systems overall performance in cases of breakdowns, thus the system keeps running.

3.2   Agent Communication Mechanism

Communication opens the door to collaborative behavior and is the basis of multi-agent systems. ZEUS agents are exchanging messages encoded in a simple ASCII character sequence. The message structure is defined by the FIPA-ACL [5]. An issue of the FIPA-ACL is to provide a pattern of communicative acts and their meanings. The message content is embedded in the ACL structure. In conjunction with FIPA-ACL the 'semantic language' is recommended and used by ZEUS to encode the message content [7]. But the semantic language (SL) itself cannot convey information among agents. Concepts of shared ontologies equip SL statements with meaning.

Obeying standards is a precondition for agents to become accepted by manufacturing companies. A major issue of FIPA is concerning interoperability of different agent systems

Network Communication Protocol
Communication is accomplished via point-to-point TCP/IP sockets. Since version 1.1 there are also implementations of IIOP or HTTP protocols.

Agent Interaction Protocols and Negotiation Strategies
An agent interaction protocol (AIP) describes a communication pattern as an allowed sequence of messages between agents and the constraints on the content of those messages [6]. ZEUS agents can be equipped by default with ContractNet protocol and iterated ContractNet protocol, which is a widely-used protocol in agent negotiations. Unfortunately other interaction protocols like the FIPA-request protocol or the FIPA-query protocol [5] are not supported yet.

3.3 Ontology and Knowledge Representation

With the term 'ontology' we refer to the "physical study of what exists. In the AI context, ontology is concerned with which categories we can usefully quantify over and how those categories relate to each other". A shared ontology contains the terms that agents will use to fill the ACL message's content with domain specific information, thus it represents significant concepts within a particular application domain. This fundamental knowledge includes definitions of concepts, their attributes, and relationships between terms and constraints. ZEUS uses the term 'fact' to describe an individual domain concept.

The ZEUS ontology editor is a tool facilitating building ontologies. Each fact of a user-defined ontology possesses attributes. These attributes are of different basic data types or of other previously defined facts. Facts are organized in a tree hierarchy wherein branches inherit attributes of their parents. The defined ontology is stored in a simple ASCII text file. Therefore it can easily be ported to other multiagent systems, according to the notion of shared ontologies.

Ontologies are not the only basis for meaningful conversations, they are also the concept of how knowledge is stored. To achieve this the Java Expert System Shell (Jess) [8] was adapted. The knowledge is stored in form of instances of 'ontology facts', relating to Jess unordered facts.

3.4 Reactive Behavior

Jess yields a rule engine that is based on the well-proven Rete algorithm. Rules can be considered as if-then-statements applied to the knowledge base. Facts that are being added to or removed from the knowledge base are tested by the rule's conditions (rules left hand sides). If all conditions of a particular rule are met, the rule becomes fired and the rule's actions (right hand side) will be performed.

Rules applied to the knowledge base are a means of equipping ZEUS agents with reactive behavior. If any rules left hand side evaluate 'true' the action will be performed immediately, i.e. parallel to concurrent running tasks.

In our implementation a shop floor resource holon consists of the agents part, the machine control and the machine itself. We have allowed the machine control to modify directly the agent's knowledge base. The agent immediately recognizes these modifications through the Rete engine. Appropriate rules provide the agent's reactive behavior. In case of machine failures the machine control initiates actions to prevent total system breakdown. These actions are de-registering the machines capabilities at the DF and re-negotiating and re-allocating the tasks that were already scheduled to this machine.

In contrast proactive behavior is driven by goals and implies a form of planning and scheduling, as described in the next two subchapters.

3.5 Tasks

ZEUS agents could be generally classified as task oriented agents. Each action an agent is able to execute is defined as a separated task, which will be performed in an own thread. When a task finishes the results are reported to the agent and the task thread terminates.

Tasks are described by 'input→ function → output' and a set of constraints. The input are precondition facts which must be available to launch the task, the 'function' is directly implemented in Java source code by the developer and the output are facts that are directly added to the knowledge base, the task effects.

In our simulated shop floor scenario production plans are stored in a production plan database. The single production steps of production plans are directly correlating with the agent's/machine's tasks.

3.6 Co-ordination Engine, Planner, and Scheduler

The Co-ordination Engine
The coordination engine drives agent interactions by executing co-ordination strategies. The co-ordination engine interprets incoming messages and dispatches them internally to the according ongoing conversations. Interaction protocols are embedded in the co-ordination engine.

How does the planner work and is it suitable for production environments?
The planner is responsible for constructing action sequences to achieve desired goals. Planning operators are defined related to the agent's task representation.

When an agent is assigned to achieve a desired goal the coordination engine invokes the planner to check if all tasks belonging to this goal are performable (checking all tasks preconditions). If not, the coordination engine automatically creates a new subgoal and initiates negotiations delegating the production of the preconditions to other agents. Thus the agent automatically cares about gathering all required preconditions that are necessary for launching a particular task.

In a first notion we thought about representing production plans in tuples of task effects and preconditions and distribute them to all resource agents. This was not practicable because of the following reason. A resource should only know its local tasks and not production plans avoiding badly maintainable production plans, which are distributed over the system.

Scheduling
Every ZEUS agent maintains its own (local) schedule. During negotiations the local schedule is checked if the requested tasks are performable in time. When the agent is awarded for a certain task, this task is scheduled in firm state at the latest possible time in the local schedule. This point of time depends on the task's desired end time.

When a time grain has elapsed, a clock tick event is generated and all scheduled tasks are reconsidered for optimizing the task sequence. The applied rescheduling algorithm originates in practical reasoning. Practical reasoning is the process of deciding, moment by moment, which action to perform in the furtherance of a goal. All scheduled tasks are reordered by two criteria: first by cost and second by duration. The best ranked is performed and the other tasks are left on their place in the schedule. Exactly this circumstance is a major problem of ZEUS regarding production environments. How the scheduling and (local) rescheduling is performed must be instructed by the system developer. There are situations where tasks constrain an order.

4 Implementing the Agent Application

In this section we describe a concrete implementation of the agent application. First we outline the basic system architecture. Then we present our approach to a machine holon implementation, depicting the holon architecture and answering the question how to connect agents to machinery.

4.1 The Multiagent System Architecture

After system requirements analysis and agent role modeling, which is very well documented in the ZEUS Case Studies [3], the multiagent system depicted in Fig. 2 was implemented. The applied architecture is related to the PROSA reference architecture [4].

An order agent is responsible for performing the assigned work correctly and on time. It manages the physical product being produced, the product state model, and all logistical information processing related to the job. Order agents are launched by the order-control-center agent, which means a new order is committed to the shop floor. The order-control-center agent replaces upper enterprise levels and is only for testing the system. First the order agent has to query the production plan database for production plans. Then negotiations with resource agents for allocating tasks are initiated.

Resource agents represent shop floor resources, in this case the three HSC machines. The HSC agents are connected by means of wrapper software to processing machines simulated in ARENA™. The benefit of the wrapper software is that agents are decoupled from the underlying software thus the simulation could easily be replaced by real machines.

4.2 Task Allocation

Applying ContractNet protocol
The order agent is responsible for awarding tasks to shop floor resources. Therefore the order agent has to figure out the optimal resource regarding the present system state. Order agents negotiate with resources based on the ContractNet protocol [6, 9].

The order agent plays the role of the negotiation initiator. Tasks are announced to resources by sending a call for proposals to the relevant resources. Which resources possess the desired task is previously requested from the DF. The call for proposals includes the desired task name, the reply time, the confirm time and the tasks end time. These times are relative to the negotiation start time. The end time specifies the latest possible date when the task has to be finished. The reply time specifies the deadline for valid replies. Agents that do not send their bids in time are no longer competing for the announced task. The confirm time is the latest time by which the requesting agent will inform the performing agent whether it has been awarded the contract or not.

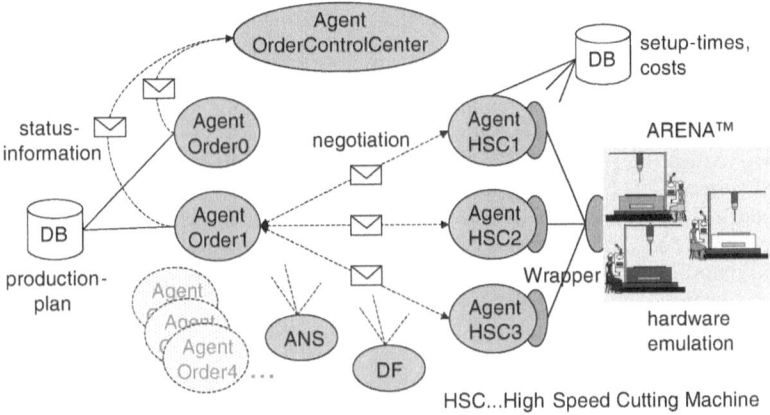

Fig. 2. System architecture

Creating Bids

The next step is creating bids. Resources attempt to schedule the requested task in tentative state in the local scheduler constrained by the end time. If there is not enough free space, the call for proposals is refused immediately. Otherwise the resource formulates a bid. Bids are based on costs expressing the machines'conditions. The total costs are composed by following addends, see (1).

$$\text{Total Costs} = \omega_1{\ast}\text{workload costs} + \omega_2{\ast}\text{setup costs}$$
$$+ \omega_3{\ast}\text{processing costs} + \omega_4{\ast}\text{machine's fix costs} \tag{1}$$

The workload costs are determined by querying the local scheduler for occupied time slots and transforming these time to cost by a proportionality factor α. Setup costs represent the effort for changing the machine's setup (i.e. the exchange of a driller). The shop floor resources setup costs and the machines fix costs are stored in the shop-floor-cost-database. The processing costs are directly derived from the processing time by multiplying with α. $\omega1\ldots\omega4$ are proportionality factors that allow an individual weighting. The calculated total costs are submitted in form of a bid to the order agent.

Task Awarding

All duly incoming bids are compared and the cheapest bid is awarded. ZEUS automatically ranks bids first by costs and second by duration, and awards the best. Therefore the calculated total costs have to include all relevant criteria for assessing bids.

The awarded agent is informed by an accept-proposal message and the remainders by a reject-proposal. Afterwards the awarded agent has to schedule the committed task in firm state. If this is possible an acknowledgement (inform message) is sent otherwise a failure is reported (failure message). A possible reason for a failure message is e.g. the negotiated task is not available any more.

4.3 Connecting Agents to Machinery

In a typical holonic manufacturing environment, resource-agents contain a physical part with which they have to communicate, the shop floor hardware. To a certain extent, these physical parts are autonomous. They have a Low Level Control (LLC) which provides the reactive, fast responsive intelligence that is necessary for time-critical systems (cf. Fig. 1). On the other hand, the physical parts need to be able to communicate to participate in the manufacturing system. Although the different physical parts can vary greatly in terms of low level control and communication capabilities, their common denominator is that they all provide services for the resource-agent they belong to.

Our approach to agent-interaction with its physical part is the implementation of a universal service layer called wrapper. By employing these abstract services, the wrapper shields an agent from hardware-specific LLC and vice versa. This has the following advantages:

- The agent does not need hardware-specific knowledge.
- The agent can be in a different location as its hardware.
- The communication path between agent and hardware can be freely chosen
- The wrapper can switch from real-mode to simulation and back without the agent's knowledge
- Every type of hardware can be used. Changes will not affect the agent.
- The agent and the physical part are not co-dependent: they can both live without eachother, minimizing system breakdown.

Figure 3 sketches the usage of the wrapper in a resource holon. Above all is the high level holonic control logic represented by a Zeus-implemented agent. The agent uses the wrapper to make a connection to the LLC of either the machining hardware or a simulation thereof. The LLC and emulation driver provide the necessary control-logic for (proprietary) machine controls that are not capable of providing the communicational or programmable control themselves.

The wrapper has the same life span as the agent. At startup it creates a connection with the hardware's LLC. When the connection has been established, the LLC sends the wrapper a list of services it is capable to provide. When one of these services is required during the manufacturing process, the agent checks its wrapper for the availability of this service and if so, participates in the negotiation process.

When the agent is asked to start the service, it signals the wrapper that it wants a specific service to be executed. The wrapper handles the execution so the agent only has to wait for a response from the wrapper, which notifies the agent at the end of the service execution.

If a machine loses one or more of its services or if a new service can be provided by the machine, this is also reflected in the wrapper.

To guarantee reusability of the wrapper, the agent-wrapper interface has been kept small. Figures 4 and 5 show the class diagrams of the interface definition in UML-notation. The wrapper (cf. Fig. 4) provides a few generic methods for initialisation, shutdown and expansion purposes (GenericWrapper). In addition to these methods, a machine-holon (ProductionResource Wrapper) also provides the methods GetSkill() and ExecuteSkill(), which are the methods that are used to inquire and execute services. All these methods are called from the agent.

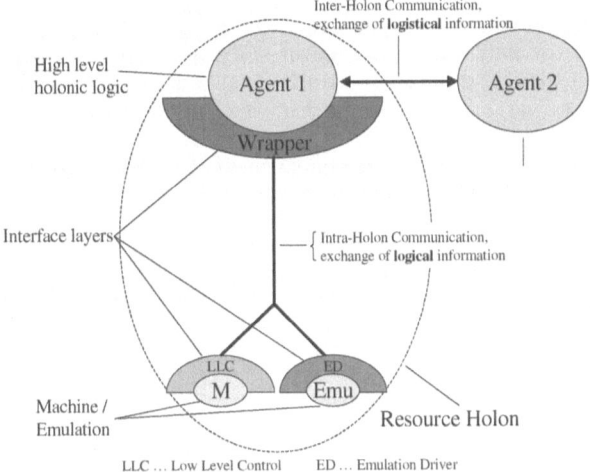

Fig. 3. Generic wrapper communication architecture

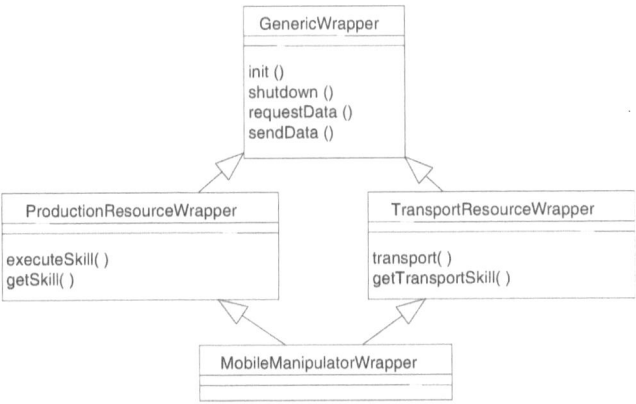

Fig. 4. Wrapper interface

Apart from these methods, Fig. 4 also shows the methods used for handling transports (TransportResource Wrapper). Transport agents provide services just like machine agents, but their service has a more complex structure. A transport service needs to include source, destination and item to transport. A third wrapper-type is built up out of a combination of the machine- and transport wrapper (MobileManipulatorWrapper). This type is used for machines that have the capabilities of both holon types. An example for such a machine is a mobile manipulator which contains a freely movable base with a robot arm connected to it.

The methods provided by the agent are depicted in Fig. 5. They also consist of generic methods for initialisation, shutdown and expansion (GenericAgent) and the machine-holon specific method FinishedExecuteSkill(), which signals the agent that the service that was executed on the hardware has finished (Production ResourceAgent).

Analog to the wrapper there are similar methods provided for the TransportResourceAgent and the MobileManipulatorAgent.

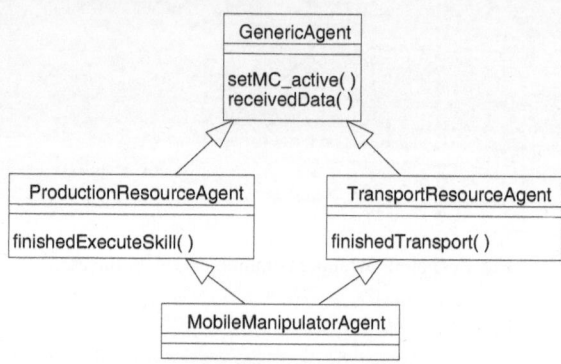

Fig. 5. Agent interface

5   Conclusion

The paper has pointed out that agent technology is an appropriate aid to implement higher level holons (above PLC level) in the manufacturing domain. Task allocation in a job shop set-up has provided the scenario for the usage of the agent building tool ZEUS to implement an agent application. Besides discussing the suitability of ZEUS for the manufacturing domain we have concentrated on the generic problem of connecting agents to machinery.

Acknowledgements. Parts of this work have been funded by the European Commission under project No. IM-26508 "Holonic Manufacturing Systems". Moreover the authors are grateful for financial contributions of the VPTÖ, the Austrian Association for Promoting Manufacturing Sciences.

References

1. Baker, A.D, Complete Manufacturing Control using a Contract Net: a simulation study, International Conference on Computer Integrated Manufacturing, May 23-25, (1988) pp. 100-109.

2. HMS European Module, Deliverable 1.1-1/2 Holonic System Architecture, University of Keele, Keele (1998)
3. Collis, J., Methodology Documentation Part II Case Study 1 - 3, Intelligent Systems Research Group British Telecom Labs, Martlesham Heath (1999).
4. Wyns, J., Reference Architecture for Holonic Manufacturing Systems, Catholic University of Leuven (1999)
5. FIPA Organisation, FIPA ACL Message Structure Specification, Geneva (2000)
6. Bauer, B., FIPA TCC Agent Communication – Extending UML for the Specification for the Agent Interaction Protocols, FIPA / OMG, (1999)
7. FIPA Organisation, FIPA SL Content Language Specification, Geneva (2000).
8. Friedman-Hill, E.J., Jess the Java Expert System Shell V5.0, Sandia National Laboratories, Livermore (2000).
9. Smith, R.G., The Contract Net Protocol: High-Level Communication and Control in a Distributed Problem Solver, IEEE Transactions on Computers, C-29, No. 12, (1980), pp. 1104-1113.
10. Barbuceanu, M., Fox, M., Integrating Communicative Action, Conversations and Decision Theory to Coordinate Agents, Proceedings of Autonomous Agents'97, Marina del Rey, (1997)
11. Bongaerts, L., Integration of scheduling and control in holonic manufacturing environments; Catholic University of Leuven, (1998)
12. Koestler, A., The Ghost in the Machine; Hutchinson, London, (1968)
13. Weiss, G., Multiagent Systems – a modern approach to Distributed Artificial Intelligence; Massachusetts Institute of Technology, London, (1999)
14. Weiming, S., Douglas, H. N., An Agent-Based Approach for Dynamic Manufacturing Scheduling; The University of Calgary, (1998)

ExPlanTech: Exploitation of Agent-Based Technology in Production Planning

Aleš Říha, Michal Pěchouček, Jiří Vokřínek, and Vladimír Mařík

Gerstner Laboratory, Department of Cybernetics
Czech Technical University in Prague
Technická 2, Prague 6, 166 27 Czech Republic
{riha,pechouc,marik}@labe.felk.cvut.cz
{xvokrine}@fel.cvut.cz

Abstract. The mission of the ExPlanTech technology transfer project is to introduce, customize and exploit the multi-agent production planning technology in two distinct industrial cases. The traditional production planning activity is substituted by agent driven service negotiations, intelligent decomposition and distributed decision-making. This paper describes a FIPA-compliant implementation of the ExPlanTech technology at the LIAZ Pattern Shop manufacturing company. We describe the structure of the agent community, types of agents, implementation of the planning strategy and its incorporation within the real production environment.

1 Introduction

This paper presents research and technology transfer activities carried out within the "ExPlanTech" Trial project (IST-1999-20171) funded by the European Commission. In the context of the ExPlanTech project, we work on transferring the already designed and implemented ProPlanT multi-agent technology [10] into industrial enterprises. The ProPlanT technology has been provided in the form of a prototype of an integrated multi-agent system (MAS) for planning of the project-oriented production. Unlike the mass-production, in the case of the project-oriented production there is always a limited series of possible products of one type manufactured (e.g. space shuttles, power turbines, TV broadcasters or unique patterns and forms). Accordingly, an important amount of resources has to be devoted to design-related activities such as quotation and configuration, design and production planning. The production-oriented planning consists of three separate (while interrelated) phases:

- **quotation and configuration**, during which the quotation engineer agrees with a customer on detailed specification of the product to be manufactured (this phase is very often supported by different areas of artificial intelligence such as, constraint programming [15], theorem proving applications [8], or possibly evolutionary computing [7]),
- **project specification**, during which the complete product configuration is transformed into the project specification and the appropriate resource speci-

V. Mařík et al. (Eds.): MASA 2001, LNAI 2322, pp. 308–322, 2002.
© Springer-Verlag Berlin Heidelberg 2002

fication (this phase is rather case specific and it is driven by the domain knowledge), and
–   **resource allocation**, where the required resources are allocated in time to appropriate resource providers, such as machines, technicians, departments, etc.

Our multi-agent solution concerns primarily the last phase, during which it becomes rather difficult to allocate a project-related resources to partially booked resource providers, to allow re-planning due to resource providers malfunction or due to scheduling of higher priority projects.

1.1   ProPlanT Production Planning Architecture

In the ProPlanT, the classical planning and scheduling mechanisms have been substituted by the processes of negotiation, job delegation and task decomposition within a community of autonomous agents, each of which represents production or information unit(s) of the factory under consideration. There is neither a central agent nor a central control mechanism. The ProPlanT system relies upon two fundamental superclasses of agents: **intra-enterprise** (IAE) and **inter-enterprise** (IEE) agents. In the category of the IAE agents we distinguish among the following basic classes:

–   **Production Planning Agent** (PPA) is in charge of project planning. Its aim is to construct an exhaustive, partially ordered set of tasks that need to be carried out in order to accomplish the given project. It contracts PMA agents.
–   **Production Management Agent** (PMA) performs project management in terms of contracting the best possible PA agent (in terms of operational costs, the delivery time and current capacity availability). PMA delegates its responsibility either to another PMA or it controls the work of a group of PA agents contracted for the considered task.
–   **Production Agent** (PA) represents the lowest level production unit that simulates or encapsulates the shop floor production process on the IAE. PA carries out the parallel-machinery scheduling of given tasks and manages resources allocation via a special type of database agents.
–   **Customer Agent** (CA) is another instance of an IEE agent that provides customers interface into the system.
–   **Meta Agent** (MA) is a special monitoring agent which visualizes information, material and work flows across the agents' community and advises on optimal system efficiency. MA provides the user with decision support regarding distributed planning of manufacturing processes.

Shall be noted that only the IAE agents have been implemented in the ProPlanT multi-agent system prototype. Special kinds of IEE agents were subject of the ExPlanTech project implementation (see Sect. 2.3).

1.2 Tri-base Acquaintance (3bA) Model Technology

As production planning is usually a problem solving activity with rather high cardi-
nality of its complexity, a coordination model that contributes to save computational
resources [13] has been suggested. As the architecture proposes, the important part of
the problem solving complexity is transferred into negotiations and job delegations
among the PMA agents. We have investigated possible ways of saving the communication traffic in the PMA coordination process, by which the overall complexity
would be reduced. Each PMA agent has been equipped with a specific knowledge
structure (tri-base acquaintance model) that administers the agent's computational
model of its social awareness. This social knowledge [3,9,12] (stored in three separate
bases) keeps precompiled important pieces of information that would have to be acquired through communication otherwise. The ProPlanT technology provides implemented mechanisms for social knowledge representation and maintenance throughout
the lifecycle of the community.

1.3 ProPlanT Multi-Agent Platform

The ProPlanT multi-agent platform provides the developers with several manda-
tory/optional agents – we call them **ProPlanT Principal Agents**. The **Facilitator**
agent maintains a white-page-list of the existing community members. Upon a registering of a newcomer, the Facilitator broadcasts its IP address and its port number
within the existing community and provides the newcomer with the white-page-list.
The **Agent Factory** constructs a community of agents by running a specific commu-
nity-description-script (equally it can stop/kill the agents). The **Meta-agent** sniffs the
communication messages among agents and re-constructs the agents' states. The
meta-agent has been primarily used for visualization of the community organizational
structure and the communication flow among the agents.

The original ProPlanT agents have been implemented mostly in C++ and they run
under WinNT 4.0 operation system. Each agent is an independently running application. The agents exchange messages via TCP/IP sockets. The agents use a specific
PMTP (ProPlanT message transport protocol), KQML as the ACL (agent communication language) [5] and KIF as the ACL content language.

2 Implementing ProPlanT in LIAZ

As already noted, this paper describes how the ProPlanT multi-agent planning technology has been applied in the plant of our industrial partner. LIAZ Pattern Shop Ltd.
(Czech Republic) belongs to the leading European producers of patterns and forms
mainly for automotive industry. LIAZ has to process approximately 120 production
orders per month with production lead time from 3 to 6 weeks. The spectrum of orders is extraordinary wide and continuously changing. Therefore the ProPlanT tech-

nology integration with the information system at the LIAZ enterprise focuses on decision-making support for the company management. The goal is to advise on the optimal production planning process with respect to customer requirements while optimally allocating available resources and while making the maximal profit.

Note: Hereafter we will talk about a particular, case specific instance of the ProPlanT multi-agent system that has been implemented in LIAZ. As this implementation is substantially different from the ProPlanT prototype we will refer to it as an **ExPlan-Tech** multi-agent system.

2.1 Role of ExPlanTech in LIAZ

The optimal production plan should balance the available LIAZ resources while maximum number of orders is processed. Considering the limited LIAZ work-shops/shop floors capacity, the decision has to be made whether the specific task/subtask will be provided internally or subcontracted externally. Such decision might be crucial in order not to threaten successful completion of other orders and not to misbalance the whole production flow. The efficient supply chain/service provision management can be handled using the agent-based approach within the *inter-enterprise and extra-enterprise level.* The technology integration (see Fig. 1) is aimed at the improved strategic decision-making, e.g. how to efficiently use available re-sources (human, material supply, workshop capacity) while the maximum number of clients' orders have been satisfied and carried out. Moreover, orders are categorized by an internal priority value ensuring that orders with a higher priority are manufac-tured before those with lower ones. The ExPlanTech system shall observe each work-shop load and consequently provide the suitability measure of the requested order.

The core of information solutions in LIAZ is their custom tailored ERP system called **ISML** (Information System Modelarna Liaz). ISML stores necessary data about the production and provides a complete business solution. The idea was not to have the ExPlanTech as a key component that others will strongly depend on.

If from any reason it ceases to operate, the human user – a project planning engineer – can develop the plan by himself and insert it into ISML.

However, once a **request for an offer** arrives to the factory, a project planning engi-neer stores it in the ISML database. After having specified the necessary production components, the respective **order specification** gets uploaded into the ExPlanTech.

This system is supposed to suggest particular resource allocation with respect to the order and planned operations of the company. This results in a distributed plan within the community of agents and its numerical and visual representation. Had the planning engineer liked the plan (i.e. deadline, costs, loads of machines) he/she downloads the **plan** back to ISML, where it is stored and further manipulated. Alter-natively, the planning manager can manipulate the capacities of workshops, change priorities of orders, cancel other planned orders in order to form a plan as he/she likes. Each update triggers the re-planning mechanism that will keep all the plans logically consistent. Once the planning manager is happy with it, the overall distrib-

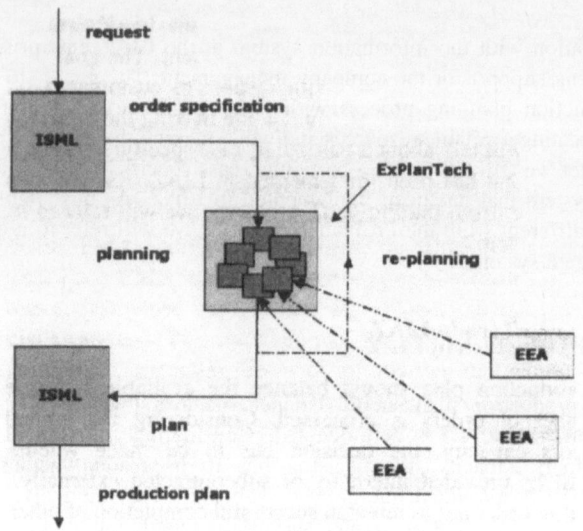

Fig. 1. Role of ExPlanTech in LIAZ

uted plan is propagated into the ISML. There are several communication flows between the ISML and the ExPlanTech:

This system is supposed to suggest particular resource allocation with respect to the order and planned operations of the company. This results in a distributed plan within the community of agents and its numerical and visual representation. Had the planning engineer liked the plan (i.e. deadline, costs, loads of machines) he/she downloads the **plan** back to ISML, where it is stored and further manipulated. Alternatively, the planning manager can manipulate the capacities of workshops, change priorities of orders, cancel other planned orders in order to form a plan as he/she likes. Each update triggers the re-planning mechanism that will keep all the plans logically consistent. Once the planning manager is happy with it, the overall distributed plan is propagated into the ISML. There are several communication flows between the ISML and the ExPlanTech:

-    order specification: ISML –>ExPlanTech
-    plan specification: ExPlanTech –> ISML
-    set of plans' modifications: ExPlanTech –>ISML
-    resources modifications: ISML –> ExPlanTech and ExPlanTech –>ISML

There are two aspects of integrating the company ERP into a MAS solution (or vice versa): **Logical Integration**, where it has to be decided upon functionality of the integrated components, relationships among components, semantics of communication and its flow, etc.

On the other hand when discussing **Physical Integration** we mean making the multi-agent system and the company ERP system interoperable in terms of physical communication – ACL, content languages, communication protocols and mechanisms (see Fig. 2).

2.2   ExPlanTech Logical Integration

The production planning process in LIAZ is simpler than envisaged in the original ProPlanT system. PA agents represent workshops. The amount of variations how a plan may be implemented in various workshops is limited (the manufacturing process is rather deterministic). The question for the system is not how to plan the order optimally, but how will the order - if accepted - affect the other planned/potential orders. The intra-enterprise ExPlanTech community in LIAZ consists of the Configurator Agent – an instance of a PPA inheriting also some properties from the PMA class, several Workshop Agents – instances of a PA, and finally a Database Agent, also an instance of a PA agent.

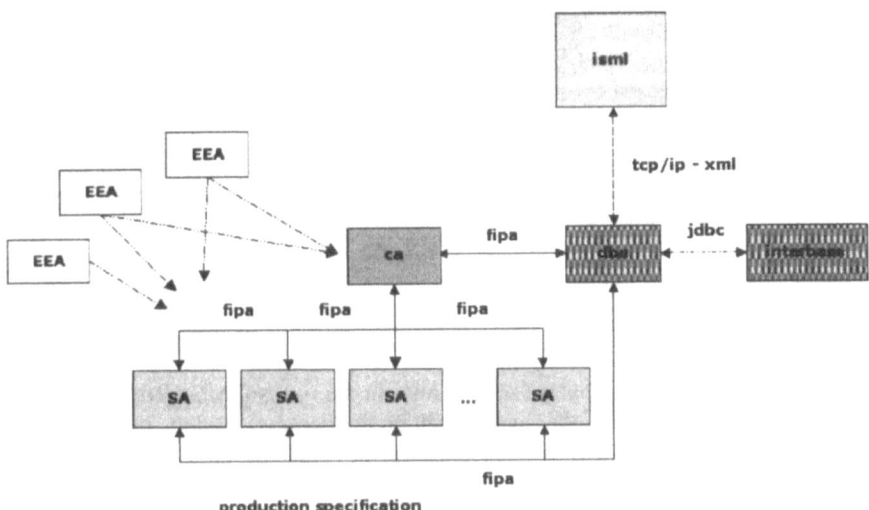

Fig. 2. The entire solution in the LIAZ Pattern Shop *(The figure depicts the architecture of the entire solution in LIAZ. ISML stands for the ERP system in LIAZ. The other blocks represent the multi-agent system ExPlanTech, CA is the Configurator Agent, SA is the Scheduler Agent, dba is the Database Agent, the block called "interbase" represents the local database and EEA stands for the instance of the extra enterprise agent – the Monitor Agent. There are also communication and data flows figured, where FIPA means the inter-agent flow of FIPA messages, TCP/IP is a communication channel between the ISML and the system ExPlantech.)*

We did not implement the ProPlanT-like meta-agent as the JADE environment [1] provides the sniffer agent that sniffs the messages and visualizes what is going on in the community.

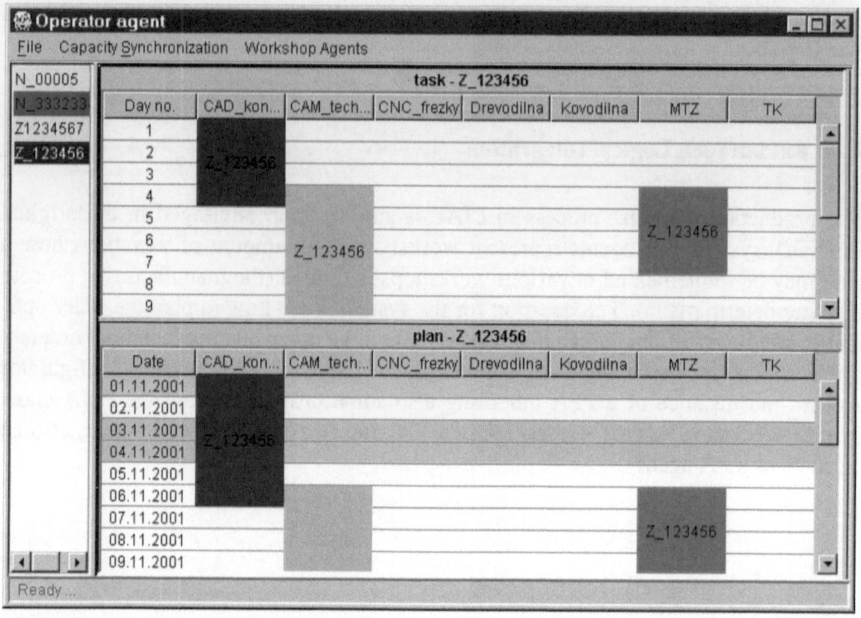

Fig. 3. Screenshot of the Configurator Agent *(the leftmost column represents the list of orders, order definition in the relative time window is placed in the upper part and the planned order in the lower part of the window)*

2.2.1   Database Agent

The Database Agent (DBA) plays several roles in the ExPlanTech agent community. The main role is to supply other agents with production data (orders, preorders, calendar, workshops), the DBA is a communication bridge between the ExPlanTech system and the ISML. The data in the XML format flow both ways between the systems via TCP/IP connection. On one side, there is sent information describing production (orders, pre-orders) from ISML to ExPlanTech, and on the other side, ready plans are sent to ISML. Received XML documents are preprocessed and then delivered to other agents (Configurator, Workshops). Preprocessing includes parsing, data extraction, storing in the local database (Interbase) and creating new XML contens for inter-agent messages. This agent doesn't have its own GUI interface. The local database, which is maintained by DBA, mirrors agents' data (knowledge) and also maintains other auxiliary data that are necessary for proper functionality of the system.

2.2.2 Configurator Agent (CA)

This agent cooperates with the group of Scheduler Agents and provides them with production data about orders. The agent itself shows two plans: a) a general plan in relative time, and b) a specific plan in absolute time (see Fig. 3). The CA agent contains a simplified 3bA model. The CA aggregates the functional aspects of both the PPA and the PMA agents. The 3bA model facilitates the agent community behavior and decreases communication traffic. It owns the information about workshops (their load, free spaces in a plan) and tasks (deadlines of orders etc.).

2.2.3 Scheduler Agent (SA)

There are as many Scheduler Agents as workshops within the factory and they stand for PA agents. The main role of this group of agents is to create plans or (better said) schedules for workshops. The Scheduler Agent tries to put a new order (pre-order) coming from ISML through both the DBA agent and the Configurator Agent into a schedule so that all constraints are met. It takes into account deadlines for each order, priorities, precedence dependencies, daily capacity of each workshop etc. The SA agent shows how could the future production look like, what order might not be finished in time because of accepting a new order. These agents help to a user to exploit production capacity in an optimal way. The optimal way is on one side to minimize void times and on the other side to accept the correct number of orders in the way that all of them are completed in time. The SA agent sends the computed plan to the DBA agent and some data about the planned tasks are sent to the Configurator Agent as well.

2.3 Extra-Enterprise Agents

The ProPlanT technology has been extended by the class of extra-enterprise agents (EEA). There are two classes of EEAs suggested: the **Monitor Agent** and the **Resource Agent**.

2.3.1 Monitor Agent

The Monitor Agent is going to serve customers of a factory, who can see the results of planning using an Internet browser (see Fig. 4). According to his/her access rights the customer is able to trace his/her orders and watch their statuses (whether the producer can make the orders in time).

Important is that data are not stored in the database but it is gathered on-line directly from the agent community. Technically, there is a web server on the side of the manufacturer exploiting ExPlanTech and a web agent that communicates between the agent community and the web server. There is going to be some sign-in authentication and security provided in the near future.

Secondly, the Monitor Agent is expected to be used by the managers of the factory, who can inspect operations of particular workshops of the factory while they are off-site. They access not only the information about particular orders, but unlike the customers they can be provided with the information about loads of the workshops and their future plans.

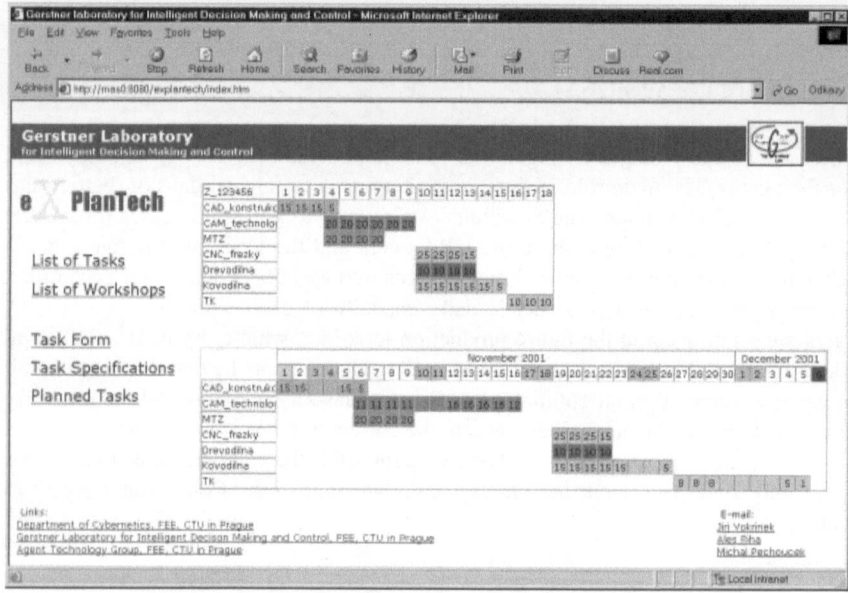

Fig. 4. Monitor Agent *(The upper table shows the order specification in the relative time and the table below represents the particular schedule for this order.)*

2.3.2 Resource Agent

This agent should work on the side of enterprise suppliers or cooperators (in the case of outsourcing). A partner enterprise (organization) could announce the status of services and resources, which are currently available. This shared (public) knowledge should be prepared in a standard form with respect to the agreed ontology. The Resource Agent could, for example, read data from the partner enterprise database or could be provided with this data by the ERP system. The ExPlanTech system can then have more precise and actual data for computation of different parameters (delivery dates, prices, amounts). The ExPlanTech could contract such an agent in case there is not enough resources and postponing of the deadline is not possible.

3   Exploration of Social Knowledge in ExPlanTech

3.1   Subcontracting, Cooperation

Even though the production planning in LIAZ has very small variability within the factory, there are possibilities to subcontract various cooperating enterprises, which may overtake responsibility for a part of an order. The LIAZ management wants the ExPlanTech to provide it with an analysis of an order that is subcontracted in part. This option significantly increases variability of the planning process and thus reveals potential for the 3bA decomposition and coordination. Thus, the concept of social knowledge-based contraction is explored specifically in the extra-enterprise coordination.

3.2   Forward/Backward Planning Strategy

The configurator (or any other PMA agent) may also exploit the stored social knowledge differently. In communities, where the number of PMAs is not critical, the agent, which is responsible for the   task decomposition may use the information stored in the acquaintance model for suggesting the most profitable request. Had the configurator known about availability of possible workshops, it may ask the contractor for keeping the proper deadline by when it wants the task to be finished. Suggesting inappropriate deadline may end up in either (i) workshop finishing the part too late even though it can be accomplished faster or (ii) workshop failing to accomplish the part at all. The decomposing agent (configurator) will than have all possible information to decide whether to ask the contractor to plan its part according the **forward** or **backward** planning policy (sometimes called eager and lazy) (see Example 1).   While forward planning tries to plan all the tasks as soon as it can – it starts from the start-time and the preceding tasks, the backward planning plans tasks as lately as possible – it plans from the due time and allocates the depending tasks first.

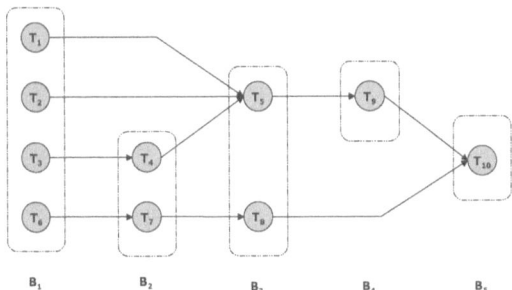

Fig. 5. Forward planning strategy

Example 1: There is a forward and backward implementation of a nonlinear plan

$$\{T_1 \rightarrow T_5, T_2 \rightarrow T_5, T_3 \rightarrow T_4, T_4 \rightarrow T_5, T_6 \rightarrow T_7, T_7 \rightarrow T_8, T_5 \rightarrow T_9, T_9 \rightarrow T_{10}, T_8 \rightarrow T_{10} \}\rangle$$

where $\rightarrow$ is a symbol for a time precedence. Figure 5 depicts the forward plan described by a totally ordered set of sets $\{B_1 \rightarrow B_2 \rightarrow B_3 \rightarrow B_4 \rightarrow B_5\}$ of a task. Tasks in each of the sets can be carried out in parallel while no task from the set B_2 can be executed before a task from a set B_1 provided that $B_1 \rightarrow B_2$. The forward instantiation of the nonlinear plan is given as follows:

$$\{\{T_1 | T_2 | T_3 | T_6\} \rightarrow \{T_4 | T_7\} \rightarrow \{T_5 | T_8\} \rightarrow \{T_9\} \rightarrow \{T_{10}\}\},$$

where the | symbol stands for tasks implementable at the same time. Analogically, Fig. 6 shows the backward solution corresponding to the sequence:

$$\{\{T_3\} \rightarrow \{T_1 | T_2 | T_4 | T_6\} \rightarrow \{T_5 | T_7\} \rightarrow \{T_8 | T_9\} \rightarrow \{T_{10}\}\}$$

Here, the tasks that have no "direct follow-ups" are executed as late as possible in order to minimize the overall "waiting" time of semi-products.

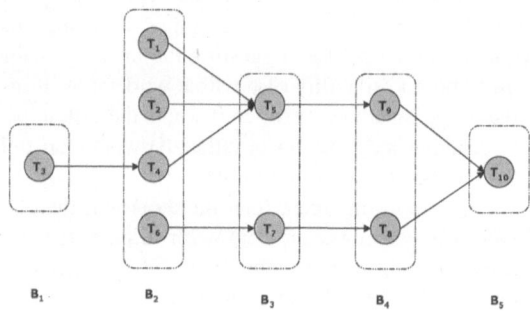

Fig. 6. Backward planning strategy

4   Implementation

We were looking for such an environment that would a) allow implementation of interoperable agents, b) standardize their communication and agent management, c) suggest ontologies and communication protocols, etc. FIPA (Foundation for Intelligent Physical Agents) [6] provides a set of such standards and reference implementations that have emerged from industrial needs and achievements of the research community. Each FIPA agent must be registered on the platform in order to interact with other agents on that platform or inside other platforms. An agent platform (AP) consists of several mandatory capability sets namely the Agent Communication Channel (ACC), Agent Management System (AMS) and Directory Facilitator (DF). AMS is an agent, which manages the lifecycle of other agents, such as creation, deletion, suspension, resumption, authentication and migration. It provides a "white pages" directory service for all the agents resident in an agent platform. It stores an address book, which maps globally unique agent names and transport addresses used by the platform. ACC is an agent, which acts as a message router among agents within the platform and towards agents resident on other platforms. DF provides a "yellow pages" directory service for the agents. It stores descriptions of the agents and the services they offer. FIPA also defines the structure of ACL (Agent Communication Language), which consists of several mandatory parameters such as for example "sender", "receiver", "content", "language" (content language) etc. In our case the messages are exchanged with the content encoded in the XML format.

The Extra Enterprise Agent is an extended JADE agent (see Sect. 4.1) similar to the intra enterprise agents in the ExPlanTech. We use the technology of servlets for assuring remote access to the ExPlanTech community (see Fig. 7). The servlet class is located on the standard web server. When the request comes from the static HTML page the servlet starts running. First, the Monitor Agent which communicates with the rest of the community by a servlet, is created. The servlet role is to dynamically create the HTML page according to the data received from the community via the Monitor Agent.

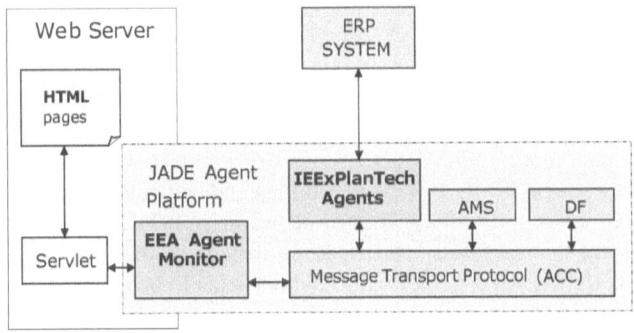

Fig. 7. Architecture of the ExPlanTech implementation

4.1 JADE

There exist several software implementations of FIPA, for instance JADE[1] (CSELT-Centro Studi e Laboratori Telecomunicazioni S.p.A), FIPA-OS (Nortel Networks), ZEUS etc. The ExPlanTech system is built using the JADE software framework, which is fully implemented in the JAVA language. The agent platform can be distributed across machines (which not even need to share the same OS) and the configuration can be controlled via a remote GUI. The configuration can be even changed at run-time by moving agents from one machine to another one, as and when required. The platform independency is an important advantage of the JAVA solutions. JADE

---

[1] http://sharon.cselt.it/projects/jade/

has several interesting features that at least make the process of implementation easier. One of these features is the availability of the Sniffer Agent that enables the user to observe the message flow among agents. The Sniffer Agent fully substitutes the role of the meta-agent used e.g. in the ProPlanT.

4.2 XML

XML is actually a language for creating markup languages that describe data and rules about the data. It requires applications to be defined before it can become truly useful. The process of defining applications is done through the use of the Document Type Definition, which defines the tags and rules within XML for a well-formed XML document. In the context of the project, and taking into account the available resources as well as the overall project aims, we head towards defining representative tags and rules for business software component interoperability in the supported applications.

Since the XML format is data base-neutral, operating system-neutral, and device-neutral, it is an effective tool for defining interoperability among heterogeneous subsystems.

4.3 Physical Integration of the ExPlanTech in LIAZ

The most standard solution for integrating the ISML with the ExPlanTech would be the implementation of the FIPA-ACC (Agent Communication Channel) on the ISML side. By doing so, the ISML would be agentified and encapsulated within FIPA-ACC (which would serve as a wrapper). That would result in ISML being a complete FIPA compliant agent that may fully participate in the life of the community. However, implementing the FIPA-ACL for FoxPro did not seem to be a perspective step (large resources required for this development). Instead we have used the DBA agent as a stand-in agent that represents the ISML to the ExPlanTech agents and communicates with the ISML using a predefined mechanism. Therefore, the ISML has no social awareness and it communicates exclusively with the DBA agent. The DBA – ISML communication flows are carried out through sockets via the TCP/IP protocol. There is no standard ACL used between the components and they exchange messages only using XML with predefined semantics.

5 Conclusions

Creating the software solution for planning of tasks is a very complex problem. We have faced a little bit different problem. We already had the production-planning tool (ProPlanT) and the task was to reuse the ProPlanT technology in the LIAZ Pattern Shop enterprise. The crucial problem is to find common language with the people from the factory and it means to understand the whole production process very well.

We defined the real task, which is to prepare the production plan for a long time horizon. The ExPlanTech gives advices and views on the production, how it could look like in the future if some order is going to be accepted or refused. It provides the information about workshops' loads, creates plans with respect to deadlines, priorities and precedence dependencies of orders. One subtask was to incorporate our system into the IT solution represented by the information system ISML that is a source of data for our planning tool. We solved this task by developing a DBA agent that serves as an interface between the ISML and the ExPlanTech. This interface DBA agent transforms the messages received via TCP/IP into the FIPA messages and vice versa. The ExPlanTech itself was implemented in the JAVA language and the FIPA compliant development tool JADE was used as a multi-agent framework.

There is an interesting problem, solution of which would improve the planning process on the side of the LIAZ Pattern Shop. The task is to observe "gaps" in the production plan and according to the previous experience to find the most suitable order (a typical order) that would fit in the best way and to contact the typical customer with a special offer. In the future, we plan to use machine learning mechanisms for this purpose.

Acknowledgements. This research work has been supported by the European Commission contract No. IST-1999-20171 (ExPlanTech) and by the Ministry of Education, Youth and Sports of the Czech Republic within the frame of the project No. MSM212300013. The authors also wish to thank and acknowledge the substantial help and assistance provided by Dr. Vojtěch Pražma and Jaroslav Körner from the LIAZ Pattern Shop Ltd.

References

1. Bellifemine, F., Poggi, A., and Rimassa, G.,: Developing Multi-agent Systems with JADE. In: *Seventh International Workshop on Agent Theories, Architectures, and Languages (ATAL-2000)*, Boston, MA, 2000
2. Camarinha-Matos, L.M., Afsarmanesh, H., and Lima, C.: Hierarchical Coordination in Virtual Enterprises. *Journal of Intelligent and Robotic Systems,* vol. 26 (1999), Issue 3/4, pp. 267-287
3. Cao, W., Bian, C.-G., and Hartvigsen, G.: Achieving Efficient Cooperation in a Multi-Agent System: The Twin-Base Modelling. In: *Co-operative Information Agents (Kandzia, P., Klusch, M. eds.)*, LNAI No. 1202, Springer Verlag, Heidelberg, 1997, pp. 210–221
4. Chandra, P.,Fisher, M.L.: Coordination of Production and Distribution Planning. *European Journal of Operational Research*, 72(1994), pp.503-517
5. Finin, T., Labrou, Y., and Mayfield, J.: KQML as an Agent Communication Language. In: *Software Agents (Jeff Bradshaw ed.)*, MIT Press, Cambridge, MA, 1995
6. FIPA: Agent Management. *In http://www.fipa.org*, Geneva, Switzerland, 1998
7. Kubalík, J., and La•anský, J.: Genetic Algorithms and their Tuning. In: *Proceedings of CASYS '98 (Dubois D., ed.)*, Liege, Belgium, 1998, pp. 217-229

8. Lowe, H., Pěchouček, M., and Bundy, A.: Proof Planning for Maintainable Configuration Systems. In: *Artificial Intelligence for Engineering Design and Manufacturing*, Cambridge University Press, Massachusetts, 12, No. 4, September 1998, pp. 345-356

9. Mařík, V., Pěchouček, M., and Štěpánková, O.: Social Knowledge in Multi-Agent Systems, In: *Multi-Agent Systems and Applications (M. Luck et. al, eds.)*, LNAI 2086 Tutorial, Springer-Verlag, 2001, pp. 211-245

10. Mařík, V., Pěchouček, M., Štěpánková, O., and La•anský, J.: ProPlanT: Multi-Agent System for Production Planning. *Applied Artificial Intelligence*, vol. 14, No.7 (2000), pp.727-762

11. Maturana, F., Shen, W., and Norrie, D. H.: MetaMorph: An Adaptive Agent-Based Architecture for Intelligent Manufacturing. *International Journal of Production Research*, vol. 37, No. 10(1999), pp. 2159-2174

12. Pěchouček, M., Mařík, V., and Štěpánková, O.: Role of Acquaintance Models in Agent-Based Production Planning Systems. In: *Cooperative Information Agents IV (M. Klusch L. Kerschberg, editors)*, LNAI No. 1860. Springer Verlag, Heidelberg, 2000, pp. 179-190.

13. Pěchouček, M., Mařík, V., and Štěpánková, O.: Towards Reducing Communication Traffic in Multi-Agent Systems. In: *Journal of Applied System Studies*, Cambridge International Science Publishing, Cambridge, UK, No.1, 2001

14. Shen, W.: Issues in Developing Agent-Based Collaborative Design and Manufacturing Systems. In: *Proceedings of the 5th International Conference on Information Sytems Analysis and Synthesis*, 1999

15. Wielinga, B. J. and Schreiber A.:Configuration-design Problem Solving. *IEEE Expert*, 12(2), 1997, pp. 49-56

A Holonic Approach to Reconfiguring Real-Time Distributed Control Systems

Robert W. Brennan[1], Martyn Fletcher[2], and Douglas H. Norrie[1]

[1] Department of Mechanical and Manufacturing Engineering
University of Calgary, 2500 University Drive NW
Calgary, Alberta T2N 1N4, Canada
{brennan,norrie}@enme.ucalgary.ca
[2] Institute for Manufacturing, University of Cambridge
Mill Lane, Cambridge CB2 1RX, United Kingdom
mf283@eng.cam.ac.uk

Abstract. In this paper we describe a general approach for dynamic and intelligent reconfiguration of real-time distributed control systems that utilises the IEC 61499 function block model. This work is central to the development of distributed intelligent control systems that are inherently adaptable and dynamically re-configurable. The approach that is used takes advantage of distributed artificial intelligence at the planning and control levels to achieve significantly shorter up-front commissioning times as well as significantly more responsiveness to change. This approach is based on object-oriented and agent-based methods and aims at overcoming the difficulties associated with managing real-time reconfiguration of a holonic manufacturing system.

1 Introduction

To remain competitive in today's global market, manufacturers require systems that are capable of quickly responding to change while maintaining stable and efficient operation. Increasingly, the manufacturing control system is viewed as being central to achieving this goal.

The main barriers to success in this area however, result from the combination of increasingly stringent customer requirements (e.g., high quality, customisable, low-cost products that can be delivered quickly) and inherent manufacturing system complexity (i.e., these systems are, by nature, distributed, concurrent and stochastic). Although manufacturing technology has become increasingly sophisticated to deal with these issues (e.g., through advanced robotics and computer numerical control), without adequate control, the result is often a collection of "islands of automation" that lack the necessary integration for truly responsive behaviour. As a result, new control software and hardware approaches are required to realise a system that is flexible (i.e., capable of reconfiguration) and responsive (i.e., capable of recovering from disturbances).

The authors' current research is intended to rectify these problems through the development of a distributed intelligent control solution that is inherently adaptable and dynamically re-configurable. This system will take advantage of distributed artificial

V. Mařík et al. (Eds.): MASA 2001, LNAI 2322, pp. 323–335, 2002.
© Springer-Verlag Berlin Heidelberg 2002

intelligence at the planning and control levels to achieve significantly shorter up-front commissioning times as well as significantly more responsiveness to change. These potential benefits, in combination with the current trend towards low-cost, distributed computing platforms, will result in a much more attractive, low-cost automation solution for future manufacturers than current centralised solutions.

In this paper we describe a general approach for dynamic and intelligent reconfiguration of real-time distributed control systems. We begin with some background on real-time distributed control. Next, we describe a function block-based operating system that is currently under development to support dynamic, intelligent reconfiguration of real-time distributed control systems. In section 4, we describe two approaches that can be used to achieve dynamic and intelligent reconfiguration and provide an example of our general approach in section 5. Finally, we provide a brief summary and discussion of our current work in section 5.

2   Real-Time Distributed Control

Distributed intelligent control involves matching the control model more closely with the physical system. This is particularly relevant to manufacturing control systems that are required to control widely distributed devices in an environment that is prone to disruptions. With this model, control is achieved by the emergent behaviour of many simple, autonomous and co-operative entities that are based on the principles of object-oriented and agent-based systems.

Although there has been a considerable amount of work on agent-based approaches to the upper/planning and scheduling level of control very little work has been done on applying these techniques to the lower, real-time control level. The main barriers at the real-time control level result from the difficulty of implementing multi-agent systems (MAS) concepts in a stochastic environment where hard real-time constraints must be met to achieve safe system operation.

The primary distinction between non-real-time and real-time systems is that real-time systems tightly link correctness with timeliness. In other words, deadlines must be met under hard real-time (i.e., tasks must finish by a specified time) and soft real-time (i.e., tasks must meet deadlines on average) constraints [1]. As well, real-time systems are typically safety-critical systems (i.e., the system should not incur too much risk to persons or equipment), and as a result, characteristics such as timeliness, responsiveness, predictability, correctness and robustness are of fundamental importance. Because of the more stringent requirements for latency, reliability and availability, it follows that the step from the non-real-time or soft real-time domain is a large one, requiring new models and methodologies for distributed control.

Recently, there have been a number of advances in this area that provide the tools to move away from the traditional centralised, scan-based programmable logic controller (PLC) architecture towards a new architecture for real-time distributed intelligent control. In particular, there have been a number of advances recently in programming languages [2], models for distributed control [3] and software methodologies [4] that are relevant.

Several authors, particularly those associated with the Holonic Manufacturing Systems (HMS) consortium, have carried-out a considerable volume of relevant research. This includes Sieverding [5] and Bussmann and Sieverding [6] who addressed the issues of an agent-based HMS and data test missions for their control systems, although it was Zhou et al. [7] who identified and rigorously defined the application of real-time principles to agent-based HMS.

Many authors have also studied the control of processes in non-holonic manufacturing (e.g., [1] and [8]). In general, these analyses are based on specific logic formalisations and are applied in particular engineering domains. Moreover, the management of such processes in real-time is used throughout the systems entire specification, design and maintenance. We feel that this metaphor would create a conflict with the emerging practice in HMS, namely that of developing the system as the seamless integration of real-time and non-real-time control components. Hence we need a unified infrastructure to support reconfiguration throughout the various echelons of functionality in an HMS.

The International Electro-technical Commission (IEC) 61499 standard addresses the need for modular software that can be used for distributed industrial process control [3]. In particular, this standard builds on the function block portion of the IEC 61131-3 standard for PLC languages [2] and extends the function block (FB) language to more adequately meet the requirements of distributed control in a format that is independent of implementation.

IEC, with the help of several HMS consortium members, have developed the Function Block Architecture as a new standard to model industrial process control systems using decentralisation and hard real-time design philosophies. The architecture permits access to the controlled manufacturing process via an IEC 61499 *system* that contains an organisation of devices. The four main models of the IEC 61499 standard are illustrated in Fig. 1. These models are organised in increasing levels of granularity: system model, device model, resource model, and application model.

A holon is represented by one or more hardware *devices*, and can interact via one or more communication networks. Each device comprises of one or more *resources* (i.e., processor with memory) and one or more interfaces. Interfaces enable the device to interact with either the controlled manufacturing process (via a process interface) or with other devices through a communication interface.

Resources are logical entities with independent control over their operations including the scheduling of their tasks. A resource can be created, configured etc (as part of the system's life-cycle) via a management model.

Applications (software functional units spanning one or more resources and over one or more devices) are networks of function blocks (FB) and variables connected by data and event flows. Such applications aid the modelling of cooperation between the autonomous holons. Function blocks receive events/data from interfaces, process them by executing algorithms and produce outputs, all handled by an event control chart.

Function blocks' algorithms can be written in either high-level programming languages (e.g., C++) or in the IEC 61131 languages for programmable controllers (e.g., Ladder Diagrams, Structured Text). A distribution model controls how applications are decomposed while ensuring that every function block is an atomic unit of distribution.

As will be discussed in section 4, the proposed model for holonic reconfiguration is based closely on the four main IEC 61499 models. For a more detailed discussion of the Function Block Architecture, Brennan and Norrie [9] may be consulted.

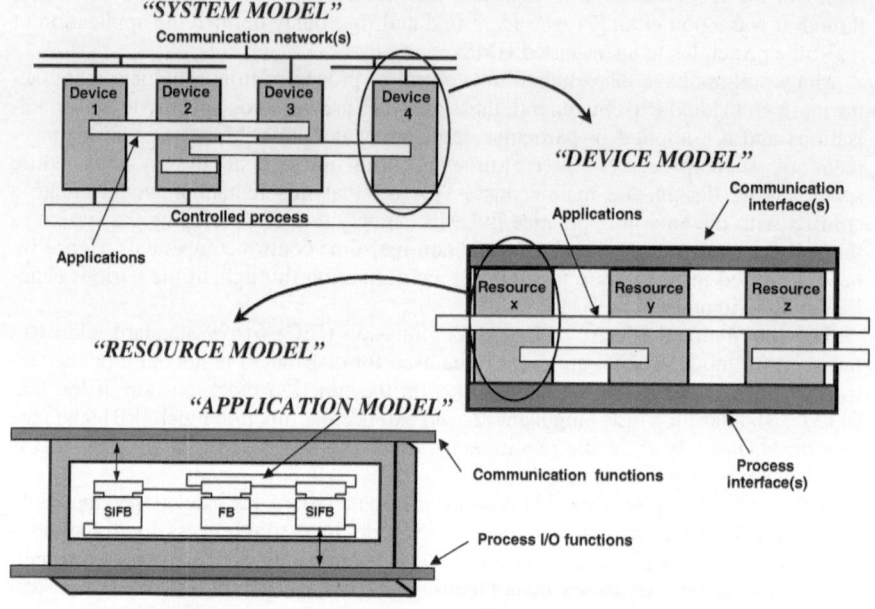

Fig. 1. The IEC 61499 system, device, resource and application models

3   A Function Block Operating System

Our motivation here is to study the key aspects of an IEC 61499 operating system as this long-term view neatly encompasses the goals of the HMS consortium [10], in which the authors are participants. Hence the operating system supports the runtime design, execution and reconfiguration of function blocks. Like many other real-time operating systems, our Function Block Operating System (FBOS) is layered with loosely coupled, highly cohesive actors. These actors act independently but monitor each other for fault detection and recovery.

Also of importance to us is the design of FBOS services to incorporate the semantics of the underlying manufacturing environment, over which currently little or no real-time control is maintained. As Balasubramanian et al. [11] remarked no manufacturing system would exhibit the desired intelligent behaviour if real-time, distribution and event-driven control requirements were not addressed. So, by considering the real-time aspects of related tasks concurrently executing within this manufacturing environment, one may reduce the opportunity to create conflicts where temporal constraints are important. These constraints are modelled as a set of predicates, called real-time guarantees, relating to where, how and when the task can be executed within the manufacturing environment and help the human expert set the HMS's control systems behavioural parameters. This behaviour must then be executed as prescribed, even in the presence of failures and errors occurring in the manufacturing environment.

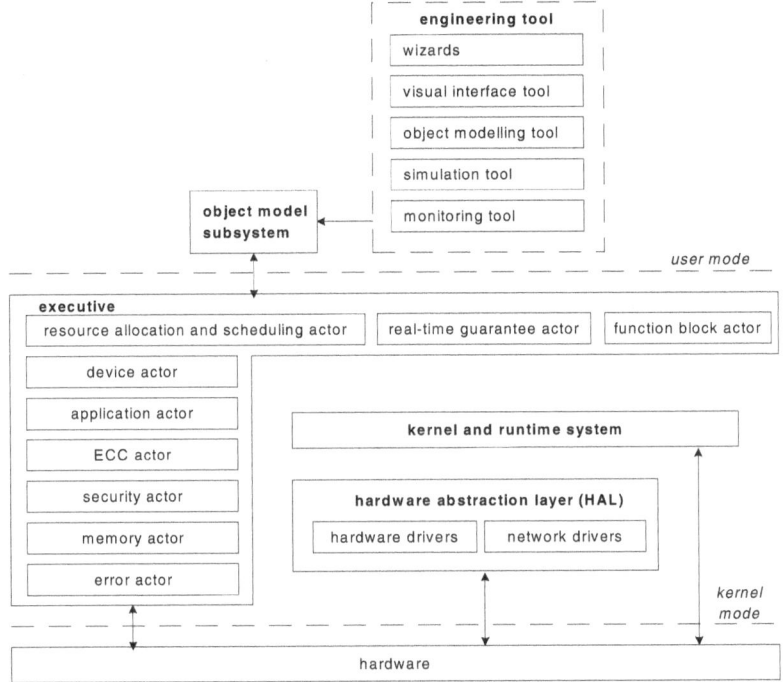

Fig. 2. The elements of the function block operating system

The FBOS encapsulates a variety of functionality associated with delivering hard real-time processing within the HMS. Broadly speaking, a function block operating system performs two main functions: resource sharing, and provision of a virtual machine for intelligent manufacturing.

Moreover, the design of FBOS should be efficient, robust and maintainable. The fundamental elements of the FBOS are shown in Fig. 2. A detailed description of all of the elements of the FBOS can be found in [12]. In the remainder of this section, we provide an overview of the major subsystems illustrated in this figure.

The goal of the *hardware abstraction layer* (HAL) is to represent the physical hardware and communication network in a uniform fashion, independent of the specific characteristics of the underlying manufacturing machinery. The *kernel* provides the major interface between the basic machinery/network (modelled by the HAL) and the FBOS executive. Its goal is to facilitate a runtime environment where real-time HMS tasks can exist and be managed.

The functionality of the *executive* is widespread, yet is modular in its design to make reconfiguration easier. The executive is actor-based to provide system support, function block support and user application support techniques. These lightweight actors collaborate together to provide reconfiguration services. For example, a service may be to migrate a function block from one hardware controller to another at run-time while still satisfying the real-time responses associated with that function block. The actors in the executive offer a variety of services to each other and to the engi-

neering tool in order to facilitate various classes of reconfiguration (e.g., adding, removing or modifying either control software or hardware). These services are based
on the classic client/server model whereby each actor has one server and at least one
client. This model enables an actor or the engineering model to acquire information
from the other actors and request the execution of methods.

The *object model* subsystem acts as an interface between the engineering tool and
the executive. Distributed control of the manufacturing system is defined as an object
model to specify parameters including timing constraints, fault monitoring and resolution mechanisms, deadline control and so forth. The object model subsystem lets the
human expert model function block applications, as defined through the engineering
model, using the Unified Modelling Language (UML) stereotype of *capsules*. For
example, Fig. 3 provides an overview of how the IEC 61499 function block, shown in
Fig. 3a, can be modelled using Real-time UML (RT-UML). As is shown in the class
diagram in Fig. 3a, an IEC 61499 basic function block is composed of a function
block body sub-capsule.

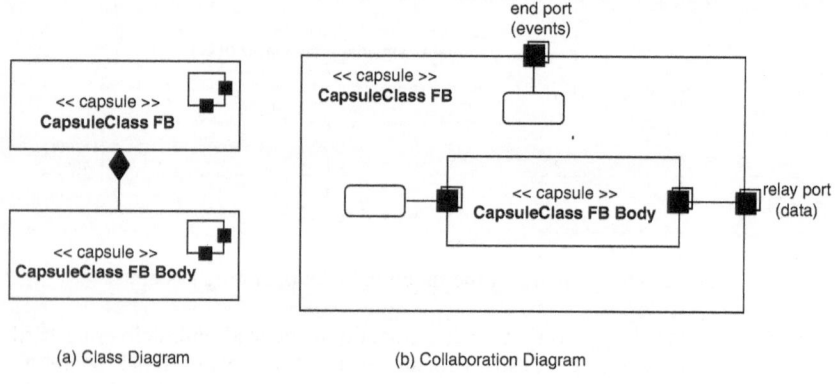

(a) Class Diagram   (b) Collaboration Diagram

Fig. 3. Real-time UML representation of an IEC 61499 function block

To provide further details of how each of the elements of the function block are
modelled, we must look at the collaboration diagram in Fig. 3b. In this figure, the
solid squares represent ports (in this case with a multiplicity factor that is greater than
one as indicated by the "shadow" square), the round-angles represent the state machine, and the rectangles represent capsules and sub-capsules.

It should be noted that the state machine is not shown explicitly in this diagram (as
is also the case with the IEC 61499 function block); as well, multiple round-angles
may be shown in a capsule, but each corresponds to the same state machine. Using the
RT-UML notation, an IEC 61499 function block is modelled as follows: event connections are represented by end ports (i.e., ports that connect to a capsule state machine), data connections are represented by relay ports (i.e., ports that connect to a
sub-capsule), and the function block body (i.e., algorithms and data) is represented by
a sub-capsule. More details of this approach to modelling real-time distributed control
systems can be found in [13].

4 Reconfiguration of Real-Time Distributed Control Systems

The primary objective of the research reported in this paper is to develop techniques to achieve automatic reconfiguration that results in predictable and stable system behaviour in a real-time environment. In conventional PLC systems, reconfiguration involves a process of first editing the control software offline while the system is running, then committing the change to the running control program. When the change is committed, severe disruptions and instability can occur as a result of high coupling between elements of the control software and inconsistent real-time synchronisation. For example, a change to an output statement can cause a chain of unanticipated events to occur throughout a ladder logic program as a result of high coupling between various rungs in the program; a change to a PID function block can result in instability when process or control values are not properly synchronised.

In order to develop appropriate methodologies, reconfiguration can be viewed in three levels of sophistication: simple, dynamic and intelligent reconfiguration. These three types of reconfiguration can be summarised as follows: (i) simple configuration utilises the IEC 61499 model to avoid software coupling issues during reconfiguration, (ii) dynamic reconfiguration uses techniques to properly synchronise software during reconfiguration, and (iii) intelligent reconfiguration exploits multi-agent techniques to allow the system to reconfigure automatically in response to change.

4.1 The Reconfiguration Model

Figure 4 provides an overview of the general model for reconfiguration that we are currently developing. With this model, function block ports (i.e., event and data connections) are objects that register with the Resource Manager (RM) associated with the function block. The resource manager looks after the interconnection of function block ports (i.e., as is specified by the application) and maintains a record of all function block ports in a FB Port table.

As discussed in Sect. 2, a device consists of one or more resources. Consequently, the relationship between resources and devices can be thought of in similar terms to the relationship between function blocks and resources: i.e., the Device Manager (DM) looks after the interconnection of the RM's function block ports and stores this information in an RM Port table. Similarly, the Application Manager (AM) looks after the interconnection of the DM's function block ports and stores this information in a DM Port table.

Using this model, a Device Manager, for example, may reconfigure the ports of its RM's to whatever new configuration is desired. The advantage of this approach is that reconfiguration can be managed at various levels (i.e., function block, resource, device, application); all that is required is a "map" of the new configuration (i.e., based on the FB, RM, and DM Port tables).

The approach described thus far allows for the "basic reconfiguration" discussed previously, but does not yet address how dynamic and intelligent reconfiguration are performed. The fundamental difference between basic and dynamic reconfiguration is the latter's recognition of timeliness as a critical aspect of correctness. The goal is to develop techniques to allow the user to change a portion of the program (e.g., simple FB, composite FB, or sub-application), while maintaining the timeliness requirements of the application. This will require freezing the state of the current FB when the change is committed, saving this state information, automatically initialising the new FB to the correct state, replacing the current FB with the new FB, and then starting the new FB. The main difference here is that matching of state information is performed automatically (rather than by the user). This is intended to result in a transparent change to the application (i.e., other FB's should see no change at the FB interface) which is intended to result in much more stable system operation than can be realised by current systems.

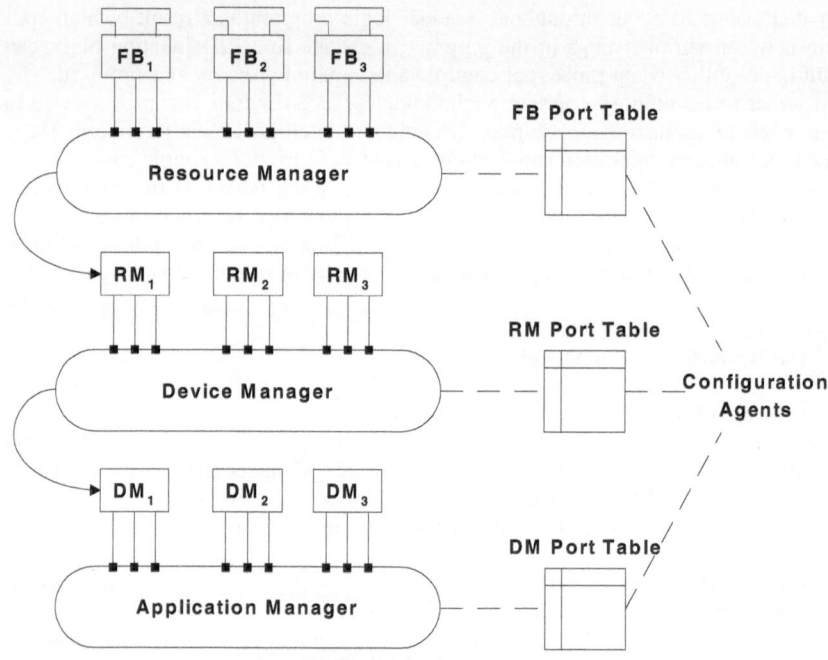

Fig. 4. The reconfiguration model

Intelligent reconfiguration builds on dynamic reconfiguration (i.e., timeliness constraints) by focusing on multi-agent techniques to allow the system to reconfigure automatically in response to change. For example, as part of a fault recovery strategy, higher-level agents will manage the reconfiguration process using diverse or homogeneous redundancy. In the following sub-sections, we describe two approaches to achieve these more advanced forms of reconfiguration: (1) a pre-programmed or "contingencies" approach, and (2) a soft-wiring approach.

4.2   Contingencies Approach to Reconfiguration

With this form of reconfiguration control, contingencies are made for all possible changes that may occur. In other words, alternate configurations are pre-programmed based on the system designer's understanding of the current configuration, possible faults that may occur, and possible means of recovery.

This approach uses pre-defined reconfiguration tables that make use of the FB, RM and DM Port tables described above. For example, in the event of a device failure, the affected portions of an application could be moved to different devices by selecting an appropriate reconfiguration table. As well, this detailed representation of the function block interconnections would allow higher-level agents to access the information required to make a smooth transition from one configuration to another, thus enabling dynamic reconfiguration.

The main disadvantage of this approach is that it is inflexible, particularly with respect to the handling of unanticipated changes. As well, this approach would require constant maintenance in order to keep the reconfiguration tables current: i.e., each change would require a change to the reconfiguration tables.

4.3 Soft-Wiring Approach to Reconfiguration

The basic idea behind this approach to reconfiguration is to enable higher layers (e.g., RM, DM, AM) to use higher-level reasoning to analyse the current configuration and plan for reconfiguration when required. Ideally, we are striving for an "integrated circuit" approach where fine grain components can be "plugged-in". Similar to Sun's Jini approach, this approach uses the directory services of the FB, RM, and DM Port tables as well as underlying Configuration Agents (CA) that handle the "wiring" between components.

These Configuration Agents use the services of the FBOS executive such as the application actors (to manage the connections of data and events between function blocks), function block actors (to model and manipulate the messages coming in and out of each function block), and real-time guarantee actors (to ensure that hard and soft real-time constraints are met). For example, function blocks will have information on how they can be connected (i.e., their interfaces) that is stored by CA's. The CA's will use this information, for example, to connect a new function block with an existing function block or to replace an existing function block with a new one while ensuring that the application's real-time requirements are met during the reconfiguration process. The primary advantage of this approach is its potential to overcome the inflexibility of the contingencies approach as well as its potential to realise intelligent reconfiguration.

5 A Worked Example

The following scenario is a simplified, though non-trivial description of the reconfiguration of an HMS. All interactions are facilitated through the FBOS.

A hardware device may receive requests to manage the function blocks running upon it from either the human expert (through the engineering model associated with the FBOS) or from other devices. Conversely, the device may become overloaded or suffer a catastrophic failure that causes it to attempt to out-source some of its tasks, totally or in part, to the other devices in the HMS.

For example, Fig. 5 illustrates one reconfiguration scenario. In this case, the user wants to change the PID_SIMPLE function block to a fuzzy logic control (FUZZY) function block. As a result of this change, Device #1 becomes overloaded and attempts to "outsource" some of its tasks to other devices.

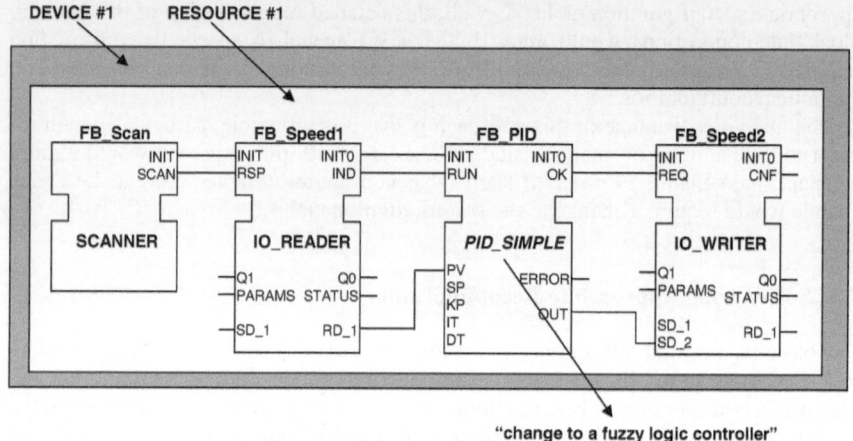

Fig. 5. Initial configuration

Using the contingencies approach, a "map" for this new configuration would have to be determined *a priori*: e.g., the data and event connections between function blocks, the procedure for adding/removing function blocks (i.e., queuing messages, stopping and killing then starting and initialising the function blocks), and the real-time constraints imposed on the function blocks. Alternatively, the soft wiring approach takes advantage of the underlying FBOS executive actors to realise a dynamic, intelligent solution to the reconfiguration problem.

For example, when a device receives a request to modify its function block configuration with given parameters (e.g., specification of deadline control mechanisms attached to the tasks the new function block configuration is to execute), an initial estimation of the real-time guarantees is made. The device actor in the FBOS corresponding to the affected device analyses the task descriptions that the revised configuration will demand to understand how this can be accomplished, taking into account the current and future load on that device (obtained via issuing a query to the resource allocation and scheduling actor) and trying to optimise the global cost. Existing ad hoc load distribution and real-time management techniques can be applied here by one or more affected device actors.

Based on the results of this evaluation, the device actor decides either to accept or reject the revised function block configuration. In the former case, the new configuration is established within the device. In the latter case, the decision is given using the acknowledgement service back to the requester's client. If the current schedule of the device allows inclusion of the tasks that the revised configuration creates then the device actor will (using the insert service of the resource allocation and scheduling actor) add the new tasks into the diary. However, it may be possible that these tasks cannot be performed locally while satisfying their attached real-time constraints (at least not all of the tasks associated with the proposed function block configuration) given the current/expected load, the availability of manufacturing resources, communication bandwidth restrictions and other technical capabilities.

If the device actor determines that (part of) the proposed configuration should be uploaded onto another device, then it will commence a negotiation with the actor(s) responsible for the remote devices as shown in Fig. 6 (in this case the negotiation is with the potential device's resource allocation and scheduling actor and security actor, expressed in standard UML notation).

The outcome of such negotiation could be success (i.e., the configuration was fully out-sourced), failure (i.e., no out-sourcing agreement could be reached), or partial (indicating that only some function blocks within the new configuration were transferred to the remote device).

An elementary negotiation scheme relies on the concepts of invitation to tender, bid and award contract; namely a Contract Net Protocol as understood in multi-agent systems could be used [14]. The device actor determines if and how to split the proposed configuration into function blocks and notifies the other device actors in the HMS about the out-sourcing requests for these different function blocks. The device actor collects quotes from the actors responsible for other devices, evaluates them and selects the optimal solution that satisfies both the device's loading criteria and any global parameters.

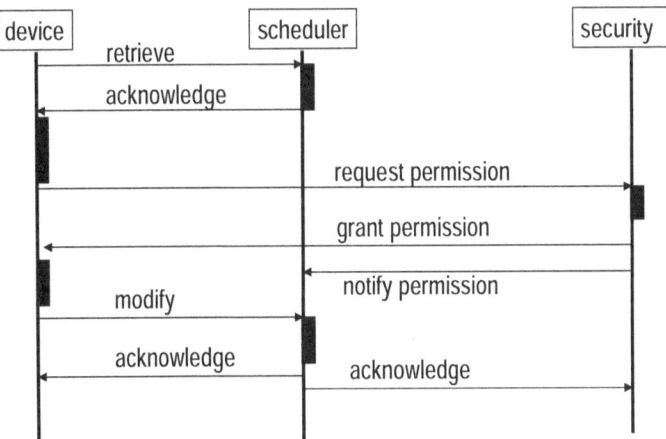

Fig. 6. An example of reconfiguration using the services of the function block operating system

The out-sourced function blocks are then sent to the device(s) that were awarded the contract. If no optimal solution could be found then the device actor may: (i) accept a sub-optimal offer (and possibly incur penalties due to the tasks not being executed by their real-time deadlines), (ii) re-distribute the function blocks with soft real-time tasks that it currently has resident on its device onto other devices in order to accept the function blocks whose tasks have hard real-time constraints attached and so execute these tasks locally, or (iii) revise how the configuration is decomposed. In any case, the process of choosing how the function blocks (and their real-time tasks) are distributed over the available devices in the HMS is a non-trivial problem. For exam-

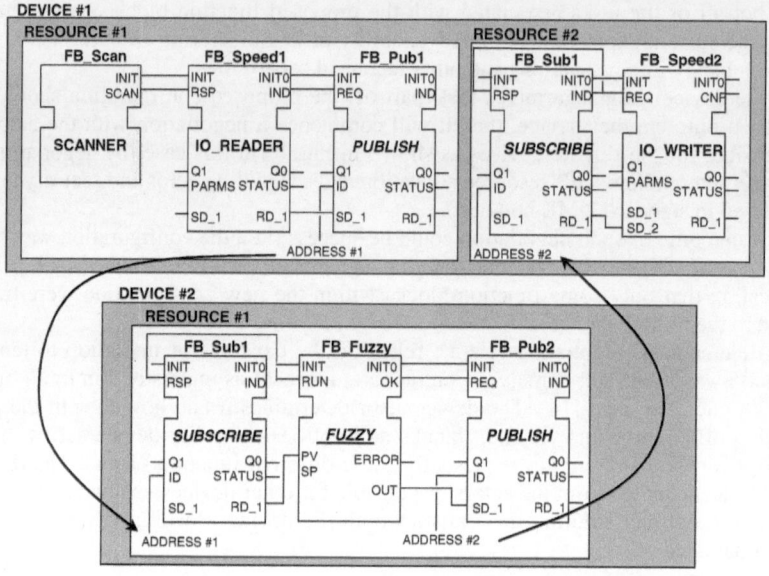

Fig. 7. One possible result of the reconfiguration process.

ple, Fig. 7 illustrates one possible final configuration the may result from this process. In this case the new configuration also required the addition of PUBLISH and SUBSCRIBE function blocks to allow communication between Device #1 and Device #2.

6 Summary and Current Work

In this paper we described a general approach for dynamic and intelligent reconfiguration that is based on the IEC 61499 model for distributed intelligent control. An important feature of this approach is that it takes advantage the holonic characteristics (i.e., modular, recursive nature) of the IEC 61499 model to allow reconfiguration to be managed at the most appropriate level. As well, the general reconfiguration model proposed here can be applied using a layered, agent-based approach to allow fault detection and recovery to occur dynamically and automatically.

Our current work in this area is focused on the development of a conceptual architecture for real-time distributed control. In particular, we are looking at how basic system functionality such as control application management and safety management (i.e., fault detection and recovery) is decomposed in a multi-layered, multi-agent environment as well as determining the nature of the agents used in this system. Our goal for future work is to completely automate this process using pseudo-intelligent behaviour within the appropriate actors. Work in this area will eventually lead to the development of a "holonic controller" that will take advantage of distributed artificial intelligence at the planning and control levels to achieve significantly shorter up-front commissioning times as well as significantly more responsiveness to change than current industrial control solutions.

References

1. Duarte, C., Maibaum, T.: A Rely-guarantee Discipline for Open Distributed System Design. Information Processing Letters, **75** (2000) 55-63
2. Lewis, R.: Programming Industrial Control Systems Using IEC 1131-3. IEE, London (1996)
3. International Electrotechnical Commission: IEC TC65/WG6, Voting Draft: Function Blocks for Industrial Process-Measurement and Control Systems, Part 1 Architecture. International Electrotechnical Commission (2000)
4. Lyons, A.: UML for Real-time Overview. Technical Report of ObjecTime Ltd. (1998)
5. Sieverding, J.: Specification of Manufacturing Test Missions. Deliverable D7.5-2 of HMS Consortium (2000)
6. Bussmann, S., Sieverding, J.: Specification of Holonic Agent Control Concepts in Manufacturing Logistics. Deliverable D7.3-1 of HMS Consortium (2000)
7. Zhou, B., Wang, L., Norrie, D.H.: Design of Distributed Real-time Control Agents for Intelligent Manufacturing Systems. Proceedings of the 2nd International Workshop on Intelligent Manufacturing Systems (1999) 237-244
8. Lam, K-Y., Law, G., Lee, V.: Priority and Deadline Assignment to Triggered Transactions in Distributed Real-time Databases. Systems and Software, **51** (2000) 57-65
9. Brennan, R.W., Norrie, D.H.: Agents, Holons and Function Blocks: Distributed Intelligent Control in Manufacturing. Journal of Applied Systems Studies Special Issue on Industrial Applications of Multi-Agent and Holonic Systems, **2**(1) (2001) 1-19
10. Holonic Manufacturing Systems Consortium: Holonic Manufacturing Systems Overview. http://hms.ifw.uni-hannover.de/ public/overview.html (2001)
11. Balasubramanian, S., Brennan, R.W., Norrie, D.H.: Requirements for Holonic Manufacturing Systems Control. The International Conference on Database and Expert System Applications (2000) 214-218
12. Fletcher, M., Norrie, D.H.: On a Function Block Operating System for Holonic Control. International Conference on Modeling, Identification and Control. (2001)
13. Fletcher, M., Brennan, R.W., Norrie, D.H.; Design or Real-time Distributed Manufacturing Control Systems using UML Capsules. 7th International Conference on Object Oriented Information Systems, Springer-Verlag, London (2001) 382-391
14. Smith, R.: The Contract Net Protocol: High-level Communication and Control in a Distributed Problem Solver. Defence Research Establishment Atlantic D.R.E.A. Report 80/1 (1982)

Rationales for Holonic Applications in Chemical Process Industries

N.N. Chokshi and D.C. McFarlane

Institute for Manufacturing, University of Cambridge, UK
{nnc20,dcm}@eng.cam.ac.uk

Abstract. This paper presents a set of rationales behind applying so called *holonic manufacturing* principles as a technological solution to the growing business concerns in chemical process industries. The anticipated benefits from holonic approach stem from the use of a distributed control systems architecture that supports flexible unit operations to dynamically integrate and collaborate with others as and when the production conditions change. A requirements deployment process is used to relate the business pressures in CPI to a set of systems requirements within key areas of *Process engineering* and *Process control*. By creating a vision of a *holonic process plant*, it is next illustrated how a holonic approach might eliminate limitations of the conventional top-down methodology of designing process control systems through a radical, bottom up approach to the structuring and operation of the process plants.

1 Introduction

Process industries today form a major part of GDP within the economy of any nation. In general, they cover a very large and diverse sector of industries including petrochemicals, polymers, bulk and specialities chemicals and related utilities sectors. Historically, these processes have evolved from small scale, simple units, which were often operated in batch or semi-continuous mode. Energy and primary raw materials were relatively available plentiful. Large and attractive profit margins were the basis on which they have grown at such a rapid rate.

Over the last two decades, however, this sector of manufacturing has also experienced an important change due primarily to increasing energy costs and increasingly strict environmental regulations [19]. Growing competitive markets demanding so-called *mass customization* of products and rapid technological innovations are replacing the old style of mass production and *me-too-electronics* type R&D structures. There is also now a growing emphasis on improving efficiency and increasing profitability of existing plants rather than creating plant expansions.

Since its conception in 1990, the field of Holonic Manufacturing is being developed as possible solution to similar challenges in next generation (discrete) manufacturing systems ([6,16,17,18]). By creating a distributed system hierarchy that is made up of dynamically collaborating manufacturing operations, it is argued that the holonic approach can provide guaranteed short-term robustness and long-term flexibility that is necessary to tackle upcoming manufacturing challenges. McFarlane et.al. [14]

V. Mařík et al. (Eds.): MASA 2001, LNAI 2322, pp. 336-350, 2002.
© Springer-Verlag Berlin Heidelberg 2002

provides a recent review of the holonic manufacturing field, with particular emphasis on production control.

Two critical observations can be made about the holonic developments to date. First, major of the researchers have concentrated on discrete manufacturing processes such as automobile and semiconductor industries, where prevailing market developments are perceived to be more stringent. Apart from a few exceptions [1,11,13], however, little research effort has been spent in continuous operations-based industries like chemical processes, where (as this paper shows) a holonic approach has significant potential. Second, there is a general shortage of business-case documents (e.g. [5]) that are available to the system designers and end-users, which enable them to connect developments in holonic research with their growing business needs.

Considering these two motivations, this paper and the direction of our overall research is aimed at bridging this gap. In this paper we consider the work of [5], which was primarily based on automobile industries, as the basic reference and extend its analysis approach to generate a similar study for chemical process industries. Particular emphasis is placed on studying the similarities and/or contrasts between discrete and process operations (and their needs) and hence how can we suitably transform the holonic developments to date in discrete industries to their continuous processing counterparts.

The analysis approach of this paper replicates the initial steps of a so-called Emerging Technology Road-mapping process [15]. A requirements analysis is first used in section 3 to link current challenges in CPI business to three key attributes, namely, improvements in *efficiency*, *responsiveness* and *variety*. Using a deployment process, we then identify the minimal properties that the underlying process operations require in order to achieve better integration of these required attributes. Particularly, we concentrate on the current research efforts in *process engineering* and *process control* areas and the trade-offs that emerge between these solutions due to current top-down methodology of process design. Using a long-term vision of a *holonic process plant,* it is next shown in section 4 & 5 that the two main holonic attributes of self-organization and collaborative behavior inherently help to eradicate the complexity of process structures and to provide sufficient robustness that is necessary to tackle production disturbances. Finally, section 6 briefs about our current research related with algorithmic issues in a test-bed level holonic control problem.

2   Process Systems

In broad terms, manufacturing processes can be divided between two main classes of continuous and discrete (parts) manufacturing. A third class, batch processes, possesses hybrid characteristics of both of them. Unlike to discrete processes (such as semiconductor or automobile), in a continuous process, materials are passed in a continuous flow through sets of processing equipment that are interconnected using piping streams. New property values are added to this common product stream when the raw-material passes further in the plant (Fig. 1 depicts an example of one such chemical process).

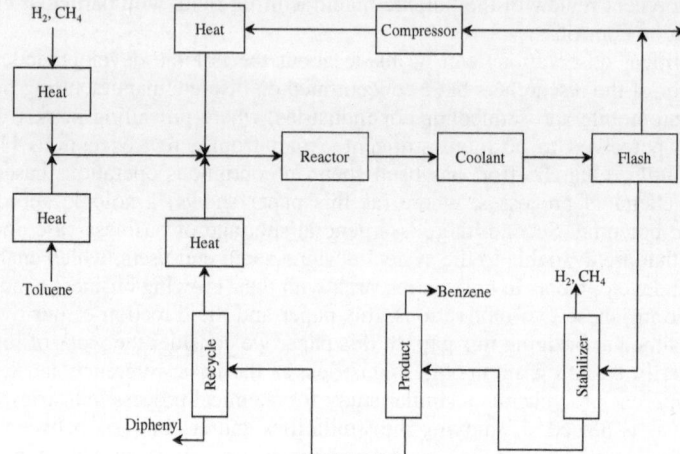

Fig. 1. Hydrodealkylation process to produce benzene from toluene [7]

Table 1 below provides a brief comparison between continuous and discrete processes. As stated therein, the main engineering and operation goals in a discrete process are to obtain an optimal network route and a schedule through which products would pass so that the desired production control values such as product due dates are achieved. On the other hand, the operational goals of a continuous process are to obtain an optimal combination of set-points, equipment modes and their transition trajectories such that desired end-product quality and quantities are achieved.

Table 1. Discrete vs. continuous process manufacturing systems

Parameter	Discrete Process	Continuous Process
System Structure	Identical or Non-identical Parallel machines having individual machining capability	Line / Series of equipments (as in flow-shop) each having defined processing capability
Production Objective/constraints	– Part or Job centered – Possibility of having intermediate buffers – Stable form of the products at intermediate stages	– Product centered – Zero or very limited intermediate buffers – Shared constraints on common utilities are important – Time critical product evolution
Process Coupling	– Time(schedule) based	– Product Based – Tight coupling between equipments due to piping streams
Product Routing Variables	– Physical Processing Routes – Machine availability/ flexibility – Route flexibility	– Equipment operational modes and control set-points – Product grade and quality
Controlled / Manipulated Variables	– Due Date – Arrival Time – Processing Time	– Process values/set points – Local control parameters
Production Control Strategy	– Discrete on-off logic based control & PLCs	– PID or Multivariable type continuous control linked with PLCs as usual overrides
Typical industry	Semiconductor, Automobile	Petrochemical, Refinery

A point worth to be emphasized here [9] is the common misunderstanding about continuous processes (and specifically of CPI) that "*these processes consist primarily of continuous or long-term, steady-state processes*". In fact, more than half of the production tonnage and revenue as in majority of polymer industries, however, is based on more discontinuous operations. Of particular interest in this paper are the so-called *campaign* processes. In a typical campaign production, a product A is made first, often in a steady-state operation, though not necessarily so, for a certain period of hours to days. Then the reaction conditions, and possibly reactant compositions, are changed to manufacture product B in the same equipment. Production systems in such processes are required to produce a whole portfolio of end-products while using the same sets of equipment. Specific production networks in such processes are required to be a combination of dedicated as well as flexible production facilities in order to cater the varying demand of product quantity and variety.

3   Requirements Analysis

Focussing specifically on a campaign type production, we next analyze emerging business performance drivers and their impact on production operations. Our aim in this section is to generate a set of requirements for CPI production operations, and specifically, to extract the resulting implications for process engineering methodology and process control systems design.

3.1   Business Drivers in CPI

As stated at the outset, many process industries are migrating from conventional mass-production based operations to customer oriented mass-customization based environments. Increasing costs of energy, growing environmental stipulations and rationalization through global mergers result in substantial business pressure on current industrial players. A recent survey (within a CAPE-21[1] program) found a range of business/legislative/technology trends that will influence future CPI operations. Considering specifically the petrochemical/polymer industry, the prominent trends (apart from current requirements of best quality and cost) will be:

Margin Compression due to intensive competition leading to demands for:
- Optimal production yield and consumption of energy/utilities
- Campaign operated plants operating in a make-to-order fashion
- More reliable, resilient and improved on-stream factors

Increasingly volatile markets making demands for:
- Improved product differentiation, novelty and non-standard products and processes
- Reduced capital and operational investment
- More flexible and responsive manufacturing, supply networks operating as *Extended enterprises* in which different links are tightly coordinated

---

[1] http://cape-21.ucl.org.uk and [5]

These trends can be broadly summarized into three different requirements for process operations, namely,
1. Increasing process *efficiency* and production throughput,
2. Dynamic *responsiveness* to external as well as internal disturbances, and
3. Continual change management and *agility* of production system

These are the generic *black-box* attributes that a business executive might desire his process system to excel in. Faced with these business objectives, and if the current level of success is to be maintained, CPI industry will need to achieve and maintain excellence throughout its life cycle from process development, plant design to production operations.

3.2   Two Main Areas for Future Improvements in CPI

Apart from developments in process technology that deal with the detail chemistry of process operations, the survival and sustainability of chemical process industries will depend on the excellence in its engineering of process systems and the excellence in the manner in which plants are operated and controlled [5]. This in turn suggests two main areas where further improvements will be necessary:

- **Improvements in Process Control**: The process is required to exhibit a number of desirable characteristics such as efficient, flexible, reliable and safe operations, and their seamless integration with supply and distribution chains. These characteristics essentially reflect the internal behavior of the plant and its underlying processes, i.e. the material and energy flows, control signals, etc.
- **Improvements in Process Engineering:** To make the improvements in process control feasible, the correct operating characteristics must have been built into the plant in the first place - consistent *design excellence* is also required, to ensure that the desired operating characteristics are *inherent* to the design and do not need to be *bolted on* by later and expensive additions.

3.3   Current Developments and Their Limitations

Although the ultimate aim of this paper is to assess the extent to which holonic manufacturing approaches can address business requirements for CPI, it is important to first review and analyze existing R & D developments and their impact on future requirements. By doing such, we can make several observations:

1. **Efficiency might increase complexity:** Increasing *efficiency* requires *minimizing* utility consumption and wastage of raw-materials/product. One approach, for example, as shown in Fig. 2 is to engineer/restructure the process paths accordingly [7]. However, this can lead to some potential difficulties such as in this case highly complex process structures (i.e. clearly more flow inter-connections) which are difficult to manage for better continual change management.
2. **Responsivenesss might create rigidity:** One approach to guarding the system against various internal or external disturbances such as supply-demand fluctuations, utilities failures etc. requires building sufficient inventory within the system.

This however conflicts with the need of frequent product changes. Also, in cases where there exists site-level sharing of utilities or intermediate products, such solutions of increased local inventories are not practical to an extent to be operated.

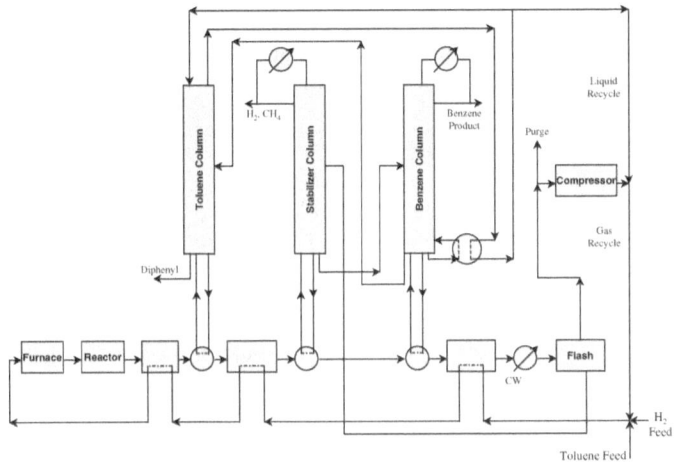

Fig. 2. A heat integrated flowsheet of the HDA process as shown in Fig. 1 [7]

3. **Flexibility/agility might require higher costs:** Requirements of constant product changes and mass-customization requires making maximum re-use of existing process equipments through their increased functional flexibility or easy reconfigurability. Such high functional flexibility, however, becomes capital intensive and is undesirable from a profitability view.

The above analysis highlights the trade-offs faced (Fig. 3) when seeking to make improvements in CPI plant design and operations. Achieving such a balance is certainly not a trivial task and requires detail understanding of the process *architectures* and the control *algorithms* through which they are operated in real-time. We next list a set of desired properties of the process systems that are necessary to be satisfied within the system design/operations phases in order to achieve this balance.

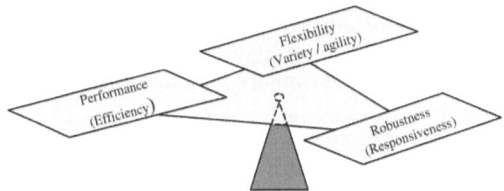

Fig. 3. Trade-offs between required attributes within a process system

3.4   Desired Properties of a Process System

Considering the future CPI business requirements and the above trade-off analysis in the current developments, we next propose a set of properties that could be as guidelines in preparing procedures for process engineering and its control design. These properties can also be used to evaluate the necessity and sufficiency of taking an alternative approach to dealing with the requirements in Fig. 3 (such as holonic manufacturing described in the later section) compared with the current approaches.

3.4.1   Process Architectural Properties

Structured Complexity: Mastering the complexity of process structures for better continual change management requires a transparent definition of unit operations and their process interactions. This issue becomes very important for mass-customization oriented production environment that uses the same sets of equipment to produce a variety of product grades.

Self-Organizing: Agility of the process requires building a reconfigurable process system that can be quickly re-organized as and when the available flexibility within process system saturates. Ideally, such reorganization should be *de facto* in that whenever necessary the process reorganizes itself with minimal human intervention

Distributed Architecture: Distributed architecture provides independent definitions to unit operations both in their structural as well as operational integration. This in turn enables, (a) the improvements in the short-term responsiveness through enabling the implementation of a decentralized control scheme, (b) the scalability of the process for its rapid expansion/reduction, and (c) the modularity through which off-the-shelf definitions of units can be made available.

3.4.2   Control Algorithmic Properties

Decentralized Control: Process control problems possess a component-wise sparse structure which can be exploited to solve large-scale/complex control (decision) problems (as in petrochemicals industry) by decomposing them into several smaller subproblems. Such a solution also avoids the inflexibility and poor responsiveness of the control architecture due primarily to the conventional top-down design methodology.

Self-Adaptive: Continuing with the above argument on decentralizing control, each controlling element should also possess some sort of intelligence through which it can measure the impact of local disturbance and hence can necessarily react by adapting its suitable parameters. It also needs to pro-actively perform a planning function to continuously perceive its future operational requirements and the interactions with other unit operations.

Dynamically Integrated: To enable the enhanced performance from a self-organizing distributed process architecture requires embedding a dynamic interaction counterpart within the unit controllers. They now have to dynamically decide with whom and how to interact in real-time, however, in a more general and abstract manner and with making very few assumptions about other unit operations and their internals.

Bottom-Up: In order to mitigate the structural complexity, the overall control layer should operate in a bottom-up fashion. This means the primitive control (execution) elements should possess capability to an extent to vertically integrate the planning (or decision making) function within their control algorithms. Behavior of such controllers can then be coordinated by a sort of higher level controller. Moving up this hierarchy the coordination takes more an advisory role on planning rather than control.

Figure 4 provides a broad comparison between a conventional process control scheme and an ideal control scheme that complies to the above mentioned control algorithmic properties. As depicted therein, the control-related decision making is now distributed between associated unit controllers that dynamically interact with other such controllers. A higher-level coordination layer enhances the global predictability of the overall process.

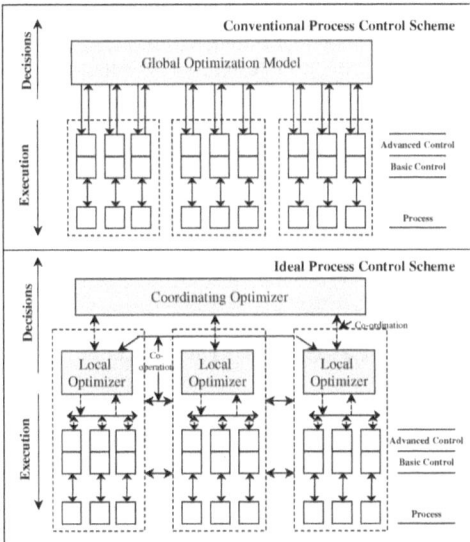

Fig. 4. Conventional vs. ideal process control scheme

In the next and the coming sections, we now examine how holonic manufacturing concepts might be applied to CPI applications and hence how and to what extent they address the above mentioned properties of process systems. The motivation for such an investigation is threefold: (a) Holonic manufacturing has been found to be successful in discrete manufacturing processes where a similar set of future requirements also exist [5], (b) holonic manufacturing can provide a new platform on which current as well as future process engineering and control procedures can be devised, and (c) holonic manufacturing can complement the current development trends (Table 2) because it reduces the migration effort necessary for their adaptation.

4   Holonic Manufacturing Concepts in the CPI

4.1   Holonic Manufacturing Systems

Holonic manufacturing is based on the concept of a *holon*, which was first proposed by the philosopher Arthur Koestler as means to explain the evolution in biological and social systems [10]. Suda in his seminal work [16,17] on future Japanese factories observed that properties in analog to a holon in biological system would be highly desirable in a manufacturing operation as well due to increasingly stringent challenges. He therefore proposed to create a visionary *holon* based manufacturing model comprising different manufacturing elements as the so-called *manufacturing holons*. A manufacturing holon effectively integrates a control part, an optional physical processing part and a human role. A holon can itself consist of other holons that are necessary for processing, information handling, and human interfaces to the outside world. A system of holons, which co-operate amongst themselves in real-time to deliver the overall manufacturing functionality, is called a *holarchy*. Ideally, holarchies remain self-organized; i.e., they are created and dissolved dynamically.

A diverse range of discrete manufacturing applications have been studied during last decade where holons have been used to describe different elements involved in manufacturing operations (e.g. resources, orders and products) and their real-time interactions. Each holon has a capability to both *decide on* and autonomously execute associated production functions. In such applications planning, scheduling as well as production operations are all performed by individual holons [4,8,18].

4.2   A Long Term Vision of a "Holonic Process Plant"

In order to demonstrate the potential benefits of holonic approach within chemical process industries, we now describe a long-term vision of how a typical *holonic process plant* might operate in the context of a campaign type production (for example, a polymer process). The vision described here is deliberately taken to its extreme in order to highlight the key elements of holonic concept.

In a unit operation based process design concept, a continuous process is built up from a set of processing elements or units that are interconnected by a network of piping streams. A unit that is such a resource or processing element is considered here as the fundamental building block and is referred as a *unit* holon. It generally comprises its underlying physical processing part, its control system and a communication interface to communicate with other such unit holons as well as with the human operator.

A holonic process network that is build up from several such unit holons consists of an assortment of dedicated and flexibly available unit operations (Fig. 5). The dedicated units such as specialty reactions or separations are designed particularly for the target of achieving sufficient production quantity at the normal efficient operational rate. The other set of units comprises unit operations which can be plugged-in and out of the process as and when required by means of mobile piping structures. Such units (i) can be designed a priory and included in the process structure with the target of redundancy or (ii) can be separately stored reaction/separation equipment as in so-called *pipeless plants*, or in an extreme case (iii) can be made up from the so-called

Micro chemical process modules (mChPM) (as described in detail by [11])[2]. All these units are structured in a process network, so-called *superstructure* [2,7], which allows them to *switch* between different most efficient production schemes.

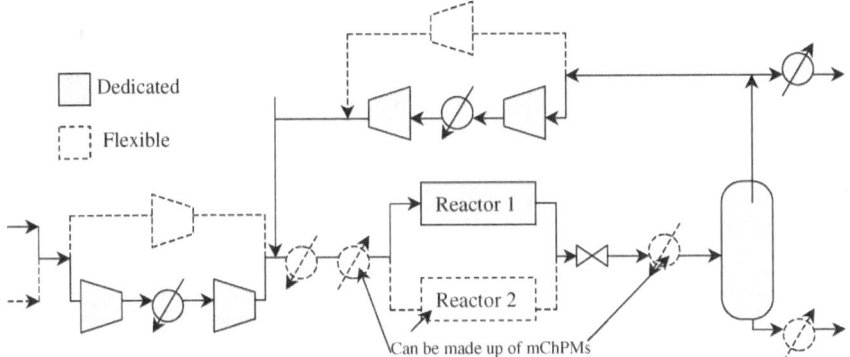

Fig. 5. An example of a holonic process network

In the beginning, a holonic process plant consists of this flexible process structure. When a new production order arrives, it creates a set of its production requirements, i.e. the product grade, processing steps and might be the allowable production cost. The unit operations within the process now carry out a co-operative interaction phase whereby they obtain suitable process network and individual optimal operation settings. In case of use of flexible operations, respective units or mChPMs are shifted or arranged in the required positions by means of AGVs. Once organized, the production starts in the usual fashion.

During operation, the units continuously monitor their operating goals and the global goals of the overall process. If any limitation is found such as an intermediate unit becomes bottleneck, such a unit in turn initiates an interaction phase. All relevant units now adjust their operational settings accordingly and in an optimal manner such that the global goals remain satisfied. If such a re-organization violates the global requirements or if there exist a redundant unit which can share the load of bottleneck unit (or if mChPMs can be used to generate a new unit immediately) then such re-organization is performed. In case of failure of utility or power which might be generated external to this plant, the units now collectively bargain for the available utility and accordingly restore the nearest optimal operational condition.

The above vision of a holonic process plant becomes more convincing when it is extended to a site or a petrochemical complex level integration. A complex (generally found in a petrochemical/refinery companies) consists different process plants that can produce entirely different products from the same set of primary raw-materials (such as ethylene) being produced by a root processing plant (such as Gas-cracker). All plants in the complex generally share a site level power production, utilities etc.

---

2 A mChPM is a simple multi-purpose chemical processing module that has capability to operate in a mixture of reaction, separation and heat exchange modes. Using simulated views based on reflex oriented swarm intelligence, Koshijima et.al. describes in [11] detail how a mChPM based Asynchronous Distributed Chemical Process plant (ADChP) can be designed, operated and self-reorganized.

Plants are also interconnected at various levels to exchange intermediate raw-materials. We consider a case when all such plants are designed using a holonic approach. When a new production order arrives at a particular plant, it collectively negotiates with the customer order for better operating costs and with other plants for sharing of utilities and common raw-materials. When the plant under consideration converges on suitable operating terms from such a negotiation, it starts its production. In case one of the plants shuts down due to unprofitable market conditions or a critical failure, the other plants now adjust their loads such that the overall performance of the whole complex remains intact.

5   Rationales for Holonic Approach as a Solution

The above description of a holonic process plant indicates that the holonic approach has the potential to effectively address the various requirements identified for the process engineering and process control. The requirements are met because of the inherent attributes of the holonic concept. We summarize here these attributes and how they satisfy the requirements.

- **Structured Complexity:** The structural integration (almost "plug and play") of unit holons allows a complex model of (ideally) any chemical process to be configured and operated just by parameterization and aggregation of the lower level unit operations.
- **Distributed Architecture and Control:** The autonomous capabilities of unit holons enables a distributed architecture where holons take local decisions for the changing dynamic conditions. This also enables them to individually adapt their behavior as required to be proactive or reactive.
- **Self-Organizing and Dynamically Integrated:** When production conditions change, the unit holons interact with others to reconfigure accordingly the process flow paths as well as reorganize their operating modes to new optimal values. Any disturbance that ordinarily requires solving a global process model in a centralized case is tackled in a distributed yet integrated fashion, and importantly is treated as "business as usual"!
- **Bottom-Up Control:** Due to the local decision making capability of a process holon, process driven by holonic control systems are inherently bottom-up based.

In summary, the flexibility and simple reconfigurability afforded by the bottom-up design philosophy of holonic approach appear to support a number of the capabilities necessary to make the current process systems more effective in the face of upcoming business challenges.

6   Current and Future Research on Holonic CPI

As mentioned in the introduction, the holonic research performed to date has been mainly concentrated on achieving improvements in discrete industries where operational agility is critical for maintaining customer orientation in volatile markets. Apart from [1], [11] and [13], there exist little research effort in the application of holonic control in continuous or more semi-continuous process industries. Based on the research in discrete manufacturing, the following issues will be critical for future research in holonic CPI:

1. **Architectural Issues:** This includes the identification, definition and description of different basic process holons, determining their attributes and specifications (both technically as well as conceptually), detailing the holonic taxonomy (for the support of process engineering) and developing the detailed interaction models through which these basic process holons will interact in order to coordinate process operations. These interaction models will provide the information exchange mechanism on which detailed coordination algorithms can be designed.
2. **Algorithmic Issues:** These include the important issues that have not been investigated so far within overall holonic research which relate to how the behavior of the individual holons will be coordinated and optimized so that the overall process moves towards a globally desirable direction and yet still maintains the bottom-up (and thus autonomous) character of individual process holons. Specifically, in the context of the process control, important issues are to investigate the implications and the requirements of this newly added coordination layer on performance and stability of the underlying device level control layer.

Various other issues which also demand the attention of future research are: (a) methodological changes to the existing process and control engineering procedures, (b) migration framework to enable existing process control systems to smoothly move towards totally holonic control architecture, and (c) international standardization of control systems components and their use as a part of holonic developments.

Our current research (as a part of first author's doctoral thesis) is to develop a test-bed level holonic process system that can reflect some of the algorithmic issues regarding the coordination of process holons and their device control algorithms. The underpinning motivation is to propose and develop a collaborative, distributed control layer within the process control architecture that would reside above the underlying physical control layer.

One particular process test-case that was suggested by one of the industrial collaborator is shown in Fig. 6. The process comprises two isolated distillation columns (possibly owned by separate companies) that separate their incoming feedstocks into respective lighter and heavier end-products. The purpose of the research is to identify the criterions and certain basic mechanisms through which the underlying (predictive) controllers should interact in order to rectify the effects of changing production conditions. One particular scenario in that regard is the case where both columns share a fixed quantity of steam supply (u_T) from a single (3rd party) supplier. The steam supply is limited in its ability to cater to the total demand (u_1 and u_2) of both columns in order to keep them operating at their desired production rate. The three main issues related to holonic control that are under investigation are:

1. What are the possible information structures that emerge due to interactions between column processes and between their local control algorithms?

2. How should the individual control problems be modified to resolve the above information structures?
3. What are the performance benefits as well as additional information overheads in implementing holonic decentralized control?

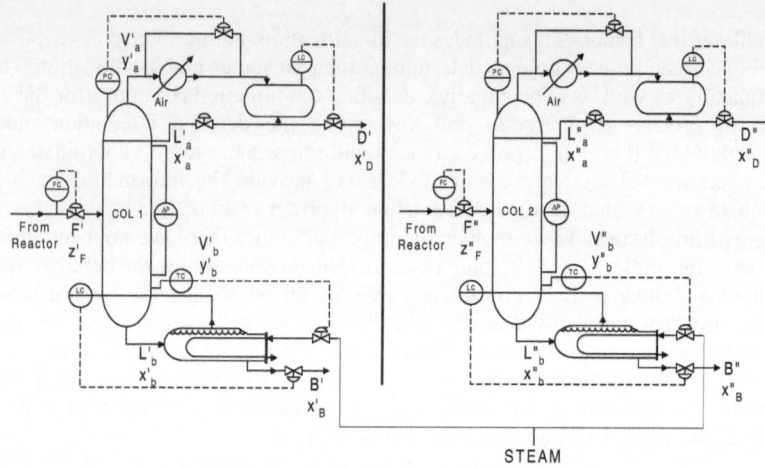

Fig. 6. Twin column process as a test-case

Figure 7 depicts two different presentations of the interaction model. In the centrally coordinated case (Fig. 7a), both columns interact directly with each other on distribution of the steam. However, their interaction is being monitored and coordinated by a higher-level coordinator (which could be a plant manager or the steam supplier or a broker of some form).

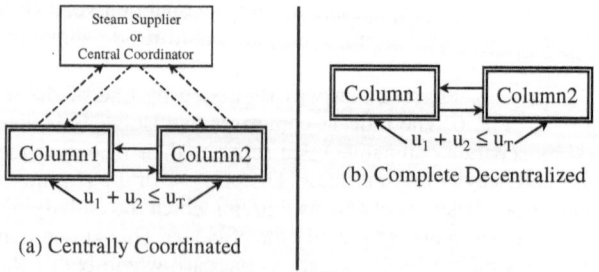

Fig. 7. Twin column optimization test-case

Case b in Fig. 7b represents a completely distributed model where both columns jointly negotiate on the steam distribution without having any central agency to coordinate them. This scenario requires further investigation on the holonic aspects of balancing the autonomy of the individual columns with the cooperative behavior required for the process holons to achieve a sensible global result. Detailed results about the performance of these two models is under development and will be reported elsewhere in the future.

7   Conclusion

This paper has developed a vision for the applications of holonic manufacturing in the chemical process industries. Although holonic manufacturing was initially intended for discrete manufacturing environment, the flexibility and simple reconfigurability afforded by its bottom-up design philosophy, and distributed control, has the potential to address a number of the business challenges faced by CPI. A simple vision of the operation of a holonic process plant has been developed to analyze the suitability of the suggested approach.

Acknowledgements. This paper is an extended version of the earlier paper "Chokshi, N.N. and McFarlane, D.C." (2001), *Rationales for Holonic Manufacturing Systems in Chemical Process Industries*", Proceedings of IEEE Conference on Database and Expert Systems, Munich, Germany, September, 2001. The authors are grateful to Stefan Bussmann (Daimler Chrysler, Germany), Andrew Ogden-Swift (Honeywell Hi-Spec Solns., UK) and Marinus Niemand (Sasol, South Africa) for providing valuable insights and suggestions in this work. The first author is supported by Cambridge Commonwealth Scholarship.

References

1.   Agre, J. A., Elsley, G., McFarlane, D.C., Cheng, J., and Gunn, B.: Holonic Control of a Water Cooling System for a Steel Rod Mill. Proceedings of Rensellaer's Fourth International Conference on Computer Integrated Manufacturing and Automation Technology. New York (1994)
2.   Biegler, L.T., Grossmann, I.E. and Westerberg, A.W.: Systematic Methods of Chemical Process Design. Prentice Hall International Series in the Physical and Chemical Engg. Sciences. Prentice Hall, New Jersey USA (1997)
3.   Bolton, L. and Perris, T.: A Vision of Future Industrial Needs and Capabilities: Process Modelling, Simulation and Control. Technical report, CAPRI Project http://cape-21.ucl.org.uk (1999)
4.   Bongaerts, L., Valckenaers, P., Van Brussel, H., Wyns, J.: Schedule Execution for a Holonic Shop Floor Control System. Preprints of the Advanced Summer Institute'95 of the Network of Excellence in Intelligent Control and Integrated Manufacturing Systems, Lisboa (1995) 115-124
5.   Bussmann, S. and McFarlane, D.C.: Rationales for Holonic Manufacturing Control. Proceedings of Intelligent Manufacturing Systems Workshop, Leuven Belgium (1999) 177-184
6.   Christensen, J.: Holonic manufacturing systems - Initial Architecture and Standard Directions. First European Conference on Holonic Manufacturing Systems, Hannover Germany (1994)
7.   Douglas, J.M.: Conceptual Design of Chemical Processes. McGrow-Hill Book Company, New York USA (1988)
8.   Heikkila, T., Järviluoma, M. and Juntunen, T.: Holonic Control for Manufacturing Systems: Functional Design of a Manufacturing Robot Cell. Int. Comp. Aid Engg. 4 (1997) 202-218

9. Keller, G. E. and Bryan, P.F.: Process Engineering: Moving in New Directions. Chem. Engg. Prog. 96(1) (2000) 41–50
10. Koestler, A.: The Ghost in the Machine. Hutchinson and Co., London UK (1967).
11. Koshijima, I., Niida, K. and Umeda, T.: A Micro Module Approach to the Design and Control of Autonomous Decentralized Chemical Plant. Jour. Proc. Cont., 6 (1996) 169-176
12. Marquardt, W.: Trends in Computer-Aided Process Modeling. Comp. Chem. Engg. 20 (1996) 591–609
13. McFarlane, D.C.: Holonic Manufacturing Systems in Continuous Processing: Concepts and Control Requirements. Proceedings of ASI'95 (1995)
14. McFarlane, D. C. and Bussmann, S.: Developments in Holonic Production Planning and Control. Prod. Plan. Cont. 11 (2000) 522-536
15. Probert, D. and Shehabuddeen, N.: Technology Road Mapping: the Issues of Managing Technology Change. Int. J. Tech Mgmt. 17 (1999) 647–661
16. Suda, H.: Future Factory System Formulated in Japan. Techno Japan, 1 (1989) 67–76
17. Suda. H.: Future Factory System Formulated in Japan (2). Techno Japan, 2 (1990) 58–66
18. Van Brussel, H., Bongaerts, L., Wyns, J., Valckenaers, P., and Van Ginderachter, T.: A Conceptual Framework for Holonic Manufacturing: Identification of Manufacturing Holons. Jour. Mfrg. Sys. 18 (1999) 35–52
19. Vision 2020.: Technology Vision 2020: The U.S. Chemical Industry, American Chemical Society, http://www.acs.org, (1996) 77 Pages.
20. Wyns, J.: Reference Architecture for Holonic Manuafacturing Systems - the key to Support to Evolution and Reconfiguration. Phd Thesis, Department Werktuigkunde Afdeling Productietechnieken, Katholieke Universiteit,, Leuven, Belgium (1999)

Distributed Deadline Control in Holonic Manufacturing Systems

Martyn Fletcher[1], Robert W. Brennan[2], and Douglas H. Norrie[2]

[1] Institute for Manufacturing, University of Cambridge
Mill Lane, Cambridge CB2 1RX, United Kingdom
mf283@eng.cam.ac.uk
[2] Department of Mechanical and Manufacturing Engineering
University of Calgary, 2500 University Drive NW
Calgary, Alberta T2N 1N4, Canada
{brennan,norrie}@enme.ucalgary.ca

Abstract. In this paper, we examine the characteristics of holons based on mobile agents that migrate to hardware controllers responsible for executing manufacturing tasks and monitoring their execution status. Appropriate compensatory actions are then initiated to ensure that task deadlines are satisfied as much as possible. It is also argued that such a conceptual model will facilitate research and development of mobile agent-based holonic manufacturing systems with respect to HMS reconfiguration in real-time.

1 Introduction

Fuelled by the rapid development of electronic commerce and customers' demands for high-variety low-volume products, systems founded on mobile and software agents [1] are among the fastest-growing areas of research and development in manufacturing science. These agents perform manufacturing tasks and aid decision-making in business activities. Many experts believe that agents provide a suitable paradigm for designing intelligent manufacturing systems [2] to improve productivity, enhance flexibility and reconfiguration of factory shop-floors, and increase responsiveness to user demands. Most notable to this paper is the application of such agents in Holonic Manufacturing Systems (HMS). Holonic manufacturing is a relatively new concept, where "smart" entities called *holons* collaborate to provide an open environment for the transformation, transport, storage and validation of knowledge and physical artefacts. HMS covers the entire scope of the manufacturing life-cycle, from ordering, through production, fixturing, assembly, resource management, handling, inspection and possibly disassembly on the shop-floor, to delivery of finished goods to customers. Every holon is characterised by their methods and knowledge (i.e., autonomy) and by their inter-holon negotiation (i.e., cooperation). Structurally, a holon comprises the following elements:

- A low-level process and machine control system that handles hard real-time decisions concerning the manufacturing hardware. This control system would typically

V. Mařík et al. (Eds.): MASA 2001, LNAI 2322, pp. 351–362, 2002.
© Springer-Verlag Berlin Heidelberg 2002

be built using the emerging IEC 61499 standard for open distributed manufacturing systems [3].

- A middle-level monitoring and activation system to observe the current execution status of manufacturing tasks and influence when these tasks are likely to terminate. We model this element with a framework that can run multiple mobile agents.
- A high-level control system responsible for planning, scheduling, configuration and other non real-time decision making actions that demand knowledge. We model this element using a software agent [4].

The focus here is on the interaction among such elements. The paper is structured as follows. A conceptual model for deadline control in mobile agent-based holonic manufacturing systems is presented in Section 2. Section 3 concentrates on a particular group of agents, namely mobile agents, and how they could function to facilitate holonic characteristics. Section 4 presents a protocol to support distributed deadline control based on the interaction between mobile and stationary agents and describes how holons synchronise their activities for deadline control. Flow and reconfiguration considerations are discussed in Section 5. Identification of future research directions is given in Section 6.

2   Conceptual Model

Various approaches to achieve intelligent behaviour in a manufacturing system are under investigation, including:

- Coping with the complexity of business innovation for small to medium enterprises (SMEs) operating in, and servicing, manufacturing enterprises. The integration of modern computer and communication technologies is leading to dramatic improvements in articulating and interacting with business-level decision making tools geared towards high-volume manufacturing.
- Next generation manufacturing systems support the complete life-cycle and will integrate all facets of globally distributed "virtual enterprises" in order to: (i) reduce lead times from production line planning to design and manufacture, (ii) encourage decentralised autonomous technologies that facilitate flexible manufacturing, and (iii) take full advantage of worldwide information technology infrastructures. Systems based on this next generation paradigm include agile manufacturing and fractal manufacturing.
- Holonic manufacturing systems that are geared towards continuous and batch processing integrating highly-flexible, agile, reusable, co-operative, modular manufacturing components. Such systems are capable of automatic reconfiguration in response to system and/or component demands, with a view towards being "plug and play".

Here we focus on HMS where the building blocks are holons. The term holon was first introduced by Koestler [5] comes from the Greek word *holos* (signifying whole) with a suffix *on* (a particle, as in proton or neutron). Holons provide all the facilities needed to control, transport, transform store artefacts within a factory. Holons can also process information such as being a server or expert system. Each holon is a dynamic system with input, processor, output and a controller. Our approach to managing an HMS is as a consequence of experimenting with an industrial test-bed where lumber (i.e., a natural material with irregular deformities) is cut in a flexible manner to construct value-added wood products for assembly into furniture. We envisage that the introduction of "holonic" ideas such manufacturing enterprises will lead to significant increases in the following: (i) robustness to disturbances; (ii) adaptability to rapid change; and (iii) efficient use of available resources. Also, it is argued that such characteristics facilitate research into holonic manufacturing systems and their augmentation with agent technology.

To put our work into context, there is now a plethora of material from other branches of agent-based research [6] and function-based research [7] that is relevant and comparable to the approach we are adopting. These branches come together to form a holon reference architecture as illustrated in Fig. 1. In this section, we present a conceptual model for deadline control in a holonic manufacturing system (using this architecture) based on *threads*.

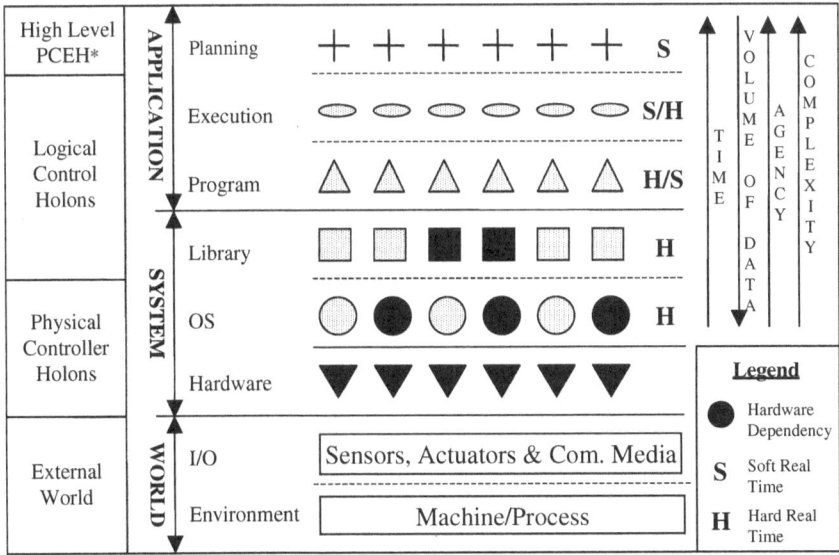

* High Level Planning, Coordinationand Execution Holons

Fig. 1. HMS reference architecture

Our motivation is to investigate inter-holon and intra-holon collaborations with a view towards supporting *deadline control*. Manufacturing tasks (of both real-time and non real-time nature) must be managed in a shop-floor environment where decentralised control is predominant. Ensuring that these tasks are completed by their scheduled end times is paramount for efficient use of the manufacturing resources. Furthermore, the failure to complete a real-time task by its cut-off time could be catastrophic and may lead to endangering the health of human operators on the shop-floor. Deadline control is the process (distributed over multiple holons and across the parallel resources within a single holon) to facilitate that tasks, as much as possible, are finished on time. Moreover deadline control takes a pro-active view of such facilitation by ensuring that if tasks appear to be running late then suitable compensatory actions are initiated by the holons to minimise any potential disruption. The guiding principles for using software agents and mobile agents in HMS for achieving such deadline control can be characterised by:

- The holonic system is distributed and demands openness so that new holons can join and existing holons can leave in an *ad hoc* fashion. Software agents provide an appropriate platform, and a rich set of flexible techniques, for letting holons be added, modified, queried and removed from the enterprise.
- Each new order entering the shop-floor creates a number of mobile agents. One mobile agent is generated per task and is then transferred to the location of the holon responsible for executing that task.
- One key advantage of an agent architecture is that the administrative decisions are not centralised in a management system, but are decentralised among the various software and mobile agents upon the shop-floor. Therefore this heterogeneous agent architecture enables the holonic system to be more scalable. Each holon has a piece of behaviour supported by its resident software agent that enables it to make local decisions that maintain the community goals, while mobile agents provide an elegant functional approach to migrate agent technology around a network while monitoring and intervening on behalf of orders.
- If an agent is unable to handle the decision making assigned to it then various holons with generic negotiation and inference facilities would be contacted.

Contrary to conventional manufacturing systems, an HMS is managed in a decentralised manner by holon interaction among the software and mobile agents as illustrated in Fig. 2.

Therefore, an HMS can support agile behaviour in the face of change; this is essential for manufacturing in the 21st Century. However how to isolate key system elements and identify efficient strategies for their interaction could be specific to particular applications. Moreover, the relationship between individual holons' behaviour and the system performance as a whole remains an open issue. Work in exploring such problems is being organised through the international HMS consortium [8], in which the authors are participating, that contributes to the Intelligent Manufacturing Systems (IMS) research and development program [2].

3   The Role of Mobile Agents in HMS

The mobile agent model used in our HMS environment is illustrated in Fig. 3. Each mobile agent consists of the following elements:

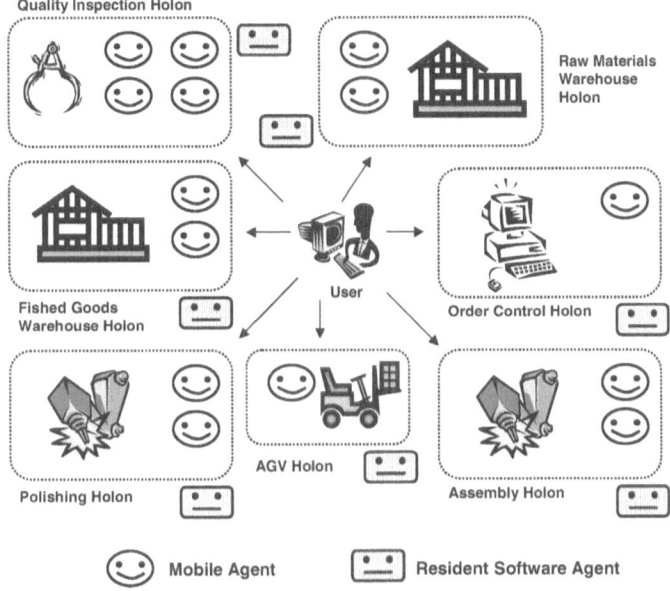

Fig. 2. HMS with software and mobile agents

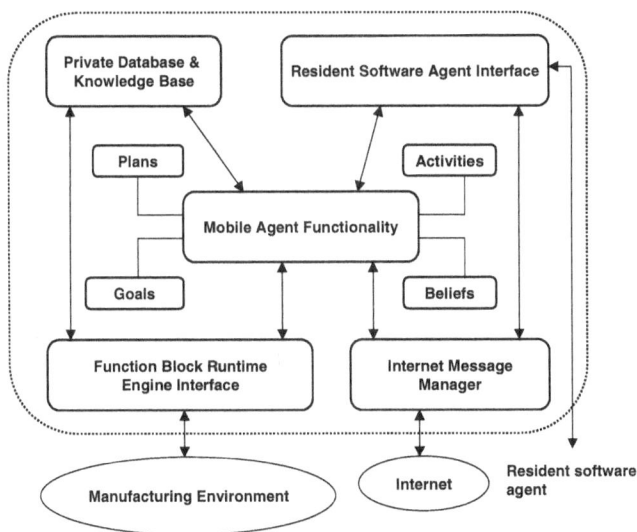

Fig. 3. Elements of the mobile agent model

- *Private Database and Knowledge base*: This retains the accumulated domain-specific and general information that the mobile-agent holon has about the manufacturing environment in which it operates, the task it is monitoring and possible compensatory actions. It also holds information concerning its acquaintances, the software agent whose location it is at and interacting with, and their network addresses. With this data as a guide, the interactions with other holons are more efficient and direct.

- *Function Block Runtime Engine Interface*: This is responsible for acting as an interface to the IEC 61499 runtime engine resident at the hardware controller. This system manipulates the sensors and actuators on the manufacturing shop-floor, is responsible for fault detection, executes responsive algorithms and handles overall control of the holon's real-time behaviour.

- *Resident Software Agent Interface*: The following control mechanisms are supported through this interface: execution service, interaction service, management service and migration service. The execution service decides the appropriate responses to external stimuli and task requests from other holons. This decision is based on criteria such as: (i) accept task requests only if the holon is idle, (ii) accept task requests from acquaintance holons involved in the same manufacturing thread before requests from any holon, and (iii) interrupt execution of a requested task to process data from local sensors. The interaction service is used to negotiate between different holons in order to coordinate their execution for the manufacture of a given artefact. Protocols such as the contract net [9] can be used to decompose and assign this manufacturing thread into a series of related tasks. The management service starts, stops, creates and kills software components within the holon, as well as querying and setting their internal information. The migration service provides a means to transport a component to another site and continue its execution.

- *Mobile Agent Functionality*: This provides the beliefs, goals, activities and plans to control the mobile agent-based holon's intelligent behaviour. Beliefs model the agent itself, its environment and other agents through a suitable set of predicates. Agents combine their activities in order to satisfy their goals which are specified either statically at conception by the user or dynamically at runtime via interaction with other agents. Activities are the lowest level of primitive action a holon can perform, with the result being atomic, i.e. either success or failure. Such activities can be divided into manufacturing activities (affecting the manufacturing environment) or communicative activities (sending and replying to inter-agent messages). Plans are used to implement the agent's goals by combining the activities with suitable sequential statements, conditional statements, and repetition statements.

- *Internet Message Manager*: In holonic manufacturing systems, a message manager is used to encrypt outgoing messages, decrypt incoming messages and process messages sent between the agent-based holons across the Internet. These messages relate to task-specific exchanges to support negotiation, conflict resolution and synchronisation during manufacture. Suitable XML document type definitions are availed upon to facilitate these WWW message exchanges and protocols.

The merits of our approach can be characterised by:

- Network load is reduced by dispatching the mobile agent to the destination host where interaction can take place locally without having to transmit numerous messages over the network.
- The deadline control scenario is heavily reliant on real-time constraints. Most stationary multi-agent approaches do not cater for such requirements due to message delivery latencies over a network. Mobile agents overcome this problem by interacting directly with the host to manipulate the manufacturing controller's operations.
- One of the key advantages of any multi-agent approach is the greater flexibility it offers with respect to adapting to its operational environment, reacting to changes in other agents and being able to dynamically adjust its interactions. Therefore, our mobile agent approach can support these features. Furthermore, it can also let the mobile agents be re-distributed over the system to balance workload.
- Fault-tolerance and reliability are two criteria essential for any pragmatic manufacturing system. The dynamic agility that agents have provides a solid foundation for the development of robust HMSs. Moreover, by migrating mobile agents away from damaged hosts, the system as a whole displays graceful degradation in the face of failures, rather than complete collapse as experienced in a centralised approach.

4   Distributed Deadline Control

Distributed deadline control of tasks is achieved among holons using the above mobile agents, a logical structure for inter-agent collaboration (called a *cooperation domain (CD)* [10]) and a protocol. An example protocol for cooperation domain formation and distributed deadline control execution is shown in Fig. 4 and Fig. 5 respectively.

Using the aforementioned concepts, each interaction between a mobile agent (representing a task within an order) and the resident software agent (responsible for governing the holon's hardware and knowledge processing) is associated with a configuration that models the thread of control used to manufacture a specific artefact. This thread is analogous to a given order received by the shop-floor and is composed of one or more tasks. Tasks are assigned to various subordinate holons (called cohorts) and is under the supervision of a managerial holon (called the coordinator). Thread synchronisation, deadline enforcement and timing at the cohorts is administrated, by the coordinator holon, through the configuration model. The software and mobile agents are jointly responsible for such administration.

The activities associated with this configuration model are sometimes referred to as being governed via a cooperation domain. The configuration model dominates the commencement and termination of the thread, and control of inter-thread synchronisation, at runtime. For intra-thread synchronisation, the whole thread is divided into milestones which can be every 10, 20, 30 etc atomic tasks (executed at the various cohort holons), or every 10, 20, 30 etc milliseconds. The principle for synchronising and reconfiguring at a milestone is as follows:

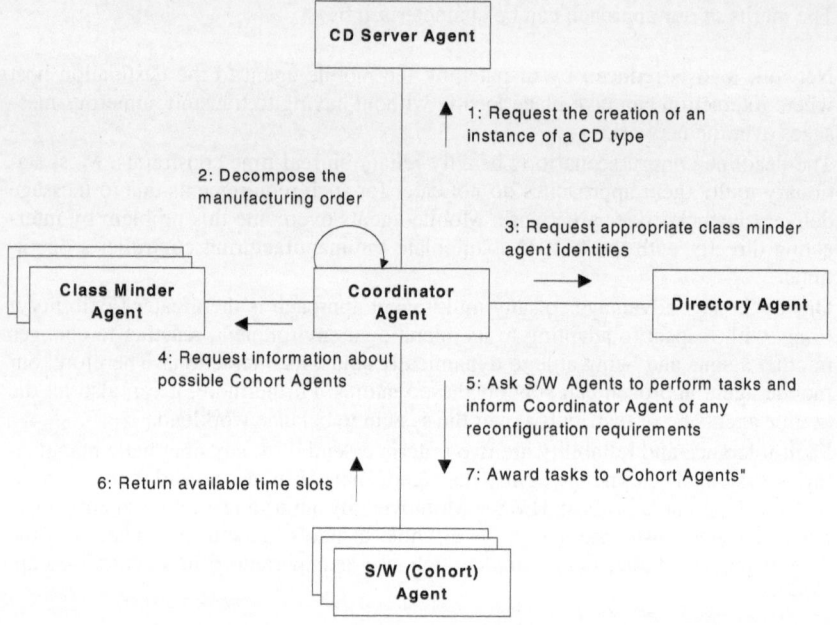

Fig. 4. A distributed deadline control protocol for cooperation domain formation

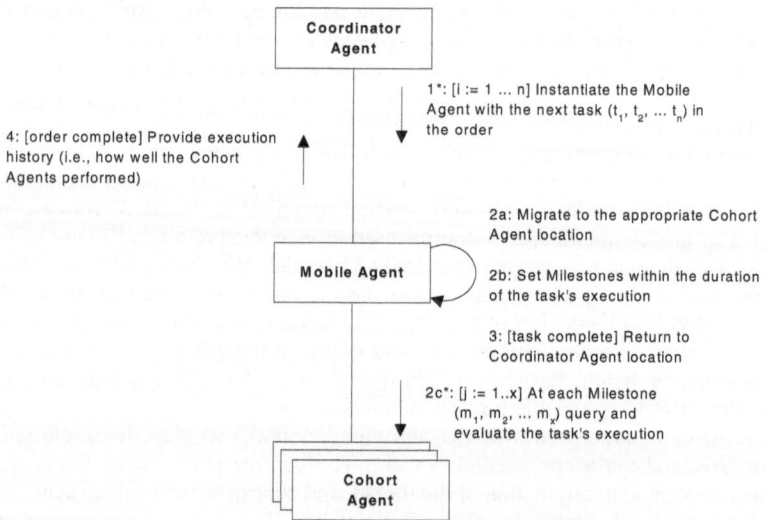

Fig. 5. A distributed deadline control protocol for task execution

1. When the execution of the configuration model's tasks that belong to a milestone are over, the other related tasks within that thread must have their execution terminated by the associated cohort holon in order to keep pace with the thread.
2. The mobile agent determines the status of execution for the task. Based on this querying, the agent discovers if the task is on schedule for completion at the due time. If needed, compensatory actions (e.g., increasing the tasks' priority on the holon's hardware controller, dispatching messages to the user and/or order holon etc) are set in motion. These actions are organised as a deadline control protocol via the CD.
3. If a cohort's software agent ends its task earlier than the time specified by the configuration model corresponding to that thread, then the holon cannot start new tasks within the thread until the next milestone is reached. Moreover common variables and objects upon the shop-floor (e.g., a work in progress artefact) cannot be altered until this next milestone has been reached. That is, the coordinator holon and its configuration model determines the optimal opportunity for the cohort agents' tasks to start and stop.

A manufacturing thread can be decomposed into a number of related tasks that are then executed by various holons. Each task is modelled as a set of activities with a prescribed set of temporal and relationship semantics. For example, the manufacturing thread presented in Fig. 6 illustrates the life cycle associated with the manufacture of a piston head for an automobile engine and its distribution, via the cooperation domain, among cohorts. The manufacturing thread is built from distinct stages that represent semantic divisions, and in the case of Fig. 6 the thread is composed of three stages. In stage 1, a grinding machine creates the piston shape from a smooth cylinder of die-cast steel and is associated with some background cutting and cleaning. In stage 2, an AGV transports and handles the piston to the next robot. In stage 3, the piston is polished and inspected. If inspection fails then the piston is returned to the grinder and processed again until it reaches sufficient quality.

According to our general classification, a manufacturing task may be composed of: (i) continuous manufacturing activities, (ii) a hybrid of continuous and discrete activities, and (iii) purely discrete activities. That is, the types of constituent activities that a holon performs within a task can be rearranged to satisfy the diverse requirements of the various stages within the thread. Each task and stage should have a master activity in the synchronisation element of our conceptual configuration model. If there are some continuous activities in a task and/or in a stage, then one of them is selected as the master activity depending on criteria such as importance, priority or current holon configuration. If there are no continuous activities then a suitable discrete activity is chosen as the master activity of the task and/or stage. Therefore the master activity is changeable depending on what types of manufacturing activities there are in the thread and which activity is more important during a stage of this thread. Therefore mobile agents synchronise their local clocks to the time of the resident software agent running the master activity. Furthermore, the mobile agents set their deadlines relative to this master activity's timing.

The designer is responsible for specifying which activity types could become the master, while it is the responsibility of the system to intelligently make the choice of instances of these types at runtime. In Fig. 6 there are seven activities and three stages.

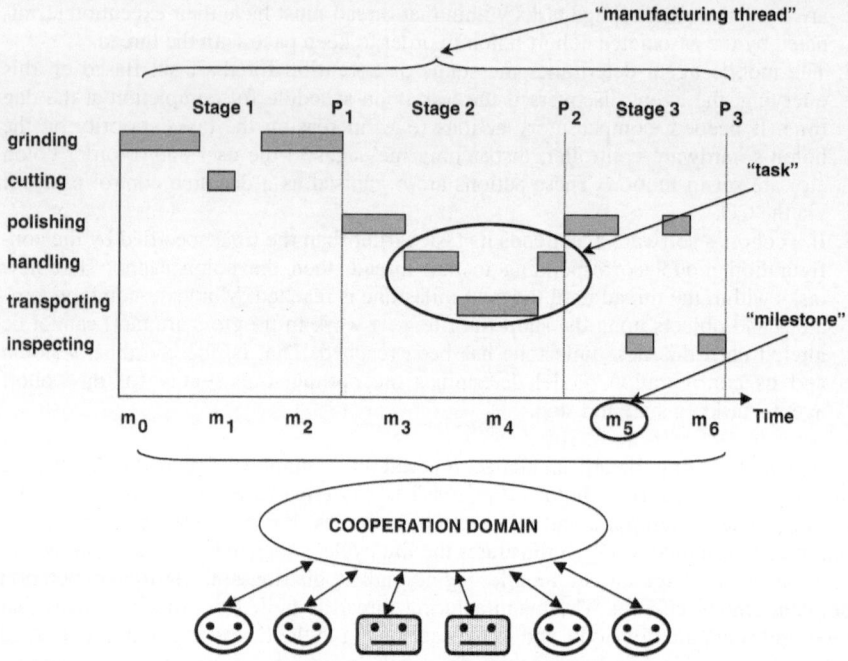

Fig. 6. Tasks and milestones in a manufacturing thread and their management via a cooperation domain

Hence grinding could be the master activity in stage 1, while transporting and polishing are the master activities of stages 2 and 3 respectively. Furthermore, timestamps called *milestones* (i.e., m_1, m_2, ..., m_x) are associated with various intervals along the time-frame of the manufacturing thread. These milestones are used to control some intra-task and inter-holon synchronisation scenarios. That is, milestones represent temporal points within the manufacturing thread where some tasks, and their subordinate activities, have synchronisation relationships based on the status of their execution. For example, several tasks (at different holons) must start execution at the same time (i.e., at reaching a milestone) or two activities (within one holon) must run simultaneously until the milestone is reached.

5   Flow and Reconfiguration Considerations

The concept of a Lagrangian *flow index* as proposed in [11] is adopted to conveniently process holon-to-holon and user-to-holon interactions concerning reconfiguration as part of the compensatory actions associated with deadline control. For example, such interactions occur to identify points where (i) contingency plans can be invoked, (ii) artefact manufacture can be rolled back to, and (iii) processing may be resumed from. The flow index provides a reference from any given point in a manufacturing thread (e.g., the activity that is being executed currently at a particular holon) with respect to the thread's start and end points. Each task is associated with a flow index counter and is incremented by the appropriate number of flow index units when the activities in that task are successfully completed. For simplicity, the length of a flow index unit is the duration needed to execute the activity. That is, the duration of the task's flow index unit is equal to that of other tasks, but the processing time and commitments needed may be different due to being instances of distinct activity and/or task classes. Hence, when an activity of task T is repeatedly performed because of the adopted intra-task synchronisation policy, T's flow index counter is still increased by one each time the activity is performed. For discrete activities in T, the flow index counter advances only once per execution.

It is not necessary that a manufacturing thread always has activities to perform throughout the thread's entire duration. For example in Fig. 6, no activities are performed between m_4 and m_5 due to delays (namely there are no available AGVs to transport the piston head). In other words, it is possible that a master activity for a given task may be idle because it does not always posses the required resources to execute itself in a specified manufacturing stage. For instance, the polishing task does not have the ability to remove imperfections from the piston head's surface between m_8 and m_9 due to its polishing head being damaged.

Suitable contingency, rollback and resumption points are isolated to aid any reconfiguration necessary for achieving the deadline control protocol's compensatory actions. In this way, reconfiguration points, e.g., in Fig. 6, can still be easily identified and manipulated to reconfigure the system on the fly if a deadline needs to be achieved. In a manufacturing thread, the holons should be interrupted, paused, replaced and resumed when either: (i) a system malfunction occurs, or (ii) when the user issues a deadline control or reconfiguration command. The thread may need to continue to be executed during this period. In essence, the configuration of a holonic manufacturing system is a specification of what tasks are being performed, how and where within the shop-floor environment.

Parameters in the configuration model used by the resident software agents and mobile agents include:

- What holons are resident in the system, what are the capabilities of the associated software agents, and what types of holons could be introduced if need be.
- What tasks are being executed now and are scheduled for execution in the future.
- What threads exist in the HMS, what mobile agents are managing tasks within these threads and where are they located.
- What are the intermediate (i.e., milestones) and final deadlines of the tasks; where are these tasks being per-formed (namely to which holon are they assigned); and what are the relationships, synchronisations and dependencies between these manufacturing tasks.
- What task monitoring and information dissemination policies are the mobile agents applying.
- What mechanisms and strategies are to be executed if the tasks are not performed by their deadlines (namely what compensatory actions are present).
- What measures are being taken to ensure the system keeps operating in the presence of faults/failures.

Reconfiguration is the compensatory process whereby the existing configuration parameters are modified by changes to the internal behaviour (i.e., autonomy) and the external interactions (i.e., cooperation) of the corresponding software and mobile agents. In an HMS, such reconfiguration must be performed while still satisfying any real-time constraints imposed on the tasks. Next we outline some avenues for future investigation within this reconfiguration process.

6   Outlook

The paper is still rather preliminary in its ideas. The following directions appear to be fruitful to clarify these ideas: (1) to prototype an implementation of the model based on software and mobile agent technologies, and (2) to explore interesting parallels with the work of [12] with respect to examining the role of product, resource, order and staff holons during real-time reconfiguration.

These investigations will draw their evidence, deployment and results from the ongoing HMS project. Furthermore, we intend to isolate hard facts from speculation, provide concrete examples of our reconfiguration ideas and outline design specifications for the implementation of our model.

References

1. Jennings, N.: Coordination Techniques for Distributed Artificial Intelligence. John Wiley and Sons (1995)
2. Intelligent Manufacturing Systems Program: Technical report. http://spuds.cpsc.ucalgary .ca/IMS/IMS.html (2000)
3. Fletcher, M., Norrie, D.H., Christensen, J.H.: A Foundation for Realtime Holonic Control Systems. Journal of Applied System Sciences, special issue on Industrial Applications of Multi-Agent and Holonic Systems 2(1) (2001) 20-43
4. Searle, J.R.: Speech Acts. Cambridge University Press (1969)
5. Koestler, A.: The Ghost in the Machine. Arkana (1967)
6. Bond, A. Gasser, L.: An Analysis of Problems and Research in DAI. Morgan Kaufman (1988)
7. Zhang, X., Balasubramanian, S., Brennan, R.W., Norrie, D.H.: Design and Implementation of a Real-Time Holonic Control System for Manufacturing. Journal of Information Sciences. 127(1-2) (2000) 23-44
8. Holonic Manufacturing Systems Consortium: Holonic Manufacturing Systems Overview. http://hms.ifw.uni-hannover.de/ public/overview.html (2001)
9. Smith, R.: The Contract Net Protocol: High-level Communication and Control in a Distributed Problem Solver. Defence Research Establishment Atlantic D.R.E.A. Report 80/1 (1982)
10. Christensen, J.H.: HMS: Initial Architecture and Standards Directions. the 1st European Conference on Holonic Manufacturing Systems (1994) 1-20
11. Luh, P.B., Hoitomt, D.J.: Scheduling of Manufacturing Systems Using the Lagrangian Relaxation Technique. IEEE Transactions on Advanced Computing and Automation journal: special edition on Meeting the Challenge of Computer Science in Industrial Applications of Control Technology. 38(7) (1993) 1066-1080
12. Van Brussel, H., Wyns, J., Valckenaers, P., Bongaerts, L., Peeters, P.: Reference Architecture for Holonic Manufacturing Systems: PROSA. Computers In Industry. 37 (1998) 255-274

CPlanT: Coalition Planning Multi-Agent System for Humanitarian Relief Operations

Michal Pěchouček, Jaroslav Bárta, and Vladimír Mařík

Gerstner Laboratory, Department of Cybernetics, Czech Technical University in Prague
Technická 2, 166 27 Prague, Czech Republic
{pechouc,barta,marik}@labe.felk.cvut.cz

Abstract. Planning humanitarian relief operations within a community of a high number of hardly collaborating and vaguely linked non-governmental organizations is a challenging problem. In this article we present an agent-oriented approach to modeling and supporting distributed decision making of agents – the humanitarian relief providers. Owing to the very special nature of this specific domain, where the agents may eventually agree to collaborate but are very often reluctant to share their knowledge and resources, we have combined classical negotiation mechanisms with the acquaintance models and social knowledge techniques.

1 Introduction

The application domain of our coalition formation research belongs to the area of **war avoidance operations** such as peace-keeping, peace-enforcing, non-combatant evacuation or disaster relief operations. Unlike in classical war operations, where the technology of control is strictly hierarchical, **operations other than war** (OOTW) are very likely to be based on cooperation of a number of different, quasi-volunteered, vaguely organized groups of people, non-governmental organizations (NGO's), institutions providing humanitarian aid but also army troops and official governmental initiatives.

Collaborative, unlike hierarchical, approach to operation planning allows greater deal of flexibility and dynamics in grouping optimal parties playing an active role in the operation. New entities shall be free to join autonomously and involve themselves in planning with respect to their capabilities. Therefore any organization framework must be essentially "open". The plan for OOTW is evaluated, according to [10], [7], with respect to multiple criteria as often there is not any one shared goal or a single type of the operation (such as political, economical, humanitarian). From the same, reason the goals across the community of entities involved in a possible coalition may be in conflict. Even if the community members share the same goal, it can be easily misunderstood due to different cultural backgrounds.

The main reason why we can hardly plan operations involving different NGO's by a central authority results from their **reluctance to provide information** about their

V. Mařík et al. (Eds.): MASA 2001, LNAI 2322, pp. 363-375, 2002.
© Springer-Verlag Berlin Heidelberg 2002

intentions, goals and resources. Consequently, besides difficulties related to planning and negotiation we have to face the problems how to assure sharing detailed information. Many institutions will be ready to share resources and information within some well specified community, whereas they will refuse to register their full capabilities and plans with a central planning system and will not follow centralized commands. They may agree to participate in executing a plan, in forming of which they played an active role.

Naturally, a paradigm of multi-agent systems, communities of heterogeneous, autonomous, proactive and collaborative agents, suits the domain of coalition planning. Multi-agent systems provide important features that will be with a great advantage applied in our problem [2]. When modeling/running a very complex system, multi-agent abstraction will allow natural decomposition of the problem into interacting components, each represented by **an agent**. By doing so, tractability, maintainability and flexibility is provided. In our interpretation, an agent is a complex, organized entity playing an active role in OOTW (NGO, humanitarian organization, army troop, etc.). Agents communicate via declarative communication languages that facilitate a wide range of interaction patterns. The important virtue of the agent-based paradigm is the fact that many courses of interaction (and resulting collaboration) are not foreseen during the system design and they can occur emergently. Agents can join and leave community upon their own decision, they do not necessarily need to be benevolent, and they improve their behavior in time. The paradigm of multi-agent systems allows integrating agents that are heterogeneous in nature and communicate in peer-to-peer manner. Let us understand a targeted multi-agent system to consist of a number of agents that group themselves in various, temporary coalitions (each solving a specific mission/part of the mission).

Firstly, let us put down several terms that will be used throughout this paper. As a **multi-agent community** we understand the whole collection of agents participating in the above-described OOTW (quasi-volunteered, vaguely organized groups of people, non-governmental organizations, institutions providing humanitarian aid, army troops or official governmental initiatives). Throughout the paper we will refer to a **coalition** as a set of agents (an agreement) who agreed to fulfill a single, well-specified goal. Agents thus commit themselves to collaboration with respect to the within-coalition-shared goal. An agent may participate in multiple coalitions. Unlike an alliance (see below), a coalition is usually regarded as a short-term agreement among collaborative agents. As a **coalition formation/planning** we understand the process of finding a coalition of agents who may participate in achieving the respective within-coalition-shared goal. As an **alliance** we understand a collection of agents that share general humanitarian objectives and all agree to form possible coalitions. Moreover, the alliance members decided to share detailed information about their statuses and resources they may provide. The alliance is regarded as a long term cooperation agreement among the agents.

2   CPlanT Multi-Agent Architecture

CPlanT is a multi-agent system for planning operations other than war where any agent can initiate the planning process [6]. Classical negotiation algorithms such as contract net protocol (CNP) are used in combination with acquaintance models techniques [4]. The CPlanT architecture consists of several specific classes of agents:

Resource Agents (R-agents) represent the in-place resources that are inevitable for delivering humanitarian aid, such as roads, airports. Unlike below-defined H-agents, the R-agents are regarded as passive and they do not initiate any kind of humanitarian effort.

In-Need Agents (IN-agents) are critical bodies in the entire simulation. They will represent the centers of conflict that call for help (e.g. cities, villages, etc.).

Humanitarian Agents (H-agents), who are computational representations of the participating humanitarian agencies. Like the R-agents, the H-agents provide humanitarian aid. Therefore, one may regard the H-agent as a subclass of R-agents. However the H-agents are proactive and they initiate providing the respective   humanitarian aid.

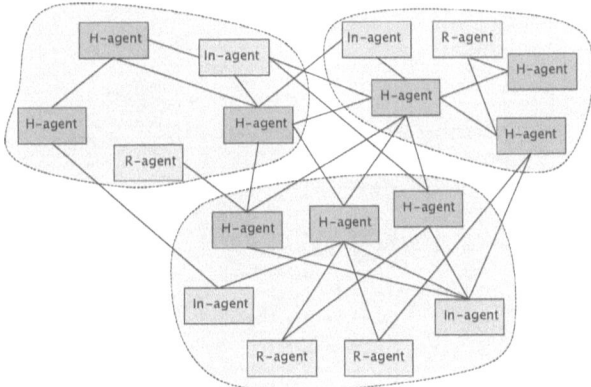

Fig. 1. CPlanT multi-agent architecture

Though the coalition formation problem is much wider and involves forming coalitions together with all the other participating agents, we will investigate coalition formation just among the H-agents.

3   H-Agent Knowledge Architecture

The H-agent may participate in one alliance only and at the same time it may be actively involved in several coalitions of agents. Computational and communication complexity of the above defined coalition formation problem depends on the amount of pre-prepared information the agents administer one about the other and on the sophistication of the agents' meta-reasoning mechanisms (as a meta-reasoning we understand agent's capability to reason about the other agent's reasoning processes). We suggest three distinct types of agent's knowledge:

Public knowledge is shared within the entire multi-agent community. This class of knowledge is freely accessible within the community. As public knowledge we understand the agent's name, the type of the organization the agent represents, the general objective of the agent's activity, the country where the agent is registered, the agent's human-human contact (telephone, fax number, email), the human-agent type of contact (usually http address), the agent-agent type of contact (the IP address, incoming port, ACL) and finally available services.

Semi-private knowledge (also referred to as alliance accessible knowledge) is shared within a specific alliance. We do not assume the knowledge to be shared within the overlapping alliances. Members of an alliance will primarily share information about free availability of their resources. This resource-oriented type of knowledge may be further divided into the description of material resources and human (professional) resources.

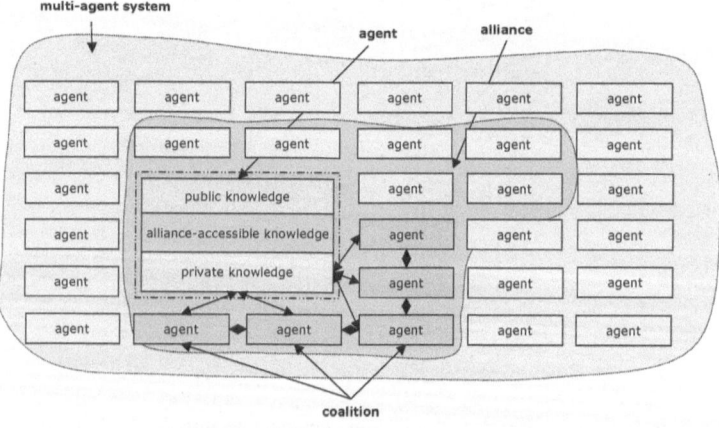

Fig. 2. Concept of the alliance and the coalition

Private knowledge is owned and administered by the agent himself. The agents share private information neither within an alliance nor within a coalition. An important type of private knowledge relates the agent's collaboration preferences, alliance restrictions, coalition leader restrictions and possible next restrictions, but also the agent's planning and scheduling algorithms.

4   Inter-agent Communication in CPlanT

Before explaining the lifecycle of the system let us comment the main communication and negotiation strategies that have been used in the CPlanT multi-agent system.

Let's remark, we have avoided the implementation of the multi-agent system with a single central communication and planning agent where the other agents' private knowledge may be sniffed and aggregated. Such a concentrated planning of all operations may result in the system bottleneck. This contradicts to our requirements listed in Sect. 1.

Contract Net Protocol: If there is no central planner, any agent (coordinating agent) can initiate the coalition forming process by requesting all agents in the community for services the coordinating agent may need within the coalition. Upon receiving proposals for collaboration, the coordinating agent carries out a computational process by which he selects the best possible collaborator(s). The coalition planning process can also be multi-staged. In this case, when the coordinating agent does not like any of the received proposals, he re-specifies his original request. This approach by its own is resource consuming and will fail in complex communities. Similarly, many agents may not want to enter the CNP negotiation as they would undertake the risk of disclosing their private knowledge.

Acquaintance Models: Each agent in a multi-agent system administers and maintains several special kinds of knowledge. Apart from his **problem-solving knowledge** that guides agent's autonomous local decision making processes, the agents usually exploit **social knowledge** [4] that expresses the other agents' behavioral patterns, their capabilities, load, experiences, resources, commitments, knowledge describing conversations or negotiation scenarios. This knowledge is usually stored separately from the agent's computational core - in agent's **acquaintance model**. There have been investigated several acquaintance models previously [5]. Based on the tri-base acquaintance model [4], the social knowledge in CPlanT is organized in four separate knowledge structures:

-   **community-base (ComB)** – is a collection of public knowledge of the community members
-   **self-belief-base (SelfBB)** – contains the agent's reflective knowledge about himself is located; here the agent stores his public knowledge that is accessible to anyone, his semi-private knowledge that is shared within the alliance and his private knowledge that is not shared by anyone,
-   **social-belief-base private (SocBB)** – where the agent stores the semi-private knowledge of his peer alliance members,
-   **coalition-base (CoalB)** – a dynamic collection of the peer coalition members and permanent coalition-formation rules (subset of the problem-solving knowledge).

Exploitation of the acquaintance model reduces the communication traffic required for collaborative activity planning. In principle, the social knowledge in the acquaintance model substantially reduces the set of agents (ideally to one) that will be requested by the coordinating agent in the Contract Net Protocol (CNP) negotiation process. An important flaw of this approach is rooted in high requirements for the social model maintenance. Providing that Θ is a set of community members, than in the worst case there is $(|\Theta|*(|\Theta|-1))$ messages required for one step of social knowledge maintenance.

Table 1. Instance of an H-agent's acquaintance model: The SelfBB knowledge structure expresses Public, Semi-Private and Private Knowledge, for example: the agent's cooperators, coalition leader restrictions etc. The CoalB provides a rule for human and material services identification and acceptable coalitions. There is knowledge about the monitored agents in SocBB and there is knowledge about all the other agents in ComBB

Self-belief-base				
Public Knowledge		**Semi-Private Knowledge**		**Private Knowledge**
port	1500	**services**	**amount**	**alliance-restriction**	("country","Suffer Terra")
ip_address	"147.32.86.167"	food	30000	**leader-restriction**	("type","Military").
country	suffer terra	nurses	50	**city-restriction**	("muslim",50)
city	north port			**cooperates-with**	("type","government")
services	food,nurses				
type	religious				
ontologies	fipa-agent-management, cplant-ontology				
Coalition Base				
coalition	coalition(task-008,[christian-suffer-terra-humanitarian-organization, suffer-terra-police])			
task	(population,degree, volacanic, 220, [["nurses",20], ["doctors",15]])		degree>=4, degree=<6, population>=0, population=<3000	
Social Belief Base				
suffer-terra police	**service**	**amount**		
	military people	30		
Community Base				
Suffer Terra Police	**Port**	2035		
	Ip	147.32.86.167		
	Type	Military		

5   CPlanT Operation Lifecycle

The CPlanT multi-agent system operates in four separate phases:
- **registration** for agents' login/logout to/from the community,
- **alliance formation** when forming alliances,
- **coalition forming** for finding a group of agents which can fulfill a well specified task and
- **team action planning** for resource allocation within the specific coalition.

5.1   Registration

Throughout the registration phase, a new-coming agent registers within the multi-agent community. The facilitator agent stores public knowledge of all agents in the community and he takes care about the agents' registration and deregistration processes. A new agent registers his public knowledge with the facilitator. Subsequently, the facilitator informs all the already registered agents about the new agent, and he also informs the new agent about all existing agents and their capabilities.

We call the list of all existing agents the agent is aware of as an **agent's total neighbourhood**. Let us define $\alpha(A)$, $\alpha(A) \subseteq \Theta$ – an agent's A total neighbourhood, that is a collection of agents the agent A is aware of. After the registration phase, all the agents will be aware of the other existing agents, formally

$$\forall A, A \in \Theta: \alpha(A) = \Theta.$$

Similarly, the agents can deregister with the facilitator. Any registered agent stores the **public knowledge** about all the members of his total neighbourhood. Public knowledge of the members of the agent's total neighbourhood are stored in the **ComB** knowledge structure.

5.2 Alliance Formation

In this phase, which follows the registration process, the agents analyze the information they have about the members of the community and attempt to form alliances. In principle, each agent is expected to compare his own private knowledge (i.e. alliance restrictions) with the public knowledge on the possible alliance members (i.e. type of organization, his objective, country of origin, etc.). Had the agent detected a possible future collaborator, the agent would propose possible collaboration. Throughout the negotiation process the agent either chooses the best alliance with respect to several criteria or starts a new alliance consisting of this agent only.

The set of agents that agreed to eventually cooperate with the given agent (say the agent A) represents the **agent's social neighbourhood** $\mu(A)$, where there is usually true that $\mu(A) \subseteq \alpha(A)$. The agent A will share the semi-private knowledge with all the alliance members. There are two specific instances of the agent's A social neighbourhood: $\mu^+(A)$ and $\mu^-(A)$. While $\mu^+(A)$ is a set of agents whose semi-private knowledge the agent A is aware of, the other type of the agent's social neighbourhood $\mu^-(A)$, is a collection of agents that keeps the agent's A **semi-private knowledge**,

$$\forall B \in \mu^-(A): A \in \mu^+(B).$$

The semi-private knowledge of the members of the agent's social neighbourhood has been stored in the **SocBB** knowledge structure. As the semi-private knowledge sharing is reciprocal, both types of agent's social neighbourhood store the same piece of information and it makes no sense to keep them separate,

$$\forall A \in \Theta : \mu^-(A) = \mu^+(A) = \mu(A).$$

Here we have talked about the alliance from the single agent's perspective. Globally, we say that an alliance is a collection of agents where all of them mutually share the semi-private information. As the alliances are not exclusive and any agent may participate in several different alliances, we say that the alliance is a set of agents κ, where

$$\exists \kappa : \forall A \in \kappa : \kappa \subseteq \mu(A).$$

5.3 Coalition Formation

In this phase, the agents group together not according to a similar mission objective but with respect to a single, well specified task that needs to be accomplished. Both the CNP and the social model are used in the coalition formation process. The simplest and the most straightforward approach to forming an effective coalition is to search for partners within the alliance members. The alliance members know the most of each other and are able to suggest a coalition that will very likely have foreseen properties. Whichever member of an alliance faces the role of coordinating the task accomplishment, he parses his social neighborhood (services the agents provide and allocation of their resources) and detects the most suitable collaborators. Upon an approval from each of the suggested agents, the respective coalition is formed. For the required task (say τ) the coordinating agent (or possible coalition leader), as well as the other agents, will maintain their **cooperation neighbourhood** (a set of agent's A collaborators) – $\varepsilon(A, \tau) \subseteq \alpha(A)$. If we disregard forming coalitions across alliances, the coordinating agent always chooses from the alliance members, therefore $\varepsilon(A, \tau) \subseteq \mu(A)$. A **coalition** is a group of agents $\chi(\tau)$ solving a task τ, where

$$\exists \chi(\tau) : \forall A \in \chi(\tau) : \chi(\tau) = \varepsilon(A, \tau)^1.$$

The agent's cooperation neighbourhood for the current, past and potential tasks has been stored in the **CoalB** knowledge structure. Maintaining the agents' social neighbourhood will save an important part of the agent's interactions. The agents will not need to broadcast a call for collaboration each time they will be required to accomplish a task. Instead, they will consult this pre-prepared knowledge and will contract the agent of which they knew he is the best to work with.

All this is true, when we disregard forming coalitions across alliances ($\forall \tau: \varepsilon(A, \tau) \subseteq \mu(A)$). If a coalition can be formed among members of different alliances, the agents can use only the public knowledge and communicate potential collaboration directly.

```
form-coalition(A, τ)
{χ₁(τ) = find-no-possible-coalitions(τ, μ(A))
  form-coalition-2(A, τ, χ₁(τ))
}

form-coalition-2(A, τ, χ₁(τ))
{repeat {χ(τ) = find_the_best_coalition(τ, μ(A))}
  until χ(τ)∉χ₁(τ)
  if χ(τ) == {} then return failure
  else ∀Aᵢ ∈ χ(τ)
    send-message(perform: request, sender: CL receiver: Aᵢ, content: χ(τ))
    if ∀Aᵢ ∈ χ(τ)
      recieve-message(perform: reply, sender: Aᵢ, receiver: CL, content: "AGREE")
      then return(coalition_leader: A, coalition χ(τ))
      else form-coalition-2(A, τ, reduce-coalitions(χ (τ)) ∪ χ₁(τ))
}
```

---

[1] provided that there is only one coalition for one task

The task of the coordinating agent, which suggests a possible coalition, is sometimes inherently complex. He has to try out substantial number of combinations. Design and implementation of intelligent algorithms for a centralized/distributed coalition formation will be part of the further research. See the coalition formation process started and lead by a coalition leader A in a general illustrative language:

5.4 Team Action Planning

Once the coalition is formed, the agents share a joint, high-level commitment to achieve the goal. Within a coalition, a team of collaborative agents, a more complicated shared state – a **team action plan** – must be achieved. The team action plan (denoted as $\pi(\tau)$), as a result of the coalition planning activity, is a joint commitment structure that defines how exactly each team member will contribute to achieving the shared goal (amount of resources, allocation time, etc.).

When constructing a coalition in a collaborative manner, the coalition formation process is initiated by a **coalition leader**. As there is no predefined hierarchy among the agents, any agent can become a coalition leader. An agent becomes a coalition leader as a result of his autonomous decision to start a mission planning process (e.g. perception from the environment, human interaction, etc). Let us assume that the coalition leader will also initiate the team action planning.

The intra-alliance team-action planning mechanism is not a pure acquaintance model based selection, where the team-action plan would be a result of the coalition leader deliberation process. The team action plan is constructed collaboratively. The coalition members advertise their services in the most informative while efficient form (such as linear approximation). Based on this knowledge, the coalition leader suggests the most optimal request decomposition and resource allocation. This is sent to the coalition members, which reply with a specific collaboration proposal. The coalition leader may find out that the suggested decomposition was not optimal and thus his social knowledge was not accurate enough. As a result of such an occurrence, the social knowledge gets updated and the coalition leader sends another proposal. After few negotiation steps, the agents are expected to form jointly a team action plan. The negotiation process lead by the coalition-leader when forming a team action plan can be algorithmically expressed in the following way:

```
repeat
{π(τ) = decompose(τ, social-knowledge)
  if π(τ) = {} return τ else
    send-message(perform: request, sender: CL, receiver: Aᵢ, content: π(τ)ᵢ)
    receive-message(perform: reply, sender: Aᵢ, receiver: CL,  content: agree-or-refuseᵢ)
    if agree-or-refuseᵢ == "AGREE" τ=τ-π(τ)ᵢ
}
until t == {}

on
receive-message(perform: request, sender: CL, receiver: Aᵢ, content: π(τ)ᵢ)
{if π(τ)ᵢ is available return "AGREE" else return  "REFUSE"}
```

5.5   Communication Flows in the CPlanT Lifecycle

As pointed above, we did not adopt one communication technique and claim that this is the best for our problem. We wanted to find a middle ground among:

- communication traffic (and computational resources) requirements in both the coalition formation and the team-action planning phases,
- periodic communication traffic in the agents idle times (mainly maintenance of the social models) and
- the amount of the private information that the agents have to disclose when forming a coalition.

Registration Phase: Any multi-agent system cannot survive without at least a tiny bit of centrality, which we try to avoid as much as possible. We have used the *central communication unit* – facilitator (see Sect. 5.1) in the registration phase only. As the agents register only their public knowledge we do not breach the requirements for confidentiality of the private information.

Alliance Formation Phase: According to their preferences in SelfBB and community public knowledge in ComB the agents carry out a selective CNP process during the alliance formation phase. As mentioned above, the alliance members create a sharing network of semi-private knowledge.

Coalition Formation Phase: When forming a coalition within one alliance, the agents exploit their *acquaintance models* consisting the other agents' semi-private knowledge stored in SocBB. If no coalition can be formed within a single alliance, the coalition leader broadcasts a *contract net* proposal among the other community members, about which he has got no social knowledge yet.

Team Action Planning: From the same reason as above, the team-action planning within the single alliance is implemented the by means of an *acquaintance-model-based* communication and the *contract net protocol* runs among alliances.

While the contract net protocol being rather inefficient, it keeps the agent from different alliances independent (they do not have to disclose their semi-private knowledge across alliances). This is why, the acquaintance-model based planning has been used exclusively within the alliances.

6   R-Agent and IN-Agent

Testing correctness of the CPlanT requires a well-defined, formal, but realistic enough scenario that can represent, model and initiate all aspects of agents' nontrivial behaviour. The above specified principles and ideas have been implemented and tested on a subset of the OOTW types of operations – humanitarian relief operations. For this purpose we have designed and implemented a hypothetical humanitarian scenario in an imaginary country – SufferTerra (inspired by [6,7]). The scenario knowledge has been encoded in XML format and the computational model of the scenario has been implemented in Allegro Common Lisp.

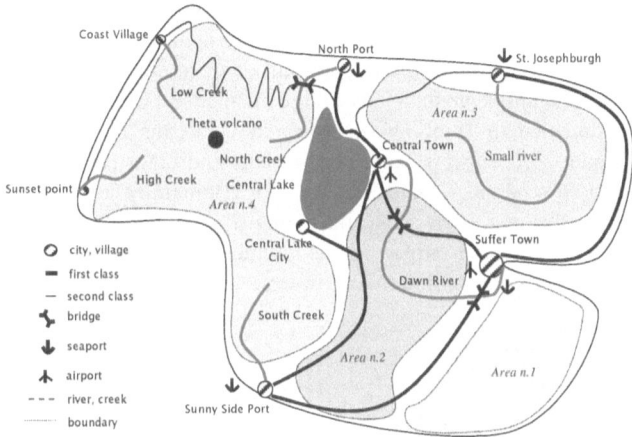

Fig. 3. Sufferterra – subject of humanitarian operations

The R-Agents specify the topological arrangements of the geographical objects and the resources they provide. The problem specification does not distinguish the level of granularity, i.e. each physical object may be implemented as an R-agent or several physical objects can creak together an R-agent. For the testing purposes, we have implemented a single R-Agent that represents the entire map of the area. The H-agents subscribe the R-Agents for a specific information, by which that subscribers are informed about any change in physical arrangements of the relevant part of the map. There is a simple IN-Agent implemented as a part of the CPlanT community. Through one of the running instances of the IN-Agent one can compose a "call-for-help" request and execute the coalition planning process. Such a request includes a type of disaster ("volcanic", "hurricane", "flood", "earthquake"), the degree of disaster (1..9), location and a targeted H–Agent. Let's present a self-explaining example of XML schema encoding a 'Suffer Town' object.

```
<city>
        <name> "Suffer Town" </name>
        <national-composition> "((christian 67) (muslim 18) (native 13) (other 2))"
        </national-composition>
        <population> "50000" </population>
        <seaport>
                <ID> "1" </ID>
                <capacity> "25" </capacity>
                <material-hour> "200000" </material-hour>
        </seaport>
        <airport>
                <ID> "1" </ID>
                <capacity> "30" </capacity>
                <material-hour> "100000" </material-hour>
                <runway> "3000" </runway>
        </airport>
</city>
```

7   Conclusion

The CPlanT multi-agent system has been successfully tested on the Sufferterra humanitarian relief scenario [12]. In this system, four agent types are considered: The Facilitator, H-agent, R-Agent and IN-Agent, all of them are implemented in Allegro Common Lisp. The implementation is complemented by a visualizing meta-agent, which is implemented in Java. This meta-agent views the logical structure of the system e.g. alliances, coalitions, team action plans and other properties of the community. There is a separate visualization tool for communication traffic monitoring. This component, that is not an agent, but rather a part of the multi-agent platform, serves mainly for debugging purposes. The community can be viewed and managed from a web server via classical Internet browsers.

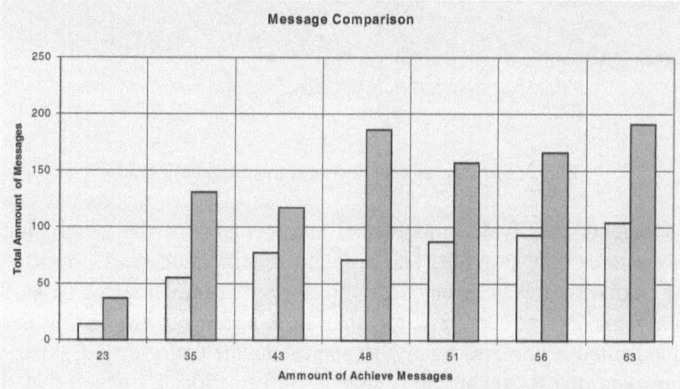

Fig. 4. Communication traffic comparison during both the coalition forming and coalition planning processes. The right column gives the number of messages for contract-net-protocol negotiations and the left column gives the number of messages for acquaintance-model-based negotiation. On the x axis we can see the number of closed contracts – achieve-type of messages that illustrates complexity of the request. On the y axis there is the total number of communicated messages per one request that illustrates the communication savings

It is hard to measure the benefit we get by maintaining confidentiality of the private and semi-private information. We have experimented with and tried to prove that communication traffic requirements are reduced (and thus an overall system response gets faster) with the acquaintance-model based communication. The graph in Fig. 4. shows the amount of the saved communication traffic with respect to complexity of the request. Experiments showed that with increasing numbers of alliances savings of communication traffic decreases, while the amount of revealed private knowledge increases.

This research effort, where we investigated potentials and possibilities of application of social knowledge and acquaintance models techniques in the humanitarian relief operations, was supported by The U.S. Air Force/European Office of Aerospace

Research and Development under contract number F61775-00-WE043 as well as by the project No. LN00B096 of the Czech Ministry for Education, Youth and Sports.

References

1. Dix J., Subrahmanian V.S., and Pick G.: Meta Agent Programs. *Journal of Logic Programming*. 46(1-2): 1-60, 2000.
2. Jennings N.: Agent Based Computing: Promises and Perils, Computer and Thought Award Lecture. In: *Proc. International Conference on Artificial Intelligence*, Stockholm, August 1999.
3. Ketchpel, S.: Coalition Formation Among Autonomous Agents. In: *Proc. 5th European Workshop on Modeling Autonomous Agents in a Multi-Agent World*, Neuchatel, Switzerland, 1993.
4. Marik V., Pechoucek M., and Stepankova O.: Social Knowledge in Multi-Agent Systems. In: *Multi-Agent Systems and Applications (M. Luck et. al, eds.)*, LNAI 2086, Tutorial, Springer-Verlag, 200, pp. 211-236.
5. Pechoucek, M., Marik, V., and Stepankova O.: Towards Reducing Communication Traffic. *Journal of Applied System Studies*, Cambridge International Science Publishing, ISSN 1466-7738, Cambridge, UK, No. 1, 2001.
6. Rathmell R.A.: A Coalition Force Scenario 'Binni – Gateway to the Golden Bowl of Africa'. Defence Evaluation Research Agency, 1999.
7. Reece G.A., and Tate A.: The Pacifica NEO Scenario. *Technical Report ARPA-RL/O-Plan2/TR/3*, Artificial Intelligence Applications Institute, University of Edinburgh, Scotland, 1993.
8. Sandholm W.: Distributed Rational Decision Making. In: *Multi-Agent Systems: Modern Approach to Distributed Artificial Intelligence (Weiss G., ed.)*, The MIT Press, Cambridge, 1999.
9. Shehory O., and Kraus S.: Methods for Task Allocation via Agent Coalition Formation. *Artificial Intelligence*, vol. 101 (1-2), pp. 165-200, 1998.
10. Walker E.C.T.: Panel Report: Coalition Planning for Operations Other Than War. In: *Proc. of the* Workshop *at AIAI*, Edinburgh, spring 1999.
11. Tambe M.: Towards flexible teamwork. *Journal of Artificial Intelligence Research*, 7:83 – 124, 1997.
12. Bárta J., Pěchouček M., and Mařik V.: Sufferterra Humanitarian Crisis Scenario. *Project Report of US Air Force Research Contract - Acquaintance Models in Operations Other Than War Coalition Formation*, project contract no.: F61775-00-WE043, (US Air Force proprietary), Department of Cybernetics, Czech Technical University, January 2001.

Author Index

Lecture Notes in Artificial Intelligence (LNAI)

Lecture Notes in Computer Science